SERMONS
— of —
GEORGE
WHITEFIELD

SERMONS
— of —
GEORGE
WHITEFIELD

George Whitefield

Sermons of George Whitefield

© 2009 Hendrickson Publishers Marketing, LLC
P. O. Box 3473
Peabody, Massachusetts 01961-3473

ISBN 978-1-61970-061-1

Printed in the United States of America

Cover art: Image of Whitefield is a detail of a frontispiece from a *Select Collection of Letters of the Late Reverend George Whitefield* and a rendering of Old South Church, where George Whitefield is buried. From the Old South Church Archive, Newburyport, Massachusetts, courtesy of Nancy Stokes.

Photo Credit: Joanna Jamieson

Library of Congress Cataloging-in-Publication Data

Whitefield, George, 1714-1770.
 [Selections. 2009]
 Sermons of George Whitefield / [sermons selected and edited by Evelyn Bence.] -- 1st Hendrickson ed.
  p. cm.
 ISBN 978-1-59856-384-9 (alk. paper)
 1. Presbyterian Church--Sermons. 2. Sermons, English--18th century.
 I. Bence, Evelyn. II. Title.
 BX9178.W5S285 2009
 252'.071--dc22
                        2009023296

Table of Contents

The Life of George Whitefield: A Timeline

1714–1770

1714	December 16: Born at Gloucester, England, the youngest of six boys, to Thomas and Elizabeth Whitefield, at the family-owned tavern, the Bell Inn.
1716	Father, Thomas, died.
1722	Mother, Elizabeth, remarried—disastrously.
1726	Transferred to the parish school: St. Mary de Crypt, where he excelled in elocution and dramatic arts. He later dropped out for several years, to help run the family inn.
1728	His mother, Elizabeth, left her husband. An older brother took over the business.
1730	With a new religious interest, returned to school to complete his secondary studies, anticipating an opportunity to go to Oxford.
1732	Entered Pembroke College, Oxford, as a servitor (a work-study program).
1733	Joined the Wesleys' Holy Club and sought holiness through charitable works, self-discipline, and deprivation, to the point of endangering his health.
1735	Received an assurance of salvation by faith.
1736	Ordained as a deacon in the Anglican Church—despite his reservations that he was not ready or fit. Graduated from Oxford. Began a London-based preaching ministry. Led the Oxford Holy Club (the Methodists), while John and Charles Wesley traveled to Georgia.
1737	Sermons first published. Ministered in Hampshire and London, but preached in various cities, with a growing following.

1738   Visited America for the first time, intending to settle as a missionary. Spent three months in Georgia and returned to England to seek ordination and raise funds for an orphanage.

1739   Ordained as an Anglican priest. Because many clergymen now disallowed him—and to accommodate the crowds—he frequently preached outdoors, without pulpit or notes. Found favor with Lady Huntington, who supported his cause (and the Wesleys') throughout her life.

Sailed to America in August. Landed in Philadelphia, for an extended preaching tour of the Colonies that prompted what history has called the Great Awakening.

1740   Established Bethesda Orphan House outside Savannah, for which he raised funds as he traveled.

Preached throughout New England. Stayed as a guest of Jonathan Edwards.

Was invited as a guest of Benjamin Franklin, commencing a lifelong friendship. Franklin published the first American volume of Whitefield's works.

1741   Arrived back in England. Theological disagreements (Calvinism vs. Arminianism) prompted a painful breech between Whitefield and the Wesleys. Continued preaching ministry despite persecutions. Supporters built a "temporary" large shed at Moorfields, to protect him from inclement weather while preaching; this "Tabernacle" remained for more than a decade, on the edge of London.

In Wales married Elizabeth James, a widow he met through (and whose affections belonged to) a fellow evangelist.

1742   Itinerated in England and traveled extensively in Scotland. Tensions started to ease between Whitefield and the Wesleys.

1743   Helped found, and then led, the Welsh Calvinistic Methodist Association.

1744   Death of his infant son. Providentially escaped a well-planned assassination attempt.

Sailed to America. Arrived in New England in critically poor health. Ministered itinerantly in the Colonies until spring 1748.

1748   Traveled to Bermuda (for improved health), where he continued to preach for two months.

Returned to Britain, where his friends were overjoyed to see him, as a magazine had reported his death in America. Overwhelmed by the debts of the Bethesda orphanage.

Appointed as Lady Huntington's personal chaplain, lessening his financial strain and giving increased access to "the great ones."

1749   Stepped down as the formal leader of the Calvinistic Methodist societies, committing himself to itinerant evangelism rather than organizational management. This further eased the Whitefield-Wesley relationship.

1750   An earthquake strikes end-times terror in London.

1751–1752   After travels in Ireland, returned to Georgia, arriving in October, but stayed in the Colonies only six months, going to England before the oppressive summer.

1753   A new, brick Moorfields Tabernacle, accommodating four thousand, completed and dedicated. A second Tabernacle dedicated at Bristol.

1754   Made his fifth voyage to America. Received an honorary master of arts degree from the College of New Jersey (Princeton), being a supporter of its founding.

1755   Arrived in England early in the year, having left Georgia in ill health. Expressed concern for Britain and the Colonies, threatened by French forces (the French and Indian War).

1755–1763   Preached throughout the British Isles, and often in London, drawing large crowds, despite persecution. Increased hopes for starting a college in Georgia. Battled bad health.

1756   Supporters built and he dedicated the Tottenham Court Road Chapel in western London

1758   Opened an almshouse for "godly widows" in western London.

1759   Paid off the long-burdensome debts of Bethesda Orphan House.

1763–1765   Returned to the Colonies. Arrived in Virginia. Traveled north, into New England, then south to Georgia and returned to England from Philadelphia. Preached as much as his health allowed, to generally receptive crowds.

1765–1769   Based in London, but traveled also, with increased respect and less resistance.

1767   Gave up his campaign to establish a chartered College of Georgia, because of the crown's demand that its president be an Anglican; Whitefield had wanted a broader foundation.

1768   Wife, Elizabeth, died. Preached her funeral sermon, using the text of Romans 8:28: "All things work together for good . . . ."

Presided at the opening of Trevecca college for preachers in Wales, founded by Lady Huntington.

1769   September 16. Preached his last sermon in London prior to voyage to America.

1770   Wintered in Georgia, then traveled north to Philadelphia, New York, and New England.

1770   Outdoors, in Exeter, New Hampshire, preached his last sermon, Saturday, September 29, weak and struggling with asthma.

September 30. Died of asthma at age 56, at Newburyport, Massachusetts, where he was buried in a crypt under the altar in the Old South Presbyterian Church.

John Wesley preached a funeral-memorial sermon in London, at Tottenham Court Road Chapel.

SERMONS

— of —

GEORGE WHITEFIELD

"I hardly ever knew him to go through a sermon without weeping more or less . . .
It was only by beholding his attitude and tears,
that one could well conceive of the effect."
—The Rev. Mr. Winter

Walking with God

—✺—

And Enoch walked with God: and he was not; for God took him.
—Genesis 5:24

Various are the pleas and arguments which men of corrupt minds frequently urge against yielding obedience to the just and holy commands of God. But, perhaps, one of the most common objections that they make is this, that our Lord's commands are not practical, because [they are] contrary to flesh and blood; and consequently, that he is "a hard master, reaping where he has not sown, and gathering where he has not strawed." These we find were the sentiments entertained by that wicked and slothful servant mentioned in St. Matthew 25, and are undoubtedly the same with many which are maintained in the present wicked and adulterous generation. The Holy Ghost, foreseeing this, has taken care to inspire holy men of old to record the examples of many holy men and women, who, even under the Old Testament dispensation, were enabled cheerfully to take Christ's yoke upon them, and counted his service perfect freedom. The large catalog of saints, confessors, and martyrs drawn up in Hebrews 11 abundantly evidences the truth of this observation. What a great cloud of witnesses have we there presented to our view? All eminent for their faith, but some shining with a greater degree of luster than do others. The proto-martyr Abel leads the van. And next to him we find Enoch mentioned, not only because he was next in order of time, but also on account of his exalted piety; he is spoken of in the words of the text in a very extraordinary manner.

We have here a short but very full and glorious account, both of his behavior in this world, and the triumphant manner of his entry into the next. The former is contained in these words: "And Enoch walked with God." The latter in these, "and he was not; for God took him." He was not; that is, he was not found; he was not taken away in the common manner; he did not see death, for God had translated him (Heb. 11:5). Who this Enoch was does not appear so plainly. To me, he seems to have been a person of public character; I suppose, like Noah, a preacher of righteousness. And, if we may credit the apostle Jude, he was a flaming preacher. For he [Jude] quotes one of his [Enoch's] prophecies, wherein he says, "Behold, the Lord cometh with ten thousands of his saints, to execute judgment upon all, and to convince all that are ungodly among them, of all their ungodly deeds which they have ungodly committed, and of all their hard speeches, which ungodly sinners have spoken against him." But whether a public or private person, he has a noble testimony given him in the lively oracles. The author of the epistle to the Hebrews says that before his [Enoch's] translation he had this testimony: "that he pleased God"; and his being translated was a proof of it beyond all doubt. And I would observe, that it was wonderful wisdom in God to translate Enoch and Elijah under the Old Testament dispensation, that hereafter, when it should be asserted that the Lord Jesus was carried into heaven, it might not seem a thing altogether incredible to the Jews; since they themselves confessed that two of their own prophets had been translated several hundred years before.

But it is not my design to detain you any longer, by enlarging, or making observations, on Enoch's short but comprehensive character: the thing I have in view being to give a discourse, as the Lord shall enable, upon a weighty and a very important subject: I mean, walking with God. "And Enoch walked with God." If so much as this can be truly said of you and me after our decease, we shall not have any reason to complain that we have lived in vain.

In handling my intended subject, I shall:

First, endeavor to show what is implied in these words: walked with God.

Second, I shall prescribe some means, upon the due observance of which, believers may keep up and maintain their walk with God.

And third, offer some motives to stir us up, if we never walked with God before, to come and walk with God now. The whole shall be closed with a word or two of application.

First, I am to show what is implied in these words, "walked with God," or, in other words, what we are to understand by walking with God.

And first, walking with God implies that the prevailing power of the enmity of a person's heart be taken away by the blessed Spirit of God. Perhaps it may seem a hard saying to some, but our own experience daily proves what the Scriptures in many places assert: that the carnal mind, the mind of the unconverted natural man, what's more, the mind of the regenerate, so far as any part of him remains unrenewed, is enmity, not only an enemy, but enmity itself, against God; so that it is not subject to the law of God, neither indeed can it be. Indeed, one may well wonder that any creature, especially that lovely creature man, made after his Maker's own image, should ever have any enmity, much less a prevailing enmity, against that very God in whom he lives and moves and has his being. But alas! so it is. Our first parents contracted it when they fell from God by eating the forbidden fruit, and the bitter and malignant contagion of it has descended to, and quite overspread, their whole posterity. This enmity discovered itself in Adam's endeavoring to hide himself in the trees of the garden. When he heard the voice of the Lord God, instead of running with an open heart, saying, "Here I am"; alas! he now wanted no communion with God, and still more discovered his lately contracted enmity, by the excuse he made to the most High: "The woman (or, this woman) thou gavest to be with me, she gave me of the tree, and I did eat." By saying thus, he in effect lays all the fault upon God; as though he had said, "If you had not given me this woman, I had not sinned against you, so you may thank yourself for my transgression."

In the same manner, this enmity works in the hearts of Adam's children. They now and again find something rising against God and saying even unto God, "What doest thou?" "It scorns any meaner competitor (says the learned Dr. Owen, in his excellent treatise on indwelling sin) than God himself." Its command is like that of the Assyrians in respect to Ahab—shoot only at the king. And it strikes against everything that has the appearance of real piety, as the Assyrians shot at Jehoshaphat in his royal clothes. But the opposition ceases when it finds that it is only an appearance, as the Assyrians left off shooting at Jehoshaphat when they perceived it was not Ahab they were shooting at. This enmity discovered itself in accursed Cain; he hated and slew his brother Abel, because Abel loved, and was peculiarly favored by, his God. And this same enmity rules and prevails in every man that is naturally engendered of the offspring of Adam. Hence that averseness to prayer and holy duties which we find in children, and very often in grown persons, who have notwithstanding been blessed with a religious education. And all that open sin and wickedness, which like a deluge has overflowed the world, are only so many streams running from this dreadful contagious fountain; I mean an enmity of man's desperately wicked and deceitful heart. He that cannot set his seal to this knows nothing yet, in a saving manner, of the holy Scriptures or of the power of God. And all that do know this will readily acknowledge that before a person can be said to walk with God, the prevailing power of this heart enmity must be destroyed; for persons do not usually walk and keep company together who entertain an irreconcilable enmity and hatred against one another. Observe me, I say, the prevailing power of this enmity must be taken away; for the in-being of it will never be totally removed, till we bow down our heads and give up the ghost. The apostle Paul, no doubt, speaks of himself—and that, too, not when he was a Pharisee, but a real Christian—when he complains that "when he would do good, evil was present with him"; not having dominion over him, but opposing and resisting his good intentions and actions, so that he could not do the things which he would, in that perfection which the new man desired. This is what he calls sin dwelling in him. And this is that φρόνημα τῆς σαρκός, "which (to use the words of the Ninth Article of our church) some do expound the wisdom, some sensuality, some the affection, some the desire, of the flesh," which does remain, yes, in them that are regenerated. But as for its prevailing power, it is destroyed in every soul that is truly born of God and gradually more and more weakened as the believer grows in grace, and the Spirit of God gains a greater and greater ascendancy in the heart.

But second, walking with God not only implies that the prevailing power of the enmity of a man's heart be taken away, but also that a person is actually reconciled to God the Father, in and through the all-sufficient righteousness and atonement of his dear Son. "Can two walk together (says Solomon [actually Amos 3:3]), unless they are agreed?" Jesus is our peace as well as our peacemaker. When we are justified by faith in Christ, then, but not till then, we have peace with God; and consequently cannot be said till then to walk with him, walking with a person being a sign and token that we are friends to that person, or at least, though we have been at variance, yet that now we are reconciled and become friends again. This is the great errand that gospel ministers are sent out upon. To us is committed the ministry of reconciliation; as ambassadors for God, we are to beseech sinners, in Christ's stead, to be reconciled unto God, and when they comply with the gracious invitation, and are actually by faith brought into a state of reconciliation with God, then, and not till then, may they be said so much as to begin to walk with God.

Further, third, walking with God implies a settled abiding communion and fellowship with God, or what in Scripture is called "The Holy Ghost dwelling in us." This is what our Lord promised when he told his disciples that "the Holy Spirit would be in and with them"; not to be like wayfaring man, to stay only for a night, but to reside and make his abode in their hearts. This, I am apt to believe, is what the apostle John would have us understand, when he talks of a person "abiding in him, in Christ, and walking as he himself also walked." And this is what is particularly meant in the words of our text. "And Enoch walked with God"; that is, he kept up and maintained a holy, settled, habitual, though undoubtedly not altogether uninterrupted communion and fellowship with God, in and through Christ Jesus. So that to sum up what has been said on this part of the first general head: walking with God consists especially in the fixed habitual bent of the will for God, in a habitual dependence upon his power and promise, in a habitual voluntary dedication of our all to his glory, in a habitual eyeing of his precept in all we do, and in a habitual complacence in his pleasure in all we suffer.

Fourth, walking with God implies our making progress or advances in the divine life. Walking, in the very first idea of the word, seems to suppose a progressive motion. A person that walks, though he move slowly, yet he goes forward and does not continue in one place. And so it is with those that walk with God. They go on, as the psalmist says, "from strength to strength"; or, in the language of the apostle Paul, "they pass from glory to glory, even by the Spirit of the Lord." Indeed, in one sense, the divine life admits of neither increase nor decrease. When a soul is born of God, to all intents and purposes he is a child of God; and though he should live to the age of Methuselah, yet he would then be only a child of God after all. But in another sense, the divine life admits of decays and additions. Hence it is, that we find the people of God charged with backslidings and losing their first love. And hence it is that we hear of babes, young men, and fathers in Christ. And upon this account it is that the apostle exhorts Timothy, "to let his progress be made known to all men." And what is here required of Timothy in particular, by St. Peter is enjoined on all Christians in general. "But grow in grace (says he), and in the knowledge of our Lord and Savior Jesus Christ." For the new creature increases in spiritual stature; and though a person can but be a new creature, yet there are some that are more conformed to the divine image than others, and will after death be admitted to a greater degree of blessedness. For want of observing this distinction, even some gracious souls, that have better hearts than heads (as well as men of corrupt minds, reprobates concerning the faith), have unawares run into downright Antinomian principles, denying all growth of grace in a believer, or any marks of grace to be laid down in the Scriptures of truth. From such principles, and more especially from practices naturally consequent on such principles, may the Lord of all lords deliver us!

From what then has been said, we may now know what is implied in the words "walked with God"; that is, our having the prevailing enmity of our hearts taken away by the power of the Spirit of God; our being actually reconciled and united to him by faith in Jesus Christ; our having and keeping up a settled communion and fellowship with him; and our making a daily progress in this fellowship, so as to be conformed to the divine image more and more.

How this is done, or, in other words, by what means believers keep up and maintain their walk with God, comes to be considered under our second general head.

And, first, believers keep up and maintain their walk with God by reading of his holy Word. "Search the Scriptures," says our blessed Lord, "for these are they that testify of me." And the royal psalmist tells us that "God's word was a light unto his feet, and a lantern unto his paths"; and he makes it one property of a good man, that "his delight is in the law of the Lord, and that he exercises himself therein day and night." "Give thyself to reading" (says Paul to Timothy); and "this book of the law (says God to Joshua) shall not go out of thy mouth." For whatsoever was written aforetime was written for our learning. And the Word of God is profitable for reproof, for correction, and for instruction in righteousness, and every way sufficient to make every true child of God thoroughly furnished unto every good work. If we once get above our Bibles, and cease making the written Word of God our sole rule both as to faith and practice, we shall soon lie open to all manner of delusion, and be in great danger of making shipwreck of faith and a good conscience. Our blessed Lord, though he had the Spirit of God without measure, yet always was governed by, and fought the devil with, "It is written." This the apostle calls the "sword of the Spirit." We may say of it, as David said of Goliath's sword, "None like this." The Scriptures are called the lively oracles of God: not only because they are generally made use of to beget in us a new life, but also to keep up and increase it in the soul. The apostle Peter, in his second epistle, prefers it even to seeing Christ transfigured upon the mount. For after he had said, "This voice which came from heaven we heard, when we were with him in the holy mount" (1:18), he adds, "We have also a more sure word of prophecy; whereunto ye do well that ye take heed, as unto a light shining in a dark place, until the day dawn, and the day star arise in your hearts": that is, till we shake off these bodies and see Jesus face to face. Till then we must see and converse with him through the glass of his Word. We must make his testimonies our counselors, and daily, with Mary, sit at Jesus' feet, by faith hearing his word. We shall then by happy experience find that they are spirit and life, meat indeed and drink indeed, to our souls.

Second, believers keep up and maintain their walk with God by secret prayer. The spirit of grace is always accompanied with the spirit of supplication. It is the very breath of the new creature, the fan of the divine life, whereby the spark of holy fire, kindled in the soul by God, is not only kept in, but raised into, a flame. A neglect of secret prayer has been frequently an inlet to many spiritual diseases and has been attended with fatal consequences. Origen observed, that the day he offered incense to an idol, he went out of his closet without making use of secret prayer. It is one of the most noble parts of the believers' spiritual armor. "Praying always," says the apostle, "with all manner of supplication." "Watch and pray," says our Lord, "that ye enter not into temptation." And he spoke a parable, that his disciples should pray and not faint. Not that our Lord would have us always upon our knees, or in our closets, to the neglect of our other relative duties. But he means that our souls should be kept in a praying frame, so that we might be able to say, as a good man in Scotland once said to his friends on his deathbed, "Could these curtains, or could these walls, speak, they would tell you what sweet communion I have had with my God here." Oh, prayer! Prayer! It brings and keeps God and man together. It raises man up to God, and brings God down to man. If you would there, O believers, keep up your walk with God; pray, pray without ceasing. Be much in secret, set prayer. And when you are about the common business of life, be much in ejaculatory prayer, and send, from time to time, short letters posted to heaven upon the wings of faith. They will reach the very heart of God, and return to you again loaded with spiritual blessings.

Third, holy and frequent meditation is another blessed means of keeping up a believer's walk with God. "Prayer, reading, temptation, and meditation," says Luther, "make a minister." And they also make and perfect a Christian. Meditation to the soul is the same as digestion to the body. Holy David found it so, and therefore he was frequently employed in meditation, even in the night season. We read also of Isaac's going out into the fields to meditate in the evening; or, as it is in the margin, to pray. For meditation is a kind of silent prayer, whereby the soul is frequently, as it were, carried out of itself to God, and in a degree made like unto those blessed spirits who, by a kind of immediate intuition, always behold the face of our heavenly Father. None but those happy souls that have been accustomed to this divine employ can tell what a blessed promoter of the divine life meditation is. "Whilst I was musing," says David, "the fire kindled." And while the believer is musing on the works and Word of God, especially that work of works, that wonder of wonders, that mystery of godliness, "God manifest in the flesh," the Lamb of God slain for the sins of the world, he frequently feels the fire of divine love kindle, so that he is obliged to speak with his tongue, and tell of the loving-kindness of the Lord to his soul. Be frequent therefore in meditation, all you that desire to keep up and maintain a close and uniform walk with the most high God.

Fourth, believers keep up their walk with God, by watching and noting his providential dealings with them. If we believe the Scriptures, we must believe what our Lord has declared therein, that "the very hairs of his disciples' heads are all numbered; and that a sparrow does not fall to the ground (either to pick up a grain of corn, or when shot by a fowler) without the knowledge of our heavenly Father." Every cross has a call in it, and every particular dispensation of divine providence has some particular end to answer in those to whom it is sent. If it be of an afflictive nature, God does thereby say, "My son, keep yourself from idols"; if prosperous, he does, as it were by a small still voice, say, "My son, give me your heart." If believers therefore would keep up their walk with God, they must from time to time hear what the Lord has to say concerning them in the voice of his providence. Thus we find that Abraham's servant, when he went to fetch a wife for his master Isaac, eyed and watched the providence of God, and by that means found out the person that was designed for his master's wife. "For a little hint from providence," says pious Bishop Hall, "is enough for faith to feed upon." And as I believe it will be one part of our happiness in heaven, to take a view of, and look back upon, the various links of the golden chain which drew us there, so those that enjoy most of heaven below, I believe, will be the most minute in remarking God's various dealings with them, in respect to his providential dispensations here on earth.

Fifth, in order to walk closely with God, his children must not only watch the motions of God's providence without them, but the motions also of his blessed Spirit in their hearts. "As many as are the sons of God, are led by the Spirit of God," and give up themselves to be guided by the Holy Ghost, as a little child gives its hand to be led by a nurse or parent. It is no doubt in this sense that we are to be converted and become like little children. And though it is the quintessence of enthusiasm to pretend to be guided by the Spirit without the written Word, yet it is every Christian's bounden duty to be guided by the Spirit in conjunction with the written Word of God. Watch, therefore, I pray you, O believers, the motions of God's blessed Spirit in your souls, and always try the suggestions or impressions that you may at any time feel, by the unerring rule of God's most holy Word: and if they are not found to be agreeable to that, reject them as diabolical and delusive. By observing this caution, you will steer a middle course between the two dangerous extremes many of this generation are in danger of running into; I mean, enthusiasm, on the one hand, and deism, and downright infidelity, on the other.

Sixth, they that would maintain a holy walk with God must walk with him in ordinances as well as providences, etc. It is therefore recorded of Zachariah and Elizabeth, that "they walked in all God's ordinances, as well as commandments, blameless." And all rightly informed Christians will look upon ordinances not as beggarly elements, but as so many conduit pipes, whereby the infinitely condescending Jehovah conveys his grace to their souls. They will look upon them as children's bread and as their highest privileges. Consequently they will be glad when they hear others say, "Come, let us go up to the house of the Lord." They will delight to visit the place where God's honor dwells, and be very eager to embrace all opportunities to show forth the Lord Christ's death till he comes.

Seventh and last, if you would walk with God, you will associate and keep company with those that do walk with him. "My delight," says holy David, "is in them that do excel" in virtue. They were, in his sight, the excellent ones of the earth. And the primitive Christians, no doubt, kept up their vigor and first love, by continuing in fellowship one with another. The apostle Paul knew this full well, and therefore exhorts the Christians to see to it, that they did not forsake the assembling of themselves together. For how can one be warm alone? And has not the wisest of men told us, that "as iron sharpeneth iron, so doth the countenance of a man his friend"? If we look therefore into church history, or make a just observation of our own times, I believe we shall find that as the power of God prevails, Christian societies and fellowship meetings prevail proportionably. And as one decays, the other has insensibly decayed and dwindled away at the same time. So necessary is it for those that would walk with God, and keep up the life of religion, to meet together as they have opportunity, in order to provoke one another to love and good works.

Proceed we now to the third general thing proposed: to offer some motives to excite all to come and walk with God. And, first, walking with God is a very honorable thing. This generally is a prevailing motive to persons of all ranks, to stir them up to any important undertaking. Oh, that it may have its due weight and influence with you in respect to the matter now before us! I suppose you would all think it a very high honor to be admitted into an earthly prince's privy council, to be trusted with his secrets, and to have his ear at all times and at all seasons. It seems Haman thought it so when he boasted, in Esther 5:11–12, that besides his being "advanced above the princes and servants of the king; yea, moreover, Esther the queen did let no man come in with the king unto the banquet that she had prepared, but myself; and tomorrow am I invited unto her also with the king." And when afterward a question was put to this same Haman, "What shall be done unto the man whom the king delighteth to honor?" (6:6), he answered, "Let the royal apparel be brought which the king used to wear, and the horse that the king rideth upon, and the crown royal which is set upon his head; and let this apparel and horse be delivered to the hand of one of the king's most noble princes, that they may array the man withal whom the king delighteth to honor, and bring him on horseback through the street of the city and proclaim before him, 'Thus shall it be done to the man whom the king delighteth to honor'" (6:8–9). This was all, then, it seems, that an ambitious Haman could ask, and the most valuable thing that he thought Ahasuerus, the greatest monarch upon earth, could give. But alas, what is this honor in comparison of that which the meanest of those enjoy that walk with God! Think it a small thing, sirs, to have the secret of the Lord of lords with you, and to be called the friends of God? And such honor have all God's saints. The secret of the Lord is with them that fear him; and "Henceforth (says the blessed Jesus) call I you no longer servants, but friends; for the servant knoweth not the will of his master." Whatever you may think of it, holy David was so sensible of the honor attending a walk with God that he declares, he "had rather be a doorkeeper in his house, than to dwell even in the tents of ungodliness." Oh, that all were like-minded with him!

But, second, as it is an honorable, so it is a pleasing, thing to walk with God. The wisest of men has told us, that "wisdom's ways are ways of pleasantness, and all her paths peace." And I remember pious Mr. [Matthew] Henry, when he was about to expire, said to a friend, "You have heard many men's dying words, and these are mine: a life spent in communion with God is the pleasantest life in the world." I am sure I can set to my seal that this is true. Indeed, I have been listed under Jesus' banner only for a few years; but I have enjoyed more solid pleasure in one moment's communion with my God, than I should or could have enjoyed in the ways of sin, though I had continued to have gone on in them for thousands of years. And may I not appeal to all you that fear and walk with God, for the truth of this? Has not one day in the Lord's courts been better to you than a thousand? In keeping God's commandments, have you not found a present, and very great, reward? Has not his Word been sweeter to you than the honey or the honeycomb? Oh, what have you felt, when, Jacob-like, you have been wrestling with your God? Has not Jesus often met you when meditating in the fields, and been made known to you over and over again in breaking of bread? Has not the Holy Ghost frequently shed the divine love abroad in your hearts abundantly and filled you with joy unspeakable, even joy that is full of glory? I know you will answer all these questions in the affirmative, and freely acknowledge the yoke of Christ to be easy and his burden light; or (to use the words of one of our collects), "His service is perfect freedom." And what need we then any further motive to excite us to walk with God?

But I think I hear some among you say, "How can these things be? For if walking with God, as you say, is such an honorable and pleasant thing, from where is it that the name of the people of this way is cast out as evil, and everywhere spoken against? How comes it to pass that they are frequently afflicted, tempted, destitute, and tormented? Is this the honor, this the pleasure, that you speak of?" I answer, "Yes. Stop a while; be not over hasty. Judge not according to appearance, but judge righteous judgment, and all will be well." It is true, we acknowledge the "people of this way," as you, and Paul before you, when a persecutor, called them, have their names cast out as evil, and are a sect everywhere spoken against. But by whom? Even by the enemies of the most high God. And do you think it is disgrace to be spoken evil of by them? Blessed be God, we have not so learned Christ. Our royal Master has pronounced those "blessed, who are persecuted, and have all manner of evil spoken against them falsely." He has commanded them "to rejoice and be exceeding glad," for it is the privilege of their discipleship, and that their reward will be great in heaven. He himself was thus treated. And can there be a greater honor put upon a creature than to be conformed to the ever-blessed Son of God? And further, it is equally true that the people of this way are frequently afflicted, tempted, destitute, and tormented. But what of all this? Does this destroy the pleasure of walking with God? No, in no wise; for those that walk with God are enabled, through Christ strengthening them, to joy even in tribulation, and to rejoice when they fall into diverse temptations. And I believe I may appeal to the experience of all true and close walkers with God, whether or not their suffering times have not frequently been their sweetest times, and that they enjoyed most of God when most cast out and despised by men? This we find was the case of Christ's primitive servants, when threatened by the Jewish Sanhedrin and commanded to preach no more in the name of Jesus; they rejoiced that they were accounted worthy to suffer shame for the sake of Jesus. Paul and Silas sang praises even in a dungeon; and the face of Stephen, that glorious proto-martyr of the Christian church, shone like the face of an angel. And Jesus is the same now as he was then and takes care so to sweeten sufferings and afflictions with his love, that his disciples find, by happy experience, that as afflictions abound, consolations do much more abound. And therefore these objections, instead of destroying, do only enforce the motives before urged, to excite you to walk with God.

But supposing the objections were just, and walkers with God were as despicable and unhappy as you would represent them to be, yet I have a third motive to offer, which if weighed in the balance of the sanctuary, will overweigh all objections, namely, that there is a heaven at the end of this walk. For, to use the words of pious Bishop Beveridge, "Though the way be narrow, yet it is not long: and though the gate be strait, yet it opens into everlasting life." Enoch found it so. He walked with God on earth, and God took him to sit down with him forever in the kingdom of heaven. Not that we are to expect to be taken away as he was: no, I suppose we shall all die the common death of all men. But after death, the spirits of those who have walked with God shall return to God that gave them; and at the morning of the resurrection, soul and body shall be forever with the Lord; their bodies shall be fashioned like unto Christ's glorious body, and their souls filled with all the fullness of God. They shall sit on thrones; they shall judge angels. They shall be enabled to sustain an exceeding and eternal weight of glory, even that glory which Jesus Christ enjoyed with the Father before the world began. *O gloriam quantam et qualem*, said the learned and pious Arndt, just before he bowed down his head, and gave up the ghost. The very thought of it is enough to make us "wish to leap our seventy years," as good Dr. Watts expresses himself, and to make us break out into the earnest language of the royal psalmist, "My soul is athirst for God, yea, for the living God. When shall I come to appear in the presence of my God?" I wonder not that a sense of this, when under a more than ordinary irradiation and influx of divine life and love, causes some persons to faint away, and even for a time lose the power of their senses. A less sight than this, even the sight of Solomon's glory, made Sheba's queen astonished; and a still lesser sight than that, even a sight of Joseph's wagons, made holy Jacob faint and for a while, as it were, die away. Daniel, when admitted to a distant view of this excellent glory, fell down at the feet of the angel as one dead. And if a distant view of this glory be so excellent, what must the actual possession of it be? If the firstfruits are so glorious, how infinitely must the harvest exceed in glory?

And now, what shall I, or, indeed, what can I well say more to excite you, even you that are yet strangers to Christ, to come and walk with God? If you love honor, pleasure, and a crown of glory, come, seek it where alone it can be found. Come, put on the Lord Jesus. Come, haste away and walk with God, and make no longer provision for the flesh, to fulfill the lust thereof. Stop, stop, O sinner! Turn, turn, O you unconverted men, for the end of that way you are now walking in, however right it may seem in your blinded eyes, will be death, even eternal destruction both of body and soul. Make no longer tarrying, I say: at your peril I charge you, step not one step further on in your present walk. For how know you, O man, but the next step you take may be into hell? Death may seize you, judgment find you, and then the great gulf will be fixed between you and endless glory forever and ever. Oh, think of these things, all you that are unwilling to walk with God. Lay them to heart. Show yourselves men, and in the strength of Jesus say, "Farewell, lust of the flesh, I will no more walk with you! Farewell, lust of the eye, and pride of life! Farewell, carnal acquaintance and enemies of the cross, I will no more walk and be intimate with you! Welcome, Jesus, welcome your Word, welcome your ordinances, welcome your Spirit, welcome your people, I will henceforth walk with you." Oh, that there may be in you such a mind! God will set his almighty fiat to it, and seal it with the broad seal of heaven, even the signet of his holy Spirit. Yes, he will, though you have been walking with, and following after, the devices and desires of your desperately wicked hearts ever since you have been born. "I, the high and lofty One," says the great Jehovah, "that inhabiteth eternity, will dwell with the humble and contrite heart, even with the man that trembleth at my word." The blood, even the precious blood of Jesus Christ, if you come to the Father in and through him, shall cleanse you from all sin.

But the text leads me to speak to you that are saints as well as to you that are open and unconverted sinners. I need not tell you that walking with God is not only honorable, but pleasant and profitable also; for you know it by happy experience and will find it more and more so every day. Only give me leave to stir up your pure minds by way of remembrance, and to beseech you by the mercies of God in Christ Jesus, to take heed to yourselves, and walk closer with your God than you have in days past: for the nearer you walk with God, the more you will enjoy of him whose presence is life, and be the better prepared for being placed at his right hand, where are pleasures forevermore. Oh, do not follow Jesus afar off! Oh, be not so formal, so dead and stupid in your attendance on holy ordinances! Do not so shamefully forsake the assembling yourselves together, or be so tightfisted or indifferent about the things of God. Remember what Jesus says of the church of Laodicea, "Because thou art neither hot nor cold, I will spew thee out of my mouth." Think of the love of Jesus, and let that love constrain you to keep near unto him; and though you die for him, do not deny him, do not keep at a distance from him in anywise.

One word to my brethren in the ministry that are here present, and I am done. You see, my brethren, my heart is full; I could almost say it is too big to speak, and yet too big to be silent, without dropping a word to you. For does not the text speak in a particular manner to those who have the honor of being styled the ambassadors of Christ and stewards of the mysteries of God. I observed at the beginning of this discourse, that Enoch in all probability was a public person and a flaming preacher. Though he be dead, does he not yet speak to us, to quicken our zeal, and make us more active in the service of our glorious and ever-blessed Master? How did Enoch preach! How did Enoch walk with God, though he lived in a wicked and adulterous generation! Let us then follow him, as he followed Jesus Christ, and before long, where he is there shall we be also. He is not entered into his rest: yet a little while and we shall enter into ours, and that too much sooner than he did. He sojourned here below three hundred years; but blessed be God, the days of man are now shortened, and in a few days our walk will be over. The Judge is before the door: he that is to come will come and will not tarry; his reward is with him. And we shall all (if we are zealous for the Lord of hosts) before long shine as the stars in the firmament, in the kingdom of our heavenly Father, forever and ever. To him, the blessed Jesus, and eternal Spirit, be all honor and glory, now, and to all eternity. Amen and amen.

Abraham's Offering Up His Son Isaac

And he said, "Lay not thine hand upon the lad, neither do thou anything unto him, for now I know that thou fearest God, seeing thou hast not withheld thy son, thine only son from me." —GENESIS 22:12

The great apostle Paul, in one of his epistles, informs us that "whatsoever was written aforetime was written for our learning, that we through patience and comfort of the holy Scripture might have hope." And as without faith it is impossible to please God, or be accepted in Jesus, the Son of his love, we may be assured that whatever instances of a more than common faith are recorded in the Book of God, they were more immediately designed by the Holy Spirit for our learning and imitation, upon whom the ends of the world are come. For this reason, the author of the Epistle to the Hebrews, in chapter 11, mentions such a noble catalog of Old Testament saints and martyrs, "who subdued kingdoms, wrought righteousness, stopped the mouths of lions, etc., and are gone before us to inherit the promises." A sufficient confutation, I think, of their error, who lightly esteem the Old Testament saints, and would not have them mentioned to Christians, as persons whose faith and patience we are called upon more immediately to follow. If this was true, the apostle would never have produced such a cloud of witnesses out of the Old Testament, to excite the Christians of the first, and consequently purest, age of the church, to continue steadfast and unmoveable in the profession of their faith. Amid this catalog of saints, I think the patriarch Abraham shines the brightest, and differs from the others, as one star differs from another star in glory; for he shone with such distinguished luster that he was called the "friend of God," the "father of the faithful"; and those who believe on Christ are said to be "sons and daughters of, and to be blessed with, faithful Abraham." Many trials of his faith did God send this great and good man, after he had commanded him to get out from his country, and from his kindred, unto a land which he should show him; but the last was the most severe of all, I mean, that of offering up his only son. This, by the divine assistance, I propose to make the subject of your present meditation, and, by way of conclusion, to draw some practical inferences, as God shall enable me, from this instructive story.

The sacred penman begins the narrative thus (Gen. 22:1): "And it came to pass, after these things, God did tempt Abraham." "After these things," that is, after he had undergone many severe trials before, after he was old, full of days, and might flatter himself perhaps that the troubles and toils of life were now finished; "after these things, God did tempt Abraham." Christians, you know not what trials you may meet with before you die: notwithstanding you may have suffered and been tried much already, yet, it may be, a greater measure is still behind, which you are to fill up. "Be not high-minded, but fear." Our last trials, in all probability, will be the greatest; and we can never say our warfare is accomplished, or our trials finished, till we bow down our heads, and give up the ghost. "And it came to pass, after these things, that God did tempt Abraham."

"God did tempt Abraham." But can the Scripture contradict itself? Does not the apostle James tell us that "God tempts no man"; and God does tempt no man to evil, or on purpose to draw him into sin; for, when a man is thus tempted, he is drawn away of his own heart's lust and enticed. But in another sense, God may be said to tempt, I mean, to try his servants; and in this sense we are to understand that passage of Matthew, where we are told that "Jesus was led up by the Spirit (the good Spirit) into the wilderness, to be tempted of the devil." And our Lord, in that excellent form of prayer which he has been pleased to give us, does not require us to pray that we may not absolutely be led into temptation, but delivered from the evil of it; from which we may plainly infer that God sees it fit sometimes to lead us into temptation, that is, to bring us into such circumstances as will try our faith and other Christian graces. In this sense we are to understand the expression before us: "God did tempt or try Abraham."

How God was pleased to reveal his will at this time to his faithful servant, whether by the Shekinah, or divine appearance, or by a small still voice, as he spoke to Elijah, or by a whisper, like that of the Spirit to Philip, when he commanded him to join himself to the eunuch's chariot, we are not told, nor is it material to inquire. It is enough that we are informed, "God said unto him, 'Abraham'"; and that Abraham knew it was the voice of God: for he said, "Behold, here I am." Oh, what a holy familiarity (if I may so speak) is there between God and those holy souls that are united to him by faith in Christ Jesus! God says, "Abraham"; and Abraham said (it should seem without the least surprise), "Behold, here I am." Being reconciled to God by the death and obedience of Christ, which he rejoiced in, and saw by faith afar off; he did not, like guilty Adam, seek the trees of the garden to hide himself from, but takes pleasure in conversing with, God, and talks with him, as a man talks with his friend. Oh, that Christless sinners knew what it is to have fellowship with the Father and the Son! They would envy the happiness of saints and count it all joy to be termed enthusiasts and fools for Christ's sake.

But what does God say to Abraham? Verse 2: "Take now thy son, thine only son Isaac, whom thou lovest, and get thee into the land of Moriah, and offer him there for a burnt offering upon one of the mountains which I shall tell thee of."

Every word deserves our particular observation. Whatever he was to do, he must do it now, immediately, without conferring with flesh and blood. But what must he do? "Take now thy son." Had God said, take now a firstling or choicest lamb or beast of your flock, and offer it up for a burnt offering, it would not have appeared so ghastly; but for God to say, "Take now thy son, and offer him up for a burnt offering," one would imagine, was enough to stagger the strongest faith. But this is not all: it must not only be a son, but "thine only son Isaac, whom thou lovest." If it must be a son, and not a beast, that must be offered, why will not Ishmael do, the son of the bondwoman? No, it must be his only son, the heir of all, his Isaac, by interpretation "laughter," the son of his old age, in whom his soul delighted, "whom thou lovest," says God, in whose life his own was wrapped up; and this son, this only son, this Isaac, the son of his love, must be taken now, even now, without delay, and be offered up by his own father, for a burnt offering, upon one of the mountains of the which God would tell him.

Well might the apostle, speaking of this man of God, say that "against hope he believed in hope, and, being strong in faith, gave glory to God." For, had he not been blessed with faith which man never before had, he must have refused to comply with this severe command. For how many arguments might nature suggest, to prove that such a command could never come from God or to excuse himself from obeying it? "What! (might the good man have said) butcher my own child! It is contrary to the very law of nature; much more to butcher my dear son Isaac, in whose seed God himself has assured me of a numerous posterity. But supposing I could give up my own affections and be willing to part with him, though I love him so dearly, yet, if I murder him, what will become of God's promise? Besides, I am now like a city built upon a hill; I shine as a light in the world, in the midst of a crooked and perverse generation. How then shall I cause God's name to be blasphemed, how shall I become a byword among the heathen, if they hear that I have committed a crime which they abhor? But, above all, what will Sarah my wife say? How can I ever return to her again, after I have imbrued my hands in my dear child's blood? Oh, that God would pardon me in this thing, or take my life in the place of my son's!" Thus, I say, Abraham might have argued, and that too seemingly with great reason, against complying with the divine command. But as before by faith he considered not the deadness of Sarah's womb, when she was past age, but believed on him who said, "Sarah thy wife shall bear thee a son indeed"; so now, being convinced that the same God spoke to and commanded him to offer up that son, and knowing that God was able to raise him from the dead, without delay he obeys the heavenly call.

Oh, that unbelievers would learn of faithful Abraham and believe whatever is revealed from God, though they cannot fully comprehend it! Abraham knew God commanded him to offer up his son, and therefore believed, notwithstanding carnal reasoning might suggest many objections. We have sufficient testimony that God has spoken to us by his son; why should we not also believe, though many things in the New Testament are above our reason? For where reason ends, faith begins. And, however infidels may style themselves reasoners, of all men they are the most unreasonable; for is it not contrary to all reason to measure an infinite by a finite understanding, or think to find out the mysteries of godliness to perfection?

But to return to the patriarch Abraham: we observed before what plausible objections he might have made; but he answered not a single word; no, without replying against his Maker, we are told that "Abraham rose up early in the morning, and saddled his ass, and took two of his young men with him, and Isaac his son, and clave the wood for the burnt offering, and rose up and went unto the place of which God had told him" (v. 3).

From this verse we may gather that God spoke to Abraham in a dream or vision of the night: for it is said, he rose up early. Perhaps it was near the fourth watch of the night, just before break of day, when God said, "Take now thy son"; and Abraham rises up early to do so; as I doubt not but he used to rise early to offer up his morning sacrifice of praise and thanksgiving. It is often remarked of people in the Old Testament, that they rose early in the morning; and particularly of our Lord in the New, that he rose a great while before day to pray. The morning befriends devotion; and if people cannot use so much self-denial as to rise early to pray, I know not how they will be able to die at a stake (if called to it) for Jesus Christ.

The humility as well as the piety of the patriarch is observable: he saddled his own ass (great men should be humble) and to show the sincerity, though he took two of his young men with him, and Isaac his son, yet he keeps his design as a secret from them all: what's more, he does not so much as tell Sarah his wife; for he knew not but she might be a snare unto him in this affair; and, as Rebekah afterward, on another occasion, advised Jacob to flee, so Sarah also might persuade Isaac to hide himself; or the young men, had they known of it, might have forced him away, as in after ages the soldiers rescued Jonathan out of the hands of Saul. But Abraham fought no such evasion, and therefore, like an Israelite indeed, in whom there was no guile, he himself resolutely "clave the wood for the burnt offering, rose up and went unto the place of which God had told him." In the second verse God commanded him to offer up his son upon one of the mountains which he would tell him of. He commanded him to offer his son up, but would not then directly tell him the place where: this was to keep him dependent and watching unto prayer, for there is nothing like being kept waiting upon God; and, if we do, assuredly God will reveal himself unto us yet further in his own time. Let us practice what we know, follow providence so far as we can see already; and what we know not, what we see not as yet, let us only be found in the way of duty, and the Lord will reveal even that unto us. Abraham knew not directly where he was to offer up his son; but he rises up and sets forward, and behold now God shows him: "And he went to the place of which God had told him." Let us go and do likewise.

Verse 4: "Then on the third day Abraham lifted up his eyes, and saw the place afar off."

So that the place, of which God had told him, was no less than three days' journey distant from the place where God first appeared to him, and commanded him to take his son. Was not this to try his faith, and to let him see that what he did was not merely from a sudden pang of devotion, but a matter of choice of deliberation? But who can tell what the aged patriarch felt during these three days? Strong as he was in faith, I am persuaded his bowels often yearned over his dear son Isaac. I think I see the good old man walking with his dear child in his hand, and now and then looking upon him, loving him, and then turning aside to weep. And perhaps, sometimes he stays a little behind to pour out his heart before God, for he had no mortal to tell his case to. Then, I think, I see him join his son and servants again, and talking to them of the things pertaining to the kingdom of God, as they walked by the way. At length, "on the third day, he lifted up his eyes, and saw the place afar off." And, to show that he was yet sincerely resolved to do whatsoever the Lord requested of him, he even now will not discover his design to his servants, but "said to his young men (as we should say to our worldly thoughts, when about to tread the courts of the Lord's house), 'Abide ye here with the ass; and I and the lad will go up yonder and worship, and come again to you'" (v. 5). This was a sufficient reason for their staying behind; and, it being their master's custom to go frequently to worship, they could have no suspicion of what he was going about. And by Abraham's saying that he and the lad would come again, I am apt to think he believed God would raise him from the dead, if so be he permitted him to offer his child up for a burnt offering.

However that be, he is yet resolved to obey God to the uttermost; and therefore: "Abraham took the wood of the burnt offering, and laid it upon Isaac his son; and he took the fire in his hand, and a knife, and they went both of them together" (v. 6). Little did Isaac think that he was to be offered on that very wood which he was carrying upon his shoulders; and therefore Isaac innocently, and with a holy freedom (for good men should not keep their children at too great a distance), "spake unto Abraham his father, and said, 'My father'; and he (with equal affection and holy condescension) said, 'Here am I, my son.'" And to show how careful Abraham had been (as all Christian parents ought to do) to instruct his Isaac how to sacrifice to God, like a youth trained up in the way wherein he should go, Isaac said, "Behold the fire and the wood; but where is the lamb for a burnt offering?" How beautiful is early piety! How amiable, to hear young people ask questions about sacrificing to God in an acceptable way! Isaac knew very well that a lamb was wanting, and that a lamb was necessary for a proper sacrifice: "Behold the fire and the wood; but where is the lamb for a burnt offering?" Young men and maidens, learn of him.

So far, it is plain, Isaac knew nothing of his father's design: but I believe, by what his father said in answer to his question, that now was the time Abraham revealed it unto him.

Verse 8: "And Abraham said, 'My son, God will provide himself a lamb for a burnt offering.'" Some think that Abraham by faith saw the Lord Jesus afar off, and here spoke prophetically of that Lamb of God already slain in decree, and hereafter to be actually offered up for sinners. This was a lamb of God's providing indeed (we dared not have thought of it) to satisfy his own justice, and to render him just in justifying the ungodly. What is all our fire and wood, the best preparations and performances we can make or present, unless God had provided himself this lamb for a burnt offering? He could not away with them. The words will well hear this interpretation. But, whatever Abraham might intend, I cannot but think he here made an application, and acquainted his son, of God's dealing with his soul; and at length, with tears in his eyes, and the utmost affection in his heart, cried out, "You are to be the lamb, my son"; God has commanded me to provide you for a burnt offering, and to offer you upon the mountain which we are now ascending. And, as it appears from a subsequent verse, Isaac, convinced that it was the divine will, made no resistance at all. For it is said, "They went both of them together"; and again, when we are told that Abraham bound Isaac, we do not hear of his complaining or endeavoring to escape, which he might have done, being (as some think) near thirty years of age and, it is plain, capable of carrying wood enough for a burnt offering. But he was partaker of the like precious faith with his aged father, and therefore is as willing to be offered as Abraham is to offer him: and "so they went both of them together."

Verse 9: At length "they came to the place of which God had told Abraham. He built an altar there, and laid the wood in order, and bound Isaac his son, and laid him on the altar upon the wood."

And here let us pause a while, and by faith take a view of the place where the father has laid him. I doubt not but that blessed angels hovered around the altar and sang, "Glory be to God in the highest," for giving such faith to man. Come, all you tenderhearted parents, who know what it is to look over a dying child: fancy that you saw the altar erected before you, and the wood laid in order, and the beloved Isaac bound upon it; fancy that you saw the aged parent standing by weeping. (For why may we not suppose that Abraham wept, since Jesus himself wept at the grave of Lazarus?) Oh, what pious, endearing expressions passed now alternately between the father and the son! Josephus records a pathetic speech made by each, whether genuine I know not; but I think I see the tears trickle down the patriarch Abraham's cheeks; and out of the abundance of the heart, he cries, "Adieu, adieu, my son; the Lord gave you to me, and the Lord calls you away; blessed be the name of the Lord; adieu, my Isaac, my only son, whom I love as my own soul; adieu, adieu." I see Isaac at the same time meekly resigning himself into his heavenly Father's hands, and praying to the most High to strengthen his earthly parent to strike the stroke. But why do I attempt to describe what either son or father felt? It is impossible; we may indeed form some faint idea of, but shall never full comprehend, it, till we come and sit down with them in the kingdom of heaven, and hear them tell the pleasing story over again. Hasten, O Lord, that blessed time! Oh, let thy kingdom come!

And now, the fatal blow is going to be given. "And Abraham stretched forth his hand, and took the knife to slay his son." But do you not think he intended to turn away his head, when he gave the blow? What's more, why may we not suppose he sometimes drew his hand in, after it was stretched out, willing to take another last farewell of his beloved Isaac, and desirous to defer it a little, though resolved at last to strike home? Be that as it will, his arm is now stretched out, the knife is in his hand, and he is about to put it to his dear son's throat.

But sing, O heavens! And rejoice, O earth! Man's extremity is God's opportunity; for behold, just as the knife, in all probability, was near his throat, "the angel of the Lord (or rather the Lord of angels, Jesus Christ, the angel of the everlasting covenant) called unto him (probably in a very audible manner) from heaven, and said, 'Abraham, Abraham.' (The word is doubled, to engage his attention; and perhaps the suddenness of the call made him draw back his hand, just as he was going to strike his son.) And Abraham said, 'Here am I'" (v. 11).

"And he said, 'Lay not thine hand upon the lad, neither do thou anything unto him: for now know I that thou fearest God, seeing thou hast not withheld thy son, thine only son from me.'"

Here then it was that Abraham received his son Isaac from the dead in a figure. He was in effect offered upon the altar, and God looked upon him as offered and given unto him. Now it was that Abraham's faith, being tried, was found more precious than gold purified seven times in the fire. Now as a reward of grace, though not of debt, for this signal act of obedience, by an oath, God gives and confirms the promise, "that in his seed all the nations of the earth should be blessed" (v. 18). With what comfort may we suppose the good old man and his son went down from the mount and returned unto the young men! With what joy may we imagine he went home and related all that had passed to Sarah! And above all, with what triumph is he now exulting in the paradise of God and adoring rich, free, distinguishing, electing, everlasting love, which alone made him to differ from the rest of mankind, and rendered him worthy of that title which he will have so long as the sun and the moon endure, "the father of the faithful"!

But let us now draw our eyes from the creature, and do what Abraham, if he was present, would direct to: I mean, fix them on the Creator, God blessed forevermore.

I see your hearts affected; I see your eyes weep. (And indeed, who can refrain weeping at the relation of such a story?) But behold, I show you a mystery, hid under the sacrifice of Abraham's only son, which, unless your hearts are hardened, must cause you to weep tears of love, and that plentifully too. I would willingly hope you even prevent me here, and are ready to say, "It is the love of God, in giving Jesus Christ to die for our sins." Yes; that is it. And yet perhaps you find your hearts, at the mentioning of this, not so much affected. Let this convince you that we are all fallen creatures, and that we do not love God or Christ as we ought to do; for, if you admire Abraham offering up his Isaac, how much more ought you to extol, magnify, and adore the love of God, who so loved the world, as to give his only begotten Son Christ Jesus our Lord, "that whosoever believeth on him should not perish, but have everlasting life"? May we not well cry out, "Now know we, O Lord, that you have loved us, since you have not withheld your Son, your only Son from us"? Abraham was God's creature (and God was Abraham's friend) and therefore under the highest obligation to surrender up his Isaac. But, oh, stupendous love! While we were his enemies, God sent forth his Son, made of a woman, made under the law, that he might become a curse for us. Oh, the freeness, as well as the infinity, of the love of God our Father! It is unsearchable: I am lost in contemplating it; it is past finding out. Think, O believers, think of the love of God, in giving Jesus Christ to be a propitiation for our sins. And when you hear how Abraham built an altar, and laid the wood in order, and bound Isaac his son, and laid him on the altar upon the wood; think how your heavenly Father bound Jesus Christ his only Son, and offered him upon the altar of his justice, and laid upon him the iniquities of us all. When you read of Abraham's stretching forth his hand to slay his son, think, oh, think, how God actually suffered his Son to be slain, that we might live forevermore. Do you read of Isaac carrying the wood upon his shoulders, upon which he was to be offered? Let this lead you to Mount Calvary (this very mount of Moriah where Isaac was offered, as some think) and take a view of the antitype Jesus Christ, the Son of God, bearing and ready to sink under the weight of that cross, on which he was to hang for us. Do you admire Isaac so freely consenting to die, though a creature, and therefore obliged to go when God called? Oh, do not forget to admire infinitely more the dear Lord Jesus, that promised seed, who willingly said, "Lo, I come," though under no obligation so to do, "to do thy will," to obey and die for men, "O God!" Did you weep just now, when I bid you fancy you saw the altar, and the wood laid in order, and Isaac laid bound on the altar? Look by faith, behold the blessed Jesus, our all-glorious Emmanuel, not bound, but nailed on an accursed tree; see how he hangs crowned with thorns, and had in derision of all that are round about him; see how the thorns pierce him, and how the blood in purple streams trickle down his sacred temples! Hark how the God of nature groans! See how he bows his head, and at length humanity gives up the ghost! Isaac is saved, but Jesus, the God of Isaac, dies; a ram is offered up in Isaac's room, but Jesus has no substitute; Jesus must bleed, Jesus must die; God the Father provided this Lamb for himself from all eternity. He must be offered in time or man must be damned forevermore. And now, where are your tears? Shall I say, refrain your voice from weeping? No; rather let me exhort you to look to him whom you have pierced, and mourn, as a woman mourns for her firstborn; for we have been the betrayers; we have been the murderers of this Lord of glory, and shall we not bewail those sins, which brought the blessed Jesus to the accursed tree? Having so much done, so much suffered for us, so much forgiven, shall we not love much? Oh! let us love him with all our hearts, and minds, and strength, and glorify him in our souls and bodies, for they are his. Which leads me to a second inference I shall draw from the foregoing discourse.

From hence we may learn the nature of true, justifying faith. Whoever understands and preaches the truth, as it is in Jesus, must acknowledge that salvation is God's free gift, and that we are saved, not by any or all the works of righteousness which we have done or can do: no, we can neither wholly nor in part justify ourselves in the light of God. The Lord Jesus Christ is our righteousness; and if we are accepted with God, it must be only in and through the personal righteousness, the active and passive obedience, of Jesus Christ his beloved Son. This righteousness must be imputed, or counted over to us, and applied by faith to our hearts, or else we can in nowise be justified in God's sight: and that very moment a sinner is enabled to lay hold on Christ's righteousness by faith, he is freely justified from all his sins, and shall never enter into condemnation, notwithstanding he was a firebrand of hell before. Thus it was that Abraham was justified before he did any good work: he was enabled to believe on the Lord Christ; it was accounted to him for righteousness; that is, Christ's righteousness was made over to him, and so accounted his. This, this is the gospel; this is the only way of finding acceptance with God: good works have nothing to do with our justification in his sight. We are justified by faith alone, as says the article of our church; agreeable to which the apostle Paul says, "By grace ye are saved, through faith; and that not of yourselves; it is the gift of God." Notwithstanding, good works have their proper place: they justify our faith, though not our persons; they follow it, and evidence our justification in the sight of men. Hence it is that the apostle James asks, "Was not Abraham justified by works?" (alluding no doubt to the story on which we have been discoursing); that is, did he not prove he was in a justified state, because his faith was productive of good works? This declarative justification in the sight of men is what is directly to be understood in the words of the text: "'Now know I,' says God, 'that thou fearest me, since thou hast not withheld thy son, thine only son from me.'" Not but that God knew it before; but this is spoken in condescension to our weak capacities and plainly shows that his offering up his son was accepted with God, as an evidence of the sincerity of his faith, and for this was left on record to future ages. Hence then you may learn, whether you are blessed with, and are sons and daughters of, faithful Abraham. You say you believe; you talk of free grace and free justification: you do well; the devils also believe and tremble. But has the faith, which you pretend to, influenced your hearts, renewed your souls, and, like

Abraham's, worked by love? Are your affections, like his, set on things above? Are you heavenly minded, and like him do you confess yourselves strangers and pilgrims on the earth? In short, has your faith enabled you to overcome the world and strengthened you to give up your Isaacs, your laughter, your most beloved lusts, friends, pleasures, and profits for God? If so, take the comfort of it; for justly may you say, "We know, assuredly, that we do fear and love God, or rather are loved of him." But if you are only talking believers, have only a faith of the head, and never felt the power of it in your hearts, however you may bolster yourselves up, and say, "We have Abraham for our father, or Christ is our Savior," unless you get a faith of the heart, a faith working by love, you shall never sit with Abraham, Isaac, Jacob, or Jesus Christ, in the kingdom of heaven.

But I must draw one more inference, and with that I shall conclude.

Learn, O saints! From what has been said, to sit loose to all your worldly comforts and stand ready prepared to part with everything, when God shall require it at your hand. Some of you perhaps may have friends, who are to you as your own souls; and others may have children, in whose lives your own lives are bound up: all, I believe, have their Isaacs, their particular delights of some kind or other. Labor, for Christ's sake, labor, you sons and daughters of Abraham, to resign them daily in affection to God, that, when he shall require you really to sacrifice them, you may not confer with flesh and blood, any more than the blessed patriarch now before us. And as for you that have been in any measure tried like unto him, let his example encourage and comfort you. Remember, Abraham your father was tried so before you; think, oh, think of the happiness he now enjoys, and how he is incessantly thanking God for tempting and trying him when here below. Look up often by the eye of faith, and see him sitting with his dearly beloved Isaac in the world of spirits. Remember, it will be but a little while, and you shall sit with them also, and tell one another what God has done for your souls. There I hope to sit with you, and hear this story of his offering up his son from his own mouth, and to praise the Lamb that sits upon the throne, for what he has done for all our souls, forever and ever.

The Great Duty of Family Religion

—✕—

"As for me and my house, we will serve the Lord." —JOSHUA 24:15

These words contain the holy resolution of pious Joshua, who, having in a most moving, affectionate discourse recounted to the Israelites what great things God had done for them, in the verse immediately preceding the text comes to draw a proper inference from what he had been delivering; and acquaints them, in the most pressing terms, that since God had been so exceedingly gracious unto them, they could do not less than out of gratitude for such uncommon favors and mercies dedicate both themselves and families to his service. "Now therefore, fear the Lord, and serve him in sincerity and truth, and put away the gods which your fathers served on the other side of the flood." And by the same engaging motive does the prophet Samuel afterward enforce their obedience to the commandments of God: "Only fear the Lord, and serve him in truth, with all your heart; for consider how great things he hath done for you" (1 Sam. 12:24). But then, that they might not excuse themselves (as too many might be apt to do) by his giving them a bad example, or think he was laying heavy burdens upon them, while he himself touched them not with one of his fingers, he tells them in the text that whatever regard they might pay to the doctrine he had been preaching, yet he (as all ministers ought to do) was resolved to live up to and practice it himself: "Choose you therefore whom you will serve, whether the gods which your fathers served, or the gods of the Amorites, in whose land ye dwell: but as for me and my house, we will serve the Lord."

A resolution this, worthy of Joshua, and no less becoming, no less necessary for every true son of Joshua that is entrusted with the care and government of a family in our day: and, if it was ever seasonable for ministers to preach up, or people to put in practice family religion, it was nevermore so than in the present age; since it is greatly to be feared, that out of those many households that call themselves Christians, there are but few that serve God in their respective families as they ought.

It is true indeed. Visit our churches, and you may perhaps see something of the form of godliness still subsisting among us; but even that is scarcely to be met with in private houses. So that were the blessed angels to come, as in the patriarchal age, and observe our spiritual economy at home, would they not be tempted to say as Abraham to Abimilech, "Surely, the fear of God is not in this place" (Gen. 20:11)?

How such a general neglect of family religion first began to overspread the Christian world is difficult to determine. As for the primitive Christians, I am positive it was not so with them. No, they had not so learned Christ, as falsely to imagine religion was to be confined solely to their assemblies for public worship; but, on the contrary, behaved with such piety and exemplary holiness in their private families, that St. Paul often styles their house a church: "Salute such a one," says he, "and the church which is in his house." And, I believe, we must forever despair of seeing a primitive spirit of piety revived in the world, till we are so happy as to see a revival of primitive family religion; and persons unanimously resolving with good old Joshua, in the words of the text, "As for me and my house, we will serve the Lord."

From which words, I shall beg leave to insist on these three things.

First, that it is the duty of every governor of a family to take care that not only he himself, but also that those committed to his charge, "serve the Lord."

Second, I shall endeavor to show after what manner a governor and his household ought to serve the Lord.

And third, I shall offer some motives, in order to excite all governors, with their respective households, to serve the Lord in the manner that shall be recommended.

And first, I am to show that it is the duty of every governor of a family to take care that not only he himself, but also that those committed to his charge, should serve the Lord.

And this will appear, if we consider that every governor of a family ought to look upon himself as obliged to act in three capacities: as a prophet, to instruct; as a priest, to pray for and with; as a king, to govern, direct, and provide for them. It is true indeed, the latter of these, their kingly office, they are not so frequently deficient in (what's more, in this they are generally too solicitous), but as for the two former, their priestly and prophetic offices, like Gallio, they care for no such things. But however indifferent some governors may be about it, they may be assured that God will require a due discharge of these offices at their hands. For if, as the apostle argues, "He that does not provide for his own house," in temporal things, "has denied the faith, and is worse than an infidel," to what greater degree of apostasy must he have arrived who takes no thought to provide for the spiritual welfare of his family?

But further, persons are generally very liberal of their invectives against the clergy and think they justly blame the conduct of that minister who does not take heed to and watch over the flock, of which the Holy Ghost has made him overseer; but may not every governor of a family be in a lower degree liable to the same censure, who takes no thought for those souls that are committed to his charge? For every house is as it were a little parish, every governor (as was before observed) a priest, every family a flock; and if any of them perish through the governor's neglect, their blood will God require at their hands.

Was a minister to disregard teaching his people publicly, and from house to house, and to excuse himself by saying that he had enough to do to work out his own salvation with fear and trembling, without concerning himself with that of others; would you not be apt to think such a minister to be like the unjust judge, "one that neither feared God, nor regarded man"? And yet, odious as such a character would be, it is no worse than that governor of a family deserves, who thinks himself obliged only to have his own soul, without paying any regard to the souls of his household. For (as was above hinted) every house is as it were a parish, and every master is concerned to secure, as much as in him lies, the spiritual prosperity of everyone under his roof, as any minister whatever is obliged to look to the spiritual welfare of every individual person under his charge.

What precedents men who neglect their duty in this particular can plead for such omission, I cannot tell. Doubtless not the example of holy Job, who was so far from imagining that he had no concern, as governor of a family, with anyone's soul but his own, that the Scripture acquaints us, "When the days of his children's feasting were gone about, that Job sent and sanctified them, and offered burnt offerings, according to the number of them all; for Job said, 'It may be that my sons have sinned and cursed God in their hearts: thus did Job continually.'" Nor can they plead the practice of good old Joshua, whom, in the text, we find as much concerned for his household's welfare as his own. Nor, last, that of Cornelius, who feared God, not only himself, but with all his house: and were Christians but of the same spirit of Job, Joshua, and the Gentile centurion, they would act as Job, Joshua, and Cornelius did.

But alas! If this be the case, and all governors of families ought not only to serve the Lord themselves, but likewise to see that their respective households do so too; what will then become of those who not only neglect serving God themselves, but also make it their business to ridicule and scoff at any of their house that do? Who are not content with "not entering into the kingdom of heaven themselves; but them also that are willing to enter in, they hinder." Surely such men are factors for the devil indeed. Surely their damnation slumbers not: for although God, in his good providence, may suffer such stumbling blocks to be put in his children's way, and suffer their greatest enemies to be those of their own households, for a trial of their sincerity, and improvement of their faith; yet we cannot but pronounce a woe against those masters by whom such offenses come. For if those that only take care of their own souls can scarcely be saved, where will such monstrous profane and wicked governors appear?

But hoping there are but few of this unhappy stamp, proceed we now to the second thing proposed: to show after what manner a governor and his household ought to serve the Lord.

1. And the first thing I shall mention is reading the Word of God. This is a duty incumbent on every private person. "Search the Scriptures, for in them ye think ye have eternal life" is a precept given by our blessed Lord indifferently to all: but much more so ought every governor of a family to think it in a peculiar manner spoken to himself, because (as has been already proved) he ought to look upon himself as a prophet and therefore, agreeably to such a character, bound to instruct those under his charge in the knowledge of the Word of God.

This we find was the order God gave to his peculiar people Israel: for thus speaks his representative Moses, "These words," that is, the Scripture words, "which I command thee this day, shall be in thy heart, and thou shalt teach them diligently unto thy children," that is, as it is generally explained, servants, as well as children, "and shalt talk of them when thou sittest in thy house" (Deut. 6:6–7). From where we may infer that the only reason why so many neglect to read the words of Scripture diligently to their children is because the words of Scripture are not in their hearts; for if they were, out of the abundance of the heart their mouth would speak.

Besides, servants as well as children are, for the generality, very ignorant and mere novices in the laws of God: and how shall they know, unless someone teach them? And what more proper to teach them by than the lively oracles of God, "which are able to make them wise unto salvation"? And who more proper to instruct them by these lively oracles than parents and masters, who (as has been more than once observed) are as much concerned to feed them with spiritual, as with bodily bread, day by day?

But if these things be so, what a miserable condition are those unhappy governors in, who are so far from feeding those committed to their care with the sincere milk of the Word, to the intent they may grow thereby, that they neither search the Scriptures themselves nor are careful to explain them to others? Such families must be in a happy way indeed to do their Master's will, who take such prodigious pains to know it! Would not one imagine that they had turned converts to the Church of Rome, that they thought ignorance to be the mother of devotion, and that those were to be condemned as heretics who read their Bibles? And yet how few families are there among us who do not act after this unseemly manner! But shall I praise them in this? I praise them not; brethren, this thing ought not so to be.

2. Pass we on now to the second means whereby every governor and his household ought to serve the Lord: family prayer.

This is a duty, though as much neglected, yet as absolutely necessary as the former. Reading is a good preparative for prayer, as prayer is an excellent means to render reading effectual. And the reason why every governor of a family should join both these exercises together is plain, because a governor of a family cannot perform his priestly office (which we before observed he is in some degree invested with) without performing this duty of family prayer.

We find it therefore remarked, when mention is made of Cain and Abel's offering sacrifices, that they brought them. But to whom did they bring them? Why, in all probability, to their father Adam, who, as priest of the family, was to offer sacrifice in their names. And so ought every spiritual son of the second Adam, who is entrusted with the care of a household, to offer up the spiritual sacrifices of supplications and thanksgivings, acceptable to God through Jesus Christ, in the presence and name of all who wait upon, or eat meat at, his table.

Thus we read our blessed Lord behaved, when he tabernacled among us: for it is said often that he prayed with his twelve disciples, which was then his little family. And he himself has promised a particular blessing to joint supplications: "Wheresoever two or three are gathered together in my name, there am I in the midst of them." And again, "If two or three are agreed touching anything they shall ask, it shall be given them." Add to this, that we are commanded by the apostle to "pray always, with all manner of supplication," which doubtless includes family prayer. And holy Joshua, when he set up the good resolution in the text, that he and his household would serve the Lord, certainly resolved to pray with his family, which is one of the best testimonies they could give of their serving him.

Besides, there are no families but what have some common blessings, of which they have been all partakers, to give thanks for; some common crosses and afflictions, which they are to pray against; some common sins, which they are all to lament and bewail; but how this can be done, without joining together in one common act of humiliation, supplication, and thanksgiving, is difficult to devise.

From all which considerations put together, it is evident that family prayer is a great and necessary duty; and consequently, those governors that neglect it are certainly without excuse. And it is much to be feared, if they live without family prayer, they live without God in the world.

And yet, such a hateful character as this is, it is to be feared that were God to send out an angel to destroy us, as he did once to destroy the Egyptian first-born, and withal give him a commission, as then, to spare no houses but where they saw the blood on the lintel, sprinkled on the doorpost, so now, to let no families escape, but those that called upon him in morning and evening prayer; few would remain unhurt by his avenging sword. Shall I term such families Christians or heathens? Doubtless they deserve not the name of Christians; and heathens will rise up in judgment against such profane families of this generation; for they had always their household gods, whom they worshiped and whose assistance they frequently invoked. And a pretty pass those families surely are arrived at, who must be sent to school to pagans. But will not the Lord be avenged on such profane households as these? Will he not pour out his fury upon those that call not upon his name?

3. But it is time for me to hasten to the third and last means I shall recommend, whereby every governor ought with his household to serve the Lord, catechizing and instructing their children and servants, and bringing them up in the nurture and admonition of the Lord.

That this, as well as the two former, is a duty incumbent on every governor of a house, appears from that famous encomium or commendation God gives of Abraham: "I know that he will command his children and his household after him, to keep the way of the Lord, to do justice and judgment." And indeed scarce anything is more frequently pressed upon us in holy Writ, than this duty of catechizing. Thus, says God in a passage before cited, "Thou shalt teach these words diligently unto thy children." And parents are commanded in the New Testament to "bring up their children in the nurture and admonition of the Lord." The holy psalmist acquaints us that one great end why God did such great wonders for his people was "to the intent that when they grew up, they should show their children, or servants, the same." And in Deuteronomy 6:20 and following verses, God strictly commands his people to instruct their children in the true nature of the ceremonial worship, when they should inquire about it, as he supposed they would do, in time to come. And if servants and children were to be instructed in the nature of Jewish rites, much more ought they now to be initiated and grounded in the doctrines and first principles of the gospel of Christ: not only because it is a revelation, which has brought life and immortality to a fuller and clearer light, but also because many seducers are gone abroad into the world, who do their utmost endeavor to destroy not only the superstructure, but likewise to sap the very foundation of our most holy religion.

Would then the present generation have their posterity be true lovers and honorers of God, masters and parents must take Solomon's good advice and train up and catechize their respective households in the way wherein they should go.

I am aware but of one objection that can, with any show of reason, be urged against what has been advanced; which is that such a procedure as this will take up too much time and hinder families too long from their worldly business. But it is much to be questioned, whether persons that start such an abjection are not of the same hypocritical spirit as the traitor Judas, who had indignation against devout Mary for being so profuse of her ointment, in anointing our blessed Lord, and asked why it might not be sold for two hundred pence, and given to the poor. For has God given us so much time to work for ourselves, and shall we not allow some small pittance of it, morning and evening, to be devoted to his more immediate worship and service? Have not people read that it is God who gives men power to get wealth, and therefore that the best way to prosper in the world is to secure his favor? And has not our blessed Lord himself promised that if we seek first the kingdom of God and his righteousness, all outward necessaries shall be added unto us?

Abraham, no doubt, was a man of as great business as such objectors may be; but yet he would find time to command his household to serve the Lord. What's more, David was a king, and consequently had a great deal of business upon his hands; yet notwithstanding, he professes that he would walk in his house with a perfect heart. And, to instance but one more, holy Joshua was a person certainly engaged very much in temporal affairs; and yet he solemnly declares before all Israel that as for him and his household, they would serve the Lord. And did persons but redeem their time, as Abraham, David, or Joshua did, they would no longer complain that family duties kept them too long from the business of the world.

But my third and last general head, under which I was to offer some motives, in order to excite all governors, with their respective households, to serve the Lord in the manner before recommended, I hope, will serve, instead of a thousand arguments, to prove the weakness and folly of any such objection.

1. And the first motive I shall mention is the duty of gratitude, which you that are governors of families owe to God. Your lot, everyone must confess, is

cast in a fair ground: providence has given you a goodly heritage, above many of your fellow creatures, and therefore, out of a principle of gratitude, you ought to endeavor, as much as in you lies, to make every person of your respective households to call upon him as long as they live: not to mention that the authority, with which God has invested you as parents and governors of families, is a talent committed to your trust, and which you are bound to improve to your Master's honor. In other things we find governors and parents can exercise lordship over their children and servants readily and frequently enough can say to one, "'Go,' and he goeth"; and to another, "'Come,' and he cometh"; to a third, "'Do this,' and he doeth it." And shall this power be so often employed in your own affairs and never exerted in the things of God? Be astonished, O heavens, at this!

Thus did not faithful Abraham; no, God says that he knew Abraham would command his servants and children after him. Thus did not Joshua: no, he was resolved not only to walk with God himself, but to improve his authority in making all about him do so too: "As for me and my household, we will serve the Lord." Let us go and do likewise.

2. But second, if gratitude to God will not, I think love and pity to your children should move you, with your respective families, to serve the Lord.

Most people express a great fondness for their children: what's more, so great that very often their own lives are wrapped up in those of their offspring. "Can a woman forget her sucking child, that she should not have compassion on the son of her womb?" says God by his prophet Isaiah. He speaks of it as a monstrous thing and scarcely credible, but the words immediately following affirm it to be possible, "Yes, they may forget"; and experience also assures us they may. Father and mother may both forsake their children; for what greater degree of forgetfulness can they express toward them than to neglect the improvement of their better part, and not bring them up in the knowledge and fear of God?

It is true indeed, parents seldom forget to provide for their children's bodies (though, it is to be feared, some men are so far sunk beneath the beasts that perish, as to neglect even that), but then how often do they forget, or, rather, when do they remember, to secure the salvation of their immortal souls? But is this their way of expressing their fondness for the fruit of their bodies? Is this the best testimony they can give of their affection to the darling of their hearts? Then was Delilah fond of Samson, when she delivered him up into the hands of the Philistines? Then were those ruffians well affected to Daniel, when they threw him into a den of lions?

3. But third, if neither gratitude to God nor love and pity to your children will prevail on you, yet let a principle of common honesty and justice move you to set up the holy resolution in the text.

This is a principle which all men would be thought to act upon. But certainly, if any may be truly censured for their injustice, none can be more liable to such censure, than those who think themselves injured if their servants withdraw themselves from their bodily work, and yet they in return take no care of their inestimable souls. For is it just that servants should spend their time and strength in their master's service, and masters not at the same time give them what is just and equal for their service?

It is true, some men may think they have done enough when they give unto their servants food and raiment, and say, "Did not I bargain with you for so much a year?" But if they give them no other reward than this, what do they less for their very beasts? But are not servants better than they? Doubtless they are; and however masters may put off their convictions for the present, they will find a time will come when they shall know they ought to have given them some spiritual as well as temporal wages; and the cry of those that have mowed down their fields will enter into the ears of the Lord of Sabaoth.

4. But fourth, if neither gratitude to God, pity to children, nor a principle for common justice to servants are sufficient to balance all objections; yet let that darling, that prevailing, motive of self-interest turn the scale and engage you with your respective households to serve the Lord.

This weighs greatly with you in other matters: be then persuaded to let it have a due and full influence on you in this; and if it has, if you have but faith as a grain of mustard seed, how can you avoid believing that promoting family religion will be the best means to promote your own temporal as well as eternal welfare? For "godliness has the promise of the life that now is, as well as that which is to come."

Besides, you all doubtless wish for honest servants and pious children; and to have them prove otherwise would be as great a grief to you, as it was to Elisha to have a treacherous Gehazi, or David to be troubled with a rebellious Absalom. But how can it be expected they should learn their duty, except those set over them take care to teach it to them? Is it not as reasonable to expect you should reap where had not sown, or gather where you had not strewed?

Did Christianity, indeed, give any countenance to children and servants to disregard their parents and masters according to the flesh, or represent their duty to them, as inconsistent with their entire obedience to their Father and Master who is in heaven, there might then be some pretense to neglect instructing them in the principles of such a religion. But since the precepts of this pure and undefiled religion are all of them holy, just, and good; and the more they are taught their duty to God, the better they will perform their duties to you; I think to neglect the improvement of their souls, out of a dread of spending too much time in religious duties, is acting quite contrary to your own interest as well as duty.

5. Fifth and last, if neither gratitude to God, love to your children, common justice to your servants, nor even that most prevailing motive self-interest, will excite; yet let a consideration of the terrors of the Lord persuade you to put in practice the pious resolution in the text. Remember, the time will come, and that perhaps very shortly, when we must all appear before the judgment seat of Christ; where we must give a solemn and strict account how we have had our conversation, in our respective families in this world. How will you endure to see your children and servants (who ought to be your joy and crown of rejoicing in the day of our Lord Jesus Christ) coming out as so many swift witnesses against you; cursing the father that begot them, the womb that bore them, the paps which they have sucked, and the day they ever entered into your houses? Think you not, the damnation which men must endure for their own sins will be sufficient that they need load themselves with the additional guilt of being accessory to the damnation of others also? Oh, consider this, all you that forget to serve the Lord with your respective households, "lest he pluck you away, and there be none to deliver you"!

But God forbid, brethren, that any such evil should befall you: no, rather will I hope that you have been in some measure convinced by what has been said of the great importance of family religion; and therefore are ready to cry out in the words immediately following the text, "God forbid that we should forsake the Lord"; and again: "Nay, but we will (with our several households) serve the Lord" (v. 21).

And that there may be always such a heart in you, let me exhort all governors of families, in the name of our Lord Jesus Christ, often to reflect on the inestimable worth of their own souls, and the infinite ransom, even the precious blood of Jesus Christ, which has been paid down for them. Remember, I beseech you to remember that you are fallen creatures; that you are by nature lost and estranged from God; and that you can never be restored to your primitive happiness, till by being born again of the Holy Ghost, you arrive at your primitive state of purity, have the image of God restamped upon your souls, and are thereby made meet to be partakers of the inheritance with the saints in light. Do, I say, but seriously and frequently reflect on and act as persons that believe such important truths, and you will no more neglect your family's spiritual welfare than your own. No, the love of God, which will then be shed abroad in your hearts, will constrain you to do your utmost to preserve them; and the deep sense of God's free grace in Christ Jesus (which you will then have) in calling you will excite you to do your utmost to save others, especially those of your own household. And though, after all your pious endeavors, some may continue unreformed, yet you will have this comfortable reflection to make, that you did what you could to make your families religious, and therefore may rest assured of sitting down in the kingdom of heaven, with Abraham, Joshua, and Cornelius, and all the godly householders, who in their several generations shone forth as so many lights in their respective households upon earth. Amen.

Thankfulness for Mercies Received, a Necessary Duty

—⁓—

A farewell sermon, preached on board the *Whitaker,* at anchor near Savannah, in Georgia, Sunday, May 17, 1738.

O that men would therefore praise the Lord for his goodness, and declare the wonders that he doeth for the children of men. —PSALM 107:31

Numberless marks does man bear in his soul, that he is fallen and estranged from God; but nothing gives a greater proof thereof, than that backwardness, which everyone finds within himself, to the duty of praise and thanksgiving.

When God placed the first man in paradise, his soul no doubt was so filled with a sense of the riches of the divine love that he was continually employing that breath of life, which the Almighty had not long before breathed into him, in blessing and magnifying that all-bountiful, all-gracious God, in whom he lived, moved, and had his being.

And the brightest idea we can form of the angelical hierarchy above, and the spirits of just men made perfect, is that they are continually standing around the throne of God and cease not, day and night, saying, "Worthy art thou, O Lamb that was slain, to receive power and riches, and wisdom, and strength, and honor, and glory, and blessing" (Rev. 5:12).

That then, which was man's perfection when time first began and will be his employment when death is swallowed up in victory, and time shall be no more, without controversy, is part of our perfection and ought to be our frequent exercise on earth; and I doubt not but those blessed spirits, who are sent forth to minister to them who shall be heirs of salvation, often stand astonished when they encamp around us or find our hearts so rarely enlarged, and our mouths so seldom opened, to show forth the loving-kindness of the Lord, or to speak of all his praise.

Matter for praise and adoration can never be wanting to creatures redeemed by the blood of the Son of God; and who have such continual scenes of his infinite goodness presented to their view, that were their souls duly affected with a sense of his universal love, they could not but be continually calling on heaven and earth, men and angels, to join with them in praising and blessing that "high and lofty one, who inhabiteth eternity, who maketh his sun to shine on the evil and on the good," and daily pours down his blessings on the whole race of mankind.

But few are arrived to such a degree of charity or love, as to rejoice with those that do rejoice, and to be as thankful for other mercies as their own. This part of Christian perfection, though begun on earth, will be consummated only in heaven, where our hearts will glow with such fervent love toward God and one another, that every fresh degree of glory communicated to our neighbor will also communicate to us a fresh topic of thankfulness and joy.

That which has the greatest tendency to excite the generality of fallen men to praise and thanksgiving is a sense of God's private mercies and particular benefits bestowed upon ourselves. For as these come nearer our own hearts, so they must be more affecting; and as they are peculiar proofs, whereby we may know that God does in a more especial manner favor us above others, so they cannot but sensibly touch us; and if our hearts are not quite frozen, like coals of a refiner's fire, they must melt us down into thankfulness and love. It was a consideration of the distinguishing favor God had shown to his chosen people Israel, and the frequent and remarkable deliverance worked by him in behalf of "those who go down to the sea in ships, and occupy their business in great matters," that made the holy psalmist break out so frequently as he does in this psalm, into this moving, pathetical exclamation, "that men would therefore praise the Lord for his goodness, and declare the wonders that he doeth for the children of men!"

His expressing himself in so fervent a manner implies both the importance and neglect of the duty. As when Moses in another occasion cried out, "O that they were wise, that they understood this, that they would practically consider their latter end!" (Deut. 32:29).

I say, importance and neglect of the duty—for out of those many thousands that receive blessings from the Lord, how few give thanks in remembrance of his holiness? The account given us of the ungrateful lepers is but too lively a representation of the ingratitude of mankind in general, who like them, when under any humbling providence, can cry, "Jesus, Master, have mercy on us!" (Luke 17:13). But when healed of their sickness, or delivered from their distress, scarce one in ten can be found "returning to give thanks to God."

And yet as common as this sin of ingratitude is, there is nothing we ought more earnestly to pray against. For what is more absolutely condemned in holy Scripture than ingratitude? Or what more peremptorily required than the contrary temper? Thus says the apostle, "Rejoice evermore . . . in everything give thanks" (1 Thess. 5:16, 18). "Be careful for nothing; but in everything by prayer and supplication, with thanksgiving, let your requests be made known unto God" (Phil. 4:6).

On the contrary, the apostle mentions it as one of the highest crimes of the Gentiles, that they were not thankful. "Neither were they thankful" (Rom. 1:21). As also in another place (2 Tim. 3:2), he numbers the "unthankful" among those unholy, profane persons, who are to have their portion in the lake of fire and brimstone.

As for our sins, God puts them behind his back; but his mercies he will have acknowledged. "There is virtue gone out of me," says Jesus Christ (Luke 8:46), and the woman who was cured of her bloody issue must confess it. And we generally find, when God sent any remarkable punishment upon a particular person, he reminded him of the favors he had received, as so many aggravations of his ingratitude. Thus when God was about to visit Eli's house, he thus expostulates with him by his prophet: "'Did I plainly appear unto the house of thy fathers, when they were in Egypt, in Pharaoh's house? And did I choose him out of all the tribes of Israel, to be my priest, to offer upon mine altar, to burn incense, and to wear an ephod before me? Wherefore kick ye at my sacrifice, and at mine offering, which I have commanded in my habitation, and honorest thy sons above me; so make yourselves fat with the chiefest of all the offerings of Israel my people?' Wherefore the Lord God of Israel saith, 'I said indeed, that thy house, and the house of thy father, should walk before me forever'; but now the Lord saith, 'Be it far from me, for them that honor me will I honor, and they that despise me shall be lightly esteemed'" (1 Sam. 2:27–30).

It was this and suchlike instances of God's severity against the unthankful that inclined me to choose the words of the text, as the most proper subject I could discourse on at this time.

Four months, my good friends, we have now been upon the sea in this ship, and "have occupied our business in the great waters." At God Almighty's word, we have seen the stormy wind arise, which has lifted up the waves thereof. We have been carried up to the heaven, and down again to the deep, and some of our souls melted away because of the trouble; but I trust we cried earnestly unto the Lord, and he delivered us out of our distress. For he made the storm to cease, so that the waves thereof were still. And now we are glad, because we are at rest, for God has brought us to the haven where we would be. Oh, that you would therefore praise the Lord for his goodness, and declare the wonders that he has done for us, the unworthiest of the sons of men [see Ps. 107:23–31].

Thus Moses, thus Joshua behaved. For when they were about to take their leave of the children of Israel, they recounted to them what great things God had done for them, as the best arguments and motives they could urge to engage them to obedience. And how can I copy after better examples? What fitter, what more noble motives, to holiness and purity of living, can I lay before you, than they did?

Indeed, I cannot say that we have seen the "pillar of a cloud by day, or a pillar of fire by night," going visibly before us to guide our course; but this I can say, that the same God who was in that pillar of a cloud, and pillar of fire, which departed not from the Israelites, and who has made the sun to rule the day, and the moon to rule the night, has, by his good providence, directed us in our right way, or else the pilot had steered us in vain.

Neither can I say that we have seen the "sun stand still," as the children of Israel did in the days of Joshua. But surely God, during part of our voyage, has caused it to withhold some of that heat, which it usually sends forth in these warmer climates, or else it had not failed, but some of you must have perished in the sickness that has been and does yet continue among us.

We have not seen the waters stand purposely on a heap, that we might pass through, neither have we been pursued by Pharaoh and his host, and delivered out of their hands; but we have been led through the sea as through a wilderness and were once remarkably preserved from being run down by another ship, which, had God permitted, the waters, in all probability, would immediately have overwhelmed us, and like Pharaoh and his host, we should have sunk, as stones, into the sea.

We may, indeed, atheist like, ascribe all these things to natural causes, and say, "Our own skill and foresight has brought us here in safety." But as certainly as Jesus Christ, the angel of the covenant, in the days of his flesh, walked upon the water, and said to his sinking disciples, "Be not afraid, it is I," so surely has the same everlasting I AM, "who decketh himself with light as with a garment, who spreadeth out the heavens like a curtain, who claspeth the winds in his fist, who holdeth the waters in the hollow of his hands," and guided the wise men by a star in the east; so surely, I say, has he spoken, and at his command the winds have blown us where we are not arrived. For his providence ruleth all things. "Wind and storms obey his word"; he said to it at one time, "Go," and it goeth; at another, "Come," and it cometh; and at a third time, "Blow this way," and it bloweth.

It is he, my brethren, and not we ourselves, that has of late sent us such prosperous gales, and made us to ride, as it were, on the wings of the wind, into the haven where we would be.

"Oh, that you would therefore praise the Lord for his goodness," and by your lives declare that you are truly thankful for the wonders he had shown to us, who are less than the least of the sons of men.

I say, declare it by your lives; for to give him thanks barely with your lips, while your hearts are far from him, is but a mock sacrifice, even an abomination unto the Lord.

This was the end, the royal psalmist says, God had in view, when he showed such wonders, from time to time, to the people of Israel, "That they might keep his statutes, and observe his laws" (Ps. 105:45); and this, my good friends, is the end God would have accomplished in us, and the only return he desires us to make him, for all the benefits he has conferred upon us.

Oh then, let me beseech you, give to God your hearts, your whole hearts; and suffer yourselves to be drawn by the cords of infinite love, to honor and obey him.

Assure yourselves you can never serve a better master; for his service is perfect freedom, his yoke, when worn a little while, is exceedingly easy, his burden light, and in keeping his commandments there is great reward: love, peace, joy in the Holy Ghost here, and a crown of glory that fades not away, hereafter.

You may, indeed, let other lords have dominion over you, and Satan may promise to give you all the kingdoms of the world, and the glory of them, if you will fall down and worship him; but he is a liar and was so from the beginning; he has not so much to give you as you may tread on with the sole of your foot; or could he give you the whole world, yes, that could not make you happy without God. It is God alone, my brethren, whose we are, in whose name I now speak, and who has of late showed us such mercies in the deep, that can give solid lasting happiness to your souls; and he for this reason only desires your hearts, because without him you must be miserable.

Suffer me not then to go away without my errand; as it is the last time I shall speak to you, let me not speak in vain; but let a sense of the divine goodness lead you to repentance.

Even Saul, that abandoned wretch, when David showed him his skirt, which he had cut off, when he might have also taken his life, was so melted down with his kindness that he lifted up his voice and wept. And we must have hearts harder than Saul's, even harder than the nether millstone, if a sense of God's late loving-kindnesses, notwithstanding he might so often have destroyed us, does not even compel us to lay down our arms against him and become his faithful servants and soldiers unto our lives' end.

If they have not this effect upon us, we shall, of all men, be most miserable; for God is just as well as merciful; and the more blessings we have received here, the greater damnation, if we do not improve them, shall we incur hereafter.

But God forbid that any of those should ever suffer the vengeance of eternal fire, among whom I have, for these four months, been preaching the gospel of Christ; but yet thus must it be, if you do not improve the divine mercies: and instead of your being my crown of rejoicing in the day of our Lord Jesus Christ, I must appear as a swift witness against you.

But, brethren, I am persuaded better things of you, and things that accompany salvation, though I thus speak.

Blessed be God, some marks of a partial reformation at least have been visible among all you that are soldiers. And my weak though sincere endeavors, to build you up in the knowledge and fear of God, have not been altogether in vain in the Lord.

Swearing, I hope is in a great measure abated with you; and God, I trust, has blessed his late visitations, by making them the means of awakening your consciences, to a more solicitous inquiry about the things which belong to your everlasting peace.

Fulfill you then my joy, by continuing thus minded, and labor to go on to perfection. For I shall have no greater pleasure than to see, or hear, that you walk in the truth.

Consider, my good friends, you are now, as it were, entering on a new world, where you will be surrounded with multitudes of heathens; and if you take not heed to "have your conversation honest amongst them" and to "walk worthy of the holy vocation wherewith you are called," you will act the hellish part of Herod's soldiers over again; and cause Christ's religion, as they did his person, to be had in derision of those that are round about you.

Consider further, what peculiar privileges you have enjoyed, above many others that are entering on the same land. They have had, as it were, a famine of the word, but you have rather been in danger of being surfeited with your spiritual manna. And therefore, as more instructions have been given you, so from you men will most justly expect the greater improvement in goodness.

Indeed, I cannot say, I have discharged my duty toward you as I ought. No, I am sensible of many faults in my ministerial office, and for which I have not failed, nor, I hope, ever shall fail, to humble myself in secret before God. However, this I can say, that except a few days that have been spent necessarily on other persons whom God immediately called me to write and minister unto, and the two last weeks wherein I have been confined by sickness, all the while I have been aboard, I have been either actually engaged in or preparing myself for instructing you. And though you are now to be committed to the care of another (whose labors I heartily beseech God to bless among you), yet I trust I shall, at all seasons, if need be, willingly spend, and be spent, for the good of your souls, though the more abundantly I love you, the less I should be loved.

As for your military affairs, I have nothing to do with them. Fear God, and you must honor the king. Nor am I well acquainted with the nature of that land which you are now come over to protect; only this I may venture to affirm in the general, that you must necessarily expect upon your arrival at a new colony, to meet with many difficulties. But your very profession teaches you to endure hardship: be not therefore fainthearted, but "quit yourselves like men, and be strong" (1 Sam. 4:9). Be not like those cowardly persons, who were affrighted at the report of the false spies (Num. 14) that came and said that there were people tall as the Anakims to be grappled with, but be like unto Caleb and Joshua, all heart; and say, "We will act valiantly, for we shall be more than conquerors over all difficulties through Jesus Christ that loved us." Above all things, my brethren, take heed, and beware of murmuring, like the perverse Israelites, against those that are set over you; and "learn, whatsoever state you shall be in, therewith to be content."

As I have spoken to you, I hope your wives also will suffer the word of exhortation: your behavior on shipboard, especially the first part of the voyage, I choose to throw a cloak over; for to use the mildest terms, it was not such as became the gospel of our Lord Jesus Christ. However, of late, blessed be God, you have taken more heed to your ways, and some of you have walked all the while, as became "women professing godliness." Let those accept my hearty thanks, and permit me to entreat you all in general, as you are all now married, to remember the solemn vow you made at your entrance into the marriage state, and see that you be subject to your own husbands, in every lawful thing; beg of God to keep the door of your lips, that you offend not with your tongues; and walk in love, that your prayers be not hindered. You that have children, let it be your chief concern to breed them up in the nurture and admonition of the Lord. And live all of you so holy and unblamable, that you may not so much as be suspected to be unchaste; and as some of you have imitated Mary Magdalen in her sin, strive to imitate her also in her repentance.

As for you, sailors, what shall I say? How shall I address myself to you? How shall I do that which I so much long to do; touch your hearts? Gratitude obliges me to wish thus well to you. For you have often taught me many instructive lessons, and reminded me to put up many prayers to God for you, that you might receive your spiritual sight.

When I have seen you preparing for a storm, and reefing [could also be reesing] your sails to guard against it, how have I wished that you and I were as careful to avoid that storm of God's wrath, which will certainly, without repentance, quickly overtake us? When I have observed you catch at every fair gale, how I secretly cried, Oh, that we were as careful to know the things that belong to our peace, before they are forever hid from our eyes! And when I have taken notice, how steadily you eyed your compass in order to steer aright, how have I wished that we as steadily eyed the Word of God, which alone can preserve us from "making shipwreck of faith, and a good conscience"! In short, there is scarce anything you do, which has not been a lesson of instruction to me; and therefore it would be ungrateful in me did I not take this opportunity of exhorting you in the name of our Lord Jesus Christ, to be as wise in the things which concern your soul, as I have observed you to be in the affairs belonging to your ship.

I am sensible that the sea is reckoned but an ill school to learn Christ in: and to see a devout sailor is esteemed as uncommon a thing as to see a Saul among the prophets. But from where this wondering? From where this looking upon a godly sailor, as a man to be wondered at, as a speckled bird in the creation? I am sure, for the little time I have come in and out among you, and as far as I can judge from the little experience I have had of things, I scarce know any way of life that is capable of greater improvements than yours.

The continual danger you are in of being overwhelmed by the great waters; the many opportunities you have of beholding God's wonders in the deep; the happy retirement you enjoy from worldly temptations; and the daily occasions that are offered you, to endure hardships, are such noble means of promoting the spiritual life, that were your hearts bent toward God, you would account it your happiest, that his providence has called you, to "go down to the sea in ships, and to occupy your business in the great waters."

The royal psalmist knew this and therefore, in the words of the text, calls more especially on men of your employ to "praise the Lord for his goodness, and declare the wonders he doeth for the children of men."

And oh, that you would be wise in time, and hearken to his voice today, "whilst it is called today"! For you yourselves know how little is to be done on a sickbed. God has, in a special manner, of late, invited you to repentance: two of your crew he has taken off by death, and most of you he has mercifully visited with a grievous sickness. The terrors of the Lord have been upon you, and when burned with a scorching fever, some of you have cried out, "What shall we do to be saved?" Remember then the resolutions you made when you thought God was about to take away your souls; and see that according to your promises, you show forth your thankfulness, not only with your lips, but in your lives. For though God may bear long, he will not forbear always; and if these signal mercies and judgments do not lead you to repentance, assure yourselves there will at last come a fiery tempest, from the presence of the Lord, which will sweep away you, and all other adversaries of God.

I am positive, neither you nor the soldiers have wanted, nor will want, any manner of encouragement to piety and holiness of living from those two persons who have here the government over you; for they have been such helps to me in my ministry, and have so readily concurred in everything for your good, that they may justly demand a public acknowledgment of thanks both from you and me.

Permit me, my honored friends, in the name of both classes of your people, to return you hearty thanks for the ears and tenderness you have expressed for the welfare of their better parts.

As for the private favors you have shown to my person, I hope so deep a sense of them is imprinted on my heart that I shall plead them before God in prayer, as long as I live.

But I have still stronger obligations to intercede in your behalf. For God—ever adored be his free grace in Christ Jesus!—has set his seal to my ministry in your hearts. Some distant pangs of the new birth I have observed to come upon you; and God forbid that I should sin against the Lord, by ceasing to pray that the good work begun in your souls may be carried on till the day of our Lord Jesus Christ.

The time of our departure from each other is now at hand, and you are going out into a world of temptations. But though absent in body, let us be present with each other in spirit; and God, I trust, will enable you to be singularly good, to be ready to be accounted fools for Christ's sake; and then we shall meet never to part again in the kingdom of our Father which is in heaven.

To you, my companions and familiar friends who came over with me to sojourn in a strange land, do I in the next place address myself. For you I especially fear, as well as for myself, because as we take sweet counsel together more often than others, and as you are let into a more intimate friendship with me in private life, the eyes of all men will be upon you to note even the minutest miscarriage; and therefore it highly concerns you to "walk circumspectly toward those that are without"; I hope that nothing but a single eye to God's glory and the salvation of your own souls brought you from your native country. Remember then the end of your coming here, and you can never do amiss. Be patterns of industry, as well as of piety, to those who shall be around you; and above all things let us have such fervent charity among ourselves, that it may be said of us, as of the primitive Christians, "See how the Christians love one another."

And now I have been speaking to others particularly, I have one general request to make to all, and that with reference to myself.

You have heard, my dear friends, how I have been exhorting every one of you to show forth your thankfulness for the divine goodness, not only with your lips, but in your lives. But "Physician, heal thyself" may justly be retorted on me. For (without any false pretenses to humility) I find my own heart so little inclined to this duty of thanksgiving for the benefits I have received that I had need fear sharing Hezekiah's fate, who because he was lifted up by, and not thankful enough for, the great things God had done for him, was given up a prey to the pride of his own heart.

I need therefore and beg your most importunate petitions at the throne of grace, that no such evil may befall me; that the more God exalts me, the more I may debase myself; and that after I have preached to others, I myself may not be cast away.

And now, brethren, into God's hands I commend your spirits, who, I trust, through his infinite mercies in Christ Jesus, will preserve you blameless, till his second coming to judge the world.

Excuse my detaining you for long; perhaps it is the last time I shall speak to you: my heart is full, and out of the abundance of it, I could continue my discourse until midnight. But I must away to your new world; may God give you new hearts and enable you to put in practice what you have heard from time to time, to do your duty, and I need not wish you anything better. For then God will so bless you, that "you will build you cities to dwell in; then will you sow your lands and plant vineyards, which will yield you fruits of increase" (Ps. 107:37). "Then your oxen shall be strong to labor, there shall be no leading into captivity, and no complaining in your streets; then shall your sons grow up as the young plants, and your daughters be as the polished corners of the temple: then shall your garners be full and plenteous with all manner of store, and your sheep bring forth thousands, and ten thousands in your streets" (Ps. 144:12–14). In short, then shall the Lord be your God; and as surely as he has now brought us to this haven, where we would be, so surely, after we have passed through the storms and tempests of this troublesome world, will he bring us to the haven of eternal rest, where we shall have nothing to do, but to praise him forever for his goodness and declare, in never-ceasing songs of praise, the wonders he has done for us, and all the other sons of men.

To which blessed rest, God of his infinite mercy bring us all, through Jesus Christ our Lord! To whom with the Father and Holy Ghost be all honor and glory, might, majesty, and dominion, now, henceforth, and forevermore. Amen. Amen.

The Necessity and Benefits of Religious Society

—⟡—

Two are better than one; because they have a good reward for their labor. For if they fall, the one will lift up his fellow. —ECCLESIASTES 4:9–10

Among the many reasons assignable for the sad decay of true Christianity, perhaps the neglecting to assemble ourselves together, in religious societies, may not be one of the least. That I may therefore do my endeavor toward promoting so excellent a means of piety, I have selected a passage of Scripture drawn from the experience of the wisest of men, which being a little enlarged on and illustrated will fully answer my present design: being to show, in the best manner I can, the necessity and benefits of society in general, and of religious society in particular.

"Two are better than one . . . ," from which words I shall take occasion to prove:

First, the truth of the wise man's assertion, "Two are better than one," and that in reference to society in general, and religious society in particular.

Second, to assign some reasons why two are better than one, especially as to the last particular. 1. Because men can raise up one another when they chance to slip: "For if they fall, the one will lift up his fellow." 2. Because they can impart heat to each other: "Again, if two lie together, then they have heat, but how can one be warm alone?" 3. Because they can secure each other from those that do oppose them: "And if one prevail against him, two shall withstand him; and a threefold cord is not quickly broken."

From hence, third, I shall take occasion to show the duty incumbent on every member of a religious society.

And fourth, I shall draw an inference or two from what may be said, and then conclude with a word or two of exhortation.

First, I am to prove the truth of the wise man's assertion, that "two are better than one," and that in reference to society in general, and religious societies in particular.

And how can this be done better than by showing that it is absolutely necessary for the welfare both of the bodies and souls of men? Indeed, if we look upon man as he came out of the hands of his Maker, we imagine him to be perfect, entire, lacking nothing. But God, whose thoughts are not as our thoughts, saw something still wanting to make Adam happy. And what was that? Why, a help meet for him. For thus speaks the Scripture: "And the Lord God said, 'It is not good that the man should be alone; I will make a help meet for him.'"

Observe, God said, "It is not good," thereby implying that the creation would have been imperfect, in some sort, unless a help was found out meet for Adam. And if this was the case of man before the fall; if a help was meet for him in a state of perfection; surely since the fall, when we come naked and helpless out of our mother's womb, when our wants increase with our years, and we can scarcely subsist a day without the mutual assistance of each other, well may we say, "It is not good for man to be alone."

Society then, we see, is absolutely necessary in respect to our bodily and personal wants. If we carry our view further and consider mankind as divided into different cities, countries, and nations, the necessity of it will appear yet more evident. For how can communities be kept up, or commerce carried on, without society? Certainly not at all, since providence seems wisely to have assigned a particular product to almost each particular country, on purpose, as it were, to oblige us to be social; and has so admirably mingled the parts of the whole body of mankind together, "that the eye cannot say to the hand, I have no need of thee; nor again, the hand to the foot, I have no need of thee."

Many other instances might be given of the necessity of society, in reference to our bodily, personal, and national wants. But what are all these when weighed in the balance of the sanctuary, in comparison of the infinite greater need of it, with respect to the soul? It was chiefly in regard to this better part, no doubt, that God said, "It is not good for the man to be alone." For, let us suppose Adam to be as happy as may be, placed as the Lord of the creation in the paradise of God, and spending all his hours in adoring and praising the blessed Author of his being; yet as his soul was the very copy of the divine nature, whose peculiar property it is to be communicative, without the divine all sufficiency he could not be completely happy, because he was alone and incommunicative, nor even content in paradise, for want of a partner in his joys. God knew this, and therefore said, "It is not good that the man shall be alone; I will make a help meet for him." And though this proved a fatal means of his falling, yet that was not owing to any natural consequence of society, but partly to that cursed apostate who craftily lies in wait to deceive; partly to Adam's own folly, in rather choosing to be miserable with one he loved, than trust in God to raise him up another spouse.

If we reflect indeed on that familiar intercourse our first parent could carry on with heaven, in a state of innocence, we shall be apt to think he had as little need of society, as to his soul, as before we supposed him to have, in respect to his body. But yet, as God and the holy angels were so far above him, on the one hand, and the beasts so far beneath him, on the other, there was nothing like having one to converse with who was "bone of his bone, and flesh of his flesh."

Man, then, could not be fully happy, we see, even in paradise, without a companion of his own species, much less now he is driven out. For let us view him a little in his natural estate now, since the fall, as "having his understanding darkened, his mind alienated from the life of God"; as no more able to see his way wherein he should go, than a blind man to describe the sun: that notwithstanding this, he must receive his sight before he can see God: and that if he never sees him, he never can be happy. Let us view him in this light (or rather this darkness) and deny the necessity of society if we can. A divine revelation we find is absolutely necessary, we being by nature as unable to know, as we are to do our duty. And how shall we learn except one teach us? But was God to do this himself, how should we, but with Moses, exceedingly quake and fear? Nor would the ministry of angels in this affair be without too much terror. It is necessary therefore (at least God's dealing with us has showed it to be so) that we should be drawn with the cords of a man. And that a divine revelation being granted, we should use one another's assistance, under God, to instruct each other in the knowledge, and to exhort one another to the practice of those things which belong to our everlasting peace. This is undoubtedly the great end of society intended by God since the fall, and a strong argument it is, why "two are better than one," and why we should "not forsake the assembling ourselves together."

But further, let us consider ourselves as Christians, as having this natural veil, in some measure, taken off from our eyes by the assistance of God's Holy Spirit, and so enabled to see what he requires of us. Let us suppose ourselves in some degree to have tasted the good word of life and to have felt the powers of the world to come, influencing and molding our souls into a religious frame; to be fully and heartily convinced that we are soldiers lifted under the banner of Christ and to have proclaimed open war at our baptism against the world, the flesh, and the devil; and have, perhaps, frequently renewed our obligations so to do, by partaking of the Lord's Supper, that we are surrounded with millions of foes without, and infected with a legion of enemies within, that we are commanded to shine as lights in the world, in the midst of a crooked and perverse generation, that we are traveling to a long eternity and need all imaginable helps to show and encourage us in our way there. Let us, I say, reflect on all this, and then how shall each of us cry out, brethren, what a necessary thing it is to meet together in religious societies?

The primitive Christians were fully sensible of this, and therefore we find them continually keeping up communion with each other. For what says the Scripture? "They continued steadfastly in the apostle's doctrine and fellowship" (Acts 2:42). Peter and John were no sooner dismissed by the great council, than they haste away to their companions. "And being set at liberty, they came to their own, and told them all these things which the high priest had said unto them" (4:23). Paul, as soon as converted, "tarried three days with the disciples that were at Damascus" (9:19). And Peter afterward, when released from prison, immediately goes to the house of Mary, where there were "great multitudes assembled, praying" (12:12). And it is reported of the Christians in after ages, that they used to assemble together before daylight, to sing a psalm to Christ as God. So precious was the communion of saints in those days.

If it be asked, what advantages we shall reap from such a procedure now, I answer, much every way. "Two are better than one, because they have a good reward for their labor: for if they fall, the one will lift up his fellow; but woe be to him that is alone when he falleth, for he hath not another to help him up. Again, if two lie together, then they have heat; but how can one be warm alone? And if one prevail against him, two shall withstand him; and a threefold cord is not quickly broken."

Which directly leads me to my second general head, under which I was to assign some reasons why "two are better than one," especially in religious society.

1. As man in his present condition cannot always stand upright, but by reason of the frailty of his nature cannot but fall; one eminent reason why two are better than one, or, in other words, one great advantage of religious society is that "when they fall, the one will lift up his fellow."

And an excellent reason this, indeed! For alas! when we reflect how prone we are to be drawn into error in our judgments, and into vice in our practice, and how unable, at least how very unwilling, to espy or correct our own miscarriages; when we consider how apt the world is to flatter us in our faults, and how few there are so kind as to tell us the truth; what an inestimable privilege must it be to have a set of true, judicious, hearty friends about us, continually watching over our souls, to inform us where we have fallen, and to warn us that we fall not again for the future. Surely it is such a privilege, that (to use the words of an eminent Christian) we shall never know the value thereof, till we come to glory.

But this is not all; for supposing that we could always stand upright, yet whosoever reflects on the difficulties of religion in general, and his own propensity to lukewarmness and indifference in particular, will find that he must be zealous as well as steady, if ever he expects to enter the kingdom of heaven. Here, then, the wise man points out to us another excellent reason why two are better than one. "Again, if two lie together, then they have heat; but how can one be warm alone?" Which was the next thing to be considered.

2. A second reason why two are better than one is because they can impart heat to each other.

It is an observation no less true than common that kindled coals, if placed asunder, soon go out, but if heaped together, quicken and enliven each other, and afford a lasting heat. The same will hold good in the case now before us. If Christians kindled by the grace of God unite, they will quicken and enliven each other; but if they separate and keep asunder, no marvel if they soon grow cool or tepid. If two or three meet together in Christ's name, they will have heat: but how can one be warm alone?

Observe, "how can one be warm alone?" The wise man's expressing himself by way of question implies an impossibility, at least a very great difficulty, to be warm in religion without company, where it may be had. Behold here, then, another excellent benefit flowing from religious society; it will keep us zealous, as well as steady, in the way of godliness.

But to illustrate this a little further by a comparison or two. Let us look upon ourselves (as was above hinted) as soldiers listed under Christ's banner; as going out with "ten thousand, to meet one that cometh against us with twenty thousand"; as persons that are to "wrestle not only with flesh and blood, but against principalities, against powers, and spiritual wickednesses in high places." And then tell me, all you that fear God, if it be not an invaluable privilege to have a company of fellow soldiers continually about us, animating and exhorting each other to stand our ground, to keep our ranks, and manfully to follow the captain of our salvation, though it be through a sea of blood?

Let us consider ourselves in another view before mentioned, as persons traveling to a long eternity; as rescued by the free grace of God, in some measure, from our natural Egyptian bondage, and marching under the conduct of our spiritual Joshua, through the wilderness of this world, to the land of our heavenly Canaan. Let us further reflect how apt we are to startle at every difficulty, to cry, "There are lions! There are lions in the way! There are the sons of Anak" to be grappled with, before we can possess the promised land. How prone we are, with Lot's wife, to look wishfully back on our spiritual Sodom or, with the foolish Israelites, to long again for the fleshpots of Egypt; and to return to our former natural state of bondage and slavery. Consider this, my brethren, and see what a blessed privilege it will be to have a set of Israelites indeed about us, always reminding us of the folly of any such cowardly design and of the intolerable misery we shall run into, if we fall in the least short of the promised land.

More might be said on this particular, did not the limits of a discourse of this nature oblige me to hasten—

3. To give a third reason, mentioned by the wise man in the text, why two are better than one: because they can secure each other from enemies without. "And if one prevail against him, yet two shall withstand him: and a three-fold cord is not quickly broken."

So far we have considered the advantages of religious societies, as a great preservative against falling (at least dangerously falling) into sin and lukewarmness, and that too from our own corruptions. But what says the wise son of Sirach? "My son, when thou goest to serve the Lord, prepare thy soul for temptation," and that not only from inward but outward foes: particularly from those two grand adversaries, the world and the devil: for no sooner will your eye be bent heavenward, but the former will be immediately diverting it another way, telling you you need not be singular in order to be religious; that you may be a Christian without going so much out of the common road.

Nor will the devil be wanting in his artful insinuations, or impious suggestions, to divert or terrify you from pressing forward, "that thou mayest lay hold on the crown of life." And if he cannot prevail this way, he will try another; and, in order to make his temptation the more undiscerned, but withal more successful, he will employ, perhaps, some of your nearest relatives, or most powerful friends (as he set Peter on our blessed Master), who will always be bidding you to spare yourself; telling you you need not take so much pain; that it is not so difficult a matter to get to heaven as some people would make of it, nor the way so narrow as others imagine it to be.

But see here the advantage of religious company—for supposing you find yourself thus surrounded on every side and unable to withstand such horrid (though seemingly friendly) counsels, haste away to your companions, and they will teach you a truer and better lesson; they will tell you that you must be singular if you will be religious; and that it is as impossible for a Christian, as for a city set upon a hill, to be hidden; that if you will be an almost Christian (and as good be none at all) you may live in the same idle, indifferent manner as you see most other people do: but if you will be not only almost, but altogether a Christian, they will inform you you must go a great deal farther; that you must not only faintly seek, but "earnestly strive to enter in at the strait gate"; that there is but one way now to heaven as formerly, even through the narrow passage of a sound conversion; and that in order to bring about this mighty work, you must undergo a constant but necessary discipline of fasting, watching, and prayer. And therefore the only reason why those friends give you such advice is because they are not willing to take so much pains themselves; or, as our Savior told Peter on a like occasion, because they "savor not the things that be of God, but the things that be of men."

This then is another excellent blessing arising from religious society, that friends can hereby secure each other from those who oppose them. The devil is fully sensible of this, and therefore he has always done his utmost to suppress and put a stop to the communion of saints. This was his grand artifice at the first planting of the gospel: to persecute the professors of it in order to separate them. Which, though God, as he always will, overruled for the better, yet it shows what an enmity he has against Christians assembling themselves together. Nor has he yet left off his old stratagem, it being his usual way to entice us by ourselves, in order to tempt us, where, by being destitute of one another's help, he hopes to lead us captive at his will.

But, on the contrary, knowing his own interest is strengthened by society, he would first persuade us to neglect the communion of saints, and then bid us "stand in the way of sinners," hoping thereby to put us into the "seat of the scornful." Judas and Peter are melancholy instances of this. The former had no sooner left his company at supper, but he went out and betrayed his Master: and the dismal downfall of the latter, when he would venture himself among a company of enemies, plainly shows us what the devil will endeavor to, when he gets us by ourselves. Had Peter kept his own company, he might have kept his integrity; but a single cord, alas! how quickly was it broken? Our blessed Savior knew this full well, and therefore it is very observable, that he always sent out his disciples "two by two."

And now, after so many advantages to be reaped from religious society, may we not very justly cry out with the wise man in my text, "Woe be to him that is alone; for when he falleth, he hath not another to lift him up!" When he is cold, he has not a friend to warm him; when he is assaulted, he has not a second to help him to withstand his enemy.

I now come to my third general head, under which was to be shown the several duties incumbent on every member of a religious society, as such, which are three: 1. Mutual reproof. 2. Mutual exhortation. 3. Mutual assisting and defending each other.

1. Mutual reproof. "Two are better than one; for when they fall, the one will lift up his fellow."

Now, reproof may be taken either in a more extensive sense, and then it signifies our raising a brother by the gentlest means when he falls into sin and error, or in a more restrained significance, as reaching no farther than those miscarriages which unavoidably happen in the most holy men living.

The wise man, in the text supposes all of us subject to both: "For when they fall (thereby implying that each of us may fall) the one will lift up his fellow." From which we may infer that "when any brother is overtaken with a fault, he that is spiritual (that is, regenerate, and knows the corruption and weakness of human nature) ought to restore such a one in the spirit of meekness." And why he should do so, the apostle subjoins a reason "considering thyself, lest thou also be tempted"; that is, considering your own frailty, lest you also fall by the like temptation.

We are all frail, unstable creatures, and it is merely owing to the free grace and good providence of God that we run not into the same excess of riot with other men. Every offending brother, therefore, claims our pity rather than our resentment; and each member should strive to be the most forward, as well as most gentle, in restoring him to his former state.

But supposing a person not to be overtaken, but to fall willfully into a crime; yet who are you that denies forgiveness to your offending brother? "Let him that standeth take heed lest he fall." Take, brethren, the holy apostles as eminent examples for you to learn by, how you ought to behave in this matter. Consider how quickly they joined the right hand of fellowship with Peter, who had so willfully denied his Master: for we find John and him together but two days after (John 20:2). And in verse 19, we find him assembled with the rest. So soon did they forgive, so soon associate with their sinful yet relenting brother. "Let us go and do likewise."

But there is another kind of reproof incumbent on every member of a religious society; namely, a gentle rebuke for some miscarriage or other, which though not actually sinful, yet may become the occasion of sin. This indeed seems a more easy, but perhaps will be found a more difficult, point than the former: for when a person has really sinned, he cannot but own his brethren's reproof to be just; whereas, when it was only for some little misconduct, the pride that is in our natures will scarce suffer us to brook it. But however ungrateful this pill may be to our brother, yet if we have any concern for his welfare, it must be administered by some friendly hand or other. By all means then let it be applied; only, like a skillful physician, gild over the ungrateful pill and endeavor, if possible, to deceive your brother into health and soundness. "Let all bitterness, and wrath, and malice, and evil speaking be put away" from it. Let the patient know his recovery is the only thing aimed at, and that you delight not causelessly to grieve your brother; then you can not want [lack] success.

2. Mutual exhortation is the second duty resulting from the words of the text. "Again, if two lie together, then they have heat."

Observe, the wise man supposes it as impossible for religious persons to meet together, and not to be the warmer for each other's company, as for two persons to lie in the same bed and yet freeze with cold. But now, how is it possible to communicate heat to each other, without mutually stirring up the gift of God which is in us, by brotherly exhortation? Let every member then of a religious society write that zealous apostle's advice on the tables of his heart: "See that ye exhort, and provoke one another to love, and to good works; and so much the more, as you see the day of the Lord approaching." Believe me, brethren, we have need of exhortation to rouse up our sleepy souls, to set us upon our watch against the temptations of the world, the flesh, and the devil; to excite us to renounce ourselves, to take up our crosses, and follow our blessed Master and the glorious company of saints and martyrs, "who through faith have fought the good fight, and are gone before us to inherit the promises." A third part therefore of the time wherein a religious society meets seems necessary to be spent in this important duty; for what avails it to have our understandings enlightened by pious reading, unless our wills are at the same time inclined, and inflamed by mutual exhortation, to put it in practice? Add also, that this is the best way both to receive and impart light, and the only means to preserve and increase that warmth and heat which each person first brought with him; God so ordering this, as all other spiritual gifts, that "to him that hath—that is, improves and communicates what he has—shall be given; but from him that hath not—or does not improve what he has—shall be taken away even that which he seemed to have." So needful, so essentially necessary, is exhortation to the good of society.

3. Third, the text points out another duty incumbent on every member of a religious society, to defend each other from those that do oppose them. "And if one prevail against him, yet two shall withstand him; and a threefold cord is not quickly broken."

Here the wise man takes it for granted that offenses will come, what's more, and that they may prevail too. And this is not more than our blessed Master has long since told us. Not, indeed, that there is anything in Christianity itself that has the least tendency to give rise to, or promote, such offenses: no, on the contrary, it breathes nothing but unity and love.

But so it is, that ever since the fatal sentence pronounced by God, after our first parents' fall, "I will put enmity between thy seed and her seed"; he that is born after the flesh—the unregenerate, unconverted sinner—has in all ages "persecuted him that is born after the spirit"; and so it always will be. Accordingly we find an early proof given of this in the instance of Cain and Abel; of Ishmael and Isaac; and of Jacob and Esau. And indeed the whole Bible contains little else but a history of the great and continued opposition between the children of this world and the children of God. The first Christians were remarkable examples of this; and though those troublesome times, blessed be God, are now over, yet the apostle has laid it down as a general rule, and all who are sincere experimentally prove the truth of it; that "they that will live godly in Christ Jesus, must (to the end of the world, in some degree or other) suffer persecution." That therefore this may not make us desert our blessed Master's cause, every member should unite their forces in order to stand against it. And for the better effecting this, each would do well, from time to time, to communicate his experiences, grievances, and temptations, and beg his companions (first asking God's assistance, without which all is nothing) to administer reproof, exhortation, or comfort, as his case requires: so that "if one cannot prevail against it, yet two shall withstand it; and a threefold (much less a manyfold) cord will not be quickly broken."

But it is time for me to proceed to the fourth general thing proposed, to draw an inference or two from what has been said.

1. And first, if "two are better than one," and the advantages of religious society are so many and so great, then it is the duty of every true Christian to set on foot, establish and promote, as much as in him lies, societies of this nature. And I believe we may venture to affirm that if ever a spirit of true Christianity is revived in the world, it must be brought about by some such means as this. Motive, surely, cannot be wanting, to stir us up to the commendable and necessary undertaking; for, granting all hitherto advanced to be of no force, yet I think the single consideration, that great part of our happiness in heaven, will consist in the communion of saints; or that the interest as well as piety of those who differ from us is strengthened and supported by nothing more than their frequent meetings; either of these considerations, I say, one would think, should induce us to do our utmost to copy after their good example and settle a lasting and pious communion of the saints on earth. Add to this, that we find the kingdom of darkness established daily by

suchlike means; and shall not the kingdom of Christ be set in opposition against it? Shall the children of Belial assemble and strengthen each other in wickedness; and shall not the children of God unite and strengthen themselves in piety? Shall societies on societies be countenanced for midnight revelings and the promoting of vice, and scarcely one be found intended for the propagation of virtue? Be astonished, O heavens, at this!

2. But this leads me to a second inference; namely, to warn persons of the great danger those are in who either by their subscriptions, presence, or approbation, promote societies of a quite opposite nature to religion.

And here I would not be understood to mean only those public meetings which are designed manifestly for nothing else but revelings and banquetings, for chambering and wantonness, and at which a modest heathen would blush to be present; but also those seemingly innocent entertainments and meetings, which the politer part of the world are so very fond of and spend so much time in, but which, notwithstanding, keep as many persons from a sense of true religion, as does intemperance, debauchery, or any other crimes whatever. Indeed, while we are in this world, we must have proper relaxations to fit us both for the business of our profession and religion. But then, for persons who call themselves Christians, that have solemnly vowed at their baptism to renounce the vanities of this sinful world; that are commanded in Scripture "to abstain from all appearance of evil, and to have their conversation in heaven"—for such persons as these to support meetings which (to say no worse of them) are vain and trifling, and have a natural tendency to draw off our minds from God, is absurd, ridiculous, and sinful. Surely two are not better than one in this case: no; it is to be wished there was not one to be found concerned in it. The sooner we forsake the assembling ourselves together in such a manner, the better; and no matter how quickly, the cord that holds such societies (was it a thousandfold) is broken.

But you, brethren, have not so learned Christ; but, on the contrary, like true disciples of your Lord and Master, have by the blessing of God (as this evening's solemnity abundantly testifies) happily formed yourselves into such societies, which, if duly attended on, and improved, cannot but strengthen you in your Christian warfare, and "make you fruitful in every good word and work."

What remains for me but, as was proposed in the first place, to close what has been said, in a word or two, by way of exhortation and to beseech you, in the name of our Lord Jesus Christ, to go on in the way you have begun, and by a constant, conscientious attendance on your respective societies, to discountenance vice, encourage virtue, and build each other up in the knowledge and fear of God?

Only permit me to "stir up your pure minds, by way of remembrance" and to exhort you, "if there be any consolation in Christ, any fellowship of the spirit," again and again to consider that as all Christians in general, so all members of religious societies in particular, are in a special manner as houses built upon a hill; and that therefore it highly concerns you to walk circumspectly toward those that are without, and to take heed to yourselves, that your conversation, in common life, be as becomes such an open and peculiar profession of the gospel of Christ: knowing that the eyes of all men are upon you, narrowly to inspect every circumstance of your behavior; and that every notorious willful miscarriage of any single member will, in some measure, redound to the scandal and dishonor of your whole fraternity.

Labor, therefore, my beloved brethren, to let your practice correspond to your profession; and think not that it will be sufficient for you to plead at the last day, "Lord, have we not assembled ourselves together in your name and enlivened each other, by singing psalms and hymns and spiritual songs?" For verily, I say unto you, notwithstanding this, our blessed Lord will bid you depart from him; no, you shall receive a great damnation, if, in the mists of these great pretensions, you are found to be workers of iniquity.

But God forbid that any such evil should befall you; that there should be ever a Judas, a traitor, among such distinguished followers of our common Master. No, on the contrary, the excellency of your rule, the regularity of your meetings, and more especially your pious zeal in assembling in such a public and solemn manner so frequently in the year, persuade me to think that you are willing not barely to seem, but to be in reality, Christians; and hope to be found at the last day what you would be esteemed now: holy, sincere disciples of a crucified Redeemer.

Oh, may you always continue thus minded! And make it your daily, constant endeavor, both by precept and example, to turn all your converse with, more especially, those of your own societies into the same most blessed spirit and temper. Thus will you adorn the gospel of our Lord Jesus Christ in all things. Thus will you anticipate the happiness of a future state; and by attending on and improving the communion of saints on earth, be made meet to join the communion and fellowship of the spirits of just men made perfect, of the holy angels, what's more, of the ever-blessed and eternal God in heaven.

Which God of his infinite mercy grant through Jesus Christ our Lord; to whom with the Father and the Holy Ghost, three persons and one God, be ascribed, as is most due, all honor and praise, might, majesty, and dominion, now and forever. Amen.

Christ, the Support of the Tempted

—ɯ—

"Lead us not into temptation." —MATTHEW 6:13

The great and important duty which is incumbent on Christians is to guard against all appearance of evil; to watch against the first risings in the heart to evil; and to have a guard upon our actions, that they may not be sinful or so much as seem to be so. It is true, the devil is tempting us continually, and our own evil hearts are ready to join with the tempter, to make us fall into sins, that he thereby may obtain a victory over us, and that we, my brethren, may be his subjects, his servants, his slaves; and then by and by he will pay us our wages, which will be death temporal and death eternal. Our Lord Jesus Christ saw how his people would be tempted, and that the great enemy of their souls would lay hold of every opportunity, so he could but be a means of keeping poor sinners from coming to the Lord Jesus Christ; hurrying you with temptation, to drive you to some great sins; and then if he cannot gain you over, fall it to a smaller, and suit his temptations time after time; and when he finds none of these things will do, often transform himself into an angel of light, and by that means make the soul fall into sin, to the dishonor of God, and the wounding of itself; the Lord Jesus, I say, seeing how liable his disciples, and all others, would be to be overcome by temptation, therefore advises them, when they pray, to beg that they might not be led into temptation. It is so dangerous to engage so subtle and powerful an enemy as Satan is, that we shall be overcome as often as we engage, unless the Lord is on our side. My brethren, if you were left to yourselves, you would be overcome by every temptation with which you are beset.

These words are part of the prayer which Christ taught his disciples; and I shall, therefore, make no doubt, but that you all believe them to be true, since they are spoken by one who cannot lie. I shall,

I. Show you who it is that tempts you.

II. Shall show, my brethren, why he tempts you.

III. Mention some of the ways and means he makes use of, to draw you over to his temptations.

IV. Let you see how earnest you ought to be to the Lord, that he may preserve you from being led into temptation.

V. I shall make some application by way of entreaty unto you, to come unto Christ, that he, my brethren, may deliver you from being tempted.

I. First, we are to consider who it is that tempts us.

And the tempter is Satan, the prince of the power of the air, he that now rules in the children of disobedience; he is an enemy to God and goodness, he is a hater of all truth. Why else did he slander God in paradise? Why did he tell Eve, "You shall not surely die"? He is full of malice, envy, and revenge; for what reasons else could induce him to molest innocent man in paradise? The person that tempts you, my brethren, is remarkable for his subtlety; for having not power given him from above, he is obliged to wait for opportunities to betray us, and to catch us by guile; he therefore made use of the serpent to tempt our first parents; and to lie in wait to deceive is another part of his character. And though this character is given of the devil, if we were to examine our own hearts, we should find many of the tempter's characters legible in us.

Do not many of you love to make a lie? And if it is done in your trade, you therefore look on it as excusable; but whether you believe it or not, it is sinful, it is exceedingly sinful. Though you may value yourselves as fine rational creatures and that you are noble beings; and you were so, as you first came out of God's hands; but now you are fallen, there is nothing lovely, nothing desirable in man; his heart is a sink of pollution, full of sin and uncleanness. Yet, though a man's own heart is so desperately wicked, he is told by our modern polite preachers that there is a fitness in men, and that God seeing you a good creature gives you his grace; but this, though it is a modern, polite, and fashionable way of talking, is very unscriptural; it is very contrary to the doctrines of the Reformation, and to our own articles. But however contrary to the doctrines of the Church of England, yet our pulpits ring of nothing more than doing no one any harm, living honestly, loving your neighbor as yourselves, and do what you can, and then Christ is to make up the deficiency; this is making Christ to be half a savior, and man the other part; but I say, Christ will be your whole righteousness, your whole wisdom, your whole sanctification, or else he will never be your whole redemption. How amazing is it, that the ministers of the Church of England should speak quite contrary to what they have subscribed! Good God! If these are the guides of the ignorant; and esteemed to be the true ministers of Jesus, because they have a great share of letter learning—when at the same time they are only the blind leaders of the blind and without a special providence—they both will fall into the ditch.

No wonder at people's talking of the fitness and unfitness of things, when they can tell us that the Spirit of God is a good conscience, and the comforts of the Holy Ghost are consequent thereupon. But this is wrong; for it should be said, the Spirit of God are the comforts of the Holy Ghost, and a good conscience consequent thereupon. Seneca, Cicero, Plato, or any of the heathen philosophers would have given as good a definition as this; it means no more than reflecting we have done well.

But let these modern, polite gentlemen, and let my letter-learned brethren, paint man in as lovely colors as they please; I will not do it; I dare not make him better than the Word of God does. If I was to paint man in his proper colors, I must go to the kingdom of hell for a copy; for man is by nature full of pride, subtlety, malice, envy, revenge, and all uncharitableness; and what are these but the temper of the devil? And lust, sensuality, pleasure, these are the tempers of the beast. Thus, my brethren, man is half a beast, and half a devil, a motley mixture of the beast and devil. And this is the creature, who has made himself so obnoxious to the wrath of God and open to his indignation, that is told, that he must be part his own savior, by doing good works, and what he cannot do, Christ will do for him.

This is giving the tempter great room to come in with his temptation; he may press a soul to follow moral duties, to go to church, take the Sacrament, read, pray, meditate; the devil is well content you should do all these; but if they are done in your own strength, or if you go no farther than here, you are only going a smoother way to hell.

Thus, my brethren, you may see who it is that tempts us.

II. But why he tempts you, is the second thing I am to show you.

It is out of envy to you, and to the Lord Jesus Christ, he endeavors to keep you from closing with Jesus; and if he can but keep you from laying hold by faith on Christ, he knows he has you safe enough; and the more temptations you are under, and according to their nature and greatness, you are more hurried in your minds; and the more unsettled your thoughts and affections are, the more apt you are to conclude that if you were to go to Christ, at present, in all that hurry of mind, he would not receive you; but this is a policy of the tempter, to make you have low and dishonorable thoughts of the blessed Jesus; and so by degrees he works upon your minds, that you are careless and indifferent about Christ. This, this, my brethren, is the design of the tempter. Nothing will please him more than to see you ruined and lost forever. He tempts you for that end, that you may lose your interest in Jesus Christ, and that you may dwell with him and apostate spirits to all eternity. He knows that

Jesus Christ died for sinners, yet he would fain keep souls from seeking to this city of refuge for shelter, and from going to Gilead for the true balm.

It is he that rules in your heart, O scoffer, O Pharisee; the devil reigns there and endeavors to blind your eyes, that you shall not see what danger you are in, and how much evil there is in those hearts of yours; and as long as he can keep you easy and unconcerned about having your hearts changed, he will be easy; though if he can, he will tempt you to sin against him, until you are hardened in your iniquity. O, my brethren, do not give the devil a handle wherewith he may lay hold on you; alas! it is no wonder that the devil tempts you, when he finds you at a play, a ball, or masquerade; if you are doing the devil's work, it is no wonder if he presses you in the continuation thereof; and how can any say, "Lead us not into temptation," in the morning, when they are resolved to run into it at night? Good God! Are these persons members of the Church of England? Alas, when you have gone to church and read over the prayers, it is offering no more than the sacrifice of fools; you say amen to them with your lips, when in your hearts you are either unconcerned at what you are about, or else you think that the bare saying of your prayers is sufficient, and that then God and you have balanced accounts.

But, my dear brethren, do not deceive yourselves, God is not to be mocked. You are only ruining yourselves for time and eternity. You pray, "Lead us not into temptation," when you are tempting the devil to come and tempt you.

III. I shall now point out some of the ways and means he makes use of to draw you to himself.

But this is a field so large, and I have but just begun to be a soldier of Jesus Christ, that I cannot name many unto you. I shall therefore be very short on this head.

1. He endeavors to make you think sin is not so great as it is; that there is no occasion of being so overstrict, and that you are righteous overmuch; that you are ostentatious and will do yourself harm by it; and that you will destroy yourselves. He shows you, my brethren, the bait, but he hides the hook; he shows you the pleasure, profits, and advantages that attend abundance of this world's goods; but he does not show you crosses, losses, and vexations that you may have while you are in the enjoyment of the blessings of this world.

2. When he finds he cannot allure you by flattery, he will try you by frowns, and the terrors of this world; he will stir up people to point at you, and cry, "Here comes another troop of his followers"; he will stir them up to jeer, scoff, backbite, and hate you; but if he still finds this will not do, then he

throws doubts, my brethren, and discouragement in your mind, whether the way you are in is the true way or not; or else he will suggest, "What! Do you expect to be saved by Christ? Also, he did not die for you; you have been too great a sinner; you have lived in sin so long, and committed such sins against Christ, which he will not forgive." Thus he hurries poor sinners almost into despair.

And very often, when the people of God are met to worship him, he sends his agents, the scoffers, to disturb them. We saw an instance of their rage just now; they would fain have disturbed us; but the Lord was on our side, and so prevented all the attempts of wicked and designing men to disturb and disquiet us. Lord Jesus, forgive them who are thus persecuting your truth! Jesus, show them that they are fighting against you, and that it is hard for them to kick against the pricks! These, my brethren, are some of the ways Satan takes in his temptations, to bring you from Christ. Many more might be named; but these are sufficient, I hope, to keep you on your guard, against all that the enemy can do to hinder you from coming to Christ.

IV. I come to show you how earnest you ought to be with Jesus Christ, either not to suffer you to be led into temptations, or to preserve you under them.

And here, my dear brethren, let me beseech you to go to Jesus Christ; tell him how you are assaulted by the evil one, who lies in wait for your souls; tell him you are not able to master him in your own strength; beg his assistance, and you shall find him ready to help you; ready to assist you, and to be your guide, your comforter, your Savior, your all; he will give you strength to resist the fiery darts of the devil; and therefore you can nowhere find one so proper to relieve you, as Jesus Christ; he knows what it is to be tempted; he was tempted by Satan in the wilderness, and he will give you the assistance of his Spirit, to resist the evil one, and then he will fly from you. In Christ Jesus you shall have the strength you stand in need of, the devil shall have no power; therefore fear not, for in the name of the Lord we shall overcome all our spiritual Amalekites. Let the devil and his agents rage, let them breathe out threatenings, yes, let them breathe out slaughters, yet we can rejoice in this, that Jesus Christ has them in his power, they shall go no farther than he permits them; they may rage, they may rage horribly, but they can go no farther, until they have got more power from on high.

If they could do us what mischief they would, very few of us should be permitted to see our habitations anymore; but, blessed be God, we can commit ourselves to his protection; he has been our protector so far, he will be so still. Then earnestly entreat of the Lord to support you under those temptations, which the devil may assault you with; he is a powerful adversary, he is a cunning one too; he would be too hard for us, unless we have the strength of Christ to be with us. But let us be looking up unto Jesus, that he would send his Spirit into our hearts, and keep us from falling. O my dear brethren in Christ Jesus, how stands it now between God and your souls? Is Jesus altogether lovely to your souls? Is he precious unto you? I am sure, if you have not gone back from Christ, he will not from you; he will root out the accursed things of this world and dwell in your hearts. You are candidates for heaven; and will you mind earth? What are all the pleasures of earth, without an interest in the Lord Jesus Christ? And one smile from him is more to be desired than rubies, yes, more than the whole world.

O you who have found Jesus Christ assisting you and supporting you under all the temptations of this life, will you forsake him? Have you not found him a gracious Master? Is he not the chiefest of ten thousand and altogether lovely? Now you see a form and comeliness in Christ, which you never saw before. Oh! how do you and I wish we had known Jesus sooner, and that we had more of his love; it is condescending love, it is amazing, it is forgiving love, it is dying love, it is exalted and interceding love, and it is glorified love. I think when I am talking of the love of Jesus Christ, who loved me before I loved him: he saw us polluted in blood, full of sores, a slave to sin, to death and hell, running to destruction, then he passed by me, and said unto my soul, "live"; he snatched me as a brand plucked from the burning. It was love that saved me, it was all of the free grace of God, and that only. The little experience I have had of this love makes me amazed at the condescension, the love, and mercifulness of the blessed Jesus, that he should have mercy upon such a wretch. O my brethren, the kingdom of God is within me and this fills me so full of love, that I would not be in my natural state again, not for millions of millions of worlds; I long to be with Jesus, to live with the Lord that bought me, to live forever with the Lamb that was slain, and to sing hallelujahs unto him. Eternity itself will be too short to set forth the love of the Lord Jesus Christ. I cannot, indeed I cannot, forbear speaking again and again and again, of the Lord Jesus.

And if there are any here who are strangers to this love of the Lord Jesus Christ, do not despair; come, come unto Christ, and he will have mercy upon you, he will pardon all your sins, he will heal all your backslidings, he will love you freely, and take you to be with himself. Come therefore, O my guilty brethren, unto Jesus, and you shall find rest for your souls. You need not fear, you need not despair, when God has had mercy upon such a wretch as I; and he will save you also, if you will come unto him by faith.

Why do you delay? What! Do you say, you are poor, and therefore ashamed to come? It is not your poverty that Christ minds; come in all your rags, in all your pollution, and he will save you. Do not depend upon anything but the blood of Jesus Christ; do not stand out an hour longer, but give your hearts to Christ, give him the firstlings of the flock; come unto him now, lest he should cut you off before you are prepared, and your soul be sent to that pit from which there is no redemption.

Do not waver, but give him that which he desires, your hearts; it is the heart the Lord Jesus Christ wants; and when you have an inward principle worked in your hearts by this same Jesus, then you will feel the sweetness and pleasure of communion with God. Oh, consider, my brethren, the love of the Lord Jesus Christ, in dying for you; and are you resolved to slight his dying love? Your sins brought Christ from heaven, and I humbly pray to the Lord that they may not be a means of sending you to hell. What language will make you leave your sins and come to Christ? Oh, that I did but know! And that it lay in my power to give you this grace; not one of you, not the greatest scoffer here should go hence before he was changed from a natural to a spiritual life; then, then we would rejoice and take sweet council together; but all this is not in my power; but I tell you where you may have it, even of the Lord Jesus; he will give it to you, if you ask it of him, for he has told us, "Ask, and you shall receive"; therefore ask of him, and if you are repulsed again and again, entreat him more, and he will be unto you as he was to the poor Syrophoenician woman, who came to Christ on account of her daughter; and if she was so importunate to him for a body, how much more should we be solicitous for our souls? If you seek to him in faith, his answer will be to you as it was to her, "Thy faith hath saved thee, be it as thou wouldest have it."

Oh, do not forsake the seeking of the Lord; do not, I beseech you, neglect the opportunities which may be offered to you, for the salvation of your souls; forsake not the assembling of yourselves together, to build up and confirm and strengthen those who are weak in faith; to convince sinners that they may feel the power of God pricking them in their hearts, and make them cry out, "What must we do to be saved?"

The devil and his agents have their clubs of reveling, and their societies of drunkenness; they are not ashamed to be seen and heard doing the devil their master's works; they are not ashamed to proclaim him; and surely you are not ashamed of the Lord Jesus Christ; you dare proclaim that Jesus, who died that you might live, and who will own you before his Father and all the holy angels; therefore dare to be singularly good; be not afraid of the face of man; let not all the threats of the men of this world move you; what is the loss of all the grandeur, or pleasure, or reputation of this life, compared to the loss of heaven, of Christ and of your souls? And as for the reproaches of the world, do not mind them; when they revile you, never, never revile again; do not answer railing with railing; but let love, kindness, meekness, patience, long-suffering, be found in you, as they were in the blessed Jesus; therefore, I beseech you, do not neglect the frequent coming together and telling each other what great things Jesus Christ has done for your souls.

I do not now, as the Pharisees say I do, encourage you to leave your lawful callings and your business, in which God, by his providence, has placed you; for you have two callings, the one a general and the other a special one; it is your duty to regard your families, and if you neglect them out of any pretense whatever, as going to church or in societies, you are out of the way of your duty, and offering that to God which he commanded you not. But then, my brethren, you are to take care that the things of this life do not hinder the preparing for that which is to come; let not the business of the world make you unmindful of your souls; but in all your moral actions, in the business of life, let all be done with a view to the glory of God, and the salvation of your souls.

The night draws on, and obliges me to hasten to a conclusion; though I think I could speak until my tongue clave to the roof of my mouth, yes, until I could speak no more, if it was to save your souls from the paws of him who seeks to devour you.

Therefore let me beseech you, in all love and compassion: consider, you who are Pharisees; you who will not come to Christ but are trusting to yourselves for righteousness; who think, because you lead civil, honest, decent lives, all will go well at last; but let me tell you, O you Pharisees, that harlots, murderers, and thieves shall enter the kingdom of God before you. Do not flatter yourselves of being in the way to heaven, when you are in the broad way to hell; but if you will throw away your righteousness and come to Christ, and be contented to let Jesus Christ do all for you, and in you, then Christ is willing to be your Savior; but if you bring your good works with you and think to be justified on the account of them, you may seek to be justified by them forever and never be justified; no, it is only the blood of Jesus Christ that cleanses us from the filth and pollution of all our sins; and you must be sanctified before you are justified. As for good works, we are justified before God without any respect to them, either past, present, or to come: when we are justified, good works will follow our justification, for we can do no good works, until we are cleansed of our pollution, by the sanctification of the Spirit of God.

O you scoffers, come and see this Jesus, this Lord of glory whom you have despised; and if you will but come to Christ, he will be willing to receive you, notwithstanding all the persecution you have used toward his members; however, if you are resolved to persist in your obstinacy, remember, salvation was offered to you, that Christ and free grace were proposed; but you refused to accept of either, and therefore your blood will be required at your own hands.

I shall only say this unto you, that however you may despise either me or my ministry, I shall not regard it, but shall frequently show you your danger, and propose to you the remedy; and shall earnestly pity and pray for you, that God would show you your error, and bring you home into his sheepfold, that you, from ravenous lions, may become peaceful lambs.

And as for you, O my brethren, who desire to choose Christ for your Lord, and to experience his power upon your souls, and as you do not find your desires and prayers answered; go on, and Christ will manifest himself unto you, as he does not unto the world; you shall be made to see and feel this love of Jesus upon your souls; you shall have a witness in your own breast, that you are the Lord's; therefore, do not fear, the Lord Jesus Christ will gather you with his elect, when he comes at that great day of accounts, to judge everyone according to the deeds done in the body, whether they be good, or whether they be evil; and, oh, that the thought of answering to God for all our actions would make us more mindful about the consequences that will attend it.

And now let me address all of you, high and low, rich and poor, one with another, to accept of mercy and grace while it is offered to you; "now is the accepted time, now is the day of salvation"; and will you not accept it, now it is offered unto you? Do not stand out one moment longer; but come and accept of Jesus Christ in his own way, and then you shall be taken up at the last day and be with him forever and ever; and surely this should make you desirous of being with that Jesus who has done so much for you, and is now interceding for you, and preparing mansions for you; where may we all arrive and sit down with Jesus to all eternity!

Which God of his infinite mercy grant through Jesus Christ our Lord; to whom with the Father and the Holy Ghost, three persons and one God, be ascribed, as is most due, all honor and praise, might, majesty, and dominion, now and forever. Amen.

Marks of a True Conversion

—ɷ—

"Verily I say unto you, Except ye be converted, and become as little children, ye shall not enter into the kingdom of heaven." —MATTHEW 18:3

I suppose I may take it for granted that all of you, among whom I am now about to preach the kingdom of God, are fully convinced that it is appointed for all men once to die, and that you all really believe that after death comes the judgment, and that the consequences of that judgment will be that you must be doomed to dwell in the blackness of darkness, or ascend to dwell with the blessed God, forever and ever. I may take it for granted also that whatever your practice in common life may be, there is not one, though ever so profligate and abandoned, but hopes to go to that place, which the Scriptures call heaven, when he dies. And, I think, if I know anything of my own heart, my heart's desire, as well as my prayer to God, for you all is that I may see you sitting down in the kingdom of our heavenly Father. But then, though we all hope to go to heaven when we die, yet, if we may judge by people's lives, and our Lord says that "by their fruits we may know them," I am afraid it will be found that thousands, and ten thousands, who hope to go to this blessed place after death are not now on the way to it while they live. Though we call ourselves Christians and would consider it as an affront put upon us, for anyone to doubt whether we were Christians or not; yet there are a great many who bear the name of Christ that yet do not so much as know what real Christianity is. Hence it is that if you ask a great many upon what their hopes of heaven are founded, they will tell you that they belong to this or that or the other denomination, and party of Christians, into which Christendom is now unhappily divided. If you ask others upon what foundation they have built their hope of heaven, they will tell you that they have been baptized, that their fathers and mothers presented them to the Lord Jesus Christ in their infancy; and though, instead of fighting under Christ's banner, they have been fighting against him almost ever since they were baptized, yet because they have been admitted to church, and their names are in the register book of the parish, therefore they will make us believe that their names are also written in the Book of Life. But a great many who will not build their hopes of salvation upon such a sorry rotten foundation as this, yet if they are what we generally call "negatively good people"; if they live so as their neighbors cannot say that they do anybody harm, they do not doubt but they shall be happy when they die; what's more, I have found many such die, as the Scripture speaks, "without any bands in their death." And if a person is what the world calls an "honest moral man," if he does justly, and what the world calls "love a little mercy," is now and then good-natured, reaches out his hand to the poor, receives the Sacrament once or twice a year, and is outwardly sober and honest; the world looks upon such a one as a Christian indeed, and doubtless we are to judge charitably of every such person. There are many, likewise, who go on in a round of duties, a model of performances, that think they shall go to heaven; but if you examine them, though they have a Christ in their heads, they have no Christ in their hearts.

The Lord Jesus Christ knew this full well; he knew how desperately wicked and deceitful men's hearts were; he knew very well how many would go to hell even by the very gates of heaven, how many would climb up even to the door and go so near as to knock at it, and yet after all be dismissed with a "verily I know you not." The Lord therefore plainly tells us what great change must be worked in us, and what must be done for us, before we can have any well-grounded hopes of entering into the kingdom of heaven. Hence, he tells Nicodemus that "unless a man be born again, and from above, and unless a man be born of water and of the Spirit, he cannot enter into the kingdom of God." And of all the solemn declarations of our Lord, I mean with respect to this, perhaps the words of the text are one of the most solemn, "Except (says Christ) ye be converted, and become as little children, ye shall not enter into the kingdom of heaven." The words, if you look back to the context, are plainly directed to the disciples; for we are told that "at the same time came the disciples unto Jesus." And I think it is plain from many parts of Scripture that these disciples, to whom our Lord addressed himself at this time, were in some degree converted before. If we take the words strictly, they are applicable only to those that have already gotten some, though but weak, faith in Christ. Our Lord means that though they had already tasted the grace of God, yet there was so much of the old man, so much indwelling sin, and corruption, yet remaining in their hearts, that unless they were more converted than they were, unless a greater change passed upon their souls, and sanctification was still carried on, they could give but very little evidence of their belonging to his kingdom, which was not to be set up in outward grandeur, as they supposed, but was to be a spiritual kingdom, begun here, but completed in the kingdom of God hereafter. But though the words had a peculiar reference to our Lord's disciples; yet as our Lord makes such a declaration as this in other places of Scripture, especially in the discourse to Nicodemus, I believe the words may be justly applied to saints and sinners; and as I suppose there are two sorts of people here—some who know Christ, and some of you that do not know him, some that are converted, and some that are strangers to conversion—I shall endeavor so to speak that if God shall be pleased to assist me, and to give you a hearing ear and an obedient heart, both saints and sinners may have their portion.

First, I shall endeavor to show you in what respects we are to understand this assertion of our Lord's, that "we must be converted and become like little children."

I shall then, second, speak to those who profess a little of this childlike temper.

And last, I shall speak to you, who have no reason to think that this change has ever passed upon your souls.

First, I shall endeavor to show you, what we are to understand by our Lord's saying, "Except ye be converted, and become as little children." But I think before I speak to this point, it may be proper to premise one or two particulars.

1. I think that the words plainly imply that before you or I can have any well-grounded, scriptural hope of being happy in a future state, there must be some great, some notable, and amazing change pass upon our souls. I believe there is not one adult person in the congregation but will readily confess that a great change has passed upon their bodies, since they came first into the world and were infants dandled upon their mother's knees. It is true, you have no more members than you had then, but how are these altered! Though you are in one respect the same you were, for the number of your limbs, and as to the shape of your body, yet if a person that knew you when you were in your cradle had been absent from you for some years, and saw you when grown up, then thousand to one if he would know you at all, you are so altered, so different from what you were, when you were little ones. And as the words plainly imply that there has a great change passed upon our bodies since we were children, so before we can go to heaven, there must as great a change pass upon our souls. Our souls considered in a physical sense are still the same, there is to be no philosophical change worked on them. But then, as for our temper, habit, and conduct, we must be so changed and altered, that those who knew us the other day, when in a state of sin and before we knew Christ, and are acquainted with us now, must see such an alteration, that they may stand as much amazed at it, as a person at the alteration worked on any person he has not seen for twenty years from his infancy.

2. But I think it proper to premise something further, because this text is the grand stronghold of Arminians and others. They learn of the devil to bring texts to propagate bad principles: when the devil had a mind to tempt Jesus Christ, because Christ quoted Scripture, therefore Satan did so too. And such persons, that their doctrine and bad principles may go down the better, would fain persuade unwary and unstable souls, that they are founded upon the Word of God. Though the doctrine of original sin is a doctrine written in such legible characters in the Word of God, that he who runs may read it; and though, I think, everything without us, and everything within us, plainly proclaims that we are fallen creatures; though the very heathens, who had no other light but the dim light of unassisted reason, complained of this, for they felt the wound and discovered the disease, but were ignorant of the cause of it; yet there are too many persons of those who have been baptized in the name of Christ that dare to speak against the doctrine of original sin and are angry with those ill-natured ministers who paint man in such black colors. Say they, "It cannot be that children come into the world with the guilt of Adam's sin lying upon them." Why? Desire them to prove it from Scripture, and they will urge this very text, our Lord tells us, "Except ye be converted, and become as little children, ye shall not enter into the kingdom of heaven." Now their argument runs thus, "It is implied in the words of the text that little children are innocent, and that they come into the world like a mere blank piece of white paper, otherwise our Lord must argue absurdly, for he could never pretend to say that we must be converted and be made like wicked creatures; that would be no conversion." But, my dear friends, this is to make Jesus Christ speak what he never intended and what cannot be deduced from his words.

That little children are guilty, I mean, that they are conceived and born in sin, is plain from the whole tenor of the Book of God. David was a man after God's own heart, yet, says he, "I was conceived in sin." Jeremiah, speaking of everyone's heart, says, "The heart of man is deceitful and desperately wicked above all things." God's servants unanimously declare (and Paul cites it from one of them) that "we are altogether now become abominable, altogether gone out of the way of original righteousness, there is not one of us that doeth good (by nature), no not one." And I appeal to any of you that are mothers and fathers, if you do not discern original sin or corruption in your children as soon as they come into the world; and as they grow up, if you do not discover self-will and an aversion to goodness? What is the reason your children are so averse to instruction, but because they bring enmity into the world with them, against a good and gracious God? So then, it is plain from Scripture and fact that children are born in sin, and consequently that they are children of wrath. And for my part, I think that the death of every child is a plain proof of original sin; sickness and death came into the world by sin, and it seems not consistent with God's goodness and justice, to let a little child be sick or die, unless Adam's first sin was imputed to him. If any charge God with injustice for imputing Adam's sin to a little child, behold we have gotten a second Adam, to bring our children to him. Therefore when our Lord says, "unless ye are converted, and become as little children," we are not to understand, as though our Lord would insinuate, that little children are perfectly innocent; but in a comparative and, as I shall show you by and by, in a rational sense. Little children are innocent, compare them with grown people; but take them as they are, and as they come into the world, they have hearts that are sensual and minds which are carnal. And I mention this with the greatest concern, because I verily believe, unless parents are convinced of this, they will never take proper care of their children's education. If parents were convinced that children's hearts were so bad as they are, you would never be fond of letting them go to balls, assemblies, and plays, the natural tendency of which is to debauch their minds and make them the children of the devil. If parents were convinced of this, I believe they would pray more when they bring their children to be baptized and would not make it a mere matter of form. And I believe if they really were convinced that their children were conceived in sin, they would always put up that petition, before their children came into the world, which I have heard that a good woman always did put up: "Lord Jesus, let me never bear a child for hell or the devil." Oh, is it not to be feared that thousands of children will appear at the great day before God, and in the presence of angels and men will say, "Father and mother, next to the wickedness of mine own heart, I owe my damnation to your bad education of me"?

Having premised these two particulars, I now proceed to show in what sense we are really to understand the words that we "must be converted, and become like little children." The Evangelist tells us that "the disciples at this time came unto Jesus, saying, 'Who is the greatest in the kingdom of heaven?'" These disciples had imbibed the common prevailing notion that the Lord Jesus Christ was to be a temporal prince; they dreamed of nothing but being ministers of state, of sitting on Christ's right hand in his kingdom, and lording it over God's people; they thought themselves qualified for state offices, as generally ignorant people are apt to conceive of themselves. Well, say they, "Who is the greatest in the kingdom of heaven?" Which of us shall have the chief management of public affairs? A pretty question for a few poor fishermen, who scarcely knew how to drag their nets to shore, much less how to govern a kingdom. Our Lord therefore in the second verse, to mortify them, calls a little child and sets him in the midst of them. This action was as much as if our Lord had said, "Poor creatures! Your imaginations are very towering; you dispute who shall be greatest in the kingdom of heaven; I will make this little child preach to you, or I will preach to you by him. Verily I say unto you (I who am truth itself, I know in what manner my subjects are to enter into my kingdom; I say unto you, you are so far from being in a right temper for my kingdom, that), except you be converted, and become as this little child, you shall not enter into the kingdom of heaven (unless you are, comparatively speaking, as loose to the world, as loose to crowns, scepters, and kingdoms and earthly things, as this poor little child I have in my hand), you shall not enter into my kingdom." So that what our Lord is speaking of, is not the innocence of little children, if you consider the relation they stand in to God, and as they are in themselves, when brought into the world; but what our Lord means is, that as to ambition and lust after the world, we must in this sense become as little children. Is there never a little boy or girl in this congregation? Ask a poor little child that can barely speak, about a crown, scepter, or kingdom, the poor creature has no notion about it: give a little boy or girl a small thing to play with, it will leave the world to other people. Now in this sense we must be converted and become as little children; that is, we must be as loose to the world, comparatively speaking, as a little child.

Do not mistake me, I am not going to persuade you to shut up your shops, or leave your business; I am not going to persuade you that if you will be Christians, you must turn hermits and retire out of the world; you cannot leave your wicked hearts behind you, when you leave the world; for I find when I am alone, my wicked heart has followed me, go where I will. No, the religion of Jesus is a social religion. But though Jesus Christ does not call us to go out of the world, shut up our shops, and leave our children to be provided for by miracles, yet this must be said to the honor of Christianity: if we are really converted, we shall be loose from the world. Though we are engaged in it and are obliged to work for our children; though we are obliged to follow trades and merchandise and to be serviceable to the commonwealth, yet if we are real Christians, we shall be loose to the world, though I will not pretend to say that all real Christians have attained to the same degree of spiritual-mindedness. This is the primary meaning of these words, that we must be converted and become as little children; nevertheless I suppose the words are to be understood in other senses.

When our Lord says, we must be converted and become as little children, I suppose he means also that we must be sensible of our weakness, comparatively speaking, as a little child. Everyone looks upon a little child as a poor weak creature; as one that ought to go to school and learn some new lesson every day; and as simple and artless, one without guile, having not learned the abominable art called dissimulation. Now in all these senses, I believe we are to understand the words of the text. Are little children sensible of their weakness? Must they be led by the hand? Must we take hold of them or they will fall? So, if we are converted, if the grace of God be really in our hearts, my dear friends, however we may have thought of ourselves once, whatever were our former high-exalted imaginations, yet we shall now be sensible of our weakness; we shall no more say, "We are rich and increased with goods and lack nothing"; we shall be inwardly poor; we shall feel "that we are poor, miserable, blind, and naked." And as a little child gives up its hand to be guided by a parent or a nurse, so those who are truly converted and are real Christians will give up the heart, their understandings, their wills, their affections, to be guided by the word, providence, and the Spirit of the Lord. Hence it is that the apostle, speaking of the sons of God, says, "As many as are led by the Spirit of God, they are (and to be sure he means they only are) the sons of God."

And as little children look upon themselves to be ignorant creatures, so those that are converted do look upon themselves as ignorant too. Hence it is that John, speaking to Christians, calls them "little children"; "I have written unto you, little children." And Christ's flock is called a little flock, not only because little in number, but also because those who are members of his flock are indeed little in their own eyes. Hence that great man, that great apostle of the Gentiles, that spiritual father of so many thousands of souls, that man, who in the opinion of Dr. Goodwin, "fits nearest the God-man, the Lord Jesus Christ, in glory," that chosen vessel, the apostle Paul, when he speaks of himself, says, "Unto me, who am less than the least of all saints, is this grace given, that I should preach among the Gentiles the unsearchable riches of Christ." Perhaps some of you, when you read these words, will be apt to think that Paul did not speak true, that he did not really feel what he said; because you judge Paul's heart by your own proud hearts; but the more you get of the grace of God, and the more you are partakers of the divine life, the more will you see your own meanness and vileness, and be less in your own eyes. Hence it is that Mr. Flavel, in his book called *Husbandry Spiritualized*, compares young Christians to green corn; which before it is ripe shoots up very high, but there is little solidity in it: whereas an old Christian is like ripe corn; it does not lift up its head so much, but then it is more weighty and fit to be cut down, and put into the farmer's barn. Young Christians are also like little rivulets; you know rivulets are shallow yet make great noise; but an old Christian, he makes not much noise; he goes on sweetly like a deep river sliding into the ocean.

And as a little child is looked upon as a harmless creature and generally speaks true; so, if we are converted and become as little children, we shall be guileless as well as harmless. What said the dear Redeemer when he saw Nathaniel? As though it was a rare sight, he gazed upon, and would have others gaze upon, it: "Behold an Israelite indeed." Why so? "In whom is no guile." Do not mistake me; I am not saying that Christians ought not to be prudent; they ought exceedingly to pray to God for prudence, otherwise they may follow the delusions of the devil, and by their imprudence give wrong touches to the ark of God. It was the lamentation of a great man, "God has given me many gifts, but God has not given me prudence." Therefore, when I say a Christian must be guileless, I do not mean, he should expose himself and lie open to everyone's assault; we should pray for the wisdom of the serpent, though we shall generally learn this wisdom by our blunders and imprudence; and we must make some advance in Christianity, before we know our imprudence. A person really converted can say, as it is reported of a philosopher, "I wish there was a window in my breast, that everyone may see the uprightness of my heart and intentions." And though there is too much of the old man in us, yet, if we are really converted, there will be in us no allowed guile; we shall be harmless. And that is the reason why the poor Christian is too often imposed upon; he judges other people by himself; having an honest heart, he thinks everyone as honest as himself and therefore is a prey to everyone. I might enlarge upon each of these points; it is a copious and important truth; but I do not intend to multiply many marks and heads.

And therefore, as I have something to say by way of personal application, give me leave therefore, with the utmost tenderness, and at the same time with faithfulness, to call upon you, my dear friends. My text is introduced in an awful manner, "Verily I say unto you"; and what Jesus said then, he says now to you, to me, and to as many as sit under a preached gospel, and to as many as the Lord our God shall call. Let me exhort you to see whether you are converted; whether such a great and almighty change has passed upon any of your souls. As I told you before, so I tell you again, you all hope to go to heaven, and I pray God Almighty you may be all there: when I see such a congregation as this, if my heart is in a proper frame, I feel myself ready to lay down my life, to be instrumental only to save one soul. It makes my heart bleed within me, it makes me sometimes most unwilling to preach, lest that word that I hope will do good may increase the damnation of any, and perhaps of a great part of the auditorium, through their own unbelief. Give me leave to deal faithfully with your souls. I have your death warrant in my hand: Christ has said it, Jesus will stand to it; it is like the laws of the Medes and Persians, it alters not. Hark, O man! Hark, O woman! He that has ears to hear, let him hear what the Lord Jesus Christ says, "Verily I say unto you, except ye be converted, and become as little children, ye shall not enter into the kingdom of heaven." Though this is Saturday night, and you are now preparing for the Sabbath, for what you know, you may yet never live to see the Sabbath. You have had awful proofs of this lately; a woman died but yesterday, a man died the day before, another was killed by something that fell from a house, and it may be in twenty-four hours more, many of you may be carried into an unalterable state. Now then, for God's sake, for your own soul's sake, if you have a mind to dwell with God, and cannot bear the thought of dwelling in everlasting burning, before I go any further, silently put up one prayer, or say amen to the prayer I would put in your mouths: "Lord, search me and try me. Lord, examine my heart and let my conscience speak. Oh, let me know whether I am converted or not!" What say you, my dear hearers? What say you, my fellow sinners? What say you, my guilty brethren? Has God by his blessed Spirit worked such a change in your hearts? I do not ask you whether God has made you angels. That I know will never be; I only ask you whether you have any well-grounded hope to think that God has made you new creatures in Christ Jesus; so renewed and changed your natures, that you can say, I humbly hope that "as to the habitual temper and tendency of my mind, that my heart is free from wickedness; I have a husband, I have a wife, I have also children, I keep a shop, I mind my business; but I love these creatures for God's sake, and do everything for Christ: and if God was now to call me away, according to the habitual temper of my mind, I can say, 'Lord, I am ready'; and however I love the creatures, I hope I can say, 'Whom have I in heaven but thee? Whom have I in heaven, O my God and my dear Redeemer, that I desire in comparison of thee?'" Can you thank God for the creatures and say at the same time, "These are not my Christ"? I speak in plain language, you know my way of preaching: I do not want to play the orator; I do not want to be counted a scholar; I want to speak so as I may reach poor people's hearts. What say you, my dear hearers? Are you sensible of your weakness? Do you feel that you are poor, miserable, blind, and naked by nature? Do you give up your hearts, your affections, your wills, your understanding to be guided by the Spirit of God, as a little child gives up its hand to be guided by its parent? Are you little in your own eyes? Do you think meanly of yourselves? And do you want to learn something new every day? I mention these marks, because

I am apt to believe they are more adapted to a great many of your capacities. A great many of you have not that showing of affection you sometimes had, therefore you are for giving up all your evidences and making way for the devil's coming into your heart. You are not brought up to the mount as you used to be, therefore you conclude you have no grace at all. But if the Lord Jesus Christ has emptied you and humbled you, if he is giving you to see and know that you are nothing; though you are not growing upward, you are growing downward; and though you have not so much joy, yet your heart is emptying to be more abundantly replenished by and by. Can any of you follow me? Then give God thanks, and take the comfort of it.

If you are thus converted and become a little child, I welcome you, in the name of the Lord Jesus, into God's dear family; I welcome you, in the name of the dear Redeemer, into the company of God's children. O you dear souls, though the world sees nothing in you, though there be no outward difference between you and others, yet I look upon you in another light, even as so many king's sons and daughters: all hail! In the name of God, I wish every one of you joy from my soul, you sons and daughters of the King of kings. Will not you henceforth exercise a childlike temper? Will not such a thought melt down your hearts, when I tell you that the great God, who might have frowned you to hell for your secret sins that nobody knew of but God and your own souls, and who might have damned you times without number, has cast the mantle of his love over you; his voice has been, "Let that man, that woman, live, for I have found a ransom." Oh, will you not cry out, "Why me, Lord?"? Was King George to send for any of your children, and were you to hear they were to be his adopted sons, how highly honored would you think your children to be? What great condescension was it for Pharaoh's daughter to take up Moses, a poor child exposed in an ark of bulrushes, and bring him up for her child? But what is that happiness in comparison of yours, who was the other day a child of the devil, but now by converting grace are become a child of God? Are you converted? Are you become like little children? Then what must you do? My dear hearers, be obedient to God; remember God is your Father; and as every one of you must know what a dreadful cross it is to have a wicked, disobedient child, if you do not want your children to be disobedient to you, for Christ's sake be not disobedient to your heavenly parent. If God be your Father, obey him; if God be your Father, serve him; love him with all your heart, love him with all your might, with all your soul, and with all your strength. If God be your Father, fly from everything that may displease him and walk worthy of that God who has called you to his kingdom and glory. If you are converted and become like little children, then behave as little children: they long for the breast and with it will be contented. Are you newborn babes? Then desire the sincere milk of the Word, that you may grow thereby. I do not want that Arminian husks should go down with you; you are king's sons and daughters and have a more refined taste; you must have the doctrines of grace; and blessed be God that you dwell in a country where the sincere word is so plainly preached. Are you children? Then grow in grace, and in the knowledge of your Lord and Savior Jesus Christ. Have any of you children that do not grow? Do not you lament these children and cry over them; do not you say, my child will never be fit for anything in the world? Well, does it grieve you to see a child that will not grow? How much must it grieve the heart of Christ to see you grow so little? Will you be always children? Will you be always learning the first principles of Christianity and never press forward toward the mark, for the prize of the high calling of God in Christ Jesus? God forbid. Let the language of your heart be "Lord Jesus, help me to grow; help me to learn more; learn me to live so as my progress may be known to all!"

Are you God's children? Are you converted and become like little children? Then deal with God as your little children do with you; as soon as ever they want anything, or if anybody hurt them, I appeal to yourselves if they do not directly run to their parent. Well, are you God's children? Does the devil trouble you? Does the world trouble you? Go tell your Father of it, go directly and complain to God. Perhaps you may say, "I cannot utter fine words." But do any of you expect fine words from your children? If they come crying and can speak but half words, do not your hearts yearn over them? And has not God unspeakably more pity to you? If you can only make signs to him, "as a father pitieth his children, so will the Lord pity them that fear him." I pray you therefore be bold with your Father, saying, "Abba, Father, Satan troubles me; the world troubles me; my own mother's children are angry with me; heavenly Father, plead my cause!" The Lord will then speak for you some way or other.

Are you converted and become as little children? Have you entered into God's family? Then assure yourselves that your heavenly Father will chasten you now and then: "for what son is there whom the father chasteneth not? If ye are without chastisement, of which all are partakers, then are ye bastards and not sons." It is recorded of Bishop Latimer, that in the house where he came to lodge, he overheard the master of the house say, "I thank God I never had a cross in my life." "Oh," said he, "then I will not stay here." I believe there is not a child of God, when in a good frame, but has prayed for great humility; they have prayed for great faith; they have prayed for great love; they have prayed for all the graces of the Spirit. Do you know, when you put up these prayers, that you did also say, "Lord send us great trials." For how is it possible to know you have great faith, humility, and love, unless God put you into great trials, that you may know whether you have them or not. I mention this, because a great many of the children of God (I am sure it has been a temptation to me many times, when I have been under God's smarting rod), when they have great trials, think God is giving them over. If therefore you are God's children, if you are converted and become as little children, do not expect that God will be like a foolish parent; no, he is a jealous God; he loves his child too well to spare his rod. How did he correct Miriam? How did he correct Moses? How has God in all ages corrected his dearest children? Therefore if you are converted and become as little children, if God has taken away a child, or your substance, if God suffers friends to forsake you, and if you are forsaken as it were both by God and man, say, "Lord, I thank you! I am a perverse child, or God would not strike me so often and so hard." Do not blame your heavenly Father, but blame yourselves; he is a loving God and a tender Father: "He is afflicted in all our afflictions"; therefore when God spoke to Moses, he spoke out of the bush, as much as to say, "Moses, this bush represents my people; as this bush is burning with fire, so are my children to burn with affliction; but I am in the bush; if the bush burns, I will burn with it; I will be with them in the furnace; I will be with them in the water, and though the water come over them, it shall not overflow them."

Are you God's children? Are you converted and become as little children? Then will you not long to go home and see your Father? Oh, happy they that have gotten home before you; happy they that are up yonder; happy they who have ascended above this field of conflict. I know not what you may think of it, but since I heard that some, whose hearts God was pleased to work upon, are gone to glory, I am sometimes filled with grief that God is not pleased to let me go home too. How can you see so much coldness among God's people? How can you see God's people like the moon, waxing and waning? Who can but desire to be forever with the Lord? Thanks be to God, the time is soon coming; thanks be to God, he will come and will not tarry. Do not be impatient; God in his own time will fetch you home. And though you may be brought to short allowance now, though some of you may be narrow in your circumstances, yet do not repine; a God, and the gospel of Christ, with brown bread, are great riches. In your Father's house there is bread enough and to spare; though you are now tormented, yet by and by you shall be comforted; the angels will look upon it as an honor to convey you to Abraham's bosom, though you are but a Lazarus here. By the frame of my heart, I am much inclined to speak comfortably to God's people.

But I only mention one thing more, and that is, if you are converted and become as little children, then for God's sake take care of doing what children often do; they are too apt to quarrel one with another. Oh, love one another: "he that dwells in love dwells in God, and God in him." Joseph knew that his brethren were in danger of falling out, therefore when he left them, says he, "Fall not out by the way." You are all children of the same Father; you are all going to the same place; why should you differ? The world has enough against us, the devil has enough against us, without our quarreling with each other. Oh, walk in love. If I could preach no more, if I was not able to hold out to the end of my sermon, I would say, as John did when he was grown old and could not preach, "Little children, love one another." If you are God's children, then love one another. There is nothing grieves me more than the differences among God's people. Oh, hasten that time, when we shall either go to heaven or never quarrel anymore!

Would to God I could speak to all of you in this comfortable language; but my Master tells me I must "not give that which is holy to dogs, I must not cast pearls before swine"; therefore, though I have been speaking comfortably, yet what I have been saying, especially in this latter part of the discourse, belongs to children; it is children's bread, it belongs to God's people. If any of you are graceless, Christless, unconverted creatures, I charge you not to touch it; I fence it in the name of God; here is a flaming sword turning every way to keep you from this bread of life, till you are turned to Jesus Christ. And therefore, as I suppose many of you are unconverted, and graceless, go home! And away to your closets, and down with your stubborn hearts before God; if you have not done it before, let this be the night. Or do not stay till you go home; begin now, while standing here; pray to God and let the language of your heart be "Lord, convert me! Lord, make me a little child. Lord Jesus, let me not be banished from your kingdom!" My dear friends, there is a great deal more implied in the words than is expressed: when Christ says, "Ye shall not enter into the kingdom of heaven," it is as much to say, "You shall certainly go to hell; you shall certainly be damned and dwell in the blackness of darkness forever; you shall go where the worm dies not, and where the fire is not quenched." The Lord God impress it upon your souls! May an arrow (as one lately wrote me in a letter) dipped in the blood of Christ reach every unconverted sinner's heart! May God fulfill the text to every one of your souls! It is he alone that can do it. If you confess your sins and leave them and lay hold on the Lord Jesus Christ, the Spirit of God shall be given you; if you will go and say, "Turn me, O my God!" you know not, O man, what the return of God may be to you. Did I think that preaching would be to the purpose, did I think that arguments would induce you to come, I would continue my discourse till midnight. And however some of you may hate me without a cause, would to God everyone in this congregation was as much concerned for himself as at present (blessed be God) I feel myself concerned for him. Oh, that my head were waters. Oh, that mine eyes were a fountain of tears, that I might weep over an unconverted, graceless, wicked, and adulterous generation. Precious souls, for God's sake think what will become of you when you die, if you die without being converted; if you go hence without the wedding garment, God will strike you speechless, and you shall be banished from his presence forever and ever. I know you cannot dwell with everlasting burnings; behold, then I show you a way of escape; Jesus is the way, Jesus is the truth, the Lord Jesus Christ is the resurrection and the life. It is his Spirit must convert you; come to Christ, and you shall have it; and may God for Christ's sake give it to you all, and convert you, that we may all meet, never to part again, in his heavenly kingdom; even so Lord Jesus. Amen and amen.

What Think Ye of Christ?

—∭—

"What think ye of Christ?" —MATTHEW 22:42

When it pleased the eternal Son of God to tabernacle among us and preach the glad tidings of salvation to a fallen world, different opinions were entertained by different parties concerning him. As to his person, some said he was Moses; others that he was Elijah, Jeremiah, or one of the ancient prophets; few acknowledged him to be what he really was: God blessed for evermore. And as to his doctrine, though the common people, being free from prejudice, were persuaded of the heavenly tendency of his going about to do good and, for the generality, heard him gladly and said he was a good man, yet the envious, worldly minded, self-righteous governors and teachers of the Jewish church, being grieved at his success, on the one hand, and unable (having never been taught of God) to understand the purity of his doctrine, on the other; notwithstanding our Lord spoke as never man spoke, and did such miracles which no man could possibly do, unless God was with him; yet they not only were so infatuated as to say that he deceived the people, but also were so blasphemous as to affirm that he was in league with the devil himself and cast out devils by Beelzebub, the prince of devils. What's more, our Lord's own brethren and kinsmen, according to the flesh, were so blinded by prejudices and unbelief, that on a certain day, when he went out to teach the multitudes in the fields, they sent to take hold of him, urging this as a reason for their conduct, that "he was beside himself."

Thus was the King and the Lord of glory judged by man's judgment, when manifest in flesh: far be it from any of his ministers to expect better treatment. No, if we come in the spirit and power of our Master, in this, as in every other part of his sufferings, we must follow his steps. The like reproaches which were cast on him will be thrown on us also. Those that received our Lord and his doctrine will receive and hear us for his name's sake. The poor, blessed be God, as our present meeting abundantly testifies, receive the gospel, and the common people hear us gladly, while those who are sitting in Moses' chair, and love to wear long robes, being ignorant of the righteousness which is of God by faith in Christ Jesus, and having never felt the power of God upon their hearts, will be continually crying out against us, as madmen, deceivers of the people, and as acting under the influence of evil spirits.

But he is unworthy of the name of a minister of the gospel of peace who is unwilling, not only to have his name cast out as evil, but also to die for the truths of the Lord Jesus. It is the character of hirelings and false prophets, who care not for the sheep, to have all men speak well of them. "Blessed are you (says our Lord to his first apostles, and in them to all succeeding ministers) when men speak all manner of evil against you falsely for my name's sake." And indeed it is impossible but such offenses must come; for men will always judge of others, according to the principles from which they act themselves. And if they care not to yield obedience to the doctrines which we deliver, they must necessarily, in self-defense, speak against the preachers, lest they should be asked that question which the Pharisees of old feared to have retorted on them, if they confessed that John was a prophet: "Why then did you not believe on him?" In all such cases, we have nothing to do but to search our own hearts, and if we can assure our consciences, before God, that we act with a single eye to his glory, we are cheerfully to go on in our work and not in the least to regard what men or devils can say against, or do unto, us.

But to return. You have heard what various thoughts there were concerning Jesus Christ, while here on earth; nor is he otherwise treated; even now he is exalted to sit down at the right hand of his Father in heaven. A stranger to Christianity, were he to hear that we all profess to hold one Lord, would naturally infer that we all thought and spoke one and the same thing about him. But alas! to our shame be it mentioned, though Christ be not divided in himself, yet professors are sadly divided in their thoughts about him—and that not only as to the circumstances of his religion, but also of those essential truths which must necessarily be believed and received by us, if ever we hope to be heirs of eternal salvation.

Some, and I fear a multitude which no man can easily number, there are among us, who call themselves Christians, and yet seldom or never seriously think of Jesus Christ at all. They can think of their shops and their farms, their plays, their balls, their assemblies, and horse races (entertainments which directly tend to exclude religion out of the world); but as for Christ, the Author and Finisher of faith, the Lord who has bought poor sinners with his precious blood, and who is the only thing worth thinking of, alas! he is not in all, or at most in very few of their thoughts. But believe me, O you earthly, sensual, carnally minded professors, however little you may think of Christ now, or however industriously you may strive to keep him out of your thoughts, by pursuing the lust of the eye, the lust of the flesh, and the pride of life, yet there is a time coming, when you will wish you had thought of Christ more and of your profits and pleasures less. For the charmed, the polite, the rich also must die as well as others, and leave their pomps and vanities and all their wealth behind them. And oh! what thoughts will you entertain concerning Jesus Christ in that hour?

But I must not purpose these reflections: they would carry me too far from the main design of this discourse, which is to show what those who are truly desirous to know how to worship God in spirit and in truth ought to think concerning Jesus Christ, whom God has sent to be the end of the law for righteousness to all them that shall believe.

I trust, my brethren, you are more noble than to think me too strict or scrupulous, in thus attempting to regulate your thoughts about Jesus Christ: for by our thoughts, as well as our words and actions, are we to be judged at the great day. And in vain do we hope to believe in or worship Christ aright, unless our principles, on which our faith and practice are founded, are agreeable to the form of sound words delivered to us in the Scriptures of truth.

Besides, many deceivers are gone abroad into the world. Mere heathen morality, and not Jesus Christ, is preached in most of our churches. And how should people think rightly of Christ, of whom they have scarcely heard? Bear with me a little then, while, to inform your consciences, I ask you a few questions concerning Jesus Christ. For there is no other name given under heaven, whereby we can be saved, but his.

First, what think you about the person of Christ? "Whose son is he?" This is the question our Lord put to the Pharisees in the words following the text; and never was it more necessary to repeat this question than in these last days. For numbers that are called after the name of Christ, and I fear many that pretend to preach him, are so far advanced in the blasphemous chair as openly to deny his being really, truly, and properly God. But no one that ever was partaker of his Spirit will speak thus lightly of him. No; if they are asked, as Peter and his brethren were, "But whom say ye that I am?" they will reply without hesitation, "Thou art Christ the Son of the ever-living God." For the confession of our Lord's divinity is the rock upon which he builds his church. Was it possible to take this away, the gates of hell would quickly prevail against it. My brethren, if Jesus Christ be not very God of very God, I would never preach the gospel of Christ again. For it would not be gospel; it would be only a system of moral ethics. Seneca, Cicero, or any of the Gentile philosophers would be as good a Savior as Jesus of Nazareth. It is the divinity of our Lord that gives a sanction to his death and makes him such a high priest as became us, one who by the infinite mercies of his suffering could make a full, perfect, sufficient sacrifice, satisfaction, and oblation to infinitely offended justice. And whatsoever minister of the Church of England makes use of her forms and eats of her bread, and, yes, holds not this doctrine (as I fear too many such are crept in among us), such a one belongs only to the synagogue of Satan. He is not a child or minister of God; no, he is a wolf in sheep's clothing; he is a child and minister of that wicked one the devil.

Many will think these hard sayings; but I think it no breach of charity to affirm that an Arian or Socinian cannot be a Christian. The one would make us believe Jesus Christ is only a created God, which is a self-contradiction; and the other would have us look on him only as a good man; and, instead of owning his death to be an atonement for the sins of the world, would persuade us that Christ died only to seal the truth of his doctrine with his blood. But if Jesus Christ be no more than a mere man, if he be not truly God, he was the vilest sinner that ever appeared in the world. For he accepted of divine adoration from the man who had been born blind, as we read John 9:38: "And he said, 'Lord I believe,' and he worshiped him." Besides, if Christ be not properly God, our faith is vain; we are yet in our sins, for no created being, though of the highest order, could possibly merit anything at God's hands; it was our Lord's divinity that alone qualified him to take away the sins of the world; and therefore we hear St. John pronouncing so positively that "the Word (Jesus Christ) was not only with God, but was God." For the like reason, St. Paul says that "he was in the form of God"; that "in him dwelt all the fullness of the Godhead bodily." What's more, Jesus Christ assumed the title which God gave to himself, when he sent Moses to deliver his people Israel. "Before Abraham was, I AM." And again, "I and my Father are one." Which last words, though our modern infidels would evade and wrest, as they do other Scriptures, to their own damnation, yet it is evident that the Jews understood our Lord, when he spoke thus, as making himself equal with God; otherwise, why did they stone him as a blasphemer? And now, why should it be thought a breach of charity to affirm that those who deny the divinity of Jesus Christ, in the strictest sense of the word, cannot be Christians? For they are greater infidels than the devils themselves, who confessed that they knew who he was, "even the holy one of God." They not only believe, but, which is more than the unbelievers of this generation do, they tremble. And were it possible for arch-heretics to be released from their chains of darkness, under which (unless they altered their principles before they died) they are now reserved to the judgment of the great day, I am persuaded they would inform us how hell had convinced them of the divinity of Jesus Christ, and that they would advise their followers to abhor their principles, lest they should come into the same place and thereby increase each other's torments.

But, second, what think you of the manhood or incarnation of Jesus Christ? For Christ was not only God, but he was God and man in one person. Thus runs the text and context, "When the Pharisees were gathered together, Jesus asked them, saying, 'What think ye of Christ? Whose son is he?' They say unto him, 'The son of David.' 'How then,' (says our divine Master), 'does David in spirit call him Lord?'" From which passage it is evident that we do not think rightly of the person of Jesus Christ, unless we believe him to be perfect God and perfect man, or a reasonable soul and human flesh subsisting.

For it is on this account that he is called Christ, or the anointed one, who through his own voluntary offer was set apart by the Father and strengthened and qualified by the anointing or communication of the Holy Ghost to be a mediator between him and offending man.

The reason why the Son of God took upon him our nature was the fall of our first parents. I hope there is no one present so atheistic, as to think that man made himself; no, it was God that made us, and not we ourselves. And I would willingly think that no one is so blasphemous as to suppose that if God did make us, he made us such creatures as we now find ourselves to be. For this would be giving God's Word the lie, which tells us that "in the image of God (not in the image which we now bear on our souls) made he man." As God made man, so God made him perfect. He placed him in the garden of Eden, and condescended to enter into a covenant with him, promising him eternal life, upon condition of unsinning obedience; and threatening eternal death, if he broke his law and did eat the forbidden fruit.

Man did eat; and herein acting as our representative, thereby involved both himself and us in that curse which God, the righteous Judge, had said should be the consequence of his disobedience. But here begins that mystery of godliness, God manifested in the flesh. For (sing, O heavens, and rejoice, O earth!) the eternal Father, foreseeing how Satan would bruise the heel of man, had in his eternal counsel provided a means whereby he might bruise that accursed serpent's head. Man is permitted to fall and become subject to death, but Jesus, the only begotten Son of God, begotten of the Father before all worlds, Light of light, very God of very God, offers to die to make an atonement for his transgression and to fulfill all righteousness in his stead. And because it was impossible for him to do this as he was God, and yet since man had offended, it was necessary it should be done in the person of man; rather than we should perish, this everlasting God, this Prince of peace, this Ancient of Days, in the fullness of time, had a body prepared for him by the Holy Ghost and became an infant. In this body he performed a complete obedience to the law of God; whereby he, in our stead, fulfilled the covenant of works and at last became subject to death, even death upon the cross; that as God he might satisfy, as man he might obey and suffer; and being God and man in one person, might once more procure a union between God and our souls.

And now, what think you of this love of Christ? Do not you think it was wondrous great? Especially when you consider that we were Christ's bitter enemies, and that he would have been infinitely happy in himself, notwithstanding we had perished forever. Whatever you may think of it, I know the blessed angels, who are not so much concerned in this mystery of godliness as we, think most highly of it. They do, they will desire to look into and admire it, through all eternity. Why, why, O you sinners, will you not think of this love of Christ? Surely it must melt down the most hardened heart. While I am speaking, the thought of this infinite and condescending love fires and warms my soul. I could dwell on it forever. But it is expedient for you, that I should ask you another question concerning Jesus Christ.

Third, what think you about being justified by Christ? I believe I can answer for some of you; for many, I fear, think to be justified or looked upon as righteous in God's sight, without Jesus Christ. But such will find themselves dreadfully mistaken; for out of Christ, "God is a consuming fire." Others satisfy themselves with believing that Christ was God and man, and that he came into the world to save sinners in general; whereas their chief concern ought to be how they may be assured that Jesus Christ came into the world to save them in particular. "The life that I now live in the flesh (says the apostle) is by faith of the Son of God, who loved me, and gave himself for me." Observe, for me: it is this immediate application of Jesus Christ to our own hearts, and that they can be justified in God's sight, only in or through him; but then they make him only in part a savior. They are for doing what they can themselves, and then Jesus Christ is to make up the deficiencies of their righteousness. This is the sum and substance of our modern divinity. And was it possible for me to know the thoughts of most that hear me this day, I believe they would tell me, this was the scheme they had laid, and perhaps depended on for some years, for their eternal salvation. Is it not then high time, my brethren, for you to entertain quite different thoughts concerning justification by Jesus Christ? For if you think thus, you are in the case of those unhappy Jews, who went about to establish their own righteousness, and would not submit to, and consequently missed of, that righteousness which is of God by faith in Christ Jesus our Lord. What think you then, if I tell you that you are to be justified freely through faith in Jesus Christ, without any regard to any work or fitness foreseen in us at all? For salvation is the free gift of God; I know no fitness in man but a fitness to be cast into the lake of fire and brimstone forever. Our righteousnesses, in God's sight, are but as filthy rags; he cannot away with them. Our holiness, if we have any, is not the cause but the effect of our justification in God's sight. "We love God, because he first loved us." We must not come to God as the proud Pharisee did, bringing in as it were a reckoning of our services; we must come in the temper and language of the poor publican, smiting upon our breasts, and saying, "God be merciful to me a sinner"; for Jesus Christ justifies us while we are ungodly. He came not to call the righteous, but sinners to repentance. The poor in spirit only, they who are willing to go out of themselves and rely wholly on the righteousness of another, are so blessed as to be members of his kingdom. The righteousness, the whole righteousness, of Jesus Christ is to be imputed to us, instead of our own: "for we are not under the law, but under grace"; and "to as many as walk after this rule, peace be on them," for they, and they only, are the true Israel of God. In the great work of man's redemption, boasting is entirely excluded; which could not be if only one of our works was to be joined with the merits of Christ. Our salvation is all of God, from the beginning to the end; it is not of works, lest any man should boast; man has no hand in it: it is Christ who is to be made to us, of God the Father, wisdom, righteousness, sanctification, and eternal redemption. His active as well as his passive obedience is to be applied to poor sinners. He has fulfilled all righteousness in our stead, that we might become the righteousness of God in him. All we have to do is to lay hold on this righteousness by faith; and the very moment we do apprehend it by a lively faith, that very moment we may be assured that the blood of Jesus Christ has cleansed us from all sin. "For the promise is to us and to our children, and to as many as the Lord our God shall call." If we and our whole houses believe, we shall be saved as well as the jailer and his house; for the righteousness of Jesus Christ is an everlasting, as well as a perfect, righteousness. It is as effectual to all who believe in him now, as formerly; and so it will be, till time shall be no more. Search the Scriptures, as the Bereans did, and see whether these things are not so. Search St. Paul's epistles to the Romans and Galatians, and there you will find this doctrine so plainly taught you, that unless you have eyes and see not, he that runs may read. Search the Eleventh Article of our church: "We are accounted righteous before God, only for the merits of our Lord and Savior Jesus Christ by faith, and not for our own works or deservings."

This doctrine of our free justification by faith in Christ Jesus, however censured and evil spoken of by our present masters of Israel, was highly esteemed by our wise forefathers; for in the subsequent words of the aforementioned article, it is called a most wholesome doctrine, and very full of comfort; and so it is to all that are weary and heavy laden, and are truly willing to find rest in Jesus Christ.

This is gospel, this is glad tidings of great joy to all that feel themselves poor, lost, undone, damned sinners. "Ho, everyone that thirsteth, come unto the waters of life, and drink freely; come and buy without money and without price." Behold a fountain opened in your Savior's side, for sin and for all uncleanness. "Look unto him whom you have pierced"; look unto him by faith, and verily you shall be saved, though you came here only to ridicule and blaspheme and never thought of God or of Christ before.

Not that you must think God will save you because, or on account, of your faith; for faith is a work, and then you would be justified for your works; but when I tell you, we are to be justified by faith, I mean that faith is the instrument whereby the sinner applies or brings home the redemption of Jesus Christ to his heart. And to whomsoever God gives such a faith (for it is the free gift of God), he may lift up his head with boldness; he need not fear; he is a spiritual son of our spiritual David; he is passed from death to life, he shall never come into condemnation. This is the gospel which we preach. If any man or angel preach any other gospel, than this of our being freely justified through faith in Christ Jesus, we have the authority of the greatest apostle to pronounce him accursed.

And now, my brethren, what think you of this foolishness of preaching? To you that have tasted the good word of life, who have been enlightened to see the riches of God's free grace in Christ Jesus, I am persuaded it is precious and has distilled like the dew into your souls. And oh, that all were like-minded! But I am afraid, numbers are ready to go away contradicting and blaspheming. Tell me, are there not many of you saying within yourselves, "This is a licentious doctrine; this preacher is opening a door for encouragement in sin." But this does not surprise me at all. It is a stale, antiquated objection, as old the doctrine of justification itself; and (which by the way is not much to the credit of those who urge it now) it was made by an infidel. St. Paul, in his Epistle to the Romans, after he had, in the first five chapters, demonstrably proved the doctrine of justification by faith alone; in the sixth brings in an unbeliever saying, "Shall we continue in sin then, that grace may abound?" But as he rejected such an inference with a "God forbid!" so do I: for the faith which we preach is not a dead speculative faith, an assenting to things credible, as credible is commonly defined: it is not a faith of the head only, but a faith of the heart. It is a living principle worked in the soul, by the Spirit of the ever-living God, convincing the sinner of his lost, undone condition by nature; enabling him to apply and lay hold on the perfect righteousness of Jesus Christ, freely offered him in the gospel, and continually exciting him, out of a principle of love and gratitude, to show forth that faith, by abounding in every good word and work. This is the sum and substance of the doctrine that has been delivered. And if this be a licentious doctrine, judge you. No, my brethren, this is not destroying, but teaching you how to do good works, from a proper principle. For to use the words of our church in another of her articles, "Works done before the grace of Christ, and the inspiration of the Spirit, are not pleasant to God, forasmuch as they spring not of faith in Jesus Christ; rather, for that they are not done as God has willed and commanded them to be done, we doubt not but they have the nature of sin." So that they who bid you do, and then live, are just as wise as those who would persuade you to build a beautiful magnificent house, without laying a foundation.

It is true, the doctrine of our free justification by faith in Christ Jesus, like other gospel truths, may and will be abused by men of corrupt minds, reprobates concerning the faith; but they who receive the truth of God in the love if it will always be showing their faith by their works. For this reason, St. Paul, after he had told the Ephesians, "By grace they were saved through faith, not of works, lest any man should boast," immediately adds, "For we are his workmanship, created in Christ Jesus unto good works." And in his Epistle to Titus, having given him directions to tell the people they were justified by grace, directly subjoins, "I will that you affirm constantly, that they who have believed in God might be careful to maintain good works" (3:8). Agreeable to this, we are told in our Twelfth Article, "Albeit that good works, which are the fruits of faith, and follow after justification, cannot put away our sins, and endure the severity of God's judgment; yet are they pleasing and acceptable to God in Christ; and do spring necessarily out of a true and lively faith, insomuch, that a lively faith may be as evidently known by them, as a tree discerned by the fruit."

What would I give, that this article was duly understood and preached by all that have subscribed to it! The ark of the Lord would not then be driven into the wilderness, nor would so many persons dissent from the Church of England. For I am fully persuaded that it is not so much on account of rites and ceremonies, as our not preaching the truth as it is in Jesus, that so many have been obliged to go and seek for food elsewhere. Did not we fall from our established doctrines, few, comparatively speaking, would fall from the Established Church. Where Christ is preached, though it be in a church or on a common, dissenters of all denominations have, and do most freely, come. But if our clergy will preach only the law, and not show the way of salvation by faith in Christ, the charge of schism at the day of judgment, I fear, will chiefly lie at their door. The true sheep of Christ know the voice of Christ's true shepherds, and strangers they will not hear.

Observe, my dear brethren, the words of the article, "Good works are the fruits of faith, and follow after justification." How then can they precede or be any way the cause of it? Our persons must be justified before our performances can be accepted. God had respect to Abel before he had respect to his offering; and therefore the righteousness of Jesus Christ must be freely imputed to and apprehended by us through faith, before we can offer an acceptable sacrifice to God: for out of Christ, as I hinted before, God is a consuming fire: and whatsoever is not of faith in Christ, is sin.

That people mistake the doctrine of free justification, I believe, is partly owing to their not rightly considering the different persons to whom St. Paul and St. James wrote in their epistles; as also the different kind of justification each of them writes about. The former affects in line upon line, argument upon argument, that "we are justified by faith alone." The latter put this question, "Was not Abraham justified by works?" From which many, not considering the different views of these holy men, and the different persons they wrote to, have blended and joined faith and works, in order to justify us in the sight of God. But this is a capital mistake; for St. Paul was writing to the Jewish proselytes, who sought righteousness by the works, not of the ceremonial only, but of the moral law. In contradistinction to that, he tells them, they were to look for justification in God's sight, only by the perfect righteousness of Jesus Christ apprehended by faith. St. James had a different set of people to deal with; such who abused the doctrines of free justification, and thought they should be saved (as numbers among us do now) upon their barely professing to believe on Jesus Christ. These the holy apostle endeavors wisely to convince, that such a faith was only a dead and false faith; and therefore it behooved all who would be blessed with faithful Abraham to show forth their faith by their works, as he did. "For was not Abraham justified by works?" Did he not prove that his faith was a true justifying faith, by its being productive of good works? From which it is plain that St. James is talking of a declarative justification before men; show me, demonstrate, evidence to me, that you have a true faith, by your works. Whereas St. Paul is talking only of our being justified in the sight of God; and thus he proves that Abraham, as we also are to be, was justified before ever the moral or ceremonial law was given to the Jews, for it is written, "Abraham believed in the Lord, and it was accounted to him for righteousness."

Take the substance of what has been said on this head, in the few following words. Every man that is saved is justified three ways: First, meritoriously, by the death of Jesus Christ: "It is the blood of Jesus Christ alone that cleanses us from all sin." Second, instrumentally, by faith; faith is the means or instrument whereby the merits of Jesus Christ are applied to the sinner's heart: "Ye are all the children of God by faith in Christ Jesus." Third, we are justified declaratively; namely, by good works; good works declare and prove to the world that our faith is a true saving faith. "Was not Abraham justified by works?" And again, "Show me thy faith by thy works."

It may not be improper to illustrate this doctrine by an example or two. I suppose no one will pretend to say that there was any fitness for salvation in Zaccheus the publican, when he came to see Jesus out of no better principle than that whereby perhaps thousands are led to hear me preach: I mean, curiosity. But Jesus Christ prevented and called him by his free grace and sweetly, but irresistibly, inclined him to obey that call; as, I pray God, he may influence all you that come only to see who the preacher is. Zaccheus received our Lord joyfully into his house, and at the same time by faith received him into his heart; Zaccheus was then freely justified in the sight of God. But behold the immediate fruits of that justification! He stands forth in the midst, and as before he had believed in his heart, he now makes confession with his mouth to salvation: "Behold, Lord, the half of my goods I give unto the poor; and if I have taken anything from any man by false accusation, I restore him fourfold." And thus it will be with you, O believer, as soon as ever God's dear Son is revealed in you by a living faith; you will have no rest in your spirit, till out of love and gratitude for what God has done for your soul, you show forth your faith by your works.

Again, I suppose everybody will grant there was no fitness for salvation in the persecutor Saul; no more than there is in those persecuting zealots of these last days who are already breathing out threatenings and, if in their power, would breathe out slaughter also, against the disciples of the Lord.

Now our Lord, we know, freely prevented him by his grace (and oh, that he would thus effectually call the persecutors of this generation), and by a light from heaven struck him to the ground. At the same time, by his Spirit, he pricked him to the heart, convinced him of sin, and caused him to cry out, "Who art thou, Lord?" Christ replies, "I am Jesus whom thou persecutest." Faith then was instantaneously given to him and, behold, immediately Saul cries out, "Lord, what wilt thou have me to do?" And so will every poor soul that believes on the Lord Jesus with his whole heart. He will be always asking, "Lord, what shall I do for thee? Lord, what wilt thou have me to do?" Not to justify himself, but only to evidence the sincerity of his love and thankfulness to his all-merciful high priest, for plucking him as a firebrand out of the fire.

Perhaps many self-righteous persons among you may flatter yourselves, that you are not so wicked as either Zaccheus or Saul was, and consequently there is a greater fitness for salvation in you than in them. But if you think thus, indeed you think more highly of yourselves than you ought to think: for by nature we are all alike, all equally fallen short of the glory of God, all equally dead in trespasses and sins, and there needs the same almighty power to be exerted in converting any one of the most sober, good-natured, moral persons here present, as there was in converting the publican Zaccheus, or that notorious persecutor Saul. And was it possible for you to ascend into the highest heaven, and to inquire of the spirits of just men made perfect, I am persuaded they would tell you this doctrine is from God. But we have a more sure word of prophecy, to which we do well to give heed, as unto a light shining in a dark place. My brethren, the word is nigh you; search the Scriptures; beg of God to make you willing to be saved in this day of his power; for it is not flesh and blood, but the Spirit of Jesus Christ, that alone can reveal these things unto you.

Fourth and last, what think you of Jesus Christ being formed within you? For whom Christ justifies, them he also sanctifies. Although he finds, yet he does not leave us unholy. A true Christian may not so properly be said to live, as Jesus Christ to live in him. For they only that are led by the Spirit of Christ are the true sons of God.

As I observed before, so I tell you again, the faith which we preach is not a dead, but a lively active faith worked in the soul, working a thorough change, by the power of the Holy Ghost, in the whole man; and unless Christ be thus in you, notwithstanding you may be orthodox as to the foregoing principles, notwithstanding you may have good desires, and attend constantly on the means of grace; yet, in St. Paul's opinion, you are out of a state of salvation. "Know you not (says that apostle to the Corinthians, a church famous for its gifts above any church under heaven) that Christ is in you (by his Spirit), unless you are reprobates?"

For Christ came not only to save us from the guilt, but from the power of our sins; till he has done this, however he may be a Savior to others, we can have no assurance of well-grounded hope that he has saved us; for it is by receiving his blessed Spirit into our hearts, and feeling him witnessing with our spirits that we are the sons of God, that we can be certified of our being sealed to the day of redemption.

This is a great mystery; but I speak of Christ and the new birth. Marvel not at my asking you what you think about Christ being formed within you.

For either God must change his nature or we ours. For as in Adam we all have spiritually died, so all that are effectually saved by Christ must in Christ be spiritually made alive. His only end in dying and rising again, and interceding for us now in heaven, is to redeem us from the misery of our fallen nature, and, by the operation of his blessed Spirit, to make us meet to be partakers of the heavenly inheritance with the saints in light. None but those that thus are changed by his grace here shall appear with him in glory hereafter.

Examine yourselves therefore, my brethren, whether you are in the faith; prove yourselves; and think it not sufficient to say in your creed, "I believe in Jesus Christ"; many say so, who do not believe, who are reprobates, and yet in a state of death. You take God's name in vain when you call him Father, and your prayers are turned into sin, unless you believe in Christ, so as to have your life hid with him in God, and to receive life and nourishment from him, as branches do from the vine.

I know, indeed, the men of this generation deny there is any such thing as feeling Christ within them; but alas! to what a dreadful condition would such reduce us, even to the state of the abandoned heathen, who, St. Paul tells us, "were past feeling." The apostle prays that the Ephesians may abound in all knowledge and spiritual understanding or, as it might be rendered, spiritual sensation. And in the office for the visitation of the sick, the minister prays that the Lord may make the sick person know and feel that there is no other name under heaven given unto men, in whom and through whom they may receive health and salvation, but only the name of our Lord Jesus. For there is a spiritual, as well as a corporeal, feeling; and though this is not communicated to us in a sensible manner, as outward objects affect our senses, yet it is as real as any sensible or visible sensation and may be as truly felt and discerned by the soul, as any impression from without can be felt by the body. All who are born again of God, know that I lie not.

What think you, sirs, did Naaman feel when he was cured of his leprosy? Did the woman feel virtue coming out of Jesus Christ, when she touched the hem of his garment and was cured of her bloody issue? So surely may you feel, O believer, when Jesus Christ dwells in your heart. I pray God to make you all know and feel this, before you depart hence.

O my brethren, my heart is enlarged toward you. I trust I feel something of that hidden, but powerful, presence of Christ, while I am preaching to you. Indeed it is sweet; it is exceedingly comfortable. All the harm I wish you who without cause are my enemies is that you felt the like. Believe me, though it would be hell to my soul to return to a natural state again, yet I would willingly change status with you for a little while, that you might know what it is to have Christ dwelling in your hearts by faith. Do not turn your backs; do not let the devil hurry you away; be not afraid of convictions; do not think worse of the doctrine, because it is preached without the church walls. Our Lord, in the days of his flesh, preached on a mount, in a ship, and a field; and I am persuaded, many have felt his gracious presence here. Indeed we speak what we know. Do not reject the kingdom of God against yourselves; be so wise as to receive our witness. I cannot, I will not, let you go; stay a little, let us reason together. However lightly you may esteem your souls, I know our Lord has set an unspeakable value on them. He thought them worthy of his most precious blood. I beseech you therefore, O sinners, be reconciled to God. I hope you do not fear being accepted in the beloved. Behold, he calls you; behold, he prevents and follows you with his mercy, and has sent forth his servants unto the highways and hedges, to compel you to come in. Remember, then, that at such an hour of such a day, in such a year, in this place, you were all told what you ought to think concerning Jesus Christ. If you now perish, it will not be for lack of knowledge: I am free from the blood of you all. You cannot say I have been preaching damnation to you; you cannot say I have, like legal preachers, been requiring you to make brick without straw. I have not bidden you to make yourselves saints and then come to God; but I have offered you salvation on as cheap terms as you can desire. I have offered you Christ's whole wisdom, Christ's whole righteousness, Christ's whole sanctification and eternal redemption, if you will but believe on him. If you say you cannot believe, you say right; for faith, as well as every other blessing, is the gift of God; but then wait upon God, and who knows but he may have mercy on you? Why do we not entertain more loving thoughts of Christ?

Or do you think he will have mercy on others, and not on you? But are you not sinners? And did not Jesus Christ come into the world to save sinners? If you say you are the chief of sinners, I answer, that will be no hindrance to your salvation, indeed it will not, if you lay hold on him by faith. Read the Evangelists, and see how kindly he behaved to his disciples who fled from and denied him: "Go tell my brethren," says he. He did not say, "Go tell those traitors"; but, "Go tell my brethren" in general, and poor Peter in particular, that "I am risen"; oh, comfort his poor drooping heart, tell him I am reconciled to him; bid him weep no more so bitterly; for though with oaths and curses he thrice denied me, yet I have died for his sins, I am risen again for his justification: I freely forgive him all. Thus slow to anger and of great kindness was our all-merciful High Priest. And do you think he has changed his nature and forgets poor sinners, now he is exalted to the right hand of God? No, he is the same yesterday, today, and forever, and sits there only to make intercession for us. Come then, you harlots, come you publicans, come you most abandoned of sinners, come and believe on Jesus Christ. Though the whole world despise you and cast you out, yet he will not disdain to take you up. Oh, amazing, oh, infinitely condescending love! Even you he will not be ashamed to call his brethren. How will you escape if you neglect such a glorious offer of salvation? What would the damned spirits, now in the prison of hell, give, if Christ was so freely offered to their souls? And why are not we lifting up our eyes in torments? Does anyone out of this great multitude dare say, he does not deserve damnation? If not, why are we left, and others taken away by death? What is this but an instance of God's free grace and a sign of his goodwill toward us? Let God's goodness lead us to repentance!

Oh, let there be joy in heaven over some of you repenting! Though we are in a field, I am persuaded the blessed angels are hovering now around us, and do long, "as the hart panteth after the waterbrooks," to sing an anthem at your conversion. Blessed be God, I hope their joy will be fulfilled. An awful silence appears among us. I have good hope that the words which the Lord has enabled me to speak in your ears this day have not altogether fallen to the ground. Your tears and deep attention are an evidence that the Lord God is among us of a truth. Come, you Pharisees, come and see, in spite of your satanical rage and fury, the Lord Jesus is getting himself the victory. And brethren, I speak the truth in Christ; I lie not, if one soul of you, by the blessing of God, be brought to think savingly of Jesus Christ this day; I care not if my enemies were permitted to carry me to prison and put my feet fast in the stocks, as soon as I have delivered this sermon. Brethren, my heart's desire and prayer to God is that you may be saved. For this cause I follow my Master outside the camp. I care not how much of his sacred reproach I bear, so that some of you be converted from the errors of your ways. I rejoice, yes and I will rejoice. You men, you devils, do your worst: the Lord who sent will support me. And when Christ, who is our life, and whom I have now been preaching, shall appear, I also, together with his despised little ones, shall appear with him in glory. And then, what will you think of Christ? I know what you will think of him. You will then think him to be the fairest among ten thousand; you will then think and feel him to be a just and sin-avenging Judge. Be you then persuaded to kiss him lest he be angry, and so you be banished forever from the presence of the Lord.

Behold, I come to you as the angel did to Lot. Flee, flee, for your lives; haste, linger no longer in your spiritual Sodom, for otherwise you will be eternally destroyed. Numbers, no doubt, there are among you, that may regard me no more than Lot's sons-in-law regarded him. I am persuaded I seem to some of you as one that mocks: but I speak the truth in Christ, I lie not; as sure as fire and brimstone was rained from the Lord out of heaven, to destroy Sodom and Gomorrah, so surely, at the great day, shall the vials of God's wrath be poured on you. If you do not think seriously of, and act agreeable to, the gospel of the Lord's Christ. Behold, I have told you before; and I pray God, all you that forget him may seriously think of what has been said, before he pluck you away, and there be none to deliver you.

Now to God the Father, God the Son, and God the Holy Ghost, be all honor, power, glory, might, majesty, and dominion, both now and forevermore. Amen.

The Wise and Foolish Virgins

—ɯ—

"Watch therefore, for ye know neither the day nor the hour in which the Son of man cometh." —MATTHEW 25:13

The apostle Paul, in his Epistle to the Hebrews, informs us that "it is appointed for all men once to die; after that is the judgment." And I think, if any consideration be sufficient to awaken a sleeping drowsy world, it must be this: that there will be a day wherein these heavens shall be wrapped up like a scroll, this element melt with fervent heat, the earth and all things therein be burned up, and every soul, of every nation and language, summoned to appear before the dreadful tribunal of the righteous Judge of quick and dead, to receive rewards and punishments, according to the deeds done in their bodies. The great apostle just mentioned, when brought before Felix, could think of no better means to convert that sinful man, than to reason to temperance, righteousness, and more especially of a judgment to come. The first might in some measure affect, but, I am persuaded, it was the last consideration, a judgment to come, that made him to tremble: and so bad as the world is now grown, yet there are few have their consciences so far seared as to deny that there will be a reckoning hereafter. The promiscuous dispensations of providence in this life, wherein we see good men afflicted, destitute, tormented, and the wicked permitted triumphantly to ride over their heads, has been always looked upon as an indisputable argument, by the generality of men, that there will be a day in which God will judge the world in righteousness and administer equity unto his people. Some indeed are so bold as to deny it, while they are engaged in the pursuit of the lust of the eye and the pride of life. But follow them to their deathbed, ask them, when their souls are ready to launch into eternity, what they then think of a judgment to come, and they will tell you, they dare not give their consciences the lie any longer. They feel a fearful looking for of judgment and fiery indignation in their hearts. Since then these things are so, does it not highly concern each of us, my brethren, before we come on a bed of sickness, seriously to examine how the account stands between God and our souls, and how it will fare with us in that day? As for the openly profane, the drunkard, the whoremonger, the adulterer, and suchlike, there is no doubt of what will become of them; without repentance they shall never enter into the kingdom of God and his Christ: no; their damnation slumbers not; a burning fiery Tophet, kindled by the fury of God's eternal wrath, is prepared for their reception, wherein they must suffer the vengeance of eternal fire. Nor is there the least doubt of the state of true believers. For though they are despised and rejected of natural men, yet being born again of God, they are heirs of God and joint heirs with Christ. They have the earnest of the promised inheritance in their hearts and are assured that a new and living way is made open for them, into the holy of holies, by the blood of Jesus Christ, into which an abundant entrance shall be administered to them at the great day of account. The only question is, what will become of the almost Christian, one that is content to go, as he thinks, in a middle way to heaven, without being profane, on the one hand, or, as he falsely imagines, righteous overmuch, on the other? Many there are in every congregation, and consequently some here present, of this stamp. And what is worst of all, it is more easy to convince the most notorious publicans and sinners of their being out of a state of salvation, than any of these.

Notwithstanding, if Jesus Christ may be our Judge, they shall as certainly be rejected and disowned by him at the last day, as though they lived in open defiance of all his laws. For what says our Lord in the parable of which the words of the text are a conclusion, and which I intend to make the subject of my present discourse? "Then," at the day of judgment, which he had been discoursing of in the foregoing, and prosecutes in this chapter, "shall the kingdom of heaven (the state of professors in the gospel church) be likened unto ten virgins, who took their lamps, and went forth to meet the bridegroom." In which words is a manifest allusion to a custom prevailing in our Lord's time among the Jews, at marriage solemnities, which were generally at night, and at which it was customary for the persons of the bride chamber to go out in procession, with many lights, to meet the bridegroom. By the bridegroom, you are here to understand Jesus Christ. The church, that is, true believers, are his Israel; he is united to them by one spirit, even in this life; but the solemnizing of their sacred nuptials is reserved till the day of judgment, when he shall come to take them home to himself, and present them before men and angels, as his purchase, to his Father, without spot or wrinkle, or any such thing. By the ten virgins we are to understand the professors of Christianity in general. All are called virgins, because all are called to be saints. Whosoever names the name of Christ is obliged by that profession to depart from all iniquity. But the pure and chaste in heart are the only persons that will be blessed as to see God. As Christ was born of a virgin, so he can dwell in none but virgins' souls, made pure and holy by the cohabitation of his Holy Spirit. What says the apostle? "All are not Israel that are of Israel," all are not Christians that are called after the name of

Christ: No, says our Lord, in the second verse, "Five of those virgins were wise," true believers, "and five were foolish," formal hypocrites. But why are five said to be wise, and the other five foolish? Hear what our Lord says in the following verses: "They that were foolish took their lamps, and took no oil with them: but the wise took oil in their vessels with their lamps." They that were foolish took their lamps of an outward profession. They would go to church, say over several manuals of prayers, come perhaps into a field to hear a sermon, give at a collection, and receive the Sacrament constantly, no, oftener than once a month. But then here lay the mistake; they had no oil in their lamps, no principle of grace, no living faith in their hearts, without which, though we should give all our goods to feed the poor, and our bodies to be burned, it would profit us nothing. In short, they were exact, even superstitious bigots as to the form, but all the while they were strangers to, and, in effect, denied the power of godliness in their hearts. They would go to church, but at the same time think it no harm to go to a ball or an assembly, notwithstanding they promised at their baptism, to renounce the pomps and vanities of this wicked world. They were so exceedingly fearful of being righteous overmuch, that they would even persecute those that were truly devout, if they attempted to go a step farther than themselves. In one word, they never effectually felt the power of the world to come. They thought they might be Christians without so much inward feeling, and therefore, notwithstanding their high pretensions, had only a name of live.

And now, sirs, let me pause a while, and in the name of God, whom I endeavor to serve in the gospel of his dear Son, give me leave to ask one question. While I have been drawing, though in miniature, the character of these foolish virgins, have not many of your consciences made the application, and with a small, still, though articulate, voice, said, "You, man, you, woman, are one of those foolish virgins," for your sentiments and practice agree thereto? Stifle not, but rather encourage these convictions; and who knows, but that Lord who is rich in mercy to all that call upon him faithfully may so work upon you even by this foolishness of preaching, as to make you wise virgins before you return home?

What they were you shall know immediately: "But the wise took oil in their vessels with their lamps." Observe, the wise, the true believers, had their lamps as well as the foolish virgins; for Christianity does not require us to cast off all outward forms; we may use forms and yet not be formal: for instance, it is possible to worship God in a set form of prayer and yet worship him in spirit and in truth. And therefore, brethren, let us not judge one another. The wise virgins had their lamps; herein did not lie the difference between them and the foolish, that one worshiped God with a form and the other did not: no, as the Pharisee and publican went up to the temple to pray, so these wise and foolish virgins might go to the same place of worship and sit under the same ministry; but then the wise took oil in their vessels with their lamps; they kept up the form, but did not rest in it; their words in prayer were the language of their hearts, and they were no strangers to inward feelings; they were not afraid of searching doctrines, nor affronted when ministers told them they deserved to be damned; they were not self-righteous but were willing that Jesus Christ should have all the glory of their salvation; they were convinced that the merits of Jesus Christ were to be apprehended only by faith; but yet were they as careful to maintain good works, as though they were to be justified by them: in short, their obedience flowed from love and gratitude and was cheerful, constant, uniform, universal, like that obedience which the holy angels pay our Father in heaven.

Here then let me exhort you to pause again; and if any of you can faithfully apply these characters to your hearts, give God the glory, and take the comfort to your own souls, you are not false but true believers. Jesus Christ has been made of God to you wisdom, even that wisdom whereby you shall be made wise unto salvation. God sees a difference between you and foolish virgins, if natural men will not. You need not be uneasy, though one chance and fate in this may happen to you both. I say, one chance and fate; for "while the bridegroom tarried," in the space of time which passed between our Lord's ascension and his coming again to judgment, "they all slumbered and slept" (v. 5). The wise as well as foolish died, for dust we are, and to dust we must return. It is no reflection at all upon the divine goodness, that believers, as well as hypocrites, must pass through the valley of the shadow of death; for Christ has taken away the sting of death, so that we need fear no evil. It is to them a passage to everlasting life: death is only terrible to those who have no hope, because they live without faith in the world. Whosoever there are among you that have received the firstfruits of the Spirit, I am persuaded you are ready to cry out, "We would not live here always; we long to be dissolved, that we may be with Jesus Christ; and though worms must destroy our bodies as well as others', yet we are content, being assured that our Redeemer lives, that he will stand at the latter days upon the earth, and that in our flesh we shall see God."

But it is not so with hypocrites and unbelievers beyond the grave; for what says our Lord? "And at midnight"—observe, at midnight, when all was hushed and quiet, and no one dreaming of any such thing—"a cry was made," the voice of the archangel and the trump of God was heard sounding this general alarm, to things in heaven, to things in earth, and to things in the waters under the earth. "Behold!" Mark how this awful summons is ushered in with the word *behold,* to engage our attention? "Behold, the bridegroom cometh!" even Jesus Christ, the desire of nations, the Bridegroom of his spouse the church: because he tarried for a while to exercise the faith of saints and give sinners space to repent, scoffers were apt to cry out, "'Where is the promise of his coming?' But the Lord is not slack concerning his promise, as these men account slackness." For behold, he that was to come, now comes and will not tarry any longer: he comes to be glorified in his saints, and to take vengeance on them that know not God and have not obeyed his gospel; he comes not as a poor despised Galilean, not be laid in a stinking manger, not to be despised and rejected of men, not to be blindfolded, spit upon, and buffeted, not to be nailed to an accursed tree; he comes not as the Son of man, but as he really was, the eternal Son of the eternal God: he comes riding on the wings of the wind, in the glory of the Father and his holy angels, and to be had in everlasting reverence of all that shall be round about him. "Go ye forth to meet him"; arise, you dead, you foolish as well as wise virgins, arise and come to judgment. Multitudes, no doubt, that hear this awakening cry would rejoice if the rocks might fall on, and the hills cover, them from the presence of the Lamb. What would they give if, as they lived as beasts, they might now die like the beasts that perish? How would they rejoice, if those same excuses which they made on this side of eternity for not attending on holy ordinances, would serve to keep them from appearing before the heavenly bridegroom? But as Adam, notwithstanding his fig leaves and the trees of the garden, could not hide himself from God, when arrested with an "Adam, where art thou?" so now the decree is gone forth, and the trump of God has given its last sound; all tongues, peoples, nations, and languages, both wise and foolish virgins, must come into his presence and bow beneath his footstool; even Pontius Pilate, Annas and Caiaphas; even the proud persecuting high priests and Pharisees of this generation, must appear before him: for says our Lord, then (when the cry was made, Behold, the bridegroom cometh!), in a moment, in the twinkling of an eye, the graves were opened, the sea gave up its dead, and "all those virgins, both wise and foolish, arose and trimmed their lamp," or endeavored to put themselves in a proper posture to meet the bridegroom.

But how may we imagine the foolish virgins were surprised, when, notwithstanding their high thoughts and proud imaginations of their security, they now find themselves wholly naked, and void of that inward holiness and purity of heart, without which no man living at that day shall comfortably meet the Lord! I doubt not but many of these foolish virgins while in this world were clothed in purple and fine linen, fared sumptuously every day, and disdained to see the wise virgins, some of whom might be as poor as Lazarus, even with the dogs of their flock. These were looked upon by them as enthusiasts and madmen, as persons that were righteous overmuch, and who intended to turn the world upside down: but now death has opened their eyes and convinced them, to their eternal sorrow, that he is not a true Christian who is only one outwardly. Now they find (though alas! too late) they, and not the wise virgins, had been beside themselves. Now their proud hearts are made to stoop, their lofty looks are brought low; and as Dives entreated that Lazarus might dip the tip of his finger in water and be sent to cool his tongue, so these foolish virgins, these formal hypocrites, are obliged to turn beggars to those whom they once despised: "Give us of your oil"; oh, impart to us a little of that grace and holy spirit, for the insisting on which we fools accounted your lives madness; for alas! "our lamps are gone out"; we had only the form of godliness; we were whited sepulchers; we were heart hypocrites; we contented ourselves with desiring to be good; and though confident of salvation while we lived, yet our hope is entirely gone, now God has taken away our souls. Give us therefore, oh, give us, though we once despised you, give us of your oil, for our lamps of an outward profession and transient convictions, are quite gone out. "'Comfort ye, comfort ye, my people,' saith the Lord." My brethren in Christ, hear what the foolish say to the wise virgins, and learn in patience to possess your souls. If you are true followers of the lowly Jesus, I am persuaded you have your names cast out, and all manner of evil spoken falsely against you, for his name's sake; for no one ever did or will live godly in Christ Jesus without suffering persecution; what's more, I doubt not but your chief foes are those of your own household. Tell me, do not your carnal relations and friends vex your tender souls day by day, in bidding you spare yourselves, and take heed lest you go too far; and as you passed along to come and hear the word of God, have you not heard many a Pharisee cry out, "Here comes another troop of his followers!"? Brethren, be not surprised, Christ's servants were always the world's fools; you know it hated him before it hated you. Rejoice and be exceedingly glad. Yet a little while, and, behold, the Bridegroom comes, and then shall you hear these formal scoffing Pharisees saying unto you, "Give us of your oil, for our lamps are gone out." When you are reviled, revile not again: when you suffer, threaten not; commit your souls into the hands of him that judges righteously, for, behold, the day comes, when the children of God shall speak for themselves.

The wise virgins in the parable no doubt endured the same cruel mockings as you may do, but as the lamb before the shearers is dumb, so in this life opened they not their mouths; but now we find they can give their enemies an answer: "Not so, lest there be not enough for us and you; but go ye rather to them that sell, and buy for yourselves." These words are not to be understood as though they were spoken in an insulting manner; for true charity teaches us to use the worst of sinners, and our most bitter enemies, with the meekness and gentleness of Christ. Though Dives was in hell, yet Abraham does not say, "You villain," but only, "Son, remember"; and I am persuaded, had it been in the power of these wise virgins, they would have dealt with the foolish virgins as, God knows, I would willingly deal with my most inveterate enemies: not only give them of their oil, but also exalt them to the right hand of God. It was not then for want of love, but the fear of wanting a sufficiency for themselves, that made them return this answer: "Not so, lest there be not enough for us and you"; for they that have most grace have none to spare; none but self-righteous, foolish virgins think they are good enough or have already attained. Those who are truly wise are always most distrustful of themselves, pressing forward to the things that are before, and think it well if after they have done all they can make their calling and election sure. "Not so, lest there be not enough for us and you; but go ye rather to them that sell, and buy for yourselves." These words indeed seem to be spoken in a triumphant, but certainly they were uttered in the most compassionate, manner: "go ye to them that sell, and buy for yourselves"; unhappy virgins! you accounted our lives folly; while with you in the body, how often have you condemned us for our zeal in running to hear the Word of God, and looked upon us as enthusiasts, for talking and affirming that we must be led by the Spirit and walk by the Spirit and feel the Spirit of God witnessing with our spirits that we are his children? But now you would be glad to be partakers of this privilege, but it is not ours to give. You contented yourselves with seeking, when you should have been striving to enter in at the strait gate. And now go to them that sell, if you can, and buy for yourselves.

And what say you to this, you foolish formal professors? For I doubt not but curiosity and novelty has brought many such, even to this despised place, to hear a sermon. Can you hear this reply to the foolish virgins, and yet not tremble? Why, yet a little while, and thus it shall be done to you. Rejoice and bolster yourselves up in your duties and forms; endeavor to cover your nakedness with the fig leaves of an outward profession and a legal righteousness, and despise the true servants of Christ as much as you please, yet know that all your hopes will fail you when God brings you into judgment. For not he who commends himself is justified, but he whom the Lord commends.

But to return; we do not hear of any reply the foolish virgins make. No, their consciences condemned them; like the person without a wedding garment, they are struck dumb, and are now filled with anxious thoughts how they shall buy oil, that they may lift up their heads before the bridegroom. "But whilst they went to buy" (v. 10), while they were thinking what they should do, the Bridegroom, the Lord Jesus, the King, the husband of his spouse the church, comes, attended with thousands and twenty times ten thousands of saints and angels, publicly to count up his jewels; "and they that were ready," the wise virgins who had oil in their lamps and were sealed by his Spirit to the day of redemption, these having on the wedding garment of an imputed righteousness and a new nature, "went in with him to the marriage."

But who can express the transports that these wise virgins felt when they were thus admitted, in holy triumph, into the presence and full enjoyment of him whom their souls hungered and thirsted after! No doubt they had tasted of his love, and by faith had often fed on him in their hearts when sitting down to commemorate his last supper here on earth; but how full may we think their hearts and tongues were of his praises, when they see themselves seated together to eat bread in his heavenly kingdom. And what was best of all, "the door was shut," and shut them in, to enjoy the ever-blessed God, and the company of angels and the spirits of just men made perfect, without interruption forevermore. I say, without interruption; for in this life, their eyes often gushed out with water, because men kept not God's law; and they could never come to appear before the Lord or to hear his Word, but Satan and his emissaries would come also to disturb them; but now "the door is shut"; now there is a perfect communion of saints, which they in vain longed for in this lower world; now tares no longer grow up with the wheat; not one single hypocrite or unbeliever can screen himself among them. "Now the wicked cease from troubling, and now their weary souls enjoy an everlasting rest."

Once more, O believers, let me exhort you in patience to possess your souls. God, if he has freely justified you by faith in his Son and given you his Spirit, has sealed you to be his, and has secured you, as surely as he secured Noah, when he locked him in the ark. But though heirs of God, and joint heirs with Christ, and neither men nor devils can pluck you out of your heavenly Father's hand, yet you must be tossed about with manifold temptations; however, lift up your heads, the day of your perfect, complete redemption draws nigh. Behold, the Bridegroom comes to take you to himself, the door shall be shut, and you shall be forever with the Lord.

But I even tremble to tell you, O nominal Christians, that the door will be shut, I mean the door of mercy, never, never to be opened to give you admission, though you should continue knocking to all eternity. For thus speaks our Lord: "Afterward," after those that were ready went in and the door was shut;

after they had, to their sorrow, found that no oil was to be bought, no grace to be procured, "came also the other virgins" (v. 11); and as Esau, after Jacob had gotten the blessing, cried with an exceedingly bitter cry, "Bless me, even me also, O my father," so they came saying, "Lord, Lord, open to us." Observe the importunity of these foolish virgins, implied in the words, "Lord, Lord." While in the body, I suppose they only read, did not pray over, their prayers. If you now tell them, they should "pray without ceasing"—they should pray from their hearts and feel the want of what they pray for—they would answer, they could not tell what you mean by inward feelings; that God did not require us to be always on our knees, but if a man did justly and loved mercy and did as the church forms required him, it was as much as the Lord required at his hands.

I fear, sirs, too many among us are of this mind: what's more, I fear there are many so polite, so void of the love of God as to think it too great a piece of self-denial to rise early to offer up a sacrifice of praise and thanksgiving acceptable to God through Jesus Christ. If any such, by the good providence of God, are brought here this morning, I beseech you to consider your ways, and remember: if you are not awakened out of your spiritual lethargy, and live a life of prayer here, you shall but in vain cry out with the foolish virgins, "Lord, Lord, open unto us," hereafter. Observe further, the impudence, as well as importunity, of these other virgins; "Lord, Lord," say they, as though they were intimately acquainted with the holy Jesus. Like numbers among us who, because they go to church, repeat their creeds, and receive the blessed sacrament, think they have a right to call Jesus their Savior and dare call God their Father, when they put up the Lord's Prayer. But Jesus is not your Savior. The devil, not God, is your father, unless your hearts are purified by faith and you are born again from above. It is not merely being baptized by water, but being born again of the Holy Ghost that must qualify you for salvation; and it will do you no service at the great day, to say unto Christ, Lord, my name is in the register of such and such a parish. I am persuaded, the foolish virgins could say this and more; but what answer did Jesus make? He answered and said, "Verily I say unto you"; he puts the *verily* to assure them he was in earnest. "I say unto you"—I who am truth itself, I whom you have owned in words, but in works denied—"verily I say unto you, I know you not" (v. 12). These words must not be understood literally; for whatever Arians and Socinians may say to the contrary, yet we affirm that Jesus Christ is God, God blessed forever, and therefore knows all things. He saw Nathaniel, when under the fig tree: he sees, and is now looking down from heaven, his dwelling place, upon us, to see how we behave in these fields. Brethren, I know nothing of the thoughts and intents of your hearts, in coming here; but Jesus Christ knows who came like newborn babes, desirous to be fed with the sincere milk of the Word; and he knows who came to hear what the babbler says, and to run away with part of a broken sentence, that they may have whereof to accuse him. This expression then, "I know you not," must not be understood literally; no, it implies a knowledge of approbation, as though Christ has said, "You call me, 'Lord, Lord,' but you have not done the things that I have said; you desire me to open the door, but how can you come in here not having on a wedding garment? Alas, you are naked! Where is my outward righteousness imputed to you? Where is my divine image stamped upon your souls? How dare you call me, 'Lord, Lord,' when you have not received the Holy Ghost, whereby I seal all that are truly mine?" "Verily I know you not; depart from me, ye cursed, into everlasting fire, prepared for the devil and his angels."

And now, he that has ears to hear, let him hear what manner of persons these were, whom Jesus Christ dismissed with this answer. Remember, I entreat you, remember they are not sent away for being fornicators, swearers, Sabbath breakers, or prodigals. No, in all probability, as I observed before, they were, touching the outward observance of the moral law, blameless; they were constant as to the form of religion; and if they did no good, yet no one could say they did anyone any harm. The only thing for which they were condemned and eternally banished from the presence of the Lord (for so much is implied in "I know you not") was this: they had no oil in their lamps, no principle of a true living faith and holiness in their hearts. And if persons may go to church, receive the Sacrament, lead honest moral lives, and yet be sent to hell at the last day, as they certainly will be if they advance no further, Where will you, O drunkard? Where will you, O swearer? Where will you, O Sabbath breaker? Where will you that denies divine revelation and even the form of godliness? Where will you and suchlike sinners appear? I know very well. You must appear before the dreadful tribunal of Jesus Christ; however you may, like Felix, put off the prosecution of your convictions, yet you, as well as others, must arise after death and appear in judgment; you will then find, to your eternal sorrow, what I just hinted at in the beginning of this discourse, that your damnation slumbers not: sin has blinded your hearts and hardened your foreheads now, but yet a little while, and our Lord will ease him of his adversaries. I think, by faith, I see the heavens opened and the holy Jesus coming, with his face brighter than ten thousand suns, darting fury upon you from his eyes! I think I see you rising from your graves, trembling and astonished, and crying out, who can abide this day of his coming!

And now what inference shall I draw from what has been delivered? Our Lord, in the words of the text, has drawn one for me: "Watch therefore, for ye know neither the day nor the hour wherein the Son of man cometh."

"Watch," that is, be upon your guard and keep your graces in continual exercise. For as when we are commanded to watch unto prayer, it signifies that we should continue instant in that duty; so when we are required to watch in general, it means that we should put on the whole armor of God and live every day as though it was our last. And oh, that the Lord may now enable me to lift up my voice like a trumpet! For had I a thousand tongues, or could I speak so loud that the whole world might hear me, I could not sound a more useful alarm than that which is contained in the text. Watch therefore, my brethren, I beseech you by the mercies of God in Christ Jesus, watch; be upon your guard; awake, you that sleep in the dust: for you know neither the day nor the hour wherein the Son of man comes. Perhaps today, perhaps this midnight, the cry may be made: "for in a moment, in the twinkling of an eye, the trump is to sound." However, supposing the final day of judgment may yet be a great way off, the day of death is certainly near at hand, for what is our life? "It is but a vapor"; but a span long, soon passes it away, and we are gone. Blessed be God, we are all here well; but who, out of this great multitude, dares say, I shall go home to my house in safety? Who knows, but while I am speaking, God may commission his ministering spirits immediately to call some of you away by a sudden stroke, to give an account with what attention you have heard this sermon. You know, my brethren, some such instances we have lately had. And what angel or spirit has assured us that some of you shall not be the next? "Watch therefore, for ye know neither the day nor the hour wherein the Son of man will come." And it is chiefly for this reason that God has hidden the day of our deaths from us. For since I know not but I may die tomorrow, why, O my soul, may each of us say, will you not watch today? Since I know not but I may die the next moment, why will you not prepare for dying thus? Many such reflections as these, my brethren, crowd in upon my mind. At present, blessed be the Lord, who delights to magnify his strength in a poor worm's weakness, I am at a stand, not so much about what I shall say, as what I shall leave unsaid. My belly, like Elihu's, is, as it were, full of new wines; "out of the abundance of my heart my mouth speaketh." The seeing so great a multitude standing before me; a sense of the infinite majesty of that God in whose name I preach and before whom I as well as you must appear to give an account; and the uncertainty there is whether I shall live another day to speak to you anymore—these considerations, especially the presence of God, which I feel upon my soul, furnish me with so much matter that I scarce know where to begin, or where to end, my application. However, for method's sake, by the divine assistance, I will branch it into three particulars.

And first, I would remind you that are notoriously ungodly, of what our Lord says in the text: for though I have said that your damnation slumbers not, while you continue in an impenitent state, yet that was only to set you upon your watch, to convince you of your danger, and excite you to cry out, "What shall we do to be saved?" I appeal to all that hear me, whether I have said the door of mercy should be shut against you, if you believe on Jesus Christ: no, if you are the chief of sinners; if you are murderers of fathers, and murderers of mothers; if you are emphatically the dung and offscouring of all things; yet if you believe on Jesus Christ and cry unto him with the same faith as the expiring thief, "Lord, remember me, when thou art in thy kingdom," I will pawn my eternal salvation upon it, if he does not shortly translate you to his heavenly paradise. Wonder not at my speaking with so much assurance: for I know "it is a faithful and true saying, and worthy of all acceptance, that Jesus Christ came into the world to save (all truly affected and believing) sinners." What's more, so great is his love that, I am persuaded, was it necessary, he would come again into the world and die a second time for them on the cross. But, blessed be God, when our Lord bowed down his head, and gave up the ghost, our redemption was finished. It is not our sins, but our want of a lively faith in his blood that will prove our condemnation: if you draw near to him by faith, though you are the worst of sinners, yet he will not say unto you, "Verily I know you not." No, a door of mercy shall be opened to you. Look then, look then, by an eye of faith, to that God-man whom you have pierced. Behold him bleeding, panting, dying upon the cross, with arms stretched out ready to embrace you all. Hark! How he groans! See how all nature is in agony! The rocks rend, the graves open; the sun withdraws its light, ashamed as it were to see the God of nature suffer; and all this to usher in man's great redemption. What's more, the holy Jesus, in the very agonies and pangs of death, prays for his very murderers: "Father, forgive them, for they know not what they do." If then you have crucified the Son of God afresh and put him to an open shame, yet do not despair, only believe, and even this shall be forgiven. You have read, at least you have heard, no doubt, how three thousand were converted at St. Peter's preaching one single sermon after our Lord's ascension into heaven; and many of those who crucified the Lord of glory undoubtedly were among them, and why should you despair? For "Jesus Christ is the same yesterday, today, and forever." The Holy Ghost shall be sent down on you, as well as on them, if you do but believe; for Christ ascended up on high to receive this gift even for the vilest of men. Come then, all you that are weary and heavy laden with the sense of your sins, lay hold on Christ by faith, and he will give you rest; for salvation is the free gift of God to all them that believe. And though you may think this too good news to be true, yet I speak the truth in Christ. I lie not, this is the gospel, this is the glad tidings which we are commissioned to preach to every creature. Be not faithless then, but believing. Let not the devil lead you captive at his will any longer; for all the wages he gives his servants is death, death often in this life, death everlasting in the next. But the free gift of God is eternal life to all that believe in Jesus Christ. Pharisees are and will be offended at my coming here and offering you salvation on such cheap terms; but the more they bid me hold my peace, the more will I cry out and proclaim to convicted sinners that Jesus, David's Son according to the flesh, but David's Lord as he was God, will have mercy upon all that by a living faith truly turn to him. If this is to be vile, I pray God, I may be more vile. If they will not let me preach Christ crucified, and offer salvation to poor sinners in a church, I will preach him in the lanes, streets, highways, and hedges; and nothing pleases me better than to think I am now in one of the devil's strongest holds. Surely, the Lord has not sent me and all you here for nothing; no, blessed be God, the fields are white ready unto harvest, and many souls I hope will be gathered into his heavenly garner. It is true, it is the midnight of the church, especially the poor Church of England, but God has lately sent forth his servants to cry, "Behold, the bridegroom cometh." I beseech you, O sinners, hearken unto the voice! Let me espouse you by faith to my dear Master; and henceforward "watch and pray," that you may be ready to go forth to meet him.

Second, I would apply myself to those among you that are not openly profane, but by depending on a formal round of duties, deceive your own souls, and are only foolish virgins. But I must speak to your conviction, rather than your comfort. My dear brethren, do not deceive your own souls. You have heard how far the foolish virgins went and yet were answered with, "Verily I know you not." The reason is, because none but such who have a living faith in Jesus Christ, and are truly born again, can possibly enter into the kingdom of heaven. You may, perhaps, live honest and outwardly moral lives, but if you depend on that morality, or join your works with your faith, in order to justify you before God, you have no lot or share in Christ's redemption, for what is this but to deny the Lord that has bought you? What is this but making yourselves your own saviors? taking the crown from Jesus Christ and putting it on your own heads? The crime of the devil, some have supposed, consisted in this, that he would not bow to Jesus Christ, when the Father commanded all the angels to worship him; and what do you less? You will not own and submit to his righteousness; and though you pretend to worship him with your lips, yet your hearts are far from him; besides you, in effect, deny the operations of his blessed spirit; you mistake common for effectual grace; you hope to be saved, because you have good desires and a few short convictions; and what is this, but to give God, his Word, and all his saints the lie? A Jew, a Turk [Muslim], has equally as good grounds whereon to build his hopes of salvation. Need I not then to cry out to you, "Ye foolish virgins, watch"? Beg of God to convince you of your self-righteousness and the secret unbelief of your hearts; or otherwise, whensoever the cry shall be made, "Behold, the bridegroom cometh," you will find yourselves utterly unprepared to go forth to meet him. You may cry, "Lord, Lord," but the answer will be, "Verily I know you not."

Third, I would speak a word or two by way of exhortation to those who are wise virgins and are assured that they have on a wedding garment. That there are many such among you, who by grace have renounced your own righteousness and know that the righteousness of the Lord Jesus is imputed to you, I make no doubts. God has his secret ones in the worst of times; and I am persuaded he has not let so loud a gospel cry to be made among his people, as of late has been heard, for nothing. No, I am confident, the Holy Ghost has been given to many at the preaching of faith and has powerfully fallen upon many, while they have been hearing the Word. You are now then no longer foolish, but wise, virgins; notwithstanding, I beseech you also to suffer the word of exhortation, for wise virgins are too apt, while the bridegroom tarries, to slumber and sleep. Watch therefore, my dear brethren, watch and pray, at this time especially, for perhaps a time of suffering is at hand. The ark of the Lord begins already to be driven into the wilderness. Be you therefore upon your watch and still persevere in following your Lord, even outside the camp, bearing his reproach; the cry that has been lately made has awakened the devil and his servants; they begin to rage horribly; and well they may; for I hope their kingdom is in danger. Watch therefore, for if we are not always upon our guard, a time of trial may overtake us unawares, and instead of owning, like Peter we may be tempted to deny our Master. Set death and eternity often before you. Look unto Jesus, the Author and Finisher of your faith, and consider how little a while it will be, before he comes to judgment; and then our reproach shall be wiped away; the accusers of us and our brethren shall be cast down, and we all shall be lodged in heaven forever, with our dear Lord Jesus.

Last, what I say unto you, I say unto all: watch; high and low, rich and poor, young and old, one with another, I beseech you, by the mercies of Jesus, to be upon your guard: fly, fly to Jesus Christ, that heavenly Bridegroom; behold, he desires to take you to himself, miserable, poor, blind, and naked as you are; he is willing to clothe you with his everlasting righteousness and make you partakers of that glory, which he enjoyed with the Father before the world began. Do not turn a deaf ear to me; do not reject the message on account of the meanness of the messenger. I am a child, but the Lord has chosen me that the glory might be all his own. Had he sent to invite you by a learned rabbi, you might have been tempted to think the man had done something; but now God has sent a child, that the excellency of the power may be seen not to be of man, but of God. Let the learned Pharisees then despise my youth: I care not how vile I appear in the sight of such men; I glory in it. And I am persuaded, if any of you should be married to Christ by this preaching, you will have no reason to repent, when you come to heaven, that God sent a child to cry, "Behold, the bridegroom cometh!" O my brethren! The thought of being instrumental in bringing one of you to glory fills me with fresh zeal. Once more I entreat you, "Watch, watch and pray," for the Lord Jesus will receive all that call upon him faithfully. Let that cry, "Behold, the bridegroom cometh," be continually sounding in your ears; and begin now to live as though you were assured, this night you were to "go forth to meet him." I could say more, but the other business and duties of the day oblige me to stop. May the Lord give you all a hearing ear and obedient heart and so closely unite you to himself by one spirit, that when he shall come in terrible majesty, to judge mankind, you may be found having on a wedding garment and ready to go in with him to the marriage.

Grant this, O Lord, for thy dear Son's sake!

Blind Bartimeus

—⁂—

And Jesus said unto him, "Go thy way; thy faith hath made thee whole."
And immediately he received his sight, and followed Jesus in the way.
—MARK 10:52

When the apostle Peter was recommending Jesus of Nazareth, in one of his sermons to the Jews, he gave him a short, but withal a glorious and exalted, character, that "he went about doing good." He went about, he sought occasions of doing good; it was his meat and drink to do the works of him that sent him, while the day of his public administration lasted. Justly was he styled by the prophet the "Sun of righteousness." For, as the sun in the natural firmament diffuses his quickening and reviving beams through the universe, so, wherever this Sun of righteousness, the blessed Jesus, arose, he arose with healing under his wings. He was indeed a prophet like unto Moses, and proved that he was the Messiah which was to come into the world, by the miracles which he worked; though with this material difference, the miracles of Moses, agreeable to the Old Testament dispensation, were miracles of judgment; the miracles of Jesus, who came to bear our sicknesses and heal our infirmities, were miracles of mercy, and were worked not only for the cure of people's bodies, but also for the conversion of their precious and immortal souls. Sometimes, one and the same person was the subject of both these mercies. A glorious proof of this we have in the miraculous cure worked upon a poor blind beggar, named Bartimeus, who is to be the subject of the following discourse, and to whom the words of the text refer. "Jesus said unto him, 'Go thy way; thy faith hath made thee whole.' And immediately he received his sight, and followed Jesus in the way."

My design is, first, to make some observations on the matter of fact, as recorded by the Evangelists.

And then, second, to point out the improvement that may be made thereof. May Jesus so bless this following discourse that every spiritually blind hearer may receive his sight, and, after the example of Bartimeus, "follow Jesus in the way"!

If we would take a view of the whole story, we must go back to verse 46 of this chapter: "And they (our Lord and his disciples, who, we find by the context, had been conversing together) came to Jericho," a place devoted by

Joshua to the curse of God; and yet even this place yields converts to Jesus; Zaccheus had been called there formerly; and Bartimeus, as we shall hear by and by, in all probability was called now. For some good may come even out of Nazareth. Christ himself was born there, and his sovereign grace can reach and overcome the worst of people, in the very worst of places. Jesus came to Jericho. Let not his ministers, if providence points out their way, shun going to seemingly the most unlikely places to do good; some chosen vessels may be therein. Jesus and his disciples came to Jericho. They were itinerants and, as I have frequently observed, seldom stayed long in a place; not that this is any argument against the stated settlement of particular pastors over particular parishes. But however, our Lord's practice, in this respect, gives a kind of a sanction to itinerant preaching, when persons are properly called to, and qualified for, such an employ. And I believe we may venture to affirm (though we would by no means prescribe or dictate to the holy One of Israel) that, whenever there shall be a general revival of religion in any country, itinerant preaching will be more in vogue. And it is to be feared that those who condemn it now, merely on account of the meanness of its appearances, would have joined with the self-righteous scribes and Pharisees, in condemning even the Son of God himself, for such a practice.

"And as he went out of Jericho with his disciples and a great number of people"; ὄχλου ἱκανοῦ, a great number of mob, or rabble, as the high priests of that generation termed them; for these were the constant followers of Jesus of Nazareth; it was the poor that received his gospel; the common people heard him gladly and followed him from place to place. Not that all who followed him were his true disciples. No, some followed him only for his loaves, others out of curiosity, though some undoubtedly followed to hear and be edified by the gracious words that proceeded out of his mouth. Jesus knew this and was also sensible how displeasing this crowding after him was to some of the rulers of the Jewish church, who, upon every occasion, were ready to say, "Have any of the scribes and Pharisees believed on him?" But, notwithstanding, I do not hear of our blessed Lord's sending them home but once; and that was after they had been with him three days, and had nothing left to eat, he saw they were as sheep having no shepherd, and therefore had compassion on them and taught them. A sufficient warrant, this, for gospel ministers to preach to poor souls that follow to hear the Word, whatever principle their coming may proceed from. At the same time, they should caution people against thinking themselves Christians because they follow Christ's ministers. This our Lord frequently did, for there are many that followed Jesus, and now follow his ministers and hear them gladly; what's more, they perhaps do many things, as Herod did, who, it is to be feared, will never follow them into the kingdom of heaven. Much people followed Jesus out of Jericho, but how many of them were offended in him; and afterward, it may be, cried out, "Crucify him, crucify him"? Who would depend on popularity? It is like the morning cloud, or early dew, that passes away. But what a press and seemingly continued hurry of business did the blessed Jesus live in! He could not be hid; go where he would, much people followed him. He had scarce time to eat bread. Happy is it for such who are called to act in a public station in the church, and to be more abundant in labors, that their Jesus has trodden in this dangerous path before them. Popularity is a fiery furnace, and no one, but he who kept the three children amid Nebuchadnezzar's flames, can preserve popular ministers from being hurt by it. But we can do all things through Christ strengthening us. And I have often thought that there is one consideration sufficient to extinguish, or moderate at least, any excess of joy and self-complacence which the most popular preacher may feel when followed even by the greatest multitudes; and that is this: how many of these hearers will go away, without receiving any saving benefit by my preaching; what's more, how many, it may be, will only have their damnation increased by it? As we find many will say at the great day, "Hast thou not taught in our streets?" to whom Jesus shall answer, "Verily I know you not."

But to proceed, "As our Lord went out of Jericho with his disciples and a great number of people, blind Bartimeus, the son of Timeus, sat by the highway side begging." It should seem that he was a noted, though by no means what we commonly call a sturdy, beggar, having no other way, as he had lost his sight, to get his bread; his case was still the more pitiable, if he was, as some think the name imports, the blind son of a blind father. It may be, he begged for his father and himself too; and if so, then this may give us light into that passage of Matthew 20:30, where we are told that "two men spake to Jesus." It might be father and son, though only one is mentioned here, because he only followed Jesus in the way. Thus that holy, judicious, and practical expositor of holy Writ, Mr. [Matthew] Henry. But however this be, he is not blamed for begging, neither should we discommend others for so doing, when providence calls to it. It was the unjust steward that said, "To beg I am ashamed." It is our pride that often makes us unwilling to be beholden; Jesus was not thus minded; he lived, as it were, upon alms; the women that followed him ministered to him of their substance. Bartimeus, not being able to dig, begs for his living; and, in order to make a better trade of it, sat by the highway side, in all probability, outside or near the gate of the city, where people must necessarily pass in and out. But though he had lost his sight, he had his hearing perfect; and it should comfort us, if we have lost one sense, that we have the use of another, and that we are not deprived of the benefit of all. Happy was it for Bartimeus that he could hear, though not see. For in all probability, upon hearing the noise and clamor of the much people that followed after our Lord, his curiosity set him upon inquiring into the cause of it, and some one or another told him that "Jesus of Nazareth was passing by"; Jesus of Nazareth, called so because he was bred there, or out of contempt; Nazareth being either a very mean or very wicked place, or both, which made guileless Nathaniel say, "Can any good come out of Nazareth?" And what does Bartimeus do when he hears of Jesus? We are told: "And when he heard that it was Jesus of Nazareth, he began to cry out" (v. 47). This plainly denotes that, though the eyes of his body were shut, yet the eyes of his mind were, in some degree, opened, so that he saw, perhaps, more than most of the multitude that followed after Jesus; for, as soon as he heard of him, he began to cry out, which he would not have done, had he not heard of him before and believed, also, that he was both able and willing to restore sight to the blind. "He began to cry out." This implies that he had a deep sense of his own misery and the need which he had of a cure; his prayers did not freeze as they went out of his lips; he began to cry out, that Jesus might hear him, notwithstanding the noise of the throng; and he began to cry out, as soon as he heard he was passing by, not knowing whether he might ever enjoy such an opportunity anymore. "He began to cry out, 'Jesus, thou Son of David, have mercy upon me.'" The people called him Jesus of Nazareth. Bartimeus styles him, "Jesus, thou Son of David," thereby evidencing that he believed him to be the Messiah who was to come into the world, unto whom the Lord God was to give the throne of his father David, and of whose kingdom there was to be no end. "Jesus, thou Son of David"; or, as it is in the parallel place of St. Matthew 20:30, "O Lord, thou son of David," of whom it had been long foretold, in Isaiah 35, that when he should come, "the eyes of the blind should be opened." "Have mercy upon me," the natural language of a soul brought to lie down at the feet of a sovereign God. Here is no laying claim to a cure by way of merit; no proud, self-righteous, "God I thank thee that I am not as other men are"; not bringing in a reckoning of performances, nor any doubting of Jesus' power or willingness to heal him, but out of the abundance of the heart, his mouth speaks, and, in the language of the poor, brokenhearted publican, he cries out, "Jesus, thou Son of David, have mercy on me." "Jesus, you friend of sinners, you Savior, who, though you be the true God, were pleased to become the Son of David and to be made man, that you might seek and save those that were lost, have mercy upon me; let your bowels yearn toward a poor, miserable, blind beggar."

One would have thought that such a moving petition as this would have melted the whole multitude that heard his piteous cry into compassion, and induced some at least to turn suitors in his behalf, or help to carry him to the blessed Jesus. But instead of that, we are told that "many charged him" (v. 48). The word in the original seems to imply a charge, attended with threatening, and spoken in an angry manner. They charged him "to hold his peace" and, it may be, threatened to beat him if he did not. They looked upon him beneath the notice of Jesus of Nazareth and were ready enough to ask whether he thought Jesus Christ had nothing else to do but to wait upon him. This was, no doubt, very discouraging to blind Bartimeus. For opposition comes closest when it proceeds from those who are esteemed followers of the Lamb. The spouse complains, as of something peculiarly afflicting, that her own mother's children were angry with her. But opposition only serves to whet the edge of true devotion, and therefore Bartimeus, instead of being silenced by their charges and threatenings, "cried out the more a great deal, 'Thou Son of David, have mercy on me.'" Still he breaks out into the same humble language, and, if Jesus, the Son of David, will have mercy on him, he cares not much what some of his peevish followers said of or did unto him. This was not a vain repetition, but a devout reiteration of his request. We may sometimes repeat the same words and yet not be guilty of that battalogia, or vain speaking, which our Lord condemns. For our Lord himself prayed in his agony and said twice the same words: "Father, if it be possible, let this cup pass from me." Thus Bartimeus, "Jesus, thou Son of David, have mercy upon me." And how does the Son of David treat him? Does he join issue with the multitude and charge him to hold his peace? Or does he go on, thinking him beneath his notice? No; for, says St. Mark 10:49, "And Jesus stood still," though he was on a journey, and it may be in haste (for it is not losing time to stop now and then on a journey to do a good office by the way), "and commanded him to be called." Why so? To teach us to be condescending and kind even to poor, if real, beggars and tacitly to reprove the blind, misguided zeal of those who had charged him to hold his peace. By this also our Lord prepares the multitude the better to take the more notice of the blind man's faith, and of his own mercy and power exerted in the healing of him. For there are times and seasons when we are called to perform acts of charity in the most public manner and that, too, very consistently with the injunction of our Savior, "not to let our right hand know what our left hand doeth." For there is a great deal of difference between giving alms and exercising acts of charity that are seen of men, and doing them that they may be seen; the one is always sinful, the other often becomes our duty. Jesus commanded Bartimeus to be called, "and they called him." Who called him? It may be those who a little before charged him to hold his peace. For it often happens that our opposers and discouragers afterward become our friends: "When a man's ways please the Lord, he makes his enemies be at peace with him." And it is to be wished that all who have charged poor souls that are crying after Jesus to hold their peace, and to spare themselves, and not be righteous overmuch, would imitate the people here and encourage those they once persecuted and maligned. "They call the blind man, saying unto him, 'Be of good comfort, rise; he calleth thee.'" The words, and manner of speaking them, imply haste and a kind of solicitude for the blind man's relief. Oh, that we might hereby learn to be patient and long-suffering toward opposers. For it may be that many may oppose awakened souls, not out of enmity, but through prejudice and misinformation, through ignorance and unbelief, and a real, though perhaps false, persuasion that their relations are going in a wrong way. By and by they may be convinced that Christ is indeed calling them, and then they may become real and open friends to the cause and work of God; if not, it is our duty to behave with meekness toward all and not to render railing for railing, but, contrary-wise, blessing, knowing that we are thereunto called, that we may inherit a blessing; Jesus did not break out into harsh language against these opposers, neither did Bartimeus. "Our Lord stood still, and commanded him to be called. And they call the blind man, saying unto him, 'Be of good comfort, rise; he calleth thee'; and he, casting away his garment, rose and came to Jesus." Had Bartimeus not been in earnest when he cried, "Jesus, thou Son of David, have mercy upon me," he might have said, "Why do you mock me? Why bid me arise? Rise indeed I can, but after I am risen, how can I, being blind, find my way unto him? If he will come to me, it is well; if not, all your calling avails nothing, it being impossible for me to find my way." Thus thousands nowadays object to evangelical preachers, saying, "Why do you bid us come to and believe on Jesus Christ, when you tell us it is impossible of ourselves to turn to God, or to do good works; and that no one can come unto him, unless the Father draw him? Is not this like the people's calling upon Bartimeus, to arise and come to Jesus, when he could not possibly see his way before him?" True, it is so; and would to God that all who make this objection would imitate Bartimeus, and put forth the strength they have! What if we do call you to come and to believe on the Lord Jesus Christ, that you may be saved? Does this imply that you have a power in yourselves to do so? No, in nowise, no more than Jesus saying unto Lazarus' dead and stinking carcass "come forth" implied that Lazarus had a power to raise himself from the grave. We call to you, being commanded to preach the gospel to every creature, hoping and praying that

Christ's power may accompany the Word and make it effectual to the quickening and raising of your dead souls. We also call to you to believe, upon the same account as Jesus said unto the lawyer, "Do this, and thou shalt live," that you, seeing your utter inability to come, might thereby be convinced of your unbelief and be led to ask for faith of him whose gift it is, and who is therefore in Scripture emphatically styled the Author, as well as Finisher, of our faith. Add to this, that it is your duty to wait at the pool, or to make use of the strength you have, in the earnest and steady performance of all commanded duty. For though you cannot do what is spiritually good, because you want spiritual principles of action, yet you may do what is morally and materially good, inasmuch as you are reasonable creatures; and though doing your duty as you can no ways deserves mercy, or entitles you to it, yet it is the way in which you are required to walk, and the way in which God is usually found. While you are attempting to stretch out your withered arm, peradventure it may be restored; and who knows but Jesus may work faith in you, by his almighty power?

Bartimeus has set before such objectors an example. Oh, that they would once submit to be taught by a poor blind beggar! For he, casting away his garment, rose and, blind as he was, came to Jesus "casting away his garment." This seems to be a large coat or cloak that he wore to screen himself from the rain and cold; undoubtedly, it was the most necessary and valuable vestment he had and one would have thought that he should have taken this along with him; but he knew very well that if he did so, it might hang about his heels and thereby his reaching Jesus be retarded at least, if not prevented entirely. Valuable therefore as it was to him, he cast it away. The word implies that he threw it from off his shoulders, with great precipitancy and resolution, knowing that if he got a cure, which he now hoped for, by Christ's calling him, he should never want his garment again. And thus will all do that are in earnest about coming to Jesus here, or seeing and enjoying him in his kingdom eternally hereafter. They will cut off a right hand; they will pluck out a right eye; they will leave father and mother, husband and wife, yes, and their own lives also, rather than not be his disciples. The apostle Paul, therefore, exhorts Christians, to "lay aside every weight, and the sin that doth most easily beset them" or hang about their heels, as the word in the original imports; alluding to the custom of the Romans, who wore long garments. Such a one was this, which Bartimeus had wrapped round him. But he, to show that he sincerely desired to recover his sight, casting it away, arose and came to Jesus. And what treatment did Jesus give him? Did he say, "Come not nigh me, you impudent noisy beggar"? No, "he answered and said unto him, 'What wilt thou, that I should do unto thee?'" an odd question this, seemingly. For did not our Lord know what he wanted? Yes, he did; but the Lord Jesus dealt with him as he deals with us. He will make us acknowledge our wants ourselves, that we thereby may confess our dependence upon him and be made more sensible of the need we stand in, of his divine assistance. The blind man immediately replies, "Lord (thereby intimating his belief of Christ's divinity), that I might receive my sight." I think I see the poor creature listening to the voice of our Savior, and, with looks and gestures bespeaking the inward earnestness of his soul, he cries out, "Lord, that I may receive my sight." As though he had said, "I believe you are that Messiah who was to come into the world. I have heard of your fame, O Jesus! And hearing the long-wished-for glad tidings of your coming this way, I cry unto you, asking not for silver and gold, but what you, you alone, can give me, Lord, that I might receive my sight." No sooner does he ask, but he receives. For, in verse 52, "Jesus said unto him, 'Go thy way; thy faith hath made thee whole.' And immediately he received his sight." With the word there went a power; and he that spoke light out of darkness, saying, "'Let there be light,' and there was light," commanded light into this poor blind beggar's eyes, and, behold, there was light. The miracle was instantaneous; immediately he received his sight. And next to a miracle it was, that by breaking into open light all at once, he was not struck blind again; but he that gave the sight preserved it when given. Oh, happy Bartimeus! Your eyes are now opened, and the very first object you do behold is the ever-loving, altogether-lovely Jesus. I think I see you transported with wonder and admiration, and all the disciples and the multitude, gazing around you! And now, having received your sight, why do you not obey the Lord's command and go your way? Why do you not haste to fetch your garment, that you just now in a hurry did cast away? No, no! with his bodily eyes, I believe, he received also a fresh addition of spiritual sight, and though others saw no form or comeliness in the blessed Jesus, that they should desire him; yet he by an eye of faith discovered such transcendent excellencies in his royal person, and felt at the same time such a divine attraction toward his all-bountiful benefactor, that instead of going his way to fetch his garment, he "followed Jesus in the way." And by his actions says with faithful, honest-hearted Ruth, "Entreat me not to leave thee; for whither thou goest, I will go; where thou lodgest, I will lodge; thy people shall be my people; and thy God, my God." He followed Jesus in the way; the narrow way, the way of the cross; and I doubt not but long since he has followed him to his crown and is at this time sitting with him at the right hand of his Father.

And now, my dear hearers, how find you your hearts affected at the relation of this notable miracle which Jesus worked? Are you not ready to break out into the language of the song of Moses and to say, "Who is like unto thee, O Lord, glorious in holiness, fearful in praises, continually doing wonders"? Marvelous are your works, O Jesus, and that our souls know right well! But we must not stop here, in admiring what the Lord did for Bartimeus; this, no doubt, as well as other parts of Scripture, was written for our learning, upon whom the ends of the world are come; consequently, as was proposed in the—

Second place, we should see what spiritual improvement can be made of this history, upon which we have already been making some remarks.

A natural man, indeed, goes no further than the outward court of the Scripture, and reads this, and the other miracles of our blessed Savior, just in the same manner as he reads Homer's battles or the exploits of Alexander. But God forbid that we should rest in only hearing this matter of fact. For I tell you, O man, I tell you, O woman, whoever you are that sit this day under a preached gospel, that if you are in a natural state you are as blind in your soul as Bartimeus was in his body; a blind child of a blind father, even of your father Adam, who lost his sight when he lost his innocence, and entailed his blindness, justly inflicted, upon you and me and his whole posterity. Some think indeed that they see, but, alas! such talk only like men in their sleep, like persons beside themselves; the Scriptures everywhere represent fallen man, not only as spiritually blind, but dead also; and we no more know, by nature, savingly the way of salvation by Jesus Christ than Bartimeus, when he was blind, knew the colors of the rainbow. This, I trust, some of you begin to feel; I see you concerned; I see you weeping; and, were I to ask some of you what you want to have done unto you, I know your answer would be "that we may receive our sight." And God forbid that I should charge you to hold your peace, as though Jesus would not regard you! No, your being made sensible of your natural blindness, and crying thus earnestly after Jesus, is a sign, at least, that you are awakened by his Holy Spirit (though it is possible that you may cry with an exceedingly bitter cry, as Esau did, and be lost at last); however, Christian charity induces me to believe and hope the best; I will therefore, in the language of those who afterward encouraged Bartimeus, say unto you, "Arise, take comfort for, I trust, Jesus is calling you; follow therefore the example of Bartimeus; cast away your garment; lay aside every weight, and the sin which doth most easily beset you; arise, and come to Jesus." He commands me, by his written Word, to call to you and say, "Come unto him, all ye that are weary, and heavy laden, and he will refresh you; he will give you rest." Be not afraid, you seek Jesus of Nazareth; behold, he comes forth to meet you;

you are now on the highway side, and Jesus, I trust, is passing by; I feel his presence. I hope many of you feel it too. Oh, then, cry mightily to him who is mighty and willing to save you; lay yourselves at the feet of sovereign grace, say unto him, "Jesus, thou Son of David, have mercy on me," in the same frame as Bartimeus did, and Jesus will answer you; he will not cast out your prayer; according to your faith, so shall it be done unto you.

Blind as you are, you shall notwithstanding receive your sight; Satan, indeed, and unbelief will suggest many objections to you; your carnal relations will also join issue with them and charge you to hold your peace; one will tell you that your blindness is too inveterate to be cured; another, that it is too late; a third, that though Jesus can, yet he will not have mercy upon such poor, blind, despicable beggars as you are; but the more they charge you to hold your peace, do cry out so much the more a great deal, "Jesus, thou Son of David, have mercy on us." Jesus, thou Savior, thou friend of sinners, thou Son of David, and therefore a Son of man! Gracious words! Endearing appellations! Be encouraged by them, to draw nigh unto him. Though David's Lord, yet he is become David's Son, after the flesh, that you through him may be made the sons of God: no matter what you are, O woman, what you are, O man; though you are literally a poor beggar, think not your condition too mean for Jesus to take notice of; he came into the highways and hedges, to call such poor beggars in; or, if you are rich, think not yourselves too high to stoop to Jesus; for he is the King of kings; and you never will be truly rich until you are made rich in Jesus; fear not being despised or losing a little worldly honor. One sight of Jesus will make amends for all; you will find something so inviting, so attracting, so satisfying, in the altogether-lovely Lamb of God that every sublunary enjoyment will sicken and die and vanish before you; and you will no more desire your former vain and trifling amusements than Bartimeus, after he had received his sight, desired to go back again and fetch his garment. Oh, that there may be many such blind beggars among you this day!

Here is a great multitude of people following me, a poor worm, this day. I rejoice to see the fields thus white, ready unto harvest, and to spread the gospel net amid so many; but alas! I shall return home with a heavy heart, unless some of you will arise and come to my Jesus; I desire to preach him and not myself; rest not in hearing and following me. Behold, believe on, and follow the Lamb of God, who came to take away the sins of the world. Indeed, I do not despair of any of you, neither am I discouraged on account of my preaching in the highways and hedges; Jesus called Zaccheus; Jesus called Bartimeus, as he passed through Jericho; that cursed, that devoted place; and why may he not call some of you, out of these despised fields? Is his arm shortened, that he cannot save? Is he not as mighty now, and as willing to save, even to the uttermost, all that come to the Father through him, as he was seventeen hundred years ago? Assuredly he is; he has said, and he also will do it, "Whosoever cometh to me, I will in nowise cast out." In nowise, or by no means. Oh, encouraging words! Sinners, believe you this? Arise then, be of good comfort, for Jesus is indeed calling you. Some of you, I trust, have obeyed this invitation and have had a sight of him long ago; I know then, you will bless and love him; and if he should say unto you, as he did unto Bartimeus, "Go your way," your answer would be, "We love our Master, and will not go from him." But suffer the word of exhortation:

Suffer me to stir up your pure minds by way of remembrance, show that you have indeed seen him, and that you do indeed love him, by following him in the way; I mean, in the way of the cross, the way of his ordinances, and in the way of his holy commandments; for alas! the love of many waxes cold, and few there are that follow Jesus rightly in the way; few there are that cast away their garments so heartily as they should; some idol or another hangs about us and hinders us in running the race that is set before us. Awake therefore, you sleepy, though it may be wise, virgins. Awake, awake, put on strength; shake yourselves from the dust; arise and follow Jesus more closely in the way than ever you did yet. Lift up the hands that hang down, and strengthen the feeble knees. Provide right paths for your feet, lest that which is lame be turned out of the way, but rather be you healed. For though the way be narrow, yet it is not long; "though the gate be strait (to use the words of pious Bishop Beveridge), yet it opens into everlasting life." Oh, that you may get a fresh sight of him again this day! That would be like oil to the wheels of your graces and make your souls like the chariots of Aminadab. It is only owing to your losing sight of him that you go so heavily from day to day. A sight of Jesus, like the sun rising in the morning, dispels the darkness and gloominess that lies upon the soul. Take therefore a fresh view of him, O believers, and never rest until you are translated to see him as he is, and to live with him forevermore, in the kingdom of heaven. Even so, Lord Jesus, amen and amen!

Directions: How to Hear Sermons

—◁◁◁—

"Take heed, therefore, how ye hear." —LUKE 8:18

The occasion of our Lord's giving this caution was this: perceiving that much people were gathered together to hear him out of every city, and knowing (for he is God and knows all things) that many, if not most, of them would be hearers only, and not doers, of the Word, he spoke to them by a parable, wherein, under the similitude of a sower that went out to sow his seed, he plainly intimated how few there were among them who would receive any saving benefit from his doctrine or bring forth fruit unto perfection.

The application one would imagine should have been plain and obvious; but the disciples, as yet unenlightened in any great degree by the Holy Spirit, and therefore unable to see into the hidden mysteries of the kingdom of God, dealt with our Savior as people ought to deal with their ministers; they discoursed with him privately about the meaning of what he had taught them in public and, with a sincere desire of doing their duty, asked for an interpretation of the parable.

Our blessed Lord, as he always was willing to instruct those that were teachable (herein setting his ministers an example to be courteous and easy of access), freely told them the significance. And withal, to make them more cautious and more attentive to his doctrine for the future, he tells them that they were in a special manner to be the light of the world, and were to proclaim on the housetop whatsoever he told them in secret: and as their improving the knowledge already imparted was the only condition upon which more was to be given them, it therefore highly concerned them to "take heed how they heard."

From the context then it appears that the words were primarily spoken to the apostles themselves. But as it is to be feared, out of those many thousands that flock to hear sermons, but few, comparatively speaking, are effectually influenced by them, I cannot but think it very necessary to remind you of the caution given by our Lord to his disciples, and to exhort you with the utmost earnestness, to "take heed how you hear."

In prosecution of which design I shall, first, prove that everyone ought to take all opportunities of hearing sermons.

And, second, I shall lay down some cautions and directions, in order to your hearing [sermons] with profit and advantage.

First, I am to prove that everyone ought to take all opportunities of hearing sermons.

That there have always been particular persons set apart by God to instruct and exhort his people to practice what he should require of them is evident from many passages of Scripture. St. Jude tells us that "Enoch, the seventh from Adam, prophesied (or preached) concerning the Lord's coming with ten thousand of his saints to judgment." And Noah, who lived not long after, is styled by St. Peter, "a preacher of righteousness." And though in all the intermediate space between the flood and giving of the law, we hear but of few preachers, yet we may reasonably conclude that God never left himself without witness, but at sundry times, and after diverse manners, spoke to our fathers by the patriarchs and prophets.

But however it was before, we are assured that after the delivery of the law, God constantly separated to himself a certain order of men to preach to, as well as pray for, his people; and commanded them to inquire their duty at the priests' mouths. And though the Jews were frequently led into captivity, and for their sins scattered abroad on the face of the earth, yet he never utterly forsook his church, but still kept up a remnant of prophets and preachers, as Ezekiel, Jeremiah, Daniel, and others, to reprove, instruct, and call them to repentance.

Thus was it under the law. Nor has the church been worse, but infinitely better, provided for under the gospel. For when Jesus Christ, that great High Priest, had through the eternal Spirit offered himself, as a full, perfect, sufficient sacrifice and satisfaction for the sins of the whole world, and after his resurrection had all power committed to him, both in heaven and earth, he gave commission to his apostles, and in them to all succeeding ministers, to "go and preach his gospel to every creature," promising "to be with them, to guide, assist, strengthen, and comfort them always, even to the end of the world."

But if it be the duty of ministers to preach (and woe be to them if they do not preach the gospel, for a necessity is laid upon them), no doubt the people are obliged to attend to them; for otherwise, wherefore are ministers sent?

And how can we here avoid admiring the love and tender care which our dear Redeemer has expressed for his spouse the church? Who, because he could not be always with us in person, on account it was expedient he should go away and as our forerunner take possession of that glory he had purchased by his precious blood, yet would not leave us comfortless, but first settled a

*I wonder did Whitefield see "church" & Jews as Church & Israel being one & the same?

sufficient number of pastors and teachers; and afterward, according to his promise, actually did and will continue to send down the Holy Ghost, to furnish them and their successors with proper gifts and graces "for the work of the ministry, for the perfecting of the saints, for the edifying of his body in love, till we all come in the unity of the Spirit, to the fullness of the measure of the stature of Christ."

Oh, how insensible are those persons of this unspeakable gift, who do despite to the Spirit of grace, who crucify the Son of God afresh, and put him to an open shame, by willfully refusing to attend on so great a means of salvation. How dreadful will the end of such men be? How aggravating, that light should come into the world, that the glad tidings of salvation should be so very frequently proclaimed in this populous city, and that so many should loath this spiritual manna, this angels' food, and call it light bread? How much more tolerable will it be for Tyre and Sidon, for Sodom and Gomorrah, than for such sinners? Better, that men had never heard of a Savior being born than, after they have heard, not to give heed to the ministry of those who are employed as his ambassadors, to transact affairs between God and their souls.

We may, though at a distance, without a spirit of prophecy, foretell the deplorable condition of such men; behold them cast into hell, lifting up their eyes, being in torment, and crying out, "How often would our ministers have gathered us, as a hen gathers her chickens under her wings? But we would not. Oh, that we had known in that our day the things that belonged to our everlasting peace! But now they are forever hid from our eyes."

Thus wretched, thus inconceivably miserable, will such be as slight and make a mock at the public preaching of the gospel. But taking it for granted, there are but few, if any, of this unhappy stamp who think it worth their while to tread the courts of the Lord's house, I pass on now to the—

Second general thing proposed, to lay down some cautions and directions, in order to your hearing sermons with profit and advantage.

And here, if we reflect on what has been already delivered, and consider that preaching is an ordinance of God, a means appointed by Jesus Christ himself for promoting his kingdom among men, you cannot reasonably be offended, if, in order that you may hear sermons with profit and advantage, I—

1. Direct or entreat you to come to hear them, not out of curiosity, but from a sincere desire to know and do your duty.

Formality and hypocrisy in any religious exercise is an abomination unto the Lord. And to enter his house merely to have our ears entertained, and not our hearts reformed, must certainly be highly displeasing to the most high God, as well as unprofitable to ourselves.

Hence it is that so many remain unconverted, yes, unaffected with the most evangelical preaching; so that like St. Paul's companions before his conversion, they only hear the preacher's voice with their outward ears, but do not experience the power of it inwardly in their hearts. Or, like the ground near Gideon's fleece, they remain untouched, while others, who came to be fed with the sincere milk of the Word, like the fleece itself, are watered by the dew of God's heavenly blessing, and grow thereby.

Flee therefore, my brethren, flee curiosity, and prepare your hearts by a humble disposition, to receive with meekness the engrafted word, and then it will be a means, under God, to quicken, build up, purify, and save your souls.

2. A second direction I shall lay down for the same purpose is not only to prepare your hearts before you hear, but also to give diligent heed to the things that are spoken from the Word of God.

If an earthly king was to issue out a royal proclamation, on performing or not performing the conditions therein contained, the life or death of his subjects entirely depended, how solicitous would they be to hear what those conditions were? And shall not we pay the same respect to the King of kings, and Lord of lords, and lend an attentive ear to his ministers, when they are declaring, in his name, how our pardon, peace, and happiness may be secured?

When God descended on Mount Sinai in terrible majesty, to give unto his people the law, how attentive were they to his servant Moses? And if they were so earnest to hear the thunderings or threatenings of the law, shall not we be as solicitous to hear from the ministers of Christ, the glad tidings of the gospel?

While Christ was himself on earth, it is said that the people hung upon him to hear the gracious words that proceeded out of his mouth. And if we looked on ministers as we ought, as the sent of Jesus Christ, we should hang upon them to hear their words also.

Besides, the sacred truths that gospel ministers deliver are not dry insipid lectures on moral philosophy, intended only to amuse us for a while, but the great mysteries of godliness, which therefore we are bound studiously to listen to, lest through our negligence we should either not understand them, or by any other means let them slip.

But how regardless are those of this direction who, instead of hanging on the preacher to hear him, doze or sleep while he is speaking to them from God? Unhappy men! Can they not watch with our blessed Lord one hour? What? Have they never read how Eutychus fell down as he was sleeping, when St. Paul continued like discourse till midnight, and was taken up dead?

* Except to a few were His words what I would consider less than gracious—but still a sense "come" know the Truth

But to return. Though you may prepare your hearts, as you may think, by a teachable disposition, and be attentive while discourses are delivering, yet this will profit you little, unless you observe—

3. A third direction, Not to entertain any the least prejudice against the minister.

For could a preacher speak with the tongue of men and angels, if his audience was prejudiced against him, he would be but as sounding brass, or tinkling cymbal.

That was the reason why Jesus Christ himself, the eternal Word, could not do many mighty works, nor preach to any great effect, among those of his own country; for they were offended at him. And was this same Jesus, this God incarnate, again to bow the heavens, and to come down speaking as never man spoke, yet if we were prejudiced against him, as the Jews were, we should harden our hearts as the Jews did theirs.

Take heed therefore, my brethren, and beware of entertaining any dislike against those whom the Holy Ghost has made overseers over you. Consider that the clergy are men of like passions with yourselves; and though we should even hear a person teaching others to do what he has not learned himself, yet that is no sufficient reason for rejecting his doctrine, for ministers speak not in their own, but Christ's, name. And we know who commanded the people to do whatsoever the scribes and Pharisees should say unto them, though they said but did not.

4. But, fourth, as you ought not to be prejudiced against, so you should be careful not to depend too much on, a preacher, or think more highly of him than you ought to think. For though this be an extreme that people seldom run into, yet preferring one teacher in apposition to another has often been of ill consequence to the church of God. It was a fault which the great apostle of the Gentiles condemned in the Corinthians. For whereas one said, "I am of Paul; another, I am of Apollos: are ye not carnal?" says he. "For who is Paul, and who is Apollos, but instruments in God's hands by whom you believed?" And are not all ministers sent forth to be ministering ambassadors to those who shall be heirs of salvation? And are they not all therefore greatly to be esteemed for their work's sake?

The apostle, it is true, commands us to pay double honor to those who labor in the Word and doctrine: but then to prefer one minister at the expense of another (perhaps, to such a degree, as when you have actually entered a church, to come out again because he does not preach) is earthly, sensual, devilish.

Not to mention that popularity and applause cannot but be exceedingly dangerous, even to a rightly informed mind; and must necessarily fill any thinking man with a holy jealousy, lest he should take that honor to himself, which is due only to God, who alone qualifies him for his ministerial labors, and from whom alone every good and perfect gift comes.

5. A fifth direction I would recommend is to make a particular application of everything that is delivered to your own hearts.

When our Savior was discoursing at the Last Supper with his beloved disciples and foretold that one of them should betray him, each of them immediately applied it to his own heart and said, "Lord, is it I?" And would persons, in like manner, when preachers are dissuading from any sin or persuading to any duty, instead of crying, "This was designed against such-and-such a one," turn their thoughts inwardly, and say, "Lord, is it I?" How far more beneficial should we find discourses to be than now they generally are?

But we are apt to wander too much abroad; always looking at the mote which is in our neighbor's eye, rather than at the beam which is in our own.

6. Haste we now to the sixth and last direction: if you would receive a blessing from the Lord, when you hear his Word preached, pray to him, both before, in, and after every sermon, to endue the minister with power to speak, and to grant you a will and ability to put in practice what he shall show from the Book of God to be your duty.

This would be an excellent means to render the word preached effectual to the enlightening and enflaming your hearts; and without this, all the other means before prescribed will be in vain.

No doubt it was this consideration that made St. Paul so earnestly entreat his beloved Ephesians to intercede with God for him: "Praying always, with all manner of prayer and supplication in the Spirit, and for me also, that I may open my mouth with boldness, to make known the mysteries of the gospel." And if so great an apostle as St. Paul needed the prayers of his people, much more do those ministers who have only the ordinary gifts of the Holy Spirit.

Besides, this would be a good proof that you sincerely desired to do, as well as to know the will of God. And it must highly profit both ministers and people; because God, through your prayers, will give them a double portion of his Holy Spirit, whereby they will be enabled to instruct you more fully in the things which pertain to the kingdom of God.

And oh, that all who hear me this day would seriously apply their hearts to practice what has now been told them! How would ministers see Satan, like lightning, fall from heaven, and people find the Word preached sharper than a two-edged sword, and mighty, through God, to the pulling down of the devil's strongholds!

The Holy Ghost would then fall on all them that hear the word, as when St. Peter preached; the gospel of Christ would have free course, run very swiftly, and thousands again be converted by a sermon.

For "Jesus Christ is the same yesterday, today, and forever." He has promised to be with his ministers always, even unto the end of the world. And the reason why we do not receive larger effusions of the blessed Spirit of God is not because our all-powerful Redeemer's hand is shortened, but because we do not expect them, and confine them to the primitive times.

It does indeed sometimes happen, that God, to magnify his free grace in Christ Jesus, is found of them that sought him not; a notorious sinner is forcibly worked upon by a public sermon and plucked as a firebrand out of the fire. But this is not God's ordinary way of acting. No, for the generality, he only visits those with the power of his Word who humbly wait to know what he would have them to do; and sends unqualified hearers not only empty, but hardened, away.

Take heed therefore, you careless, curious professors, if any such be here present, how you hear. Remember, that whether we think of it or not, "we must all appear before the judgment seat of Christ," where ministers must give a strict account of the doctrine they have delivered, and you as strict a one, how you have improved under it. And, good God! How will you be able to stand at the bar of an angry, sin-avenging Judge and see so many discourses you have despised, so many ministers, who once longed and labored for the salvation of your precious and immortal souls, brought out as so many swift witnesses against you? Will it be sufficient then, think you, to allege that you went to hear them only out of curiosity, to pass away an idle hour, to admire the oratory or ridicule the simplicity of the preacher? No. God will then let you know that you ought to have come out of better principles, that every sermon has been put down to your account, and that you must then be justly punished for not improving by them.

But fear not, you little flock, who with meekness receive the ingrafted Word and bring forth the peaceable fruits of righteousness, for it shall not be so with you. No, you will be your minister's joy and their crown of rejoicing in the day of our Lord Jesus. And they will present you in a holy triumph, faultless, and unblamable, to our common Redeemer, saying, "Behold us, O Lord, and the children which thou hast given us."

But still take heed how you hear: for upon your improving the grace you have, more shall be given, and you shall have abundance. "He is faithful that he promised, who also will do it." What's more, God from out of Zion shall so bless

* There comes a moment when the Church/the Bride of sorts is called up and with the Church I've long thought It's Spirit of Holiness to leaves Yet the world is not ended so is Christ with those who then become preachers?

you, that every sermon you hear shall communicate to you a fresh supply of spiritual knowledge. The Word of God shall dwell in you richly; you shall go on from strength to strength, from one degree of grace unto another, till being grown up to be perfect men in Christ Jesus, and filled with all the fullness of God, you shall be translated by death to see him as he is, and to sing praises before his throne with angels and archangels, cherubim, and seraphim, and the general assembly of the firstborn, whose names are written in heaven, forever and ever.

The Care of the Soul Urged as the One Thing Needful

—⚊—

"But one thing is needful." —LUKE 10:42

It was the amiable character of our blessed Redeemer, that "he went about doing good." This great motive, which animated all his actions, brought him to the house of his friend Lazarus, at Bethany, and directed his behavior there. Though it was a season of recess from public labor, our Lord brought the sentiments and the pious cares of a preacher of righteousness into the parlor of a friend; and there his doctrine dropped as the rain, and distilled as the dew, as the little happy circle that were then surrounding him. Mary, the sister of Lazarus, with great delight made one among them; she seated herself at the feet of Jesus, in the posture of a humble disciple; and we have a great deal of reason to believe that Martha, his other sister, would gladly have been with her there; but domestic cares pressed hard upon her, and "she was cumbered with much serving," being, perhaps, too solicitous to prepare a sumptuous entertainment for her heavenly Master and the train that attended him. Happy are they, who in a crowd of business do not lose something of the spirituality of their minds, and of the composure and sweetness of their tempers. This good woman comes to our Lord with too impatient a complaint; insinuating some little reflection, not only on Mary, but on himself too. "Lord, dost thou not care that my sister hath left me to serve alone? Bid her, therefore, that she help me." Our Lord, willing to take all opportunities of suggesting useful thoughts, answers her in these words, of which the text is a part, "Martha, Martha, thou art careful and troubled about many things, but one thing is needful; and Mary has chosen that good part, which shall not be taken away from her." Alas, Martha! The concerns of the soul are of so much greater importance than those of the body, that I cannot blame your sister on this occasion: I rather recommend her to your imitation, and caution you, and all my other friends, to be much on your guard, that in the midst of your worldly cares, you do not lose sight of what much better deserves your attention.

I shall consider these words, "One thing is needful," as a kind of aphorism, or wise and weighty sentence, which dropped from the mouth of our blessed Redeemer, and is evidently worthy of our most serious regard.

I shall—

I. Consider what we are to understand by "the one thing" here spoken of.

II. Show you what is intended when it is said to be the one thing needful.

III. I will show how justly it may be so represented, or prove that it is, indeed, the one thing needful, and then conclude with some reflections.

My friends, the words which are now before us are, to this day, as true as they were seventeen hundred years ago. Set your hearts to attend to them. Oh, that you may, by divine grace, be awakened to hear them with a due regard, and be so impressed with the plain and serious things which are now to be spoken, as you probably would, if I were speaking by your dying beds, and you had the near and lively view of eternity!

First, I am to consider, what we are to understand by the "one thing needful."

Now, in a few words, it is the "care of the soul," opposed, as you see in the text, to the care, the excessive care, of the body, to which Martha was gently admonished by our Lord. This is a general answer, and it comprehends a variety of important particulars, which is the business of our ministry often to open to you at large: the care of the soul implies a readiness to hear the words of Christ, to seat ourselves with Mary at his feet, and to receive both the law and the gospel from his mouth. It supposes that we learn from this divine teacher the worth of our souls, their danger, and their remedy; and that we become above all things solicitous about their salvation. That, heartily repenting of all our sins, and cordially believing the everlasting gospel, we receive the Lord Jesus Christ for righteousness and life, resting our souls on the value of his atonement and the efficacy of his grace. It imports the sincere dedication of ourselves to the service of God and a faithful adherence to it, notwithstanding all oppositions arising from inward corruptions or outward temptations; and a resolute perseverance in the way of gospel dependence, till we receive the end of our faith in our complete salvation. This is the "one thing needful," represented indeed in various Scriptures by various names. Sometimes it is called "regeneration" or "the new creature," because it is the blessed work of God's efficacious grace; sometimes the "fear of God," and sometimes "his love, and the keeping his commandments"; and very frequently in the New Testament it is called "faith" or "receiving Christ, and believing on him," which therefore is represented as the "great work of God" (John 6:29), the great thing which God in his glorious gospel requires, as well as by his Spirit produces in us: each of these, if rightly understood and explained, comprehends all that I have said on this head. On the whole, we may say, that, as the body is one, though it has many members, and the soul is one, though it has many faculties, so in the present case, this real vital religion is "one thing," one sacred principle of divine life, bringing us to attend to the care of our souls, as of our greatest treasure. It is one thing, notwithstanding all the variety of views in which it may be considered, and of characters under which it may be described. I proceed,

Second, to consider what may be intended in the representation which is here made of it, as the "one thing needful."

Now I think it naturally includes these three particulars: it is a matter of universal concern, of the highest importance, and of so comprehensive a nature, that everything which is truly worthy of our regard may be considered as included in, or subservient to, it. Let me a little illustrate each of these particulars.

1. The care of the soul may be called the "one thing needful," as it is a matter of universal concern.

Our Lord, you see, speaks of it as needful in the general. He says not, "for this or that particular person"; or "for those of such an age, station, or circumstance in life," but needful for all. And indeed, when discoursing on such a subject, one might properly introduce it with those solemn words of the psalmist, "Give ear, all ye people, hear, all ye inhabitants of the earth, both high and low, rich and poor, together" (Ps. 49:1–2). For it is the concern of all, from the king that sits upon the throne, to the servant that grinds at the mill, or the beggar that lies upon the dunghill. It is needful for us that are ministers, for our own salvation is concerned; and woe, insupportable woe, will be to our souls, if we think it enough to recommend it to others, and to talk of it in a warm, or an awful, manner, in public assemblies or in our private converse, while it does not penetrate our hearts, as our own greatest care. Our case will then be like that of the Israelitish lord in Samaria (2 Kings 7:2), who was employed to distribute the corn when the siege was raised; though we see it with our eyes, and dispense it with our hands, we shall ourselves die miserably, without tasting the blessings we impart.

It is needful to all you that are our hearers, without the exception of one single person. It is needful to you that are rich, though it may on some accounts be peculiarly difficult for you, even as difficult, comparatively speaking, as for a "camel to go through the eye of a needle" (Matt. 19:24), yet if it be neglected, you are poor in the midst of all your wealth and miserable in all your abundance; a wretch starving for hunger, in a magnificent palace and a rich dress, would be less the object of compassion than you. It is needful for you that are poor; though you are distressed with so many anxious cares—

"what you shall eat, and what you shall drink, and wherewithal you shall be clothed?" (Matt. 6:31). The nature that makes you capable of such anxieties as these argues your much greater concern in the bread "which endures to eternal life" (John 6:27), than in that by which this mortal body must be supported. It is needful for you that are advanced in years, though your strength be impaired so that the "grasshopper is a burden," (Eccles. 12:5), and though you have, by your long continuance in sin, rendered this great work so hard that, were it less important, one would in pity let you alone without reminding you of it; yes, late as it is, it must be done, or your hoary heads will be brought down to the grave with wrath and sink under a curse aggravated by every year and by every day of your lives. It is needful to you that are young, though solicited by so many carefree vanities to neglect it, though it may be represented as an unseasonable care at present, yet I repeat it: it is needful to you, immediately needful, unless you, who walk so frequently over the dust of your brethren and companions that died in the bloom and vigor of their days, have made some secret covenant with the grave for yourselves, and found out some wonderful method, hitherto unknown, of securing this precarious life, and of answering for days and months to come, while others cannot answer for one single moment.

2. The care of the soul is a matter of the highest importance; beyond anything which can be brought into comparison with it.

As Solomon says of wisdom, that it is "more precious than rubies, and that all things which can be desired are not to be compared with her" (Prov. 3:15), so I may properly say of this great and most important branch of wisdom; whatever can be laid in the balance with it will be found altogether lighter than vanity. This is strongly implied when it is said in the text, "one thing is needful"; one thing, and one thing alone is so. Just as the blessed God is said to be "only wise" (1 Tim. 1:17), and "only holy" (Rev. 15:4). Because the wisdom and holiness of angels and men is as nothing, when compared with his. What seems most great and most important in life, what kings and senates, what the wisest and greatest of this world, are employing their time— their councils, their pens, their labors—upon are trifles, when compared with this one thing. A man may subsist; he may in some considerable measure be happy, without learning, without riches, without titles, without health, without liberty, without friends, what's more, though "the life be more than meat, and the body than raiment" (Matt. 6:25), yet may he be happy, unspeakably happy, without the body itself. But he cannot be so, in the neglect of the one thing needful. I must therefore bespeak your regard to it in the words of Moses, "it is not a light thing, but it is your life" (Deut. 32:47).

3. The care of the soul is of so comprehensive a nature, that everything truly worthy of our regard may be considered as included in it, or subservient to it.

As David observes that "the commandment of God is exceeding broad" (Ps. 119:96), so we may say of this one thing needful; or as Solomon very justly and emphatically expresses it, "to fear God and to keep his commandments is the whole duty of man" (Eccles. 12:13). His whole duty, and his whole interest, and everything which is wise and rational does in its proper place and connection make a part of it. We should judge very ill concerning the nature of this care, if we imagined that it consisted merely in acts of devotion or religious contemplation; it comprehends all the lovely and harmonious band of social and human virtues. It requires a care of society, a care of our bodies, and of our temporal concerns; but then all is to be regulated, directed, and animated by proper regards to God, Christ, and immortality. Our food and our rest, our trades and our labors, are to be attended to, and all the offices of humanity performed in obedience to the will of God, for the glory of Christ, and in a view of improving the mind in a growing meekness for a state of complete perfection. Name anything which has no reference at all to this, and you name a worthless trifle, however it may be gilded to allure the eye, or however it may be sweetened to gratify the taste. Name a thing which, instead of thus improving the soul, has a tendency to debase and pollute, to enslave and endanger it, and you name what is most unprofitable and mischievous, be the wages of iniquity ever so great; most foul and deformed, be it in the eyes of men ever so honorable, or in their customs ever so fashionable. Thus I have endeavored to show you what we may suppose implied in the expression of "one thing being needful."

I am now, third, to show you with how much propriety the care of the soul may be represented under this character, as the one thing needful, or as a matter of universal and most serious concern, to which everything else is to be considered as subservient, if at all worthy of our care and pursuit.

There let me appeal to the sentiments of those who must be allowed most capable of judging, and to the evident reason of the case itself, as it must appear to every unprejudiced mind.

1. Let me argue from the opinions of those who must be allowed most capable of judging in such an affair, and we shall quickly see that the care of the soul appears to them, the one thing needful.

Is the judgment of the blessed God "according to truth"? How evidently and how solemnly is that judgment declared? I will not say merely in this or the other particular passage of his Word, but in the whole series of his revelations to the children of men, and the whole tenor of his addresses to them—is not this the language of all, from the early days of Job and Moses to the conclusion of the canon of Scripture? "If wisdom be hid from the eyes of all the living . . . surely God understandeth the way thereof, he knoweth the place thereof"; and if he does, it is plainly pointed out, for "unto man he still saith, 'Behold, the fear of the Lord, that is wisdom, and to depart from evil, that is understanding'" (Job 28:21, 23, 28). By Moses he declared to the Israelites that "to do the commandments of the Lord would be their wisdom and their understanding in the sight of the nations, who should hear his statutes, and say, 'Surely this is a wise and an understanding people'" (Deut. 4:6). When he had raised up one man on the throne of Israel, with the character of the wisest that ever lived upon the face of the earth, he chose to make him eminently a teacher of this great truth. And though now all that he spoke on the curious and less concerning subjects of natural philosophy is lost, "though he spoke of trees from the cedar to the hyssop, and of beasts, and of fowls, and of creeping things, and of fishes" (1 Kings 4:33), that saying is preserved in which he testifies that "the fear of the Lord is the beginning of wisdom" (Prov. 1:7; 9:10), and those Proverbs, in almost every line of which they who neglect God and their own souls are spoken of as fools, as if that were the most proper significance of the word, while the religious alone are honored with the title of wise. But in this respect, as attesting this truth in the name of God and in his own, "a greater than Solomon is here."

For if we inquire what it was that our Lord Jesus Christ judged to be the one thing needful, the words of the text contain as full an answer as can be imagined; and the sense of them is repeated in a very lively and emphatical manner, in that remarkable passage wherein our Lord not only declares his own judgment, but seems to appeal to the conscience of all, as obliged by their own secret convictions to subscribe to the truth of it. "What is a man profited, if he gain the whole world, and lose his own soul; or what shall a man give in exchange for his soul?" (Matt. 16:26). If it were once lost, what would he not be willing to give to redeem it? But it depends not on the words of Christ alone. Let his actions, his sufferings, his blood, his death, speak what a value he set on the souls of men. Is it to be imagined that he would have relinquished heaven, have dwelt upon earth, have labored by night and by day, and at last have expired on the cross, for a matter of light importance? Or can we think that he, in whom "dwell all the treasures of wisdom and knowledge" and "all the fullness of the Godhead bodily" (Col. 2:3, 9), was mistaken in judgment so deliberately formed, and so solemnly declared?

If after this, there were room to mention human judgment and testimonies, how easy would it be to produce a cloud of witnesses in such a cause,

*i wonder, do those now whose souls are present where for eternity they shall remain knowing the anguish of seperation- would they not give all to have the choice again?

and to show that the wisest and best of men in all ages of the world have agreed in this point, that amid all the diversities of opinion and profession, which succeeding generations have produced, this has been the unanimous judgment, this the common and most solicitous care of those whose characters are most truly valuable, to secure the salvation of their own souls, and to promote the salvation of others.

And let me beseech you seriously to reflect: what are the characters of those who have taken the liberty, most boldly and freely, to declare their judgment on the contrary side? The number of such is comparatively few; and when you compare what you have observed of their temper and conduct, I will not say with what you read of holy men of old, but with what you have yourselves seen in the faithful, active, and zealous servants of Christ, in these latter ages, with whom you have conversed; do you on the whole find that the rejecters and deriders of the gospel are in other respects so much more prudent and judicious, so much wiser for themselves, and for others that are influenced by them, as that you can be in reason obliged to pay any great deference to the authority of a few such names as these, in opposition to those to whom they are here opposed?

But you will say, and you will say it too truly, though but a few may venture in words to declare for the neglect of the soul and its eternal interest, that the greater part of mankind do it in their actions. But are the greater part of mankind so wise, and so good, as implicitly to be followed in matters of the highest importance? And do not multitudes of these declare themselves on the other side, in their most serious moments? When the intoxications of worldly business and pleasures are over, and some languishing sickness forces men to solitude and retirement, what have you generally observed to be the affect of such a circumstance? Have they not then declared themselves convinced of the truth we are now laboring to establish? What's more, do we not sometimes see that a distemper which seizes the mind with violence, yet does not utterly destroy its reasoning faculties, fixes this conviction on the soul in a few hours, even sometimes in a few moments? Have you never seen a carefree, thoughtless creature surprised in the giddy round of pleasures and amusements, and presently brought not only to seriousness, but terror and trembling, by the near views of death? Have you never seen the man of business and care interrupted, like the rich fool in the parable, in the midst of his schemes for the present world? And have you not heard one and the other of them owning the vanity of those pleasures and cares, which but a few days ago were everything to them, confessing that religion was the one thing needful, and recommending it to others with an earnestness, as if they hoped thereby to atone for their own former neglect? We that are ministers frequently are witnesses to such things as these, and I believe few of our hearers are entire strangers to them.

Once more, what if to the testimony of the dying we could add that of the dead? What if God were to turn aside the veil between us and the invisible world and permit the most careless sinner in the assembly to converse for a few moments with the inhabitants of it? If you were to apply yourself to a happy spirit that trod the most thorny road to paradise, or passed through the most fiery trial, and to ask him, "Was it worth your while to labor so much, and to endure so much for what you now possess?" Surely if the blessed in heaven were capable of indignation, it would move them to hear that it should be made a question. And, on the other hand, if you could inquire of one tormented in that flame below, though he might once be "clothed in purple and fine linen, and fare sumptuously every day" (Luke 16:19), if you could ask him, whether his former enjoyments were an equivalent for his present sufferings and despair, what answer do you suppose he would return? Perhaps an answer of so much horror and rage, as you would not be able so much as to endure. Or if the malignity of his nature should prevent him from returning any answer at all, surely there would be a language even in that silence, a language in the darkness, and flames, and groans of that infernal prison, which would speak to your very soul what the Word of God is with equal certainty, though less forcible conviction, speaking to your ear, that "one thing is needful." You see it is so in the judgment of God the Father, and the Lord Jesus Christ, of the wisest and best of men, of many, who seemed to judge most differently of it, when they come to more deliberate and serious thought, and not only of the dying, but of the dead too, of those who have experimentally known both worlds, and most surely know what is to be preferred. But I will not rest the whole argument here; therefore —

2. I appeal to the evident reason of the case itself, as it must appear to every unprejudiced mind, that the care of the soul is indeed the one thing needful.

I still consider myself as speaking not to atheists or to deists, but to those who not only believe the existence and providence of God, and a future state of happiness and misery, but likewise who credit the truth of the Christian revelation, as many undoubtedly do, who live in a fatal neglect of God, and their own souls. Now on these principles, a little reflection may be sufficient to convince you that it is needful to the present repose of your own mind; needful, if ever you would secure eternal happiness and avoid eternal misery, which will be aggravated, rather than alleviated, by all your present enjoyments.

The care of the soul is the one thing needful, because without it you cannot secure the peace of your own mind, nor avoid the upbraidings of your conscience.

That noble faculty is indeed the vicegerent of God in the soul. It is sensible of the dignity and worth of an immortal spirit and will sometimes cry out of the violence that is offered to it, and cry so loud as to compel the sinner to hear, whether he will or not. Do you not sometimes find it yourselves? When you labor most to forget the concerns of your soul, do they not sometimes force themselves on your remembrance? You are afraid of the reflections of your own mind, but with all your artifice and all your resolution can you entirely avoid them? Does not conscience follow you to your beds, even if denied the opportunity of meeting you in your closets, and, though with an unwelcome voice, there warn you that your soul is neglected, and will quickly be lost. Does it not follow you to your shops and your fields, when you are busiest there? What's more, I will add, does it not sometimes follow you to the feast, to the club, to the dance, and perhaps, amid all resistance, to the theater too? Does it not sometimes mingle your sweetest drafts with wormwood, and your most carefree scenes with horror? So that you are like a tradesman, who, suspecting his affairs to be in a bad posture, lays by his books and his papers, yet sometimes they will come accidentally in his way. He hardly dares to look abroad for fear of meeting a creditor or an arrest: and if he labors to forget his cares and his dangers, in a course of luxury at home, the remembrance is sometimes awakened, and the alarm increased, by those very extravagancies in which he is attempting to lose it. Such probably is the case of your minds, and it is a very painful state; and while things are thus within, external circumstances can no more make you happy than a fine dress could relieve you under a violent fit of the stone. Whereas, if this great affair were secured, you might delight in reflection, as much as you now dread it; and conscience, of your bitterest enemy, would become a delightful friend, and the testimony of it your greatest rejoicing.

The care of the soul is the one thing needful, because without this your eternal happiness will be lost.

A crown of everlasting glory is not surely such a trifle as to be thrown away on a careless creature that will not in good earnest pursue it. God does not ordinarily deal thus, even with the bounties of his common providence, which are comparatively of little value. As to these, the hand of the diligent generally makes rich, and he would be thought distracted, rather than prudent, who should expect to get an estate merely by wishing for it, or without some resolute and continued application to a proper course of action for that purpose.

Now, that we may not foolishly dream of obtaining heaven, in the midst of a course of indolence and sloth, we are expressly told in the Word of God that "the kingdom of heaven suffers violence, and the violent take it by force" (Matt. 11:12), and are therefore exhorted to "strive," with the greatest intenseness, and eagerness of mind, as the word properly signifies, "to enter in at the strait gate," for this great and important reason: "because many shall another day seek to enter in, and shall not be able." What's more, when our Lord makes the most gracious promises to the humble petitioner, he does it in such a manner as to exclude the hopes of those who are careless and indifferent. "Ask, and it shall be given you; seek, and you shall find; knock, and it shall be opened unto you." If therefore you do not ask, seek, and knock, the door of mercy will not be opened, and eternal happiness will be lost. Not that heaven is to be obtained by our own good works; no, no; for having done all, we must account ourselves unprofitable servants.

And surely if I could say no more as to the fatal consequences of your neglect than this, that eternal happiness will be lost, I should say enough to impress every mind that considers what eternity means. To fall into a state of everlasting forgetfulness might indeed appear a refuge to a mind filled with the apprehension of future misery. But oh, how dreadful a refuge is it! Surely it is such a refuge, as a vast precipice (from which a man falling would be dashed to pieces in a moment) might appear to a person, pursued by the officers of justice, that he might be brought out to a painful and lingering execution. If an extravagant youth would have reason to look round with anguish on some fair and ample paternal inheritance which he had sold or forfeited merely for the riot of a few days, how much more melancholy would it be for a rational mind to think that its eternal happiness is lost for any earthly consideration whatever? Tormenting thought! "Had I attended to that one thing which I have neglected, I might have been, through the grace of God in Christ Jesus, great and happy beyond expression, beyond conception: not merely for the little span of ten thousand thousand ages, forever. A line reaching even to the remotest star would not have been able to contain the number of ages, nor would millions of years have been sufficient to figure them down; this is eternity, but I have lost it, and am now on the verge of being. This lamp, which might have outlasted those of the firmament, will presently be extinguished, and I blotted out from among the works of God, and cut off from all the bounties of his hand." Would not this be a very miserable case, if this were all? And would it not be sufficient to prove this to be the better part, which, as our Lord observes, can "never be taken away"? But God forbid that we should be so unfaithful to him, and to the souls of men, as to rest in such a representation alone.

I therefore add once more, the care of the soul is the one thing needful, because without it, you cannot avoid a state of eternal misery, which will be aggravated, rather than alleviated by all your present enjoyments.

Nothing can be more evident from the Word of the God of truth. It there plainly appears to be a determined case, which leaves no room for a more favorable conjecture or hope. "The wicked shall be turned into hell, even all the nations that forget God." "They shall go away into everlasting punishment," into a state where they shall in vain seek death, and death shall flee from them. Oh! brethren, it is a certain, but an awful truth, that your souls will be thinking and immortal beings, even in spite of themselves. They may indeed torment, but they cannot destroy themselves. They can no more suspend their power of thought and perception than a mirror its property of reflecting rays that fall off its surface. Do you suspect the contrary? Make the trial immediately. Command your minds to create from thinking but for one quarter of an hour, or for half that time, and exclude every idea and every reflection. Can you succeed in that attempt? Or rather, does not thought press in with a more sensible violence on that resistance, as an anxious desire to sleep makes us so much the more wakeful? Thus will thought follow you beyond the grave, thus will it, as an unwelcome guest, force itself upon you, when it can serve only to perplex and distress the mind. It will forever upbraid you, that notwithstanding all the kind expostulations of God and man, notwithstanding all the keen remonstrances of conscience, and the pleadings of the blood of Christ, you have gone on in your folly, till heaven is lost and damnation incurred; and all, for what? for a shadow and a dream?

Oh, think not, sinners, that the remembrance of your past pleasures, and of your success in your other cares, while that of the one thing needful was forgotten—think not that this will ease you minds. It will rather torment them the more. "Son, remember that thou in thy lifetime receivedst thy good things." Bitter remembrance! Well might the heathen poets represent the unhappy spirits in the shades below, as eagerly catching at the water of forgetfulness, yet unable to reach it. Your present comforts will only serve to give you a livelier sense of your misery, as having tasted such degrees of enjoyment, and to inflame the reckoning, as you have misimproved those talents lodged in your hands for better purposes. Surely, if these things were believed, and seriously considered, the sinner would have no more heart to rejoice in his present prosperity, than a man would have to amuse himself with the curiosities of a fine garden, through which he was led to be broken upon the rack.

But I will enlarge no further on these things. Would to God that the unaccountable stupidity of men's minds, and their fatal attachment to the pleasures and cares of the present life, did not make it necessary to insist on them so frequently and so copiously!

I now proceed to the reflections which naturally arise from hence, and shall only mention two.

1. How much reason have we to lament the folly of mankind in neglecting the one thing needful.

If religion be indeed the truest wisdom, then surely we have the most just reason to say with Solomon, "the folly and madness is in men's hearts" (Eccles. 9:3). Is it the one thing needful? Look on the conduct of the generality of mankind, and you would imagine they thought it the one thing needless: the vainest dream, and the idlest amusement of the mind. God is admonishing them by ordinances, and providences, sometimes by such as are most awful, to lay it to heart; "he speaks once, yea twice (yes a multitude of times) but man regards not" (Job 33:14). They profess perhaps to believe all that I have been saying, but act as if the contrary were self-evident; they will risk their souls and eternity for a thing of naught, for that, for the sake of which they would not risk so much as a hand or a finger or a joint, no, nor perhaps a toy that adorns it. Surely this is the wonder of angels, and perhaps of devils too, unless the observation of so many ages may have rendered it familiar to both. And can we, my Christian brethren, behold such a scene with indifference? If some epidemic madness had seized our country, or the places where we live, so that as we went from one place to another, we everywhere met with lunatics, and saw among the rest some, perhaps of the finest genius, in the most eminent stations in life, amusing themselves with others, surely were we ever so secure from the danger of infection or assault, the fight would cut us to the heart. A good-natured man would hardly be able to go abroad or even be desirous to live, if it must be among so many sad spectacles. Yet these poor creatures might, notwithstanding this, be the children of God, and the higher their frenzy rose, the nearer might their complete happiness be. But alas! the greater part of mankind are seized with a worse kind of madness, in which they are ruining their souls; and can we behold it with indifference? The Lord awaken our compassion, our prayers, and our endeavors, in dependence on divine grace, that we may be instrumental in bringing them to their mind and making them wise indeed, that is, wise to salvation!

2. How necessary is it that we should seriously inquire, how this one thing needful is regarded by us!

Let me entreat you to remember your own concern in it, and inquire: Have I thought seriously of it? Have I seen the importance of it? Has it lain with a due and abiding weight on my mind? Has it brought me to Christ, that I might lay the stress of these great eternal interests on him? And am I acting in the main of my life, as one that has these convictions? Am I willing, in fact, to give up other things, my interests, my pleasures, my passions to this? Am I conversing with God and with man, as one that believes these things; as one that has deliberately chosen the better part and is determined to abide by that choice?

Observe the answer which conscience returns to these inquiries, and you will know your own part in that more particular application, with which I shall conclude.

1. Let me address those that are entirely unconcerned about the one thing needful.

Brethren, I have been stating the case at large, and now I appeal to your consciences: are these things so, or are they not? God and your own hearts best know for what the care of your soul is neglected; but be it what it will, the difference between one grain of sand and another is not great, when it comes to be weighed against a talent of gold. Whatever it is, you had need to examine it carefully. You had need to view that commodity on all sides, of which you do in effect say, "For this will I sell my soul; for this will I give up heaven and venture hell, be heaven and hell whatever they may." In the name of God, brethren, is this the part of a man, of a rational creature? To go on with your eyes open toward a pit of eternal ruin, because there are a few gay flowers in the way; or what if you shut your eyes, will that prevent your fall? It signifies little to say, "I will not think of these things; I will not consider them." God has said, "In the last days they shall consider it perfectly" (Jer. 23:20). The revels of a drunken malefactor will not prevent nor respite his execution. Pardon my plainness; if it were a fable or a tale, I would endeavor to amuse you with words, but I cannot do it where souls are at stake.

2. I would apply to those who are, in some sense, convinced of the importance of their souls, and yet are inclined to defer that care of them a little longer, which, in the general, they see to be necessary.

I know you that are young are under peculiar temptations to do this; though it is strange that the death of so many of your companions should not be an answer to some of the most specious and dangerous of those temptations.

*To be mindful then is to consider what am I with regard exchanging an eternity with my Creator for an eternity separated from Him?

I think, if these were the least degree of uncertainty, the importance is too weighty to put matters to the venture. But here the uncertainty is great and apparent. You must surely know that there are critical seasons of life for managing the concerns of it, which are of such a nature that, if once left, they may never return; here is a critical season: "Now is the accepted time, now is the day of salvation" (2 Cor. 6:2). "Today, if ye will hear his voice, harden not your hearts" (Heb. 3:7–8). This language may not be spoken tomorrow. Talk not of a more convenient season; none can be more convenient; and that to which you would probably refer it is least of all so, a dying time. You would not choose then to have any important business in hand; and will you of choice refer the greatest business of all to that languishing, hurrying, amazing hour? If a friend were then to come to you with the balance of an intricate account, or a view of a title to an estate, you would shake your fainting head and lift up your pale trembling hand, and say, perhaps with a feeble voice, "Alas, is this a time for these things?" And is it a time for so much greater things than these? I wish you knew, and would consider, into what a strait we that are ministers are sometimes brought, when we are called to the dying beds of those who have spent their lives in the neglect of the one thing needful. On the one hand, we fear, lest, if we palliate matters and speak smooth things, we shall betray and ruin their souls; and on the other, that if we use a becoming plainness and seriousness in warning them of their danger, we shall quite overwhelm them, and hasten the dying moments, which is advancing by such swift steps. Oh, let me entreat you for our sakes, and much more for your own, that you do not drive us to such sad extremities; but if you are convinced, as I hope some of you may now be, that the care of the soul is that needful thing we have represented, let the conviction work, let it drive you immediately to the throne of grace; from there you may derive that wisdom and strength, which will direct you in all the intricacies which entangle you, and animate you in the midst of difficulty and discouragement.

3. I would in the last place address myself to those happy souls, who have in good earnest attended to the one thing needful.

I hope that when you see how commonly it is neglected, neglected indeed by many whose natural capacities, improvements, and circumstances in life appear to you superior to your own; you will humbly acknowledge that it was distinguishing grace which brought you into this happy state and formed you to this most necessary care. Bless the Lord, therefore, who has given you that counsel, in virtue of which you can say, "He is your portion." Rejoice in the thought that the great concern is secured: as it is natural for us to do, when some important affair is dispatched, which has long lain before us, and which we have been inclined to put off from one day to another, but have at length strenuously and successfully attended. Remember still to endeavor to continue acting on these great principles, which at first determined your choice; and seriously consider that those who desire their life may at last be given them for a prey, must continue on their guard, in all stages of their journey through a wilderness, where daily dangers are still surrounding them. Being enabled to secure the great concern, make yourselves easy as to others of smaller importance. You have chosen the kingdom of God and his righteousness; other things therefore shall be added unto you: and if any which you desire should not be added, comfort yourselves with this thought: that you have the good part, which can never be taken away. And, now to enlarge on these obvious hints, which must often occur: be very solicitous that others may be brought to a care about the one thing needful. If it be needful for you, it is so for your children, your friends, your servants. Let them therefore see your concern in this respect for them, as well as for yourselves. Let parents especially attend to this exhortation whose care for their offspring often exceeds in other respects, and falls in this. Remember that your children may never live to enjoy the effects of your labor and concern to get them estates and portions; the charges of their funerals may, perhaps, be all their share of what you are so anxiously careful to lay up for them. And, oh, think what a sword would pierce through your very heart, if you should stand by the corpse of a beloved child with this reflection: "This poor creature has done with life, before it learned its great business in it; and is gone to eternity, which I have seldom been warning it to prepare for, and which, perhaps, it learned of me to forget."

On the whole, may this grand care be awakened in those by whom it has been hitherto neglected: may it be revived in each of our minds. And that you may be encouraged to pursue it with greater cheerfulness, let me conclude with this comfortable thought, that in proportion to the necessity of the case, through the merits of Christ Jesus, is the provision which divine grace has made for our assistance. If you are disposed to sit down at Christ's feet, he will teach you by his Word and Spirit. If you commit this precious jewel, which is your eternal all, into his hand, he will preserve it unto that day and will then produce it richly adorned and gloriously improved to his own honor, and to your everlasting joy.

Which God of his infinite mercy grant through Jesus Christ our Lord; to whom with the Father and the Holy Ghost, three persons and one God, be ascribed, as is most due, all honor and praise, might, majesty, and dominion, now and forever. Amen.

A Penitent Heart,
the Best New Year's Gift

—◆—

"Except ye repent, ye shall all likewise perish." —LUKE 13:3

When we consider how heinous and aggravating our offenses are, in the sight of a just and holy God, that they bring down his wrath upon our heads, and occasion us to live under his indignation; how ought we thereby to be deterred from evil, or at least engaged to study to repent thereof, and not commit the same again; but man is so thoughtless of an eternal state, and has so little consideration of the welfare of his immortal soul, that he can sin without any thought that he must give an account of his actions at the day of judgment; or if he, at times, has any reflections on his behavior, they do not drive him to true repentance. He may, for a short time, refrain from falling into some gross sins which he had lately committed; but then, when the temptation comes again with power, he is carried away with the lust; and thus he goes on promising and resolving, and in breaking both his resolutions and his promises, as fast almost as he has made them. This is highly offensive to God; it is mocking of him. My brethren, when grace is given us to repent truly, we shall turn wholly unto God; and let me beseech you to repent of your sins, for the time is hastening when you will have neither time nor call to repent; there is none in the grave, where we are going. But do not be afraid, for God often receives the greatest sinner to mercy through the merits of Christ Jesus; this magnifies the riches of his free grace and should be an encouragement for you, who are great and notorious sinners, to repent, for he shall have mercy upon you, if you through Christ return unto him.

St. Paul was an eminent instance of this; he speaks of himself as "the chief of sinners," and he declares how God showed mercy unto him. Christ loves to show mercy unto sinners, and if you repent, he will have mercy upon you. But as no word is more mistaken than that of repentance, I shall—

I. Show you what the nature of repentance is.

II. Consider the several parts and causes of repentance.

III. I shall give you some reasons why repentance is necessary to salvation.

[margin handwritten note: How can this be yet it is.]

IV. Exhort all of you, high and low, rich and poor, one with another, to endeavor after repentance.

I. Repentance, my brethren, in the first place, as to its nature, is the carnal and corrupt disposition of men being changed into a renewed and sanctified disposition. A man that has truly repented is truly regenerated: it is a different word for one and the same thing; the motley mixture of the beast and devil is gone; there is, as it were, a new creation worked in your hearts. If your repentance is true, you are renewed throughout, both in soul and body; your understandings are enlightened with the knowledge of God and of the Lord Jesus Christ; and your wills, which were stubborn, obstinate, and hated all good, are obedient and comformable to the will of God. Indeed, our deists tell us that man now has a free will to do good, to love God, and to repent when he will; but indeed, there is no free will in any of you, but to sin; what's more, your free will leads you so far, that you would, if possible, pull God from his throne. This may, perhaps, offend the Pharisees; but (it is the truth in Christ which I speak, I lie not) every man by his own natural will hates God; but when he is turned unto the Lord, by evangelical repentance, then his will is changed; then your consciences, now hardened and benumbed, shall be quickened and awakened; then your hard hearts shall be melted, and your unruly affections shall be crucified. Thus, by that repentance, the whole soul will be changed; you will have new inclinations, new desires, and new habits.

You may see how vile we are by nature, that it requires so great a change to be made upon us, to recover us from this state of sin, and therefore the consideration of our dreadful state should make us earnest with God to change our condition, and that change, true repentance implies; therefore, my brethren, consider how hateful your ways are to God, while you continue in sin; how abominable you are unto him, while you run into evil: you cannot be said to be Christians while you are hating Christ and his people; true repentance will entirely change you, the bias of your souls will be changed, then you will delight in God, in Christ, in his law, and in his people; you will then believe that there is such a thing as inward feeling, though now you may esteem it madness and enthusiasm; you will not then be ashamed of becoming fools for Christ's sake; you will not regard being scoffed at; it is not then their pointing after you and crying, "Here comes another troop of his followers," will dismay you; no, your soul will abhor such proceedings, the ways of Christ and his people will be your whole delight.

It is the nature of such repentance to make a change, and the greatest change as can be made here in the soul. Thus you see what repentance implies in its own nature; it denotes an abhorrence of all evil and a forsaking of it.

I shall now proceed, second, to show you the parts of it, and the causes concurring thereto.

The parts are sorrow, hatred, and an entire forsaking of sin.

Our sorrow and grief for sin must not spring merely from a fear of wrath; for if we have no other ground but that, it proceeds from self-love and not from any love to God; and if love to God is not the chief motive of your repentance, your repentance is in vain and not to be esteemed true.

Many, in our days, think their crying, "God forgive me!" or, "Lord, have mercy upon me!" or, "I am sorry for it!" is repentance, and that God will esteem it as such; but, indeed, they are mistaken; it is not the drawing near to God with our lips, while our hearts are far from him, which he regards. Repentance does not come by fits and starts; no, it is one continued act of our lives; for as we daily commit sin, so we need a daily repentance before God, to obtain forgiveness for those sins we commit.

It is not your confessing yourselves to be sinners, it is not knowing your condition to be sad and deplorable, so long as you continue in your sins; your care and endeavors should be to get the heart thoroughly affected therewith, that you may feel yourselves to be lost and undone creatures, for Christ came to save such as are lost; and if you are enabled to groan under the weight and burden of your sins, then Christ will ease you and give you rest.

And till you are thus sensible of your misery and lost condition, you are a servant to sin and to your lusts, under the bondage and command of Satan, doing his drudgery: you are under the curse of God and liable to his judgment. Consider how dreadful your state will be at death and after the day of judgment, when you will be exposed to such miseries which the ear has not heard, neither can the heart conceive, and that to all eternity, if you die impenitent.

But I hope better things of you, my brethren, though I thus speak, and things which accompany salvation; go to God in prayer and be earnest with him, that by his Spirit he would convince you of your miserable condition by nature and make you truly sensible thereof. Oh, be humbled, be humbled, I beseech you, for your sins. Having spent so many years in sinning, what can you do less, than be concerned to spend some hours in mourning and sorrowing for the same, and be humbled before God.

Better one humbles oneself
Rather than be humbled by God

Look back into your lives, call to mind your sins, as many as possible you can, the sins of your youth, as well as of your riper years; see how you have departed from a gracious Father and wandered in the way of wickedness, in which you have lost yourselves, the favor of God, the comforts of his Spirit, and the peace of your own consciences; then go and beg pardon of the Lord, through the blood of the Lamb, for the evil you have committed, and for the good you have omitted. Consider, likewise, the heinousness of your sins; see what very aggravating circumstances your sins are attended with, how you have abused the patience of God, which should have led you to repentance; and when you find your heart hard, beg of God to soften it, cry mightily unto him, and he will take away your stony heart, and give you a heart of flesh.

Resolve to leave all your sinful lusts and pleasures; renounce, forsake, and abhor your old sinful course of life and serve God in holiness and righteousness all the remaining part of life. If you lament and bewail past sins, and do not forsake them, your repentance is in vain; you are mocking of God and deceiving your own soul; you must put off the old man with his deeds, before you can put on the new man, Christ Jesus.

You therefore who have been swearers and cursers, you who have been harlots and drunkards, you who have been thieves and robbers, you who have hitherto followed the sinful pleasures and diversions of life, let me beseech you, by the mercies of God in Christ Jesus, that you would no longer continue therein, but that you would forsake your evil ways and turn unto the Lord, for he waits to be gracious unto you; he is ready, he is willing to pardon you of all your sins; but do not expect Christ to pardon you of sin, when you run into it and will not abstain from complying with the temptations; but if you will be persuaded to abstain from evil and choose the good, to return unto the Lord, and repent of your wickedness, he has promised he will abundantly pardon you, he will heal your backslidings and will love you freely. Resolve now this day to have done with your sins forever; let your old ways and you be separated; you must resolve against it, for there can be no true repentance without a resolution to forsake it. Resolve for Christ, resolve against the devil and his works, and go on fighting the Lord's battles against the devil and his emissaries; attack him in the strongest holds he has; fight him as men, as Christians, and you will soon find him to be a coward; resist him and he will fly from you. Resolve, through grace, to do this, and your repentance is half done; but then take care that you do not ground your resolutions on your own strength, but in the strength of the Lord Jesus Christ; he is the way, he is the truth, and he is the life; without his assistance you can do nothing, but through his grace strengthening you, you will be enabled to do all things; and the more ready Christ will be to help you; and what can all the men of the world do to you when Christ is for you? You will not regard what they say against you, for you will have the testimony of a good conscience.

Resolve to cast yourself at the feet of Christ in subjection to him, and throw yourself into the arms of Christ for salvation by him. Consider, my dear brethren, the many invitations he has given you to come unto him, to be saved by him. "God has laid on him the iniquity of us all." Oh, let me prevail with you, above all things, to make choice of the Lord Jesus Christ; resign yourselves unto him, take him, oh, take him, upon his own terms, and whosoever you are, how great a sinner you have been, this evening, in the name of the great God, do I offer Jesus Christ unto you; as you value your life and soul, refuse him not, but stir up yourself to accept of the Lord Jesus, take him wholly as he is, for he will be applied wholly unto you or else not at all. Jesus Christ must be your whole wisdom. Jesus Christ must be your whole righteousness. Jesus Christ must be your whole sanctification, or he will never be your eternal redemption.

What though you have been ever so wicked and profligate, yet, if you will now abandon your sins, and turn unto the Lord Jesus Christ, you shall have him given to you, and all your sins shall be freely forgiven. Oh, why will you neglect the great work of your repentance? Do not defer the doing of it one day longer, but today, even now, take that Christ who is freely offered to you.

Now as to the causes hereof, the first cause is God; he is the Author. "We are born of God"; God has begotten us, even God, the Father of our Lord Jesus Christ; it is he that stirs us up to will and to do of his own good pleasure. And another cause is God's free grace; it is owing to the "riches of his free grace," my brethren, that we have been prevented from going down to hell long ago; it is because the compassions of the Lord fail not, they are new every morning, and fresh every evening.

Sometimes the instruments are very unlikely: a poor, despised minister, or member of Jesus Christ, may, by the power of God, be made an instrument in the hands of God, of bringing you to true evangelical repentance; and this may be done to show that the power is not in men, but that it is entirely owing to the good pleasure of God; and if there has been any good done among many of you, by preaching the Word, as I trust there has, though it was preached in a field, if God has met and owned us, and blessed his Word, though preached by an enthusiastic babbler, a boy, a madman; I do rejoice, yes, and will rejoice, let foes say what they will.

I shall now, third, show the reasons why repentance is necessary to salvation.

And this, my brethren, is plainly revealed to us in the Word of God: "The soul that does not repent and turn unto the Lord shall die in its sins, and their blood shall be required at their own heads." It is necessary, as we have sinned, we should repent; for a holy God could not, nor ever can, or will, admit anything that is unholy into his presence. This is the beginning of grace in the soul; there must be a change in heart and life, before there can be a dwelling with a holy God. You cannot love sin and God too; you cannot love God and mammon; no unclean person can stand in the presence of God; it is contrary to the holiness of his nature; there is a contrariety between the holy nature of God and the unholy nature of carnal and unregenerate men.

What communication can there be between a sinless God and creatures full of sin, between a pure God and impure creatures? If you were to be admitted into heaven with your present tempers, in your impenitent condition, heaven itself would be a hell to you; the songs of angels would be as enthusiasm [fanaticism] and would be intolerable to you; therefore you must have these tempers changed, you must be holy, as God is. He must be your God here, and you must be his people, or you will never dwell together to all eternity. If you hate the ways of God, and cannot spend an hour in his service, how will you think to be easy, to all eternity, in singing praises to him that sits upon the throne, and to the Lamb forever.

And this is to be the employment, my brethren, of all those who are admitted into this glorious place, where neither sin nor sinner is admitted, where no scoffer ever can come, without repentance from his evil ways, a turning unto God, and a cleaving unto him. This must be done before any can be admitted into the glorious mansions of God, which are prepared for all that love the Lord Jesus Christ in sincerity and truth: repent, then, of all your sins. O my dear brethren, it makes my blood run cold, in thinking that any of you should not be admitted into the glorious mansions above. Oh, ✳ that it was in my power, I would place all of you, yes, you my scoffing brethren, and the greatest enemy I have on earth, at the right hand of Jesus; but this I cannot do. However, I advise and exhort you, with all love and tenderness, to make Jesus your refuge; fly to him for relief; Jesus died to save such as you; he is full of compassion; and if you go to him, as poor, lost, undone sinners, Jesus will give you his Spirit; you shall live and reign, and reign and live, you shall love and live, and live and love with this Jesus to all eternity.

✳ O LORD that make this my heart's desire

I am, fourth, to exhort all of you, high and low, rich and poor, one with another, to repent of all your sins and turn unto the Lord.

And I shall speak to each of you; for you have either repented or you have not; you are believers in Christ Jesus or unbelievers.

And first, you who never have truly repented of your sins, and never have truly forsaken your lusts, be not offended if I speak plain to you; for it is love, love to your souls, that constrains me to speak: I shall lay before you your danger, and the misery to which you are exposed, while you remain impenitent in sin. And oh, that this may be a means of making you fly to Christ for pardon and forgiveness.

While your sins are not repented of, you are in danger of death, and if you should die, you would perish forever. There is no hope of any who live and die in their sins, but that they will dwell with devils and damned spirits to all eternity. And how do we know we shall live much longer? We are not sure of seeing our own habitations this night in safety. What mean you then being at ease and pleasure while your sins are not pardoned? As sure as ever the Word of God is true, if you die in that condition, you are shut out of all hope and mercy forever, and shall pass into ceaseless and endless misery.

What are all your pleasures and diversions worth? They last but for a moment; they are of no worth and but of short continuance. And sure it must be gross folly, eagerly to pursue those sinful lusts and pleasures, which war against the soul, which tend to harden the heart, and keep us from closing with the Lord Jesus; indeed, these are destructive of our peace here and, without repentance, will be of our peace hereafter.

Oh, the folly and madness of this sensual world; sure, if there were nothing in sin but present slavery, it would keep an ingenuous spirit from it. But to do the devils drudgery! And if we do that, we shall have his wages, which is eternal death and condemnation. O consider this, my guilty brethren, you that think it no crime to swear, whore, drink, or scoff and jeer at the people of God; consider how your voices will then be changed, and you that counted their lives madness and their end without honor, shall howl and lament at your own madness and folly, that should bring you to so much woe and distress. Then you will lament and bemoan your own dreadful condition; but it will be of no significance, for he that is not your merciful Savior will then become your inexorable Judge. Now he is easy to be entreated; but then, all your tears and prayers will be in vain, for God has allotted to every man a day of grace, a time of repentance, which if he does not improve, but neglects and despises the means which are offered to him, he cannot be saved.

* No soft serve ice cream here - no cheesy Christianity

Consider therefore while you are going on in a course of sin and unrighteousness, I beseech you, my brethren, to think of the consequence that will attend your thus misspending your precious time; your souls are worth being concerned about; for if you can enjoy all the pleasures and diversions of life, at death you must leave them; that will put an end to all your worldly concerns. And will it not be very deplorable to have your good things here—all your earthly, sensual, devilish pleasures which you have been so much taken up with—all over: and the thought for how trifling a concern you have lost eternal welfare will gnaw your very soul.

Your wealth and grandeur will stand in no stead; you can carry nothing of it into the other world: then the consideration of your uncharitableness to the poor, and the ways you did take to obtain your wealth, will be a very hell unto you.

Now you enjoy the means of grace, as the preaching of his Word, prayer, and sacraments; and God has sent his ministers out into the fields and highways, to invite, to woo you to come in; but they are tiresome to you; you would rather be at your pleasures. Before long, my brethren, they will be over, and you will be no more troubled with them; but then you would give ten thousand worlds for one moment of that merciful time of grace which you have abused; then you will cry for a drop of that precious blood which now you trample under your feet; then you will wish for one more offer of mercy, for Christ and his free grace to be offered to you again; but your crying will be in vain, for as you would not repent here, God will not give you an opportunity to repent hereafter; if you would not in Christ's time, you shall not in your own. In what a dreadful condition will you then be? What horror and astonishment will possess your souls? Then all your lies and oaths, your scoffs and jeers at the people of God, all your filthy and unclean thoughts and actions, your misspent time in balls, plays, and assemblies, your spending whole evenings at cards, dice, and masquerades, your frequenting of taverns and alehouses, your worldliness, covetousness, and your uncharitableness, will be brought at once to your remembrance, and at once charged upon your guilty soul. And how can you bear the thoughts of these things? Indeed I am full of compassion toward you, to think that this should be the portion of any who now hear me. These are truths, though awful ones; my brethren, these are the truths of the gospel; and if there was not a necessity for thus speaking, I would willingly forbear, for it is no pleasing subject to me, any more than it is to you; but it is my duty to show you the dreadful consequences of continuing in sin. I am only now acting the part of a skillful surgeon, that searches

* Is this not the whole duty of believers as some have over the years? What then becomes of us if we divert from discipling?

a wound before he heals it: I would show you your danger first, that deliverance may be the more readily accepted by you.

Consider, that however you may be for putting the evil day away from you and are now striving to hide your sins, at the day of judgment there shall be a full discovery of all; hidden things on that day shall be brought to light; and after all your sins have been revealed to the whole world, then you must depart into everlasting fire in hell, which will not be quenched night and day; it will be without intermission, without end. Oh, then, what stupidity and senselessness have possessed your hearts, that you are not frighted from your sins? The fear of Nebuchadnezzar's fiery furnace made men do anything to avoid it; and shall not an everlasting fire make men, make you, do anything to avoid it?

Oh, that this would awaken and cause you to humble yourselves for your sins, and to beg pardon for them, that you might find mercy in the Lord.

Do not go away. Let not the devil hurry you away before the sermon is over; but stay, and you shall have a Jesus offered to you, who has made full satisfaction for all your sins.

Let me beseech you to cast away your transgressions, to strive against sin, to watch against it, and to beg power and strength from Christ, to keep down the power of those lusts that hurry you on in your sinful ways.

But if you will not do any of these things, if you are resolved to sin on, you must expect eternal death to be the consequence; you must expect to be seized with horror and trembling, with horror and amazement, to hear the dreadful sentence of condemnation pronounced against you; and then you will run and call upon the mountains to fall on you, to hide you from the Lord, and from the fierce anger of his wrath.

Had you now a heart to turn from your sins unto the living God, by true and unfeigned repentance, and to pray unto him for mercy, in and through the merits of Jesus Christ, there were hope; but at the day of judgment, your prayers and tears will be of no significance; they will be of no service to you, the Judge will not be entreated by you: as you would not hearken to him when he called unto you, but despised both him and his ministers, and would not leave your iniquities; therefore on that day he will not be entreated, notwithstanding all your cries and tears; for God himself has said, "Because I have called, and you refused; I have stretched out my hand, and no man regarded, but you have set at naught all my counsel, and would have none of my reproof; I will also laugh at your calamity, and mock when your fear cometh as desolation, and your destruction cometh as a whirlwind; when distress and anguish cometh upon you, then shall they call upon me, but I will not answer, they shall seek me early, but they shall not find me."

Now you may call this enthusiasm [fanaticism] and madness; but at that great day, if you repent not of your sins here, you will find, by woeful experience, that your own ways were madness indeed; but God forbid it should be left undone till then. Seek after the Lord while he is to be found; call upon him while he is near, and you shall find mercy: repent this hour, and Christ will joyfully receive you. *Oh what an image now that makes clear these words of old, eternal death is that "forever' separation*

What say you? Must I go to my Master and tell him you will not come unto him, and will have none of his counsels? No; do not send me on so unhappy an errand. I cannot, I will not, tell him any such thing. Shall not I rather tell him, you are willing to repent and to be converted, to become new men, and take up a new course of life? This is the only wise resolution you can make. Let me tell my Master that you will come unto, and will wait upon, him, for if you do not, it will be your ruin in time, and to eternity.

You will at death wish you had lived the life of the righteous,* that you might have died his death. Be advised then; consider what is before you, Christ and the world, holiness and sin, life and death: choose now for yourselves; let your choice be made immediately, and let that choice be your dying choice.

If you would not choose to die in your sins, to die drunkards, to die adulterers, to die swearers and scoffers, etc., live not out this night in the dreadful condition you are in. Some of you, it may be, may say, you have not power, you have no strength: but have not you been wanting to yourselves in such things that were within your power? Have you not as much power to go to hear a sermon, as to go into a playhouse, or to a ball or masquerade? You have as much power to read the Bible, as to read plays, novels, and romances; and you can associate as well with the godly, as with the wicked and profane. This is but an idle excuse, my brethren, to go on in your sins; and if you will be found in the means of grace, Christ has promised he will give you strength. While Peter was preaching, the Holy Ghost fell on all that heard the Word: how then should you be found in the way of your duty? Jesus Christ will then give you strength; he will put his Spirit within you; you shall find he will be your wisdom, your righteousness, your sanctification, and your redemption. Do but try what a gracious, a kind, and loving Master he is; he will be a help to you in all your burdens: and if the burden of sin is on your soul, go to him as weary and heavy laden, and you shall find rest.

Do not say that your sins are too many and too great to expect to find mercy! No, be they ever so many, or ever so great, the blood of the Lord Jesus

* Lord my prayer, my sweet communion with you shall ever be be my Savior and my righteousness. Amen

Christ will cleanse you from all sins. God's grace, my brethren, is free, rich, and sovereign. Manassah was a great sinner, and yet he was pardoned; Zaccheus was gone far from God, and went out to see Christ with no other view but to satisfy his curiosity, and yet Jesus met him and brought salvation to his house. Manassah was an idolater and murderer, yet he received mercy; the other was an oppressor and extortioner, who had gotten riches by fraud and deceit, and by grinding the faces of the poor: so did Matthew too, and yet they found mercy.

Have you been blasphemers and persecutors of the saints and servants of God? So was St. Paul, yet he received mercy. Have you been common harlots, filthy and unclean persons? So was Mary Magdalene, and yet she received mercy. Have you been a thief? The thief upon the cross found mercy. I despair of none of you, however vile and profligate you have been; I say, I despair of none of you, especially when God has had mercy on such a wretch as I am.

Remember the poor publican, how he found favor with God, when the proud, self-conceited Pharisee, who puffed up with his own righteousness, was rejected. And if you will go to Jesus, as the poor publican did, under a sense of your own unworthiness, you shall find favor as he did: there is virtue enough in the blood of Jesus, to pardon greater sinners than he has yet pardoned. Then be not discouraged, but come unto Jesus, and you will find him ready to help in all your distresses, to lead you into all truth, to bring you from darkness to light, and from the power of Satan to God.

Do not let the devil deceive you, by telling you that then all your delights and pleasures will be over. No; this is so far from depriving you of all pleasure, that it is an inlet unto unspeakable delights, peculiar to all who are truly regenerated. The new birth is the very beginning of a life of peace and comfort; and the greatest pleasantness is to be found in the ways of holiness.

Solomon, who had experience of all other pleasures, yet said of the ways of godliness, that "all her ways are ways of pleasantness, and all her paths are paths of peace." Then surely you will not let the devil deceive you; it is all he wants; it is that he aims at, to make religion appear to be melancholy, miserable, and enthusiastic [fanatical]; but let him say what he will, give not ear to him, regard him not, for he always was and will be a liar.

What words, what entreaties shall I use, to make you come unto the Lord Jesus Christ? The little love I have experienced, since I have been brought from sin to God, is so great, that I would not be in a natural state for ten thousand worlds; and what I have felt is but little to what I hope to feel; but that little love which I have experienced is a sufficient buoy against all the storms and

† Solomon great start
Solomon lousy finish

tempests of this boisterous world: and let men and devils do their worst, I rejoice in the Lord Jesus, yes, and I will rejoice.

And oh, if you repent and come to Jesus, I would rejoice on your accounts too; and we should rejoice together to all eternity, when once passed on the other side of the grave. Oh, come to Jesus. The arms of Jesus Christ will embrace you; he will wash away all your sins in his blood and will love you freely.

Come, I beseech you to come unto Jesus Christ. Oh, that my words would pierce to the very soul! Oh, that Jesus Christ was formed in you! Oh, that you would turn to the Lord Jesus Christ, that he might have mercy upon you! I would speak till midnight, yes, I would speak till I could speak no more, so it might be a means to bring you to Jesus; let the Lord Jesus but enter your souls, and you shall find peace which the world can neither give nor take away. There is mercy for the greatest sinner among you; go unto the Lord as sinners, help-less and undone without it, and then you shall find comfort in your souls and be admitted at last among those who sing praises unto the Lord to all eternity.

Now, my brethren, let me speak a word of exhortation to those of you who are already brought to the Lord Jesus, who are born again, who do belong to God, to whom it has been given to repent of your sins, and are cleansed from their guilt: and that is, be thankful to God for his mercies toward you. Oh, admire the grace of God, and bless his name forever! Are you made alive in Christ Jesus? Is the life of God begun in your souls, and have you the evidence thereof? Be thankful for this unspeakable mercy to you: never forget to speak of his mercy. And as your life was formerly devoted to sin and to the pleasures of the world, let it now be spent wholly in the ways of God; and oh, embrace every opportunity of doing and of receiving good. Whatso-ever opportunity you have, do it vigorously, do it speedily, do not defer it. If you see one hurrying on to destruction, use the utmost of your endeavor to stop him in his course; show him the need he has of repentance, and that without it he is lost forever; do not regard his despising of you; still go on to show him his danger: and if your friends mock and despise, do not let that dis-courage you; hold on, hold out to the end, so you shall have a crown which is immutable, and that fades not away.

Let the love of Jesus to you keep you also humble; do not be high-minded, keep close unto the Lord, observe the rules which the Lord Jesus Christ has given in his Word, and let not the instructions be lost which you are capable of giving. Oh, consider what reason you have to be thankful to the Lord Jesus Christ for giving you that repentance you yourselves had need of: a repentance which works by love. Now you find more pleasure in walking with God one hour, than in all your former carnal delights, and all the pleasures of sin. Oh, the joy you feel in your own souls, which all the men of the world, and all the devils in hell, though they were to combine together, could not destroy. Then fear not their wrath or malice, for through many tribulations we must enter into glory.

A few days or weeks or years more, and then you will be beyond their reach; you will be in the heavenly Jerusalem. There is all harmony and love; there is all joy and delight; there the weary soul is at rest.

Now we have many enemies, but at death they are all lost; they cannot follow us beyond the grave; and this is a great encouragement to us not to regard the scoffs and jeers of the men of this world.

Oh, let the love of Jesus be in your thoughts continually. It was his dying that brought you life; it was his crucifixion that paid the satisfaction for your sins; his death, burial, and resurrection that completed the work; and he is now in heaven, interceding for you at the right hand of his Father. And can you do too much for the Lord Jesus Christ, who has done so much for you? His love to you is unfathomable. Oh, the height, the depth, the length, and breadth of this love, that brought the King of glory from his throne, to die for such rebels as we are, when we had acted so unkindly against him, and deserved nothing but eternal damnation. He came down and took our nature upon him; he was made of flesh and dwelt among us; he was put to death on our account; he paid our ransom: surely this should make us rejoice in him, and not do as too many do—and as we ourselves have too often—crucify this Jesus afresh. Let us do all we can, my dear brethren, to honor him.

Come, all of you, come, and behold him stretched out for you; see his hands and feet nailed to the cross. Oh, come, come, my brethren, and nail your sins thereto. Come, come and see his side pierced; there is a fountain open for sin, and for uncleanness: oh, wash, wash and be clean: come and see his head crowned with thorns, and all for you. Can you think of a panting, bleeding, dying Jesus, and not be filled with pity toward him? He underwent all this for you. Come unto him by faith; lay hold on him: there is mercy for every soul of you that will come unto him. Then do not delay; fly unto the arms of this Jesus, and you shall be made clean in his blood.

Oh, what shall I say unto you to make you come to Jesus? I have showed you the dreadful consequence of not repenting of your sins: and if after all I have said, you are resolved to persist, your blood will be required at your own heads; but I hope better things of you, and things that accompany salvation. Let me beg of you to pray in good earnest for the grace of repentance. I may never see your faces again; but at the day of judgment I will meet you: there you will either bless God that ever you were moved to repentance; or else this sermon, though in a field, will be as a swift witness against you. Repent, repent therefore, my dear brethren, as John the Baptist, and as our blessed Redeemer himself earnestly exhorted, and turn from your evil ways, and the Lord will have mercy on you.

Show them, O Father, wherein they have offended you; make them to see their own vileness, and that they are lost and undone without true repentance; and oh, give them that repentance, we beseech you, that they may turn from sin unto you, the living and true God. These things, and whatever else you see needful for us, we entreat that you would bestow upon us, on account of what the dear Jesus Christ has done and suffered; to whom, with yourself, and the Holy Spirit, three persons and one God, be ascribed, as is most due, all power, glory, might, majesty, and dominion, now, henceforth, and forevermore. Amen.

The Pharisee and Publican

———

"I tell you, this man went down to his house justified rather than the other: for everyone that exalteth himself shall be abased; and he that humbleth himself shall be exalted." —LUKE 18:14

Though there be some who dare to deny the Lord Jesus and disbelieve the revelation he has been pleased to give us, and thereby bring upon themselves swift destruction, yet I would charitably hope there are but few if any such among you, to whom I am now to preach the kingdom of God. Was I to ask you, how you expect to be justified in the sight of an offended God, I suppose you would answer, "only for the sake of our Lord Jesus Christ." But was I to come more home to your consciences, I fear that most would make the Lord Jesus but in part their Savior and go about, as it were, to establish a righteousness of their own. And this is not thinking contrary to the rules of Christian charity: for we are all self-righteous by nature; it is as natural for us to turn to a covenant of works, as for the sparks to fly upward. We have had so many legal and so few free-grace preachers, for these many years, that most professors now seem to be settled upon their lees, and rather deserve the title of Pharisees than Christians.

Thus it was with the generality of the people during the time of our Lord's public ministration: and therefore, in almost all his discourses, he preached the gospel to poor sinners, and denounced terrible woes against proud self-justifiers. The parable to which the words of the text belong looks both these ways, for the Evangelist informs us that our Lord "spake it unto certain who trusted in themselves that they were righteous, and despised others" (v. 9). And a notable parable it is; a parable worthy of your most serious attention. "He that hath ears to hear, let him hear" what Jesus Christ speaks to all visible professors in it.

Verse 10: "Two men went up to the temple to pray (and never two men of more opposite characters); the one a Pharisee and the other a publican." The Pharisees were the strictest sect among the Jews. "I was of the strictest sect, of the Pharisees," says Paul. They prayed often; not only so, but they made long prayers; and, that they might appear extraordinary devout, they would pray at the corners of the street, where two ways met, that people going or coming, both ways, might see them. "They made broad (as our Lord informs us) the borders of their phylacteries"; they had pieces of parchment sown to their long robes, on which some parts of the Scripture were written, that people might from there infer that they were lovers of the law of God. They were so very punctual and exact in outward purifications that they washed at their going out and coming in. They held the washing of pots, brazen vessels, and tables, and many other suchlike things they did. They were very zealous for the traditions of the fathers and for the observation of the rites and ceremonies of the church, notwithstanding they frequently made void the law of God by their traditions. And they were so exceedingly exact in the outward observation of the Sabbath, that they condemned our Lord for making a little clay with his spittle, and called him a sinner, and said he was not of God, because he had given sight to a man born blind, on the Sabbath day. For these reasons they were held in high veneration among the people, who were sadly misled by these blind guides: they had the uppermost places in the synagogues and greetings in the marketplaces (which they loved dearly) and were called of men, "rabbi"; in short, they had such a reputation for piety that it became a proverb among the Jews, that if there were but two men saved, the one of them must be a Pharisee.

As for the publicans, it was not so with them. It seems they were sometimes Jews, or at least proselytes of the gate; for we find one here coming up to the temple; but for the generality, I am apt to think they were Gentiles; for they were gatherers of the Roman taxes and used to amass much wealth (as appears by the confession of Zaccheus, one of the chief of them) by wronging men with false accusations. They were so universally infamous that our Lord himself tells his disciples, the excommunicated man should be to them "as a heathen man, or a publican." And the Pharisees thought it a sufficient impeachment of our Lord's character, that he was a friend to publicans and sinners and went to sit down with them at meat.

But, however they disagreed in other things, they agreed in this, that public worship is a duty incumbent upon all; for they both came up to the temple. The very heathens were observers of temple worship. We have very early notice of men's sacrificing to, and calling upon, the name of the Lord, in the Old Testament; and I find it nowhere contradicted in the New. Our Lord, and his apostles, went up to the temple; and we are commanded by the apostle, "not to forsake the assembling ourselves together," as the manner of too many is in our days; and such too, as would have us think well of them, though they seldom or never tread the courts of the Lord's house. But, though our devotions begin in our closets, they must not end there. And, if people never show their devotions abroad, I must suspect they have little or none at

Interesting it wasn't so different for Whitefield notes the Church had become a mercantile, den for thieves — antagonists

home. "Two men went up to the temple." And what went they there for? Not (as multitudes among us do) to make the house of God a house of merchandise, or turn it into a den of thieves; much less to ridicule the preacher or disturb the congregation; no, they came to the temple, says our Lord, "to pray." There should the tribes of God's spiritual Israel go up, to talk with, and pour out their hearts before the mighty God of Jacob.

"Two men went up to the temple to pray." I fear one of them forgot his errand. I have often been at a loss what to call the Pharisee's address; it certainly does not deserve the name of a prayer. He may rather be said to come to the temple to boast, than to pray; for I do not find one word of confession of his original guilt; not one single petition for pardon of his past actual sins, or for grace to help and assist him for the time to come: he only brings to God, as it were, a reckoning of his performances; and does that which no flesh can justly do, I mean, glory in his presence.

Verse 11: "The Pharisee stood, and prayed thus with himself, 'God, I thank thee that I am not as other men are, extortioners, unjust, adulterers, or even as this publican.'"

Our Lord first takes notice of his posture: "the Pharisee stood." He is not to be condemned for that, for standing, as well as kneeling, is a proper posture for prayer. "When you stand praying," says our Lord—though sometimes our Lord knelt, even lay flat on his face upon the ground; his apostles also knelt, as we read in the Acts, which has made me wonder at some who are so bigoted to standing in family, as well as public prayer, that they will not kneel, notwithstanding all kneel that are around them. I fear there is something of the Pharisee in this conduct. Kneeling and standing are indifferent, if the knee of the soul be bent and the heart upright toward God. We should study not to be particular in indifferent things, lest we offend weak minds. What the Pharisee is remarked for, is his "standing by himself," for the words may be rendered, he stood by himself, upon some eminent place, at the upper part of the temple, near the holy of holies, that the congregation might see what a devout man he was; or it may be understood as we read it, he prayed by himself, or of himself, out of his own heart; he did not pray by form; it was an extemporaneous prayer, for there are many Pharisees that pray, and preach too, extemporaneously. I do not see why these may not be acquired, as well as other arts and sciences. A man, with a good elocution, ready turn of thought, and good memory, may repeat his own or other men's sermons, and, by the help of Wilkins or Henry, may pray seemingly excellently well, and yet not have the least grain of true grace in his heart; I speak this, not to cry down extemporaneous prayer or to discourage those dear souls who really pray by the spirit; I only would hereby give a word of reproof to those who are so bigoted to extemporaneous prayer, that they condemn, at least judge, all that use forms, as though not so holy and heavenly as others who pray without them. Alas! this is wrong. Not everyone that prays extemporaneously is a spiritual, nor everyone that prays with a form, a formal man. Let us not judge one another; let not him that uses a form, judge him that prays extemporaneously, on that account; and let not him that prays extemporaneously, despise him who uses a form.

"The Pharisee stood, and prayed thus by himself," which may signify also praying inwardly in his heart; for there is a way (and that an excellent one too) of praying when we cannot speak; thus Anna prayed, when she spoke not aloud, only her lips moved. Thus God says to Moses, "Why criest thou?" when it is plain, he did not speak a word. This is what the apostle means by the "spirit making intercession (for believers) with groanings which cannot be uttered." For there are times when the soul is too big to speak; when God fills it as it were, and overshadows it with his presence, so that it can only fall down, worship, adore, and lie in the dust before the Lord. Again, there is a time when the soul is benumbed, barren, and dry, and the believer has not a word to say to his heavenly Father; and then the heart only can speak. And I mention this for the encouragement of weak Christians, who think they never are accepted but when they have a flow of words, and fancy they do not please God at the bottom, for no other reason but because they do not please themselves. Such would do well to consider that God knows the language of the heart and the mind of the spirit; and that we make use of words, not to inform God, but to affect ourselves. Whenever therefore any of you find yourselves in such a frame, be not discouraged: offer yourselves up in silence before God, as clay in the hands of the potter, for him to write and stamp his own divine image upon your souls. But I believe the Pharisee knew nothing of this way of prayer: he was self-righteous, a stranger to the divine life; and therefore either of the former explanations may be best put upon these words.

"He stood, and prayed thus with himself, 'God, I thank thee that I am not as other men are, extortioners, unjust, adulterers, or even as this publican.'" Here is some appearance of devotion, but it is only in appearance. To thank God that we are not extortioners, unjust, adulterers, and as wicked in our practices as other men are, is certainly meet, right, and our bounden duty: for whatever degrees of goodness there may be in us, more than in others, it is owing to God's restraining, preventing, and assisting grace. We are all equally conceived and born in sin; all are fallen short of the glory of God, and liable to all the curses and maledictions of the law; so that "he who glorieth, must glory only in the Lord." For none of us have anything which we did not receive; and whatever we have received, we did not in the least merit it, nor could we lay the least claim to it on any account whatever: we are wholly indebted to free grace for all. Had the Pharisee thought thus, when he said, "God, I thank thee that I am not as other men are," it would have been an excellent introduction to his prayer; but he was a free willer, as well as self-righteous (for he that is one must be the other), and thought that by his own power and strength he had kept himself from these vices. And yet I do not see what reason he had to trust in himself that he was righteous, merely because he had to trust in himself that he was righteous, merely because he was not an extortioner, unjust, adulterer; for all this while he might be, as he certainly was (as is also every self-righteous person), as proud as the devil. But he not only boasts, but lies before God (as all self-justifiers will be found liars here or hereafter). He thanks God that he was not unjust. But is it not an act of the highest injustice to rob God of his prerogative? Is it not an act of injustice to judge our neighbor? And yet of both these crimes this self-righteous vaunter is guilty.

"Even as this publican." He seems to speak with the utmost disdain; this publican! Perhaps he pointed at the poor man, that others might treat him with the like contempt. You proud, confident boaster, what had you to do with that poor publican? Supposing other publicans were unjust, and extortioners, did it therefore follow that he must be so? Or, if he had been such a sinner, how do you know but he has repented of those sins? His coming up to the temple to pray is one good sign of a reformation at least. You are therefore inexcusable, O Pharisee, who thus judges the publican—for you that judge him to be unjust are, in the very act of judging, unjust yourself: your sacrifice is only the sacrifice of a fool.

We have seen what the Pharisee's negative goodness comes to: I think, nothing at all. Let us see how far his positive goodness extends; for, if we are truly religious, we shall not only eschew evil, but also do good: "I fast twice in the week; I give tithes of all that I possess."

The Pharisee is not here condemned for his fasting, for fasting is a Christian duty. "When you fast . . . ," says our Lord, thereby taking it for granted that his disciples would fast. And "When the bridegroom shall be taken away, then shall they fast in those days." "In fasting often," says the apostle. And all that would not be castaways, will take care, as their privilege, without legal constraint, to "keep their bodies under, and bring them into subjection." The Pharisee is only condemned for making a righteousness of his fasting, and thinking that God would accept him, or that he was any better than his neighbors,

The Pharisee

[margin annotations in handwriting: "The Pharisee"; "&? so true"; " one might infer our purpose to fast is for HIS return"]*

merely on account of his fasting, and thinking that God would accept him, or that he was any better than his neighbors, merely on account of his fasting: this is what he was blamed for. The Pharisee was not to be discommended for fasting twice in a week; I wish some Christians would imitate him more in this: but to depend on fasting in the least, for his justification in the sight of God, was really abominable. "I give tithes of all that I possess." He might as well have said, I pay tithes. But self-righteous people (whatever they may say to the contrary) think they give something to God. "I give tithes of all that I possess"; I make conscience of giving tithes, not only of all that the law requires, but of my mint, anise, and cumin, of all things whatsoever I possess; this was well; but to boast of such things, or of fasting, is pharisaic and devilish. Now then let us sum up all the righteousness of this boasting Pharisee, and see what little reason he had to trust in himself, that he was righteous, or to despise others. He is not unjust (but we have only his bare word for that; I think I have proved the contrary); he is no adulterer, no extortioner; he fasts twice in the week, and gives tithes of all that he possesses; and all this he might do, and a great deal more, and yet be a child of the devil: for here is no mention made of his loving the Lord his God with all his heart, which was the "first and great commandment of the law"; here is not a single syllable of inward religion; and he was not a true Jew who was only one outwardly. It is only an outside piety at the best; inwardly he is full of pride, self-justification, free will, and great uncharitableness.

Were not the Pharisees, do you think, highly offended at this character, for they might easily know it was spoken against them? And though, perhaps, some of you may be offended at me, yet, out of love, I must tell you: I fear this parable is spoken against many of you, for are there not many of you, who go up to the temple to pray, with no better spirit than this Pharisee did? And because you fast, it may be in the Lent or every Friday, and because you do nobody any harm, receive the Sacrament, pay tithes, and give an alms now and then, you think that you are safe, and trust in yourselves that you are righteous, and inwardly despise those who do not come up to you in these outward duties. This, I am persuaded, is the case of many of you, though alas! it is a desperate one, as I shall endeavor to show at the close of this discourse.

Let us now take a view of the publican, in verse 13: "And the publican, standing afar off, would not lift up so much as his eyes unto heaven, but smote upon his breast, saying, 'God be merciful to me a sinner.'"

"The publican, standing afar off," perhaps in the outward court of the temple, conscious to himself that he was not worthy to approach the holy of

Was he Jew or Gentile?

To have the heart of a publican! O Lord

holies; so conscious and so weighed down, with a sense of his own unworthiness, that he would not so much as lift up his eyes unto heaven, which he knew was God's throne. Poor heart! What did he feel at this time? None but returning publicans, like himself, can tell. I think I see him standing afar off, pensive, oppressed, and even overwhelmed with sorrow; sometimes he attempts to look up; but then, thinks he, the heavens are unclean in God's sight, and the very angels are charged with folly; how then shall such a wretch as I dare to lift up my guilty head! And to show that his heart was full of holy self-resentment, and that he sorrowed after a godly sort, "he smote upon his breast"; the word in the original implies that he struck hard upon his breast. He will lay the blame upon none but his own wicked heart. He will not, like unhumbled Adam, tacitly lay the fault of his vileness upon God, and say, "The passions which you gave me, they deceived me, and I sinned." He is too penitent thus to reproach his Maker; he smites upon his breast, his treacherous, ungrateful, desperately wicked breast, a breast now ready to burst.

And at length, out of the abundance of his heart, I doubt not, with many tears, he at last cries out, God be merciful to me a sinner. Not "God be merciful to yonder proud Pharisee"; he found enough in himself to vent his resentment against, without looking abroad upon others. Not "God be merciful to me a saint," for he knew "all his righteousnesses were but filthy rags." Not "God be merciful to such or such a one"; but God be merciful to me, even to me a sinner—a sinner by birth, a sinner in thought, word, and deed; a sinner as to my person, a sinner as to all my performances; a sinner in whom is no health, in whom dwells no good thing, a sinner, poor, miserable, blind and naked, from the crown of the head to the sole of the feet, full of wounds, and bruises, and putrefying sores; a self-accused, self-condemned sinner." What think you? Would this publican have been offended if any minister had told him that he deserved to be damned? Would he have been angry, if anyone had told him that by nature he was half a devil and half a beast? No, he would have confessed a thousand hells to have been his due, and that he was an earthly, devilish sinner. He felt now what a dreadful thing it was to depart from the living God; he felt that he was inexcusable every way; that he could in nowise, upon account of anything in himself, be justified in the sight of God; and therefore lays himself at the feet of sovereign mercy. "God be merciful to me a sinner." Here is no confidence in the flesh, no plea fetched from fasting, paying tithes, or the performance of any other duty; here is no boasting that he was not an extortioner, unjust, or an adulterer. Perhaps he had been guilty of all these crimes, at least he knew he would have been guilty of all these, had he been left to follow the devices and desires of his own heart;

and therefore, with a broken and contrite spirit, he cries out, "God be merciful to me a sinner."

This man came up to the temple to pray, and he prayed indeed. And a broken and contrite heart God will not despise. "I tell you," says our Lord—I who lay in the bosom of the Father from all eternity; I who am God, and therefore know all things; I who can neither deceive, nor be deceived, whose judgment is according to right—I tell you, whatever you may think of it, or think of me for telling you so, "this man," this publican, this despised, sinful, but brokenhearted man, "went down to his house justified (acquitted, and looked upon as righteous in the sight of God) rather than the other."

Let Pharisees take heed that they do not pervert this text: for when it is said, "This man went down to his house justified rather than the other," our Lord does not mean that both were justified, and that the publican had rather more justification than the Pharisee; but it implies either that the publican was actually justified, but the Pharisee was not; or that the publican was in a better way to receive justification than the Pharisee, according to our Lord's saying, "The publicans and harlots enter the kingdom of heaven before you." That the Pharisee was not justified is certain, for "God resisteth the proud"; and that the publican was at this time actually justified (and perhaps went home with a sense of it in his heart) we have great reason to infer from the latter part of the text, "For everyone that exalteth himself shall be abased, and he that humbleth himself shall be exalted."

The parable therefore now speaks to all who hear me this day: for that our Lord intended it for our learning is evident, from his making such a general application: "For everyone that exalteth himself shall be abased, and he that humbleth himself shall be exalted."

The parable of the publican and Pharisee is but as it were a glass, wherein we may see the different disposition of all mankind; for all mankind may be divided into two general classes. Either they trust wholly in themselves, or in part, that they are righteous, and then they are Pharisees; or they have no confidence in the flesh, are self-condemned sinners, and then they come under the character of the publican just now described. And we may add also, that the different reception these men meet with points out to us, in lively colors, the different treatment the self-justified and self-condemned criminal will meet with at the terrible day of judgment: "Everyone that exalts himself shall be abased, but he that humbleth himself shall be exalted."

"Everyone," without exception, young or old, high or low, rich or poor (for God is no respecter of persons); "everyone," whosoever he be that exalts himself and not free grace; everyone that trusts in himself that he is righteous,

Pharisee-minded

that rests in his duties, or thinks to join them with the righteousness of Jesus Christ, for justification in the sight of God, though he be no adulterer nor extortioner, though he be not outwardly unjust, even though he fast twice in the week, and give tithes of all that he possesses; yet shall he be abased in the sight of all good men who know him here, and before men and angels, and God himself, when Jesus Christ comes to appear in judgment hereafter. How low, none but the almighty God can tell. He shall be abased to live with devils, and make his abode in the lowest hell forevermore.

Hear this, all ye self-justifiers, tremble, and behold your doom! a dreadful doom, more dreadful than words can express or thought conceive! If you refuse to humble yourselves, after hearing this parable, I call heaven and earth to witness against you this day, that God shall visit you with all his storms, and pour all the vials of his wrath upon your rebellious heads; you exalted yourselves here, and God shall abase you hereafter; you are as proud as the devil, and with devils shall you dwell to all eternity. "Be not deceived, God is not mocked"; he sees your hearts, he knows all things. And, notwithstanding you may come up to the temple to pray, your prayers are turned into sin, and you go down to your houses unjustified, if you are self-justifiers; and do you know what it is to be unjustified? Why, if you are unjustified, the wrath of God abides upon you; you are in your blood; all the curses of the law belong to you: cursed are you when you go out, cursed are you when you come in; cursed are your thoughts; cursed are your words; cursed are your deeds; everything you do, say, or think, from morning to night, is only one continued series of sin. However highly you may be esteemed in the sight of men, however you may be honored with the uppermost seats in the synagogues, in the church militant, you will have no place in the church triumphant. "Humble yourselves therefore under the mighty hand of God": pull down every self-righteous thought and every proud imagination that now exalts itself against the perfect, personal, imputed righteousness of the dear Lord Jesus: "For he (and he alone) that humbleth himself shall be exalted."

He that humbles himself, whatever he be: if, instead of fasting twice in the week, he has been drunk twice in the week; if, instead of giving tithes of all that he possesses, he has cheated the minister of his tithes, and the king of his taxes; notwithstanding he be unjust, an extortioner, an adulterer; what's more, notwithstanding the sins of all mankind center and unite in him; yet if through grace, like the publican, he is enabled to humble himself, he shall be exalted; not in a temporal manner, for Christians must rather expect to be abased and to have their names cast out as evil and to lay down their lives for Christ Jesus in this world; but he shall be exalted in a spiritual sense; he shall

It was never enough to merely sing about it; one must experience this "Peace With God"

be freely justified from all his sins by the blood of Jesus; he shall have peace with God, a peace which passes all understanding; not only peace, but joy in believing; he shall be translated from the kingdom of Satan, to the kingdom of God's dear Son: he shall dwell in Christ and Christ in him: he shall be one with Christ, and Christ one with him: he shall drink of divine pleasures, as out of a river; he shall be sanctified throughout in spirit, soul, and body; in one word, he shall be filled with all the fullness of God. Thus shall the man that humbles himself be exalted here; but oh, how high shall he be exalted hereafter! As high as the highest heavens, even to the right hand of God: there he shall sit, happy both in soul and body, and judge angels; high, out of the reach of all sin and trouble, eternally secure from all danger of falling. O sinners, did you but know how highly God intends to exalt those who humble themselves and believe in Jesus, surely you would humble yourselves, at least beg of God to humble you; for it is he that must strike the rock of your hearts and cause floods of contrite tears to flow therefrom. Oh, that God would give this sermon such a commission, as he once gave to the rod of Moses! I would strike you through and through with the rod of his word, until each of you was brought to cry out with the poor publican, "God be merciful to me a sinner." What pleasant language would this be in the ears of the Lord of Sabaoth!

Are there no poor sinners among you? What, are you all Pharisees? Surely, you cannot bear the thoughts of returning home unjustified, can you? What if a fit of the apoplexy should seize you, and your souls be hurried away before the awful Judge of quick and dead? What will you do without Christ's righteousness? If you go out of the world unjustified, you must remain so for ever. Oh, that you would humble yourselves! Then would the Lord exalt you; it may be that, while I am speaking, the Lord might justify you freely by his grace. I observed that perhaps the publican had a sense of his justification before he went from the temple, and knew that his pardon was sealed in heaven. And who knows but you may be thus exalted before you go home, if you humble yourselves? Oh, what peace, love, and joy, would you then feel in your hearts! You would have a heaven upon earth. Oh, that I could hear any of you say (as I once heard a poor sinner, under my preaching, cry out), "He is come. He is come!" How would you then, like him, extol a precious, a free-hearted Christ! How would you magnify him for being such a friend to publicans and sinners? Greater love can no man show, than to lay down his life for a friend: but Christ laid down his life for his enemies, even for you, if you are enabled to humble yourselves, as the publican did. Sinners, I know not how to leave off talking with you; I would fill my mouth with arguments. I would plead with you. "Come, let us reason together"; though your

Never have I connected friend-love to enemy-love

sins be as scarlet, yet, if you humble yourselves, they shall be as white as snow. One act of true faith in Christ justifies you forever and ever; he has not promised you what he cannot perform; he is able to exalt you: for God has exalted and given him a name above every name; that at the name of Jesus every knee shall bow; what's more, God has exalted him to be not only a Prince, but a Savior. May he be a Savior to you! And then I shall have reason to rejoice, in the day of judgment, that I have not preached in vain, not labored in vain. You, sir, were not in vain, Countless now are souls, saved, as credited to your faithfulness to proclaim the Gospel.

The Conversion of Zaccheus

—m—

And Jesus said unto him, "This day is salvation come to this house; forasmuch as he also is a son of Abraham. For the Son of man is come to seek and to save that which was lost." —LUKE 19:9–10 Note: Messiah does not say Abraham, Isaac & Jacob, only a son of Abraham. Likely he wasn't an Israelite

Salvation, everywhere through the whole Scripture, is said to be the free gift of God, through Jesus Christ our Lord. Not only free, because God is a sovereign agent, and therefore may withhold it from, or confer it on, whom he pleases; but free, because there is nothing to be found in man that can any way induce God to be merciful unto him. The righteousness of Jesus Christ is the sole cause of our finding favor in God's sight: this righteousness apprehended by faith (which is also the gift of God) makes it our own; and this faith, if true, will work by love.

These are parts of those glad tidings which are published in the gospel; and of the certainty of them, next to the express Word of God, the experience of all such as have been saved, is the best, and, as I take it, the most undoubted proof. That God might teach us every way, he has been pleased to leave upon record many instances of the power of his grace exerted in the salvation of several persons, that we, hearing how he dealt with them, might from there infer the manner we must expect to be dealt with ourselves, and learn in what way we must look for salvation, if we truly desire to be made partakers of the inheritance with the saints in light.

The conversion of the person referred to in the text, I think, will be of no small service to us in this matter, if rightly improved. I would hope most of you know who the person is, to whom the Lord Jesus speaks; it is the publican Zaccheus, to whose house the blessed Jesus said salvation came, and whom he pronounces a son of Abraham.

It is my design (God helping) to make some remarks upon his conversion recorded at large in the preceding verses, and then to enforce the latter part of the text, as an encouragement to poor undone sinners to come to Jesus Christ. "For the Son of man is come to seek and to save that which was lost."

The evangelist Luke introduces the account of this man's conversion thus: "And Jesus entered and passed through Jericho" (v. 1). The holy Jesus made it his business to go about doing good. As the sun in the firmament is continually spreading his benign, quickening, and cheering influences over the natural, so the Sun of righteousness arose with healing under his wings, and was daily and hourly diffusing his gracious influences over the moral world. The preceding chapter acquaints us of a notable miracle worked by the holy Jesus, on poor blind Bartimeus; and in this, a greater presents itself to our consideration. The Evangelist would have us take particular notice of it; for he introduces it with the word *behold*: "And, behold, there was a man named Zaccheus, who was the chief among the publicans, and he was rich."

Well might the Evangelist usher in the relation of this man's conversion with the word *behold*! For, according to human judgment, how many insurmountable obstacles lay in the way of it! Surely no one will say there was any fitness in Zaccheus for salvation; for we are told that he was a publican, and therefore in all probability a notorious sinner. The publicans were gatherers of the Roman taxes; they were infamous for their abominable extortion; their very name therefore became so odious, that we find the Pharisees often reproached our Lord as very wicked, because he was a friend unto and sat down to meat with them. Zaccheus then, being a publican, was no doubt a sinner; and, being chief among the publicans, consequently was chief among sinners. What's more, "he was rich." One inspired apostle has told us that "not many mighty, not many noble are called." Another said, "God has chosen the poor of this world, rich in faith." And he who was the Maker and Redeemer of the apostles assures us that "it is easier for a camel (or cable rope) to go through the eye of a needle, than for a rich man to enter into the kingdom of God." Let not therefore the rich glory in the multitude of their riches.

But rich as he was, we are told, in verse 3, that "he sought to see Jesus." A wonder indeed! The common people heard our Lord gladly, and the poor received the gospel. The multitude, the ὄχλος, the mob, the people that know not the law, as the proud high priests called them, used to follow him on foot into the country, and sometimes stayed with him three days together to hear him preach. But did the rich believe or attend on him? No. Our Lord preached up the doctrine of the cross; he preached too searching for them, and therefore they counted him their enemy, persecuted, and spoke all manner of evil against him falsely. Let not the ministers of Christ marvel, if they meet with the like treatment from the rich men of this wicked and adulterous generation. I should think it no scandal (supposing it true) to hear it affirmed that none but the poor attended my ministry. Their souls are as precious to our Lord Jesus Christ, as the souls of the greatest men. They were the poor that attended him in the days of his flesh; these are they whom he has chosen to be rich in faith, and to be the greatest in the kingdom of heaven. Were the rich in this world's goods generally to speak well of me, woe be unto me; I should think it a dreadful sign that I was only a wolf in sheep's clothing, that I spoke peace, peace, when there was no peace, and prophesied smoother things than the gospel would allow of. Hear this, O you rich. Let who will dare to do it, God forbid that I should despise the poor; in doing so, I should reproach my Maker. The poor are dear to my soul; I rejoice to see them fly to the doctrine of Christ, like the doves to their windows. I only pray, that the poor who attend may be evangelized and turned into the spirit of the gospel: if so, "Blessed are ye; for yours is the kingdom of heaven."

But we must return to Zaccheus. "He sought to see Jesus." That is good news. I heartily wish I could say it was out of a good principle: but, without speaking contrary to that charity which hopes and believes all things for the best, we may say that the same principle drew him after Christ, which now draws multitudes (to speak plainly, it may be multitudes of you) to hear a particular preacher, even curiosity; for we are told that he came not to hear his doctrine, but to view his person, or, to use the words of the Evangelist, "to see who he was." Our Lord's fame was now spread abroad through all Jerusalem, and all the country round about: "Some said he was a good man; others, 'Nay, but he deceiveth the people.'" And therefore curiosity drew out this rich publican Zaccheus, to see who this person was, of whom he had heard such various accounts. But it seems he could not conveniently get a sight of him for the press [of the crowd], and because he was little of stature. Alas! How many are kept from seeing Christ in glory, by reason of the press! I mean, how many are ashamed of being singularly good, and therefore follow a multitude to do evil, because they have a press or throng of polite acquaintance! And, for fear of being set at naught by those with whom they used to sit at meat, they deny the Lord of glory, and are ashamed to confess him before men. This base, this servile, fear of man, is the bane of true Christianity; it brings a dreadful snare upon the soul and is the ruin of ten thousands: for I am fully persuaded, numbers are rationally convicted of gospel truths; but, not being able to brook contempt, they will not prosecute their convictions nor reduce them to practice. Happy those who in this respect, like Zaccheus, are resolved to overcome all impediments that lie in their way to a sight of Christ; for, finding he could not see Christ because of the press and the littleness of his natural stature, he did not smite upon his breast, and depart, saying, "It is in vain to seek after a sight of him any longer; I can never attain unto it." No, finding he could not see Christ, if he continued in the midst of, he ran before the multitude, and climbed up into a sycamore tree, to see him, for he was to pass that way." There is no seeing Christ in glory, unless we run before the multitude and are willing to be in the number of those despised few, who take the kingdom of

[handwritten: with the Kingdom of Satan]

[handwritten: Peace with God comes by violence of breaking]

God by violence The broad way, in which so many go, can never be that strait and narrow way which leads to life. Our Lord's flock was, and always will be, comparatively a little one; and unless we dare to run before the multitude in a holy singularity and can rejoice in being accounted fools for Christ's sake, we shall never see Jesus with comfort, when he appears in glory. From mentioning the sycamore tree, and considering the difficulty with which Zaccheus must climb it, we may further learn that those who would see Christ must undergo other difficulties and hardships, besides contempt, Zaccheus, without doubt, went through both. Did not many, think you, laugh at him as he ran along, and in the language of Michal, Saul's daughter, cry out, "How glorious did the rich Zaccheus look today, when, forgetting the greatness of his station, he ran before a pitiful, giddy mob, and climbed up a sycamore tree, to see an enthusiastic preacher!" But Zaccheus cares not for all that; his curiosity was strong: if he could but see who Jesus was, he did not value what scoffers said of him. Thus, and much more, will it be with all those who have an effectual desire to see Jesus in heaven: they will go on from strength to strength, break through every difficulty lying in their way, and care not what men or devils say of or do unto them. May the Lord make us all thus minded, for his dear Son's sake!

At length, after taking much pains, and going (as we may well suppose) through much contempt, Zaccheus has climbed the tree; and there he sits, as he thinks, hid in the leaves of it, and watching when he should see Jesus pass by: "For he was to pass by that way."

But sing, O heavens, and rejoice, O earth! Praise, magnify, and adore sovereign, electing, free, preventing love! Jesus the everlasting God, the Prince of peace, who saw Nathanael under the fig tree, and Zaccheus from eternity, now sees him in the sycamore tree, and calls him in time. *[handwritten: God's into trees.]*

Verse 5: "And when Jesus came to the place, he looked up, and saw him, and said unto him, 'Zaccheus, make haste and come down; for this day I must abide at thy house.'" Amazing love! Well might Luke usher in the account with "behold"! It is worthy of our highest admiration. When Zaccheus thought of no such thing, what's more, thought that Christ Jesus did not know him; behold, Christ does what we never hear he did before or after, I mean, invite himself to the house of Zaccheus, saying, "Zaccheus, make haste and come down; for this day I must abide at thy house." Not "pray, let me abide," but "I must abide" this day at your house. He also calls him by name, as though he was well acquainted with him, and indeed well he might; for his name was written in the Book of Life, he was one of those whom the Father had given him from all eternity: therefore he must abide at his house that day. "For whom he did predestinate, them he also called."

[handwritten: • Messiah calls to Zaccheus "Let Me In" the Choice was Zaccheus' and rightly he chose! ▢ Jesus doesn't just "get us"; HE knows us to the soul]

Here then, as through a glass, we may see the doctrine of free grace evidently exemplified before us. Here was not fitness in Zaccheus. He was a publican, chief among the publicans, not only so, but rich, and came to see Christ only out of curiosity; but sovereign grace triumphs over all. And if we do God justice, and are effectually worked upon, we must acknowledge there was no more fitness in us than in Zaccheus; and, had not Christ prevented us by his call, we had remained dead in trespasses and sins and alienated from the divine life, even as others. "Jesus looked up, and saw him, and said unto him, 'Zaccheus, make haste and come down; for this day I must abide at thy house.'"

With what different emotions of heart may we suppose Zaccheus received this invitation? Think you not that he was surprised to hear Jesus Christ call him by name, and not only so, but invite himself to his house? Surely, thinks Zaccheus, I dream: it cannot be; how should he know me? I never saw him before. Besides, I shall undergo much contempt if I receive him under my roof. Thus, I say, we may suppose Zaccheus thought within himself. But what says the Scripture? "I will make a willing people in the day of my power." With this outward call, there went an efficacious power from God, which sweetly overruled his natural will; and therefore: "He made haste, and came down, and received him joyfully" (v. 6), not only into his house, but also into his heart.

Thus it is the great God brings home his children. He calls them by name, by his Word, or providence; he speaks to them also by his Spirit. Hereby they are enabled to open their hearts and are made willing to receive the King of glory. For Zaccheus' sake, let us not entirely condemn people that come under the Word out of no better principle than curiosity. Who knows but God may call them? It is good to be where the Lord is passing by. May all who are now present out of this principle hear the voice of the Son of God speaking to their souls, and so hear that they may live! Not that men ought therefore to take encouragement to come out of curiosity. For perhaps a thousand more, at other times, came to see Christ out of curiosity, as well as Zaccheus, who were not effectually called by his grace. I only mention this for the encouragement of my own soul and the consolation of God's children, who are too apt to be angry with those who do not attend on the Word out of love to God; but let them alone. Brethren, pray for them! How do you know but Jesus Christ may speak to their hearts? A few words from Christ, applied by his Spirit, will save their souls. "'Zaccheus,'" says Christ, "'make haste, and come down.' And he made haste, and came down, and received him joyfully."

I have observed, in holy Scripture, how particularly it is remarked that persons rejoiced upon believing in Christ. Thus the converted eunuch went on his way rejoicing; thus the jailer rejoiced with his whole house; thus Zaccheus received Christ joyfully. And well may those rejoice who receive Jesus Christ; for with him they receive righteousness, sanctification, and eternal redemption. Many have brought up an ill report upon our good land and would fain persuade people that religion will make them melancholy mad. So far from it, that joy is one ingredient of the kingdom of God in the heart of a believer: "The kingdom of God is righteousness, peace, and joy in the Holy Ghost." To rejoice in the Lord is a gospel duty. "Rejoice in the Lord always, and again I say, rejoice." And who can be so joyful as those who know that their pardon is sealed before they go hence and are no more seen? The godly may, but I cannot see how any ungodly men can, rejoice: they cannot be truly cheerful. What if wicked men may sometimes have laughter among them? It is only the laughter of fools; in the midst of it there is heaviness. At the best, it is but like the cracking of thorns under a pot; it makes a blaze, but soon goes out. But, as for the godly, it is not so with them; their joy is solid and lasting. As it is a joy that a stranger meddles not with, so it is a joy that no man takes from them: it is a joy in God, a "joy unspeakable and full of glory."

It should seem that Zaccheus was under soul distress but a little while; perhaps (says Guthrie, in his book titled *The Trial Concerning a Saving Interest in Christ*) not above a quarter of an hour. I add, perhaps not so long; for, as one observes, sometimes the Lord Jesus delights to deliver speedily. God is a sovereign agent and works upon his children in their effectual calling, according to the counsel of his eternal will. It is with the spiritual, as natural birth: all women have not the like pangs; all Christians have not the like degree of conviction. But all agree in this, that all have Jesus Christ formed in their hearts: and those who have not so many trials at first may be visited with the greater conflicts hereafter; though they never come into bondage again, after they have once received the spirit of adoption. "We have not (says Paul) received the spirit of bondage again unto fear." We know not what Zaccheus underwent before he died; however, this one thing I know: he now believed in Christ and was justified, or acquitted, and looked upon as righteous in God's sight, though a publican, chief among the publicans, not many moments before. And thus it is with all that, like Zaccheus, receive Jesus Christ by faith into their hearts: the very moment they find rest in him, they are freely justified from all things from which they could not be justified by the law of Moses; "for by grace are we saved, through faith, and that not of ourselves, it is the gift of God."

Say not within yourselves, this is a licentious Antinomian doctrine; for this faith, if true, will work by love and be productive of the fruits of holiness. See an instance in this convert Zaccheus; no sooner had he received Jesus Christ by faith into his heart, but he evidences it by his works; for in verse 8 we are told, "Zaccheus stood forth, and said unto the Lord, 'Behold, Lord, the half of my goods I give unto the poor; and if I have taken anything from any man by false accusation, I restore him fourfold.'"

Having believed on Jesus in his heart, he now makes confession of him with his mouth to salvation. "Zaccheus stood forth"; he was not ashamed, but stood forth before his brother publicans; for true faith casts out all servile, sinful fear of man. And he said, "Behold, Lord." It is remarkable, how readily people in Scripture have owned the divinity of Christ immediately upon their conversion. Thus the woman at Jacob's well: "Is not this the Christ?" Thus the man born blind: "'Lord, I believe'; and worshiped him." Thus Zaccheus: "Behold, Lord." An incontestable proof, this to me, that those who deny our Lord's divinity never effectually felt his power; if they had, they would not speak so lightly of him; they would scorn to deny his eternal power and Godhead. "Zaccheus stood forth, and said, 'Behold, Lord, the half of my goods I give to the poor; and if I have taken anything from any man by false accusation, I restore him fourfold.'" Noble fruits of a true living faith in the Lord Jesus! Every word calls for our notice. Not some small, not the tenth part, but the half. Of what? "My goods"; things that were valuable. "My goods," his own, not another's. "I give"; not "I will give when I die, when I can keep them no longer"; but, "I give", now, even now. Zaccheus would be his own executor. For while we have time we should do good.

But to whom would he give half of his goods? Not to the rich, not to those who were already clothed in purple and fine linen, of whom he might be recompensed again; but to the poor, the maimed, the halt, the blind, from which he could expect no recompense till the resurrection of the dead. "I give to the poor." But knowing that he must be just before he could be charitable, and conscious to himself that in his public administrations he had wronged many persons, he adds, "And if I have taken anything from any man by false accusation, I restore him fourfold." Hear this, all you that make no conscience of cheating the king of his taxes, or of buying or selling run goods. If ever God gives you true faith, you will never rest, till, like Zaccheus, you have made restitution to the utmost of your power. I suppose, before his conversion, he thought it no harm to cheat thus, no more than you may do now, and pleased himself frequently, to be sure, that he got rich by doing so: but now he is grieved for it at his heart; he confesses his injustice before men, and promises to make ample restitution. Go, you cheating publicans, learn of Zaccheus; go away and do likewise. If you do not make restitution here, the Lord Jesus shall make you confess your sins before men and angels, and condemn you for it, when he comes in the glory of his Father to judgment hereafter.

After all this, with good reason might our Lord say unto him, "This day is salvation come to this house, forasmuch as he also is a son of Abraham"; not so much by a natural as by a spiritual birth. He was made partaker of like precious faith with Abraham; like Abraham he believed on the Lord, and it was accounted to him for righteousness; his faith, like Abraham's, worked by love; and I doubt not, but he has been long since sitting in Abraham's harbor.

And now, are you not ashamed of yourselves, who speak against the doctrines of grace, especially that doctrine of being justified by faith alone, as though it led to licentiousness? What can be more unjust than such a charge? Is not the instance of Zaccheus a sufficient proof to the contrary? Have I strained it to serve my own turn? God forbid. To the best of my knowledge I have spoken the truth in sincerity, and the truth as it is in Jesus. I do affirm that we are saved by grace, and that we are justified by faith alone: but I do also affirm that faith must be evidenced by good works, where there is an opportunity of performing them.

What therefore has been said of Zaccheus may serve as a rule, whereby all may judge whether they have faith or not. You say you have faith; but how do you prove it? Did you ever hear the Lord Jesus call you by name? Were you ever made to obey the call? Did you ever, like Zaccheus, receive Jesus Christ joyfully into your hearts? Are you influenced by the faith you say you have, to stand up and confess the Lord Jesus before men? Were you ever made willing to own, and humble yourselves for, your past offenses? Does your faith work by love, so that you conscientiously lay up, according as God has prospered you, for the support of the poor? Do you give alms of all things that you possess? And have you made due restitution to those you have wronged? If so, happy are you; salvation is come to your souls; you are sons, you are daughters of, you shall shortly be everlastingly blessed with, faithful Abraham. But if you are not thus minded, do not deceive your own souls. Though you may talk of justification by faith, like angels, it will do you no good; it will only increase your damnation. You hold the truth, but it is in unrighteousness: your faith being without works is dead; you have the devil, not Abraham, for your father. Unless you get a faith of the heart, a faith working by love, with devils and damned spirits shall you dwell forevermore.

But it is time now to enforce the latter part of the text: "For the Son of man is come to seek and to save that which was lost." These words are spoken by our Savior in answer to some self-righteous Pharisees, who, instead of rejoicing with the angels in heaven at the conversion of such a sinner, murmured, "That he was gone to be a guest with a man that was a sinner." To vindicate his conduct, he tells them that this was an act agreeable to the design of his coming: "For the Son of man is come to seek and to save that which was lost." He might have said, the Son of God. But, oh, the wonderful condescension of our Redeemer! He delights to style himself the Son of man. He came not only to save, but to seek and to save that which was lost. He came to Jericho to seek and save Zaccheus; for otherwise Zaccheus would never have been saved by him. But from where came he? Even from heaven, his dwelling place, to this lower earth, this vale of tears, to seek and save that which was lost, or all that feel themselves lost and are willing, like Zaccheus, to receive him into their hearts to save them. With how great a salvation? Even from the guilt and also from the power of their sins; to make them heirs of God, and joint heirs with himself, and partakers of that glory which he enjoyed with the Father before the world began. Thus will the Son of man save that which is lost. He was made the Son of man, on purpose that he might save them. He had no other end but this in leaving his Father's throne, in obeying the moral law, and hanging upon the cross: all that was done and suffered merely to satisfy and procure a righteousness for poor, lost, undone sinners, and that too without respect of persons. "That which was lost"; all of every nation and language that feel, bewail, and are truly desirous of being delivered from their lost state did the Son of man come down to seek and to save: for he is mighty, not only so, but willing, to save to the uttermost all that come to God through him. He will in nowise cast out: for he is the same today as he was yesterday. He comes now to sinners, as well as formerly; and, I hope, has sent me out this day to seek, and, under him, to bring home some of you, the lost sheep of the house of Israel. *of Israel? Whitefield is not in Israel*

What say you? Shall I go home rejoicing, saying, that many like sheep *Amazing* have gone astray, but they have now believed on Jesus Christ, and so returned *thought* home to the great Shepherd and Bishop of their souls? If the Lord would be pleased thus to prosper my handiwork, I care not how many legalists and self-righteous Pharisees murmur against me for offering salvation to the worst of sinners: for I know the Son of man came to seek and to save them; and the Lord Jesus will now be a guest to the worst publican, the vilest sinner that is among you, if he does but believe on him. Make haste then, O sinners, make haste, and come by faith to Christ. Then this day, even this hour, even this moment, if you believe, Jesus Christ shall come and make his eternal abode in your hearts. Which of you is made willing to receive the King of glory? Which *on* of you obeys his call, as Zaccheus did? Alas! why do you stand still? How know *that* you, whether Jesus Christ may ever call you again? Come then, poor, guilty *all would*

sinners; come away, poor, lost, undone publicans: make haste, I say, and come away to Jesus Christ. The Lord condescends to invite himself to come under the filthy roofs of the houses of your souls. Do not be afraid of entertaining him; he will fill you with all peace and joy in believing. Do not be ashamed to run before the multitude, and to have all manner of evil spoken against you falsely for his sake: one sight of Christ will make amends for all. Zaccheus was laughed at; and all that will live godly in Christ Jesus shall suffer persecution. But what of that? Zaccheus is now crowned in glory; as you also shall shortly be, if you believe on, and are reproached for, Christ's sake. Do not, therefore, put me off with frivolous excuses: there's no excuse can be given for your not coming to Christ. You are lost, undone, without him; and if he is not glorified in your salvation, he will be glorified in your destruction; if he does not come and make his abode in your hearts, you must take up an eternal abode with the devil and his angels. Oh, that the Lord would be pleased to pass by some of you at this time! Oh, that he may call you by his Spirit, and make you a willing people in this day of his power! For I know my calling will not do, unless he, by his efficacious grace, compel you to come in. Oh, that you once felt what it is to receive Jesus Christ into your hearts! You would soon, like Zaccheus, give him everything. You do not love Christ, because you do not know him; you do not come to him, because you do not feel your want of him: you are whole, and not brokenhearted; you are not sick, at least not sensible of your sickness; and therefore no wonder you do not apply to Jesus Christ, that great, that almighty physician. You do not feel yourselves lost, and therefore do not seek to be found in Christ. Oh, that God would wound you with the sword of his Spirit, and cause his arrows of conviction to stick deep in your hearts! Oh, that he would dart a ray of divine light into your souls! For if you do not feel yourselves lost without Christ, you are of all men most miserable: your souls are dead; you are not only an image of hell, but in some degree hell itself: you carry hell about with you, and you know it not. Oh, that I could see some of you sensible of this, and hear you cry out, "Lord, break this hard heart; Lord, deliver me from the body of this death; draw me, Lord, make me willing to come after you; I am lost; Lord, save me, or I perish!" Was this your case, how soon would the Lord stretch forth his almighty hand, and say, "Be of good cheer, it is I; be not afraid"? What a wonderful calm would then possess your troubled souls! Your fellowship would then be with the Father and the Son: your life would be hid with Christ in God.

Some of you, I hope, have experienced this, and can say, "I was lost, but I am found; I was dead, but am alive again: the Son of man came and sought me in the day of his power and saved my sinful soul." And do you repent that

Yea!
&
Amen!

✻ Oh Lord embolden me to make known the Gospel to a people who are not not now sensible to their sickness. Call them by the sword of your Spirit Amen

you came to Christ? Has he not been a good Master? Is not his presence sweet to your souls? Has he not been faithful to his promise? And have you not found, that even in doing and suffering for him, there is an exceeding present great reward? I am persuaded you will answer yes. O, then, you saints, recommend and talk of the love of Christ to others, and tell them, oh, tell them what great things the Lord has done for you? This may encourage others to come unto him. And who knows but the Lord may make you fishers of men? The story of Zaccheus was left on record for this purpose. No truly convicted soul, after such an instance of divine grace has been laid before him, need despair of mercy. What if you are publicans? Was not Zaccheus a publican? What if you are chief among the publicans? Was not Zaccheus likewise? What if you are rich? Was not Zaccheus rich also? And yet almighty grace made him more than conqueror over all these hindrances. All things are possible to Jesus Christ; nothing is too hard for him: he is the Lord almighty. Our mountains of sins must all fall before this great Zerubbabel. On him God the Father has laid the iniquities of all that shall believe on him; and in his own body he bare them on the tree. There, there, by faith, O mourners in Zion, may you see your Savior hanging with arms stretched out, and hear him, as it were, thus speaking to your souls: "Behold how I have loved you! Behold my hands and my feet! Look, look into my wounded side, and see a heart flaming with love: love stronger than death. Come into my arms, O sinners, come wash your spotted souls in my heart's blood. See here is a fountain opened for all sin and all uncleanness! See, O guilty souls, how the wrath of God is now abiding upon you: come, haste away, and hide yourselves in the clefts of my wounds; for I am wounded for your transgressions; I am dying that you may live forevermore. Behold, as Moses lifted up the serpent in the wilderness, so am I here lifted up upon a tree. See how I am become a curse for you: the chastisement of your peace is upon me. I am thus scourged, thus wounded, thus crucified, that you by my stripes may be healed. Oh, look unto me, all you trembling sinners, even to the ends of the earth! Look unto me by faith, and you shall be saved: for I came thus to be obedient even unto death, that I might save that which was lost."

And what say you to this, O sinners? Suppose you saw the King of glory dying, and thus speaking to you; would you believe on him? No, you would not, unless you believe on him now; for though he is dead, he yet speaks all this in the Scripture; what's more, in effect, says all this in the words of the text: "The Son of man is come to seek and to save that which is lost." Do not therefore any longer crucify the Lord of glory. Bring those rebels, your sins, which will not have him to reign over them, bring them out to him; though you cannot slay them yourselves, yet he will slay them for you. The power of his death and resurrection is as great now as formerly. Make haste therefore, make haste, O you publicans and sinners, and give the dear Lord Jesus your hearts, your whole hearts. If you refuse to hearken to this call of the Lord, remember your damnation will be just. I am free from the blood of you all; you must acquit my Master and me at the terrible day of judgment. Oh, that you may know the things that belong to your everlasting peace, before they are eternally hid from your eyes! Let all that love the Lord Jesus Christ in sincerity say, "Amen."

*LORD show me whose blood is on my hands whose blood convicts for not proclaiming the day of salvation is at hand? Show me LORD that if it is possible even these sins be covered under Christ's precious blood that I might be forgiven my utter failures. Amen

The Marriage of Cana

—ₘₗ—

This beginning of miracles did Jesus in Cana of Galilee, and manifested forth his glory; and his disciples believed on him. —JOHN 2:11

I have more than once had occasion to observe that the chief end St. John had in view, when he wrote his gospel, was to prove the divinity of Jesus Christ, [that Word, who not only was from everlasting with God, but also was really God blessed forevermore] against those archheretics Ebion and Cerinthus, whose pernicious principles too many follow in these last days. For this purpose, you may take notice, that he is more particular than any other Evangelist in relating our Lord's divine discourses, and also the glorious miracles which he worked, not by a power derived from another, like Moses and other prophets, but from a power inherent in himself.

The words of the text have a reference to a notable miracle which Christ performed, and thereby gave proof of his eternal power and Godhead. "This beginning of miracles did Jesus in Cana of Galilee, and manifested forth his glory; and his disciples believed on him."

The miracle here spoken of, is that of our Lord's turning water into wine at a marriage feast. I design, at present, by God's help, to make some observations on the circumstances and certainty of the miracle, and then conclude with some practical instructions, that you, by hearing how Jesus Christ has showed forth his glory, may, by the operation of God's Spirit upon your hearts, with the disciples mentioned in the text, be brought to believe on him.

First, then, I would make some observations on the miracle itself.

Verses 1 and 2: "And the third day there was a marriage in Cana of Galilee; and the mother of Jesus was there. And both Jesus was called, and his disciples, to the marriage." By our Lord's being at a feast we may learn that feasting upon solemn occasions is not absolutely unlawful: but then we must be exceedingly careful at such seasons, that the occasion be solemn, and that we go not for the sake of eating and drinking, but to edify one another in love. Feasting in any other manner I think absolutely unlawful for the followers of Jesus Christ: because if we eat and drink out of any other view, it cannot be to the glory of God. The Son of man, we know, "came eating and drinking." If a Pharisee asked him to come to his house, our Lord went, and sat down with him. But then we find his discourse was always such as tended to the use of edifying. We may then, no doubt, go and do likewise.

We may observe further, that if our Lord was present at a marriage feast, then, to deny marriage to any order of men is certainly a "doctrine of devils." "Marriage (says the apostle) is honorable in all." Our Lord graced a marriage feast with his first public miracle. It was an institution of God himself, even in paradise: and therefore, no doubt, lawful for all Christians, even for those who are made perfect in holiness through the faith of Jesus Christ. But then, we may learn the reason why we have so many unhappy marriages in the world; it is because the parties concerned do not call Jesus Christ by prayer, nor ask the advice of his true disciples when they are about to marry. No; Christ and religion are the last things that are consulted; and no wonder then if matches of the devil's making (as all such are, which are contracted only on account of outward beauty, or for filthy lucre's sake) prove most miserable, and grievous to be borne.

I cannot but dwell a little on this particular, because I am persuaded the devil cannot lay a greater snare for young Christians, than to tempt them unequally to yoke themselves with unbelievers; as are all who are not born again of God. This was the snare wherein the sons of God were entangled before the flood, and one great cause why God brought that flood upon the world. For what says Moses in Genesis 6:2–3? "The sons of God (the posterity of pious Seth) saw the daughters of men (or the posterity of wicked Cain) that they were fair (not that they were pious) and they took them wives of all which they chose," not which God chose for them. What follows? "And the Lord saith, 'My spirit shall not always strive with man, for that he also is flesh'"; that is, even the few righteous souls being now grown carnal by their ungodly marriages; the whole world had altogether become abominable and had made themselves vessels of wrath fitted for destruction. I might instance further the care the ancient patriarchs took to choose wives for their children out of their own religious families, and it was one great mark of Esau's rebellion against his father, that he took unto himself wives of the daughters of the Canaanites, who were strangers to the covenant of promise made unto his fathers. But I forbear. Time will not permit me to enlarge here. Let it suffice to advise all, whenever they enter into a marriage state, to imitate the people of Cana in Galilee, to call Christ to the marriage; he certainly will hear and choose for you; and you will always find his choice to be the best. He then will direct you to such yoke-fellows as shall be helps meet for you in the great work of your salvation, and then he will also enable you to serve him without distraction, and cause you to walk, as Zachariah and Elizabeth, in all his commandments and ordinances blameless.

But to proceed. Who these persons were that called our Lord and his disciples to the marriage, is not certain. Some (because it is said that the mother of Jesus was there) have supposed that they were related to the Virgin, and that therefore our Lord and his disciples were invited on her account. However that be, it should seem they were not very rich (for what had rich folks to do with a despised Jesus of Nazareth, and his mean followers?), because we find they were unfurnished with a sufficient quantity of wine for a large company, and therefore, "when they wanted wine, the mother of Jesus"—having, as it should seem by her applying to him so readily on this occasion, even in his private life, seen some instances of his miraculous power—"saith unto him, 'They have no wine.'" She thought it sufficient only to inform him of the wants of the host, knowing that he was as ready to give as she to ask. In this light the blessed Virgin's request appears to us at the first view; but if we examine our Lord's answer, we shall have reason to think there was something which was not right; for Jesus said unto her, "Woman, what have I to do with thee?" (v. 4). Observe, he calls her "woman," not mother; to show her that, though she was his mother, as he was man, yet she was his creature, as he was God. "What have I to do with thee?" Think you that I must work miracles at your bidding? Some have thought that she spoke as though she had an authority over him, which was a proud motion, and our Lord therefore checks her for it. And if Jesus Christ would not turn a little water into wine, while he was here on earth, at her command, how idolatrous is that church, and how justly do we separate from her, which prescribes forms wherein the Virgin is desired to command her Son to have compassion on us!

But notwithstanding the holy Virgin was blamable in this respect, yet she has herein set rich and poor an example which it is your duty to follow. You that are rich, and live in ceiled [covered] houses, learn of her to go into the cottages of the poor; your Lord was not above it, and why should you? And when you do visit them, like the virgin mother, examine their wants; and when you see they have no wine and are ready to perish with hunger, shut not up your bowels of compassion, but bless the Lord for putting it in your power to administer to their necessities. Believe me, such visits would do you good. You would learn then to be thankful that God has given you bread enough, and to spare. And I am persuaded, every mite that you bestow on feeding the hungry and clothing the naked disciples of Jesus Christ will afford you more satisfaction at the hour of death, and in the day of judgment, than all the thousands squandered away in balls and assemblies and suchlike entertainments.

You that are poor in this world's goods, and thereby are disabled from helping, yet you may learn from the Virgin, to pray for one another. She could not turn the water into wine, but she could entreat her son to do it: and so may you; and doubt not of the Lord's hearing you; for God has chosen the poor in this world, rich in faith: and by your servant prayers, you may draw down many a blessing on your poor fellow creatures. Oh, that I may ever be remembered by you before the throne of our dear Lord Jesus! But what shall we say? Will our Lord entirely disregard this motion of his mother? No; though he check her with, "Woman, what have I to do with thee?" yet he intimates that he would do as she desired by and by: "Mine hour is not yet come." As though he had said, "The wine is almost, but not quite out; when they are come to an extremity, and sensible of the want of my assistance, then will I show forth my glory, that they may behold it, and believe on me."

Thus, sirs, has our Lord been frequently pleased to deal with me, and, I doubt not, with many of you also. Often, often when I have found his presence as it were hidden from my soul, and his comforts well nigh gone, I have gone unto him complaining that I had no visit and token of his love, as usual. Sometimes he has seemed to turn a deaf ear to my request, and as it were said, "What have I to do with thee?" which has made me go sorrowing all the day long; so foolish was I and faithless before him: for I have always found he loved me notwithstanding, as he did Lazarus, though he stayed two days after he heard he was sick. But when my hour of extremity has been come, and my will broken, then has he lifted up the light of his blessed countenance afresh; he has showed forth his glory and made me ashamed for disbelieving him, who often has turned my water into wine. Be not then discouraged, if the Lord does not immediately seem to regard the voice of your prayer when you cry unto him. The holy Virgin we find was not; no, she was convinced his time was the best time, and therefore, "saith unto the servants (oh, that we could follow her advice!), 'Whatsoever he saith unto you, do it'" (v. 5).

And now, behold the hour is come, when the eternal Son of God will show forth his glory. The circumstance of the miracle is very remarkable: "And there were set six waterpots of water, after the manner of the purifying of the Jews, containing two or three firkins apiece" (v. 6). The manner of this purifying we have an account of in the other Evangelists, especially St. Mark, who inform us that the Pharisees, and all the Jews, except they wash their hands often, eat not; and when they come from the market, except they wash, they eat not. This was a superstitious custom; but, however, we may learn from it, whenever we come in from conversing with those that are without, to purify our hearts by self-examination and prayer; for it is hard to go through the world and to be kept unspotted from it.

Observe further, verse 7: "Jesus saith unto them"—not to his own disciples, but unto the servants of the house, who were strangers to the holy Jesus, and whom the Virgin had before charged to do whatsoever he said unto them—"'Fill the waterpots with water.' And they filled them to the brim. And he saith unto them, 'Draw out now, and bear to the governor of the feast.' And they bear it." How our Lord turned the water into wine we are not told. What have we to do with that? Why should we desire to be wise above what is written? It is sufficient for the manifestation of his glorious Godhead, that we are assured he did do it. For we are told, "When the ruler of the feast had tasted the water that was made wine, and knew not whence it was (but the servants that drew the water knew), the governor of the feast called the bridegroom, and saith unto him, 'Every man at the beginning doth set forth good wine, and when they have well drunk, then that which is worse; but thou hast kept the good wine until now'" (vv. 9–10).

To explain this passage, you must observe, it was the custom of the Jews, what's more, even of the heathens themselves (to the shame of our Christian baptized heathens be it spoken) at their public feasts to choose a governor, who was to oversee and regulate the behavior of the guests, and to take care that all things were carried on with decency and order. To this person then did the servants bear the wine; and we may judge how rich it was by his commendation of it, "Every man at the beginning. . . ." Judge you then, whether Jesus did not show forth his glory, and whether you have not good reason, like the disciple here mentioned, to believe on him.

Thus, my brethren, I have endeavored to make some observations on the miracle itself. But alas! this is only the outward court thereof, the veil is yet before our eyes; turn that aside, and we shall see such mysteries under it, as will make our hearts to dance for joy, and fill our mouths with praise forevermore!

But here I cannot help remarking what a sad inference one of our masters of Israel, in a printed sermon, has lately drawn from this commendation of the bridegroom. His words are these: "Our blessed Savior came eating and drinking, was present at weddings and other entertainments (though I hear of his being only at one); what's more, at one of them (which I suppose is that of which I am now discoursing) worked a miracle to make wine, when it is plain there had been more drunk than was absolutely necessary for the support of nature, and consequently something had been indulged to pleasure and cheerfulness."

I am sorry such words should come from the mouth and pen of a dignified clergyman of the Church of England. Alas! How is she fallen! Or at least, in what danger must her tottering ark be, when such unhallowed hands are stretched out to support it! Well may I bear patiently to be styled a blasphemer, and a setter forth of strange doctrine, when my dear Lord Jesus is thus traduced; and when those who pretend to preach in his name urge this example to patronize licentiousness and excess. It is true (as I observed at the beginning of this discourse) our blessed Savior did come eating and drinking; he was present at a wedding and other entertainments; what's more, at one of them worked a miracle to make wine (you see I have been making some observations on it), but then it is not plain there had been more wine drunk than was absolutely necessary for the support of nature; much less does it appear that something had been indulged to pleasure and cheerfulness.

The governor does indeed say, "When men have well drunken," but it nowhere appears that they were the men. Is it to be supposed that the most holy and unspotted Lamb of God, who was manifested to destroy the works of the devil, and who, when at a Pharisee's house, took notice of even the gestures of those with whom he sat at meat; is it to be supposed that our dear Redeemer, whose constant practice it was to tell people they must deny themselves, and take up their crosses daily; who bid his disciples to take heed, lest at any time their hearts might be overcharged with surfeiting and drunkenness; can it be supposed that such a self-denying Jesus should now turn six large waterpots of water into the richest wine, to encourage excess and drunkenness in persons, who, according to this writer, had indulged to pleasure and cheerfulness already? Had our Lord sat by and seen them indulge, without telling them of it, would it not be a sin? But to insinuate he not only did this, but also turned water into wine, to increase that indulgence—this is making Christ a minister of sin indeed. What is this, but using him like the Pharisees of old, who called him a glutton and a winebibber? Alas! how may we expect our dear Lord's enemies will treat him, when he is thus wounded in the house of his seeming friends? Sirs, if you follow such doctrine as this, you will not be righteous, but I am persuaded you will be wicked overmuch.

But God forbid you should think our Lord behaved so much unlike himself in this matter. No, he had nobler ends in view, when he worked this miracle. One, the Evangelist mentions in the words of the text, "to show forth his glory," or to give a proof of his eternal power and Godhead.

Here seems to be an allusion to the appearance of God in the tabernacle, which this same Evangelist takes notice of in his first chapter, where he says, "The Word (Jesus Christ) was made flesh, and dwelt (or, as it is rendered in the margin, tabernacled) among us." Our dear Lord, though very God of very God, and also most perfect and glorious in himself as man, was pleased to throw a veil of flesh over this his great glory, when he came to make his soul an offering for sin. And that the world might know and believe in him as the Savior of all men, he performed many miracles, and this in particular; for thus speaks the Evangelist: "This first. . . ." (miracle)

This then was the chief design of our Lord's turning the water into wine. But there are more which our Lord may be supposed to have had in view, some of which I shall proceed to mention.

Second, he might do this to reward the host for calling him and his disciples to the marriage. Jesus Christ will not be behindhand [tardy or slow to recognize] with those who receive him or his followers, for his name's sake. Those who thus honor him, he will honor. A cup of cold water given in the name of a disciple, shall in nowise lose its reward. He will turn water into wine. Though those who abound in almsdeeds, out of a true faith in, and love for Jesus, may seem as it were to throw their bread upon the waters, yet they shall find it again after many days. For they who give to the poor out of this principle, lend unto the Lord; and look, whatsoever they lay out, it shall be repaid them again. Even in this life, God often orders good measure pressed down and running over, to be returned into his servants' bosoms. It is the same in spirituals. To him that has, and improves what he has, for the sake of Christ and his disciples, shall be given, and he shall have abundance. Brethren, I would not boast; but, to my Master's honor and free grace be it spoken, I can prove this to be true by happy experience. When I have considered that I am a child, and cannot speak, and have seen so many of you come out into the wilderness to be fed, I have often said within myself, what can I do with my little stock of grace and knowledge among so great a multitude? But, at my Lord's command, I have given you to eat of such spiritual food as I had, and before I have done speaking, have had my soul richly fed with the bread which comes down from heaven. Thus shall it be done to all such who are willing to spend and be spent for Christ or his disciples; for there is no respect of persons with God.

Third, our Lord's turning the water, which was poured out so plentifully, into wine, is a sign of the plentiful pouring out of his Spirit into the hearts of believers. The Holy Spirit is in Scripture compared unto wine; and therefore the prophet calls us to buy wine as well as milk, that is, the spirit of love, which fills and gladdens the soul as it were with new wine. The apostle alludes to this, when he bids the Ephesians "not to be drunk with wine, wherein is excess, but be filled with the Spirit." And our Lord shows us thus much by choosing wine; to show forth the strength and refreshment of his blood, in the blessed sacrament. I know these terms are unintelligible to natural men; they can no more understand me, than if I spoke to them in an unknown tongue, for they are only to be spiritually discerned. To you then that are spiritual do I speak, to you who are justified by faith, and feel the blessed Spirit of Jesus Christ working upon your hearts, you can judge of what I say; you have already (I am persuaded) been as it were filled with new wine by the inspiration of his Holy Spirit. But alas! You have not yet had half your portion; these are only earnests, and in comparison but shadows of good things to come; our Lord keeps his best wine for you till the last; and though you have drunk deep of it already, yet he intends to give you more. He will not leave you, till he has filled you to the brim, till you are ready to cry out, Lord, stay your hand, your poor creatures can hold no more! Be not straitened in your own bowels [inner man], since Jesus Christ is not straitened in his. Open your hearts as wide as ever you will, the Spirit of the Lord shall fill them. Christ deals with true believers, as Elijah did with the poor woman whose oil increased to pay her husband's debts; as long as she brought pitchers, the oil continued. It did not cease till she ceased bringing vessels to contain it. My brethren, our hearts are like those pitchers; open them freely by faith, and the oil of God's free gift, the oil of gladness, the love of God through Christ, shall be continually pouring in; for believers are to be filled with all the fullness of God.

Fourth, our Lord's turning water into wine, and keeping the best until last, may show forth the glory of the latter days of his marriage feast with his church. Great things God has done already, of which millions of saints have rejoiced, and do yet rejoice. Great things God is doing now, but yet, my brethren, we shall see greater things than these. It is meet, right, and our bounden duty, to give thanks unto God, even the Father; for many righteous men have desired to see the things which we see, and have not seen them; and to hear the things which we hear, and have not heard them. But still there are more excellent things behind. Glorious things are spoken of these times, "when the earth shall be filled with the knowledge of the Lord, as the waters cover the sea." There is a general expectation among the people of God, when the partition wall between Jew and Gentile shall be broken down, and all Israel be saved. Happy those who live when God does this. They shall see Satan, like lightning, fall from heaven. They shall not weep, as the Jews did at the building of the second temple. No, they shall rejoice with exceedingly great joy. For all the former glory of the Christian church shall be nothing in comparison of that glory which shall excel. Then shall they cry out with the governor of the feast: "Thou hast kept the good wine until now!"

Fifth, and last, this shows us the happiness of that blessed state, when we shall all sit together at the marriage supper of the Lamb, and drink of the new wine in his eternal and glorious kingdom!

The rewards which Jesus Christ confers on his faithful servants, and the comforts of his love wherewith he comforts them, while pilgrims here on earth, are often so exceedingly great, that was it not promised, it were almost presumption for them to hope for any reward hereafter. But, my brethren, all the manifestations of God that we can possibly be favored with here, when compared with the glory that is to be revealed in us, are no more than a drop of water when compared with an unbounded ocean. Though Christ frequently fills his saints even to the brim, yet their corruptible bodies weigh down their souls and cause them to cry, "Who shall deliver us from these bodies of death?" These earthly tabernacles can hold no more: But, blessed be God, these earthly tabernacles are to be dissolved; this corruptible is to put on incorruption; this mortal is to put on immortality: and when God shall cause all his glory to pass before us, then shall we cry out, "Lord, you have kept your good wine until now. We have drunk deeply of your spirit; we have heard glorious things spoken of this your city, O God! But we now find that not the half, not the thousandth part has been told us." Oh, the invisible realities of the world of faith! Eye has not seen, ear has not heard, neither has it entered into the heart of the greatest saint to conceive how Christ will show forth his glory there! St. Paul, who was carried up into the third heavens, could give us little or no account of it. And well he might not—for he heard and saw such things as is not possible for a man clothed with flesh and blood to utter. While I am thinking, and only speaking of those things unto you, I am almost carried beyond myself. I think I now receive some little foretastes of that new wine which I hope to drink with you in the heavenly kingdom forever and ever.

And wherefore do you think I have been saying these things? Many, perhaps, may be ready to say, "to manifest your own vainglory." But it is a small matter with me to be judged of man's judgment. He that judges me is the Lord. He knows that I have spoken of his miracle, only for the same end for which he at first performed it, and which I at first proposed, that is, "to show forth his glory," that you also may be brought to believe on him.

Did I come to preach myself, and not Christ Jesus my Lord, I would come to you, not in this plainness of speech, but with the enticing words of man's wisdom. Did I desire to please natural men, I need not preach here in the wilderness. I hope my heart aims at nothing else, than what our Lord's great forerunner aimed at, and which ought to be the business of every gospel minister, that is, to point out to you the God-man Christ Jesus. "Behold then (by faith behold) the Lamb of God, who taketh away the sins of the world." Look unto him, and be saved. You have heard how he manifested, and will yet manifest, his glory to true believers; and why then, O sinners, will you not believe in him? I say, "O sinners," for now I have spoken to the saints, I have many things to say to you. And may God give you all a hearing ear and an obedient heart! Amen!

The Lord Jesus who showed forth his glory above seventeen hundred years ago, has made a marriage feast, and offers to espouse all sinners to himself, and to make them flesh of his flesh, and bone of his bone. He is willing to be united to you by one spirit. In every age, at sundry times, and after diverse manners, he has sent forth his servants, and they have bidden many, but yet, my brethren, there is room. The Lord therefore now has given a commission in these last days to others of his servants, even to compel poor sinners by the cords of love to come in. For our Master's house must and shall be filled. He will not shed his gracious blood in vain. Come then, come to the marriage. Let this be the day of your espousals with Jesus Christ; he is willing to receive you, though other lords have had dominion over you. Come then to the marriage. Behold, the oxen and fatlings are killed, and all things are ready; let me hear you say—as Rebecca did when they asked her whether she would go and be a wife to Isaac—oh, let me hear you say, "We will come." Indeed you will not repent it. The Lord shall turn your water into wine. He shall fill your souls with marrow and fatness and cause you to praise him with joyful lips.

Do not say, you are miserable and poor and blind and naked, and therefore ashamed to come, for it is to such that this invitation is now sent. The polite, the rich, the busy, self-righteous Pharisees of this generation have been bidden already, but they have rejected the counsel of God against themselves. They are too deeply engaged in going, one to his country house, another to his merchandise. They are so deeply wedded to the pomps and vanities of this wicked world, that they, as it were with one consent, have made excuse. And though they have been often called in their own synagogues, yet all the return they make is to thrust us out and thereby in effect say, they will not come. But God forbid, my brethren, that you should learn of them; no, since our Lord condescends to call first (because if left to yourselves you would never call after him), let me beseech you to answer him, as he answered for you, when called upon by infinite offended justice to die for your sins: "Lo! I come to do thy will, O God!" What if you are miserable and poor and blind and naked, that is no excuse; faith is the only wedding garment which Christ requires; he does not call you because you already are, but because he intends to make you, saints. It pities him to see you naked. He wants to cover you with his righteousness. In short, he desires to show forth his glory, that is, his free love through your faith in him. Not but that he will be glorified, whether you believe in him or not; for the infinitely free love of Jesus Christ will be ever the same, whether you believe it, or so receive it, or the contrary. But our Lord will not always send out his servants in vain, to call you; the time will come when he will say, "None of those which were bidden, and would not come, shall taste of my supper." Our Lord is a God of justice, as well as of love; and if sinners will not take hold of his golden scepter, verily he will bruise them with his iron rod. It is for your sakes, O sinners, and not his own, that he thus condescends to invite you: suffer him then to show forth his glory, even the glory of the exceeding riches of his free grace, by believing on him: "For we are saved by grace through faith." It was grace, free grace, that moved the Father so to love the world, as to "give his only begotten Son, that whosoever believeth in him should not perish, but have everlasting life"! It was grace that made the Son to come down and die. It was grace, free grace, that moved the Holy Ghost to undertake to sanctify the elect people of God: and it was grace, free grace, that moved our Lord Jesus Christ to send forth his ministers to call poor sinners this day. Let me not then, my brethren, go without my errand. Why will you not believe in him? Will the devil do such great and good things for you as Christ will? No indeed, he will not. Perhaps, he may give you to drink at first of a little brutish pleasure; but what will he give you to drink at last? A cup of fury and of trembling; a never-dying worm, a self-condemning conscience, and the bitter pains of eternal death. But as for the servants of Jesus Christ, it is not so with them. No, he keeps his best wine till the last. And though he may cause you to drink of the brook in the way to heaven and of the cup of affliction, yet he sweetens it with a sense of his goodness and makes it pleasant drink, such as their souls do love. I appeal to the experience of any saint here present (as I doubt not but there are many such in this field), whether Christ has not proved faithful, ever since you have been espoused to him? Has he not showed forth his glory, ever since you have believed on him?

[margin note: open field preaching view]

  And now, sinners, what have you to object? I see you are all silent, and well you may. For if you will not be drawn by the cords of infinite and everlasting love, what will draw you? I could urge many terrors of the Lord to persuade you; but if the love of Jesus Christ will not constrain you, your case is desperate. Remember then this day I have invited all, even the worst of sinners, to be married to the Lord Jesus. If you perish, remember you do not perish for lack of invitation. You yourselves shall stand forth at the last day, and I here give you a summons to meet me at the judgment seat of Christ, and to clear both my Master and me. Would weeping, would tears, prevail on you, I could wish my head were waters, and my eyes fountains of tears, that I might weep out every argument and melt you into love. Would anything I could do, or suffer, influence your hearts, I think I could bear to pluck out my eyes, or even to lay down my life, for your sakes. Or was I sure to prevail on you by importunity, I could continue my discourse till midnight, I would wrestle with you even till the morning watch, as Jacob did with the angel, and would not go away till I had overcome. But such power belongs only unto the Lord, I can only invite; it is he only can work in you both to will and to do after his good pleasure; it is his property to take away the heart of stone and give you a heart of flesh; it is his Spirit that must convince you of unbelief, and of the everlasting righteousness of his dear Son; it is he alone must give faith to apply his righteousness to your hearts; it is he alone can give you a wedding garment and bring you to sit down and drink new wine in his kingdom. As to spirituals we are quite dead, and have no more power to turn to God of ourselves than Lazarus had to raise himself, after he had lain stinking in the grave four days. If you can go, O man, and breathe upon all the dry bones that lie in the graves and bid them live; if you can take your mantle and divide yonder river, as Elijah did the river Jordan; then will we believe you have a power to turn to God of yourself; but as you must despair of the one, so you must despair of the other, without Christ's quickening grace; in him is your only help; fly to him then by faith; say unto him, as the poor leper did, "Lord, if thou wilt," thou canst make me willing; and he will stretch forth the right hand of his power to assist and relieve you. He will sweetly guide you by his wisdom on earth and afterward take you up to partake of his glory in heaven.

To his mercy therefore, and almighty protection, do I earnestly, humbly, and most affectionately commit you: the Lord bless you and keep you; the Lord lift up the light of his blessed countenance upon you, and give you all peace and joy in believing, now and forevermore!

The Duty of Searching the Scriptures

—m—

"Search the Scriptures." —JOHN 5:39

When the Sadducees came to our blessed Lord, and put to him the question, "Whose wife that woman should be in the next life, who had seven husbands in this?" he told them they "erred, not knowing the Scriptures." And if we would know from where all the errors that have overspread the church of Christ first arose, we should find that, in a great measure, they flowed from the same fountain: ignorance of the Word of God.

Our blessed Lord, though he was the eternal God, yet as man, he made the Scriptures his constant rule and guide. And therefore, when he was asked by the lawyer, "Which was the great commandment of the law?" he referred him to his Bible for an answer, "What readest thou?" And thus, when led by the Spirit to be tempted by the devil, he repelled all his assaults with "it is written."

A sufficient confutation, this, of their opinion who say, "The Spirit only, and not the Spirit by the Word, is to be our rule of action." If so, our Savior, who had the Spirit without measure, needed not always have referred to the written Word.

But how few copy after the example of Christ? How many are there who do not regard the Word of God at all, but throw the sacred oracles aside, as an antiquated book, fit only for illiterate men?

Such do greatly err, not knowing what the Scriptures are. I shall therefore—

First, show that it is everyone's duty to search them.

And second, lay down some directions for you to search them with advantage.

I. I am to show that it is every person's duty to search the Scriptures.

By the Scriptures, I understand the Law and the Prophets, and those books which have in all ages been accounted canonical, and which make up that volume commonly called the Bible.

These are emphatically styled the Scriptures, and, in one place, the Scriptures of Truth, as though no other books deserved the name of true writings or Scripture in comparison of them.

They are not of any private interpretation, authority, or invention, but holy men of old wrote them, as they were moved by the Holy Ghost.

The fountain of God's revealing himself thus to mankind was our fall in Adam, and the necessity of our new birth in Christ Jesus. And if we search the Scriptures as we ought, we shall find the sum and substance, the alpha and omega, the beginning and end of them, is to lead us to a knowledge of these two great truths.

All the threats, promises and precepts, all the exhortations and doctrines contained therein, all the rites, ceremonies and sacrifices appointed under the Jewish law, what's more, almost all the historical parts of holy Scripture, suppose our being fallen in Adam and either point out to us a mediator to come or speak of him as already come in the flesh.

Had man continued in a state of innocence, he would not have needed an outward revelation, because the law of God was so deeply written in the tables of his heart. But having eaten the forbidden fruit, he incurred the displeasure of God and lost the divine image, and therefore without an external revelation, could never tell how God would be reconciled unto him or how he should be saved from the misery and darkness of his fallen nature.

That these truths are so, I need not refer you to any other book, than your own hearts.

For unless we are fallen creatures, whence those abominable corruptions which daily arise in our hearts? We could not come thus corrupt out of the hands of our Maker, because he being goodness itself could make nothing but what is like himself, holy, just, and good. And that we want to be delivered from these disorders of our nature is evident, because we find an unwillingness within ourselves to own we are thus depraved, and are always striving to appear to others of a quite different frame and temper of mind than what we are.

I appeal to the experience of the most learned disputer against divine revelation, whether he does not find in himself, that he is naturally proud, angry, revengeful, and full of other passions contrary to the purity, holiness, and long-suffering of God. And is not this a demonstration that some way or other he is fallen from God? And I appeal also, whether at the same time that he finds these hurtful lusts in his heart, he does not strive to seem amiable, courteous, kind, and affable; and is not this a manifest proof, that he senses he is miserable and wants, he knows not how, to be redeemed or delivered from it?

Here then, God by his Word steps in and opens to his view such a scene of divine love, and infinite goodness in the holy Scriptures, that none but men of such corrupt and reprobate minds as our modern deists would shut their eyes against it.

What does God in his written Word do more or less, than show you, O man, how you are fallen into that blindness, darkness, and misery, of which you feel and complain? And, at the same time, he points out the way to what you desire, even how you may be redeemed out of it by believing in, and copying after, the Son of his love.

As I told you before, so I tell you again, upon these two truths rest all divine revelation. It being given us for no other end, but to show our misery and our happiness; our fall and recovery; or, in one word, after what manner we died in Adam, and how in Christ we may again be made alive.

Hence, then arises the necessity of searching the Scriptures; for since they are nothing else but the grand charter of our salvation, the revelation of a covenant made by God with men in Christ, and a light to guide us into the way of peace; it follows that all are obliged to read and search them, because all are equally fallen from God, all equally stand in need of being informed how they must be restored to, and again united with, him.

How foolishly then do the disputing infidels of this generation act, who are continually either calling for signs from heaven or seeking for outward evidence to prove the truth of divine revelation? Whereas what they so earnestly seek for is nigh unto, even within, them. For let them but consult their own hearts, they cannot but feel what they want. Let them but consult the lively oracles of God, and they cannot but see a remedy revealed for all their wants, and that the written Word does as exactly answer the wants and desires of their hearts, as face answers to face in the water. Where then is the scribe, where is the wise, where is the solidity of the reasoning of the disputers of this world? Has not God revealed himself unto them, as plain as their own hearts could wish? And yet they require a sign, but there shall no other sign be given them. For if they believe not a revelation which is every way so suited to their wants, neither will they be persuaded though one should rise from the dead.

But this discourse is not designed so much for them that believe not as for them, who both know and believe that the Scriptures contain a revelation which came from God, and that it is their duty, as being chief parties concerned, not only to read but search them also.

II. I pass on, therefore, in the second place, to lay down some directions, how you may search them with advantage.

First, have always in view, the end for which the Scriptures were written, even to show us the way of salvation, by Jesus Christ.

"Search the Scriptures," says our blessed Lord, "for they are they that testify of me." Look, therefore, always for Christ in the Scripture. He is the treasure hid in the field, both of the Old and New Testaments. In the Old you

Looking for Jesus in all the Bible OT & NT

will find him under prophecies, types, sacrifices, and shadows; in the New, manifested in the flesh, to become a propitiation for our sins as a priest, and as a prophet to reveal the whole will of his heavenly Father.

Have Christ, then, always in view when you are reading the Word of God, and this, like the star in the east, will guide you to the Messiah, will serve as a key to everything that is obscure, and unlock to you the wisdom and riches of all the mysteries of the kingdom of God.

Second, search the Scriptures with a humble childlike disposition.

For whosoever does not read them with this temper shall in nowise enter into the knowledge of the things contained in them. For God hides the sense of them, from those that are wise and prudent in their own eyes, and reveals them only to babes in Christ: who think they know nothing yet as they ought to know; who hunger and thirst after righteousness and humbly desire to be fed with the sincere milk of the Word, that they may grow thereby.

Fancy yourselves therefore, when you are searching the Scriptures, especially when you are reading the New Testament, to be with Mary sitting at the feet of the holy Jesus; and be as willing to learn what God shall teach you, as Samuel was, when he said, "Speak, Lord, for thy servant heareth."

Oh, that the unbelievers would pull down every high thought and imagination that exalts itself against the revealed will of God! Oh, that they would, like newborn babes, desire to be fed with the pure milk of the Word! Then we should have them no longer scoffing at divine revelation, nor would they read the Bible anymore with the same intent the Philistines brought our Samson, to make sport at it; but they would see the divine image and superscription written upon every line. They would hear God speaking unto their souls by it and consequently be built up in the knowledge and fear of him, who is the Author thereof.

Third, search the Scriptures, with a sincere intention to put in practice what you read.

A desire to do the will of God is the only way to know it; if any man will do my will, says Jesus Christ, "he shall know of my doctrine, whether it be of God, or whether I speak of myself." As he also speaks in another place to his disciples, "To you (who are willing to practice your duty) it is given to know the mysteries of the kingdom of God, but to those that are without (who only want to raise cavils against my doctrine) all these things are spoken in parables, that seeing they may see and not understand, and hearing they may hear and not perceive." *Oh that I would see & understand*

Oh that I would hear & perceive

For it is but just in God to send those strong delusions, that they may believe a lie, and to conceal the knowledge of himself from all such as do not seek him with a single intention.

Jesus Christ is the same now, as formerly, to those who desire to know from his Word, who he is that they may believe on and live by; and to him he will reveal himself as clearly as he did to the woman of Samaria, when he said, "I that speak to thee am he," or as he did to the man that was born blind, whom the Jews had cast out for his name's sake, "He that talketh with thee, is he." But to those who consult his Word with a desire neither to know him nor keep his commandments, but either merely for their entertainment or to scoff at the simplicity of the manner in which he is revealed, to those, I say, he never will reveal himself, though they should search the Scriptures to all eternity. As he never would tell those whether he was the Messiah or not, who put that question to him either out of curiosity or that they might have whereof to accuse him.

Fourth, in order to search the Scriptures still more effectually, make an application of everything you read to your own hearts.

For whatever was written in the Book of God was written for our learning. And what Christ said unto those in times past, we must look upon as spoken to us also: for since the holy Scriptures are nothing but a revelation from God, how fallen man is to be restored by Jesus Christ: all the precepts, threats, and promises, belong to us and to our children, as well as to those to whom they were immediately made known.

Thus the apostle, when he tells us that he lived by the faith of the Son of God, adds, "who died and gave himself for me." It is this application of Jesus Christ to our hearts that makes his redemption effectual to each of us.

And it is this application of all the doctrinal and historical parts of Scripture when we are reading them over, that must render them profitable to us, as they were designed for reproof, for correction, for instruction in righteousness, and to make every child of God perfect, thoroughly furnished to every good work.

I dare appeal to the experience of every spiritual reader of holy Writ, whether or not, if he consulted the Word of God in this manner, he was not at all times and at all seasons as plainly directed how to act, as though he had consulted the Urim and Thummim, which was upon the high priest's breast. For this is the way God now reveals himself to man: not by making new revelations but by applying general things that are revealed already to every sincere reader's heart.

Oh that I could inquire of the pious Mr. Whitefield, why then in NT teaching does exist the office of Prophet?

And this, by the way, answers an objection made by those who say, "The Word of God is not a perfect rule of action, because it cannot direct us how to act or how to determine in particular cases, or what place to go to, when we are in doubt, and therefore, the Spirit, and not the Word, is to be our rule of action."

But this I deny, and affirm on the contrary, that God at all times, circumstances, and places, though never so minute, never so particular, will, if we diligently seek the assistance of his Holy Spirit, apply general things to our hearts, and thereby, to use the words of the holy Jesus, will lead us into all truth and give us the particular assistance we want.

But this leads me to a fifth direction how to search the Scriptures with profit: Labor to attain that Spirit by which they were written.

For the natural man discerns not the words of the Spirit of God, because they are spiritually discerned; the words that Christ has spoken, they are spirit, and they are life, and can be no more understood as to the true sense and meaning of them, by the mere natural man, than a person who never had learned a language can understand another speaking in it. The Scriptures therefore have not unfitly been compared, by some, to the cloud which went before the Israelites; they are dark and hard to be understood by the natural man, as the cloud appeared dark to the Egyptians; but they are light, they are life, to Christians indeed, as that same cloud which seemed dark to Pharaoh and his house appeared bright and altogether glorious to the Israel of God.

It was the want of the assistance of this Spirit that made Nicodemus, a teacher of Israel, and a ruler of the Jews, so utterly ignorant in the doctrine of regeneration: for being only a natural man, he could not tell how that thing could be; it was the want of this Spirit that made our Savior's disciples, though he so frequently conversed with them, daily mistake the nature of the doctrines he delivered; and it is because the natural veil is not taken off from their hearts that so many who now pretend to search the Scriptures still see no farther than into the bare letter of them, and continue entire strangers to the spiritual meaning couched under every parable and contained in almost all the precepts of the Book of God. *as Christ told Peter, men did not reveal this to you

Indeed, how should it be otherwise, for God being a Spirit, he cannot communicate himself any otherwise than in a spiritual manner to the hearts of men; and consequently if we are strangers to his Spirit, we must continue strangers to his Word, because it is altogether like himself, spiritual. Labor therefore earnestly for to attain this blessed Spirit; otherwise, your understandings will never be opened to understand the Scriptures aright; and remember, prayer is one of the most immediate means to get this Holy Spirit.

Therefore, sixth, let me advise you, before you read the Scriptures, to pray that Christ, according to his promise, would send his Spirit to guide you into all truth; intersperse short ejaculations while you are engaged in reading; pray over every word and verse, if possible; and when you close up the Book, most earnestly beseech God, that the words which you have read may be inwardly engrafted into your hearts and bring forth in you the fruits of a good life.

Do this, and you will, with a holy violence, draw down God's Holy Spirit into your hearts; you will experience his gracious influence, and feel him enlightening, quickening, and inflaming your souls by the Word of God; you will then not only read, but mark, learn, and inwardly digest what you read: and the Word of God will be meat indeed, and drink indeed unto your souls; you then will be as Apollos was, powerful in the Scriptures; be scribes ready instructed to the kingdom of God, and bring out of the good treasures of your heart, things both from the Old and New Testaments, to entertain all you converse with.

One direction more, which shall be the last, seventh: read the Scripture constantly, or, to use our Savior's expression in the text, "search the Scriptures"; dig in them as for hid treasure; for here is a manifest allusion to those who dig in mines; and our Savior would thereby teach us that we must take as much pains in constantly reading his Word, if we would grow wise thereby, as those who dig for gold and silver. The Scriptures contain the deep things of God, and therefore can never be sufficiently searched into by a careless, superficial, cursory way of reading them, but by an industrious, close, and humble application.

The psalmist makes it the characteristic of a good man, that he "meditates on God's law day and night." And "this book of the law (says God to Joshua) shall not go out of thy mouth, but thou shalt meditate therein day and night"; for then you shall make your way prosperous, and you shall have good success. Search therefore the Scriptures, not only devoutly but daily, for in them are the words of eternal life; wait constantly at wisdom's gate, and she will then, and not till then, display and lay open to you her heavenly treasures. You that are rich are without excuse if you do not; and you that are poor ought to take heed and improve that little time you have: for by the Scriptures you are to be acquitted, and by the Scriptures you are to be condemned at the last day.

But perhaps you have no taste for this despised Book; perhaps plays, romances, and books of polite entertainment suit your taste better; if this be your case, give me leave to tell you, your taste is vitiated, and unless corrected by the Spirit and Word of God, you shall never enter into his heavenly kingdom: for unless you delight in God here, how will you be made meet to dwell with him hereafter? Is it a sin then, you will say, to read useless impertinent books? I answer, yes. And that for the same reason, as it is a sin to indulge useless conversation, because both immediately tend to grieve and quench that Spirit, by which alone we can be sealed to the day of redemption. You may reply, "How shall we know this?" Why, put in practice the precept in the text; search the Scripture in the manner that has been recommended, and then you will be convinced of the danger, sinfulness, and unsatisfactoriness of reading any others than the Book of God, or such as are written in the same spirit. You will then say, "When I was a child, and ignorant of the excellency of the Word of God, I read what the world calls harmless books, as other children in knowledge, though old in years, have done, and still do; but now that I have tasted the good word of life, and am come to a more perfect knowledge of Christ Jesus my Lord, I put away these childish, trifling things, and am determined to read no other books but what lead me to a knowledge of myself and of Christ Jesus."

Search therefore the Scriptures, my dear brethren; taste and see how good the Word of God is, and then you will never leave that heavenly manna, that angel's food, to feed on dry husks, that light bread, those trifling, sinful compositions, in which men of false taste delight themselves: no, you will then disdain such poor entertainment, and blush that yourselves once were fond of it. The Word of God will then be sweeter to you than honey, and the honeycomb, and dearer than gold and silver; your souls by reading it, will be filled as it were, with marrow and fatness, and your hearts insensibly molded into the spirit of its blessed Author. In short, you will be guided by God's wisdom here, and conducted by the light of his divine Word into glory hereafter.

Saul's Conversion

—〰—

But Saul increased the more in strength, and confounded the Jews which dwelt at Damascus, proving that this is very Christ. —ACTS 9:22

It is an undoubted truth, however paradoxical it may seem to natural men, that "whosoever will live godly in Christ Jesus, shall suffer persecution." And therefore it is very remarkable that our blessed Lord, in his glorious Sermon on the Mount, after he had been pronouncing those blessed who were poor in spirit, meek, pure in heart, and suchlike, immediately adds (and spends no less than three verses in this beatitude): "Blessed are they who are persecuted for righteousness' sake." No one ever was, or ever will be, endowed with the forementioned graces in any degree, but he will be persuaded for it in a measure. There is an irreconcilable enmity between the seed of the woman and the seed of the serpent. And if we are not of the world, but show by our fruits that we are of the number of those whom Jesus Christ has chosen out of this world, for that very reason the world will hate us. As this is true of every particular Christian, so it is true of every Christian church in general. For some years past we have heard but little of a public persecution. Why? Because but little of the power of godliness has prevailed among all denominations. The strong man armed has had full possession of most professors' hearts, and therefore he has let them rest in a false peace. But we may assure ourselves, when Jesus Christ begins to gather in his elect in any remarkable manner, and opens an effectual door for preaching the everlasting gospel, persecution will flame out, and Satan and his emissaries will do their utmost (though all in vain) to stop the work of God. Thus it was in the first ages, thus it is in our days, and thus it will be, till time shall be no more.

Christians and Christian churches must then expect enemies. Our chief concern should be to learn how to behave toward them in a Christian manner, for, unless we make good heed to ourselves, we shall embitter our spirits and act unbecoming the followers of that Lord "who, when he was reviled, reviled not again; when he suffered, threatened not; and, as a lamb before his shearers is dumb, so opened he not his mouth." But what motive shall we make use of to bring ourselves to this blessed lamblike temper? Next to the immediate operation of the Holy Spirit upon our hearts, I know of no consideration more conducive to teach us long-suffering toward our most bitter persecutors, than this, that, for all we know to the contrary, some of those very persons, who are now persecuting, may be chosen from all eternity by God, and hereafter called in time, to edify and build up the church of Christ.

The persecutor Saul, mentioned in the words of the text (and whose conversion, God willing, I propose to treat on in the following discourse), is a noble instance of this kind.

I say a persecutor, and that a bloody one, for see how he is introduced in the beginning of this chapter: "And Saul, yet breathing out threatenings and slaughter against the disciples of our Lord, went unto the high priest, and desired of him letters to Damascus to the synagogues, that if he found any of this way, whether they were men or women, he might bring them bound to Jerusalem."

"And Saul, yet breathing out." This implies that he had been a persecutor before. To prove which, we need only look back to the seventh chapter, where we shall find him so very remarkably active at Stephen's death, that "the witnesses laid down their clothes at a young man's feet, whose name was Saul." He seems, though young, to be in some authority. Perhaps, for his zeal against the Christians, he was preferred in the church and was allowed to sit in the great council or Sanhedrin; for we are told that "Saul was consenting unto his death" (Acts 8:1); and again, at verse 3, he is brought in as exceeding all in his opposition; for thus speaks the Evangelist, "As for Saul, he made havoc of the church, entering into every house, and haling men and women, committed them to prison." One would have imagined that this should have satisfied, at least abated, the fury of this young zealot. No; being exceedingly mad against them, as he himself informs Agrippa, and having made havoc of all in Jerusalem, he now is resolved to persecute the disciples of the Lord, even to strange cities; and therefore yet breathing out threatenings. "Breathing out"— the words are very emphatic and expressive of his bitter enmity. It was as natural to him now to threaten the Christians, as it was for him to breathe: he could scarce speak, but it was some threatenings against them. What's more, he not only breathed out threatenings, but slaughters also (and those who threaten would also slaughter, if it were in their power) against the disciples of the Lord. Insatiable therefore as hell, finding he could not confute or stop the Christians by force of argument, he is resolved to do it by force of arms; and therefore went to the high priest (for there never was a persecution yet without a high priest at the head of it) and desired of him letters, issued out of his spiritual court, to the synagogues or ecclesiastical courts at Damascus, giving him authority, that "if he found any of this way, whether they were men or women, he might bring them bound unto Jerusalem," I suppose, there

*only here does it occur to me that the great Evangelist Paul, had a "blood thirst" once having part in Stephen's execution

to be arraigned and condemned in the high priest's court. Observe how he speaks of the Christians. Luke, who wrote the Acts, calls them "disciples of the Lord," and Saul styles them "men and women of this way." I doubt not but he represented them as a company of upstart enthusiasts, that had lately gotten into a new method or way of living; that would not be content with the temple service, but they must be righteous overmuch, and have their private meetings or conventicles, and break bread, as they called it, from house to house, to the great disturbance of the established clergy, and to the utter subversion of all order and decency. I do not hear that the high priest makes any objection: no, he was as willing to grant letters as Saul was to ask them; and wonderfully pleased within himself to find he had such an active zealot to employ against the Christians.

Well then, a judicial process is immediately issued out, with the high priest's seal affixed to it. And now I think I see the young persecutor finely equipped, and pleasing himself with thoughts, how triumphantly he should ride back with the "men and women of this way," dragging them after him to Jerusalem.

What a condition may we imagine the poor disciples at Damascus were in at this time! No doubt they had heard of Saul's imprisoning and making havoc of the saints at Jerusalem, and we may well suppose they were apprised of his design against them. I am persuaded this was a growing, because a trying, time with these dear people. Oh, how did they wrestle with God in prayer, beseeching him either to deliver them from, or give them grace sufficient to ✱ enable them to bear up under, the fury of their persecutors? The high priest, doubtless with the rest of his reverend brethren, flattered themselves, that they should now put an effectual stop to this growing heresy and waited with impatience for Saul's return.

But "he that sitteth in heaven laughs them to scorn, the Lord has them in derision." And therefore, "As Saul journeyed, and came even near unto Damascus," perhaps to the very gates (our Lord permitting this, to try the faith of his disciples, and more conspicuously to baffle the designs of his enemies), "suddenly (at midday, as he acquaints Agrippa) there shined round about him a light from heaven," a light brighter than the sun; "and he fell to the earth (why not into hell?) and heard a voice saying unto him, Saul, Saul, why persecutest thou me?'" (Acts 9:3–4). The word is doubled, Saul, Saul, like that of our Lord to Martha, "Martha, Martha," or the prophet, "O earth, earth, earth." Perhaps these words came like thunder to his soul; that they were spoken audibly, we are assured from verse 7: "His companions heard the voice." Our Lord now arrests the persecuting zealot, calling him by name; for the

✱ Oh Lord like them we see what is coming, Lord deliver us or increase Your grace toward us to fulfil Your commission & thank You Father

For word never does us good, till we find it spoken to us in particular. "Saul, Saul, why persecutest thou me?" Put the emphasis upon the word *why*. What evil have I done? Put it upon the word *persecutest*. Why *persecutest*? I suppose Saul thought he was not persecuting; no, he was only putting the laws of the ecclesiastical court into execution; but Jesus, whose eyes are as a flame of fire, saw through the hypocrisy of his heart, that, notwithstanding his specious pretenses, all this proceeded from a persecuting spirit, and secret enmity of heart against God; and therefore says, "Why *persecutest* thou me?" Put the emphasis upon the word *me*. Why persecutest thou *me*? Alas! Saul was not persecuting Christ, was he? He was only taking care to prevent innovations in the church, and bringing a company of enthusiasts to justice, who otherwise would overturn the established constitution. But Jesus says, "Why persecutest thou me?" For what is done to Christ's disciples, he takes as done to himself, whether it be good, or whether it be evil. He that touches Christ's disciples, touches the apple of his eye; and they who persecute the followers of our Lord would persecute our Lord himself, was he again to come and tabernacle among us.

I do not find that Saul gives any reason why he did persecute; no, he was struck dumb; as every persecutor will be, when Jesus Christ puts this same question to them at the terrible day of judgment. But being pricked at the heart, no doubt with a sense not only of this, but of all his other offenses against the great God, he said, "Who art thou, Lord?" (v. 5). See how soon God can change the heart and voice of his most bitter enemies. Not many days ago, Saul was not only blaspheming Christ himself, but, as much as in him lay, compelling others to blaspheme also; but now he, who before was an impostor, is called Lord: "Who art thou, Lord?" This admirably points out the way in which God's Spirit works upon the heart: it first powerfully convinces of sin, and of our damnable state; and then puts us upon inquiring after Jesus Christ. Saul being struck to the ground, or pricked to the heart, cries out after Jesus, "Who art thou, Lord?" As many of you that were never so far made sensible of your damnable state, as to be made feelingly to seek after Jesus Christ; were never yet truly convicted by, much less converted to, God—may the Lord, who struck Saul, effectually now strike all my Christless hearers, and set them upon inquiring after Jesus, as their all in all! Saul said, "'Who art thou, Lord?' And the Lord said, 'I am Jesus whom thou persecutest.'" Never did anyone inquire truly after Jesus Christ, but Christ made a saving discovery of himself, to his soul. It should seem, our Lord appeared to him in person; for Ananias, afterward, says, "The Lord who appeared to thee in the way which thou camest"; though this may only imply Christ's meeting him in the way, it is not much matter: it is plain Christ here speaks to him, and says, "I am Jesus, whom thou persecutest." It is remarkable, how our Lord takes to himself the name of Jesus; for it is a name in which he delights, I am Jesus, a Savior of my people, both from the guilt and power of their sins; "a Jesus, whom thou persecutest." This seems to be spoken to convince Saul more and more of his sin; and I doubt not but that every word was sharper than a two-edged sword, and came like so many daggers to his heart. Oh, how did these words affect him! A Jesus! A Savior! And yet I am persecuting him! This strikes him with horror; but then the word *Jesus,* though he was a persecutor, might give him some hope. However, our dear Lord, to convince Saul that he was to be saved by grace, and that he was not afraid of his power and enmity, tells him, "It is hard for thee to kick against the pricks." As much as to say, though he was persecuting, yet he could not overthrow the church of Christ: for he would sit as King upon his holy hill of Zion; the malice of men or devils should never be able to prevail against him.

Verse 6: "And he, trembling and astonished, said, 'Lord, what wilt thou have me to do?'" Those who think Saul had a discovery of Jesus made to his heart before, think that this question is the result of his faith, and that he now desires to know what he shall do, out of gratitude for what the Lord had done for his soul; in this sense it may be understood; and I have made use of it as an instance to prove that faith will work by love; but perhaps it may be more agreeable to the context, if we suppose that Saul had only some distant discovery of Christ made to him, and not of full assurance of faith, for we are told, "he trembling and astonished," trembling at the thoughts of his persecuting a Jesus, and astonished at his own vileness, and the infinite condescension of this Jesus, cries out, "Lord, what wilt thou have me to do?" Persons under soul trouble, and sore conviction, would be glad to do anything, or comply on any terms, to get peace with God. "Arise (says our Lord), and go into the city, and it shall be told thee what thou shalt do."

And here we will leave Saul a while, and see what is become of his companions. But what shall we say? God is a sovereign agent; his sacred Spirit blows when and where it lists; "he will have mercy on whom he will have mercy." Saul is taken, but, as far as we know to the contrary, his fellow travelers are left to perish in their sins, for we are told that "the men who journeyed with him stood, indeed, speechless, and hearing a confused voice" (v. 7); I say, "a confused voice," for so the word signifies, and must be so interpreted, in order to reconcile it with Acts 22:9, where Saul, giving an account of these men, tells Agrippa, "They heard not the voice of him that spake to me." They heard a voice, a confused noise, but not the articulate voice of him that spoke to Saul, and therefore remained unconverted. For what are all ordinances, all, even the most extraordinary dispensations of providence, without that Christ speaks to the soul in them? Thus it is now under the word preached: many, like Saul's companions, are sometimes so struck with the outgoings of God appearing in the sanctuary, that they even stand speechless; they hear the preacher's voice, but not the voice of the Son of God, who, perhaps, at the same time is speaking effectually to many other hearts; this I have known often; and what shall we say to these things? Oh, the depth of the sovereignty of God! It is past finding out. Lord, I desire to adore what I cannot comprehend. "Even so, Father, for so it seemeth good in thy sight!"

But to return to Saul: the Lord bids him, "Arise and go into the city"; and we are told that "Saul arose from the earth; and when his eyes were opened (he was so overpowered with the greatness of the light that shone upon them, that) he saw no man; but they led him by the hand, and brought him into Damascus" (v. 8), that very city which was to be the place of his executing or imprisoning the disciples of the Lord. "And he was three days without sight, and neither did eat nor drink." But who can tell what horrors of conscience, what convulsions of soul, what deep and pungent convictions of sin he underwent during these three long days? It was this took away his appetite (for who can eat or drink when under a sense of the wrath of God for sin?) and, being to be greatly employed hereafter, he must be greatly humbled now; therefore the Lord leaves him three days groaning under the spirit of bondage and buffeted, no doubt, with the fiery darts of the devil, that, being tempted like unto his brethren, he might be able hereafter to succor those that were tempted. Had Saul applied to any of the blind guides of the Jewish church, under these circumstances, they would have said he was mad, or going beside himself, just as many carnal teachers and blind Pharisees now deal with, and so more and more distress, poor souls laboring under awakening convictions of their damnable state. But God often at our first awakenings visits us with sore trials, especially those who are, like Saul, to shine in the church, and to be used as instruments in bringing many sons to glory: those who are to be highly exalted must first be deeply humbled; and this I speak for the comfort of such, who may be now groaning under the spirit of bondage, and perhaps, like Saul, can neither eat nor drink; for I have generally observed that those who have had the deepest convictions have afterward been favored with the most precious communications, and enjoyed most of the divine presence in their souls. This was afterward remarkably exemplified in Saul, who was three days without sight, and neither did eat nor drink.

But will the Lord leave his poor servant in this distress? No; his Jesus (though Saul persecuted him) promised (and he will perform) that "it should be told him what he must do. And there was a certain disciple at Damascus, named Ananias; and unto him, said the Lord, in a vision, 'Ananias'; and he said, 'Behold, I am here, Lord.'" What a holy familiarity is there between Jesus Christ and regenerate souls! Ananias had been used to such love visits, and therefore knew the voice of his beloved. The Lord says, "Ananias"; Ananias says, "Behold, I am here, Lord." Thus it is that Christ now, as well as formerly, often talks with his children at sundry times and after diverse manners, as a man talks with his friend. But what has the Lord to say to Ananias?

Verse 11: "And the Lord said unto him, 'Arise, and go into the street, which is called Straight, and inquire in the house of Judas, for one called Saul of Tarsus' (see here for your comfort, O children of the most high God, what notice Jesus Christ takes of the street and the house where his own dear servants lodge), 'for, behold, he prayeth.'" But why is this ushered in with the word *behold*? What, was it such a wonder, to hear that Saul was praying? Why, Saul was a Pharisee, and therefore, no doubt, tasted and made long prayers; and, since we are told that he profited above many of his equals, I doubt not but he was taken notice of for his gift in prayer; and yet it seems that before these three days, Saul never prayed in his life. And why? Because, before these three days, he never felt himself a condemned creature: he was alive in his own opinion, because without a knowledge of the spiritual meaning of the law, he felt not a want of, and therefore before now cried not after, a Jesus; and consequently, though he might have said or made a prayer (as many Pharisees do nowadays) he never prayed a prayer; but now, "behold, he prayed indeed"; and this was urged as one reason why he was converted. None of God's children, as one observes, comes into the world stillborn; prayer is the very breath of the new creature: and therefore, if we are prayerless, we are Christless; if we never had the spirit of supplication, it is a sad sign that we never had the spirit of grace in our souls: and you may be assured you never did pray, unless you have felt yourselves sinners and seen the want of Jesus to be your Savior. May the Lord, whom I serve in the gospel of his dear Son, prick you all to the heart, and may it be said of you all, as it was of Saul, "Behold, they pray."

The Lord goes on to encourage Ananias to go to Saul; says he: "For he hath seen in a vision a man named Ananias, coming in, and putting his hand on him, that he might receive his sight" (v. 12). So that though Christ converted Saul immediately by himself, yet he will carry on the work, thus begun, by a minister. Happy they, who under soul troubles have such experienced guides, and as well acquainted with Jesus Christ as Ananias was; you that have such, make much of and be thankful for them; and you who have them not, trust in God; he will carry on his own work without them.

Doubtless, Ananias was a good man; but shall I commend him for his answer to our Lord? I commend him not, for says he: "Lord, I have heard by many of this man, how much evil he hath done to thy saints at Jerusalem: and here he hath authority from the chief priests to bind all that call upon thy name" (v. 13). I fear this answer proceeded from some relics of self-righteousness, as well as infidelity, that lay undiscovered in the heart of Ananias. "Arise (said our Lord), and go into the street, which is called Straight, and inquire in the house of Judas, for one called Saul of Tarsus; for, behold, he prayeth." One would think this was sufficient to satisfy him; but says Ananias, "Lord, I have heard by many of this man (he seems to speak of him with much contempt; for even good men are apt to think too contemptuously of those who are yet in their sins), how much evil he hath done to thy saints in Jerusalem: and here he hath authority from the chief priests to bind all that call upon Christ's name," should bind him [Ananias] also, if he went unto him; but the Lord silences all objections, with a "Go thy way, for he is a chosen vessel unto me, to bear my name before the Gentiles, and kings, and the children of Israel. For I will show him how great things he must suffer for my name's sake." Here God stops his mouth immediately, by asserting his sovereignty, and preaching to him the doctrine of election. And the frequent conversion of notorious sinners to God to me is one great proof, among a thousand others, of that precious, but too much exploded and sadly misrepresented, doctrine of God's electing love; for whence is it that such are taken, while thousands, not near so vile, die senseless and stupid? All the answer that can be given is, they are chosen vessels; "Go thy way (says God), for he is a chosen vessel unto me, to bear my name before the Gentiles, and kings, and the children of Israel. For I will show him how great things he must suffer for my name's sake." Observe what a close connection there is between doing and suffering for Christ. If any of my brethren in the ministry are present, let them bear what preferment we must expect, if we are called out to work remarkably for God: not great prebendaries or bishoprics, but great sufferings for our Lord's name's sake; these are the fruits of our labor: and he that will not contentedly suffer great things for preaching Christ is not worthy of him. Suffering will be found to be the best preferment, when we are called to give an account of our ministry at the great day.

I do not hear that Ananias quarreled with God concerning the doctrine of election. No (oh, that all good men would, in this, learn of him!), he "went his way, and entered into the house; and put his hands on him, and said, 'Brother Saul'"; just now it was "this man"; now it is "Brother Saul": it is no matter what a man has been, if he be now a Christian; the same should be our brother, our

By this time Ananias has tried to lodge 3 times why he shouldn't; but God persists sister and mother; God blots out every convert's transgressions as with a thick cloud, and so should we; the more vile a man has been, the more should we love him when believing in Christ, because Christ will be more glorified on his behalf. I doubt not, but Ananias was wonderfully delighted to hear that so remarkable a persecutor was brought home to God: I am persuaded he felt his soul immediately united to him by love, and therefore addresses him not with, "Thou persecutor, thou murderer that came to butcher me and my friends"; but, "Brother Saul." It is remarkable that the primitive Christians much used the word *brother* and *brethren*; I know it is a term now much in reproach; but those who despise it, I believe, would be glad to be of our brotherhood, when they see us sitting at the right hand of the Majesty on high. "Brother Saul, the Lord, even Jesus that appeared unto thee in the way as thou camest, hath sent me, that thou mightest receive thy sight, and be filled with the Holy Ghost." At this time, we may suppose, he laid his hands upon him. See the consequences. *So after his ascension He appears to Paul*

Verse 18: "Immediately there fell from his eyes as it had been scales, and *and* he received sight forthwith"; not only bodily, but spiritual sight; he emerged as *we speak* it were into a new world; he saw, and felt too, things unutterable: he felt a *of his* union of soul with God; he received the spirit of adoption; he could now, with *return w/o* a full assurance of faith, cry, "Abba, Father." Now was he filled with the Holy *regard* Ghost; and had the love of God shed abroad in his heart; now were the days *to He* of his mourning ended; now was Christ formed in his soul; now he could give *is here* men and devils the challenge, knowing that Christ had justified him; now he saw the excellencies of Christ, and esteemed him the fairest among ten thousand. You only know how to sympathize with the apostle in his joy, who, after a long night of bondage, have been set free by the Spirit, and have received joy in the Holy Ghost. May all that are now mourning, as Saul was, be comforted in like manner!

The scales are now removed from the eyes of Saul's mind; Ananias has done that for him, under God: he must now do another office, baptize him, and so receive him into the visible church of Christ; a good proof to me of the necessity of baptism where it may be had: for I find here, as well as elsewhere, that baptism is administered even to those who had received the Holy Ghost; Saul was convinced of this, and therefore arose and was baptized; and now it is time for him to recruit the outward man, which, by three days' abstinence and spiritual conflicts, had been much impaired; we are therefore told, "when he had received meat, he was strengthened" (v. 19).

But oh, with what comfort did the apostle now eat his food? I am sure it was with singleness. I am persuaded also with gladness of heart; and why? He knew that he was reconciled to God; and, for my own part, did I not know how blind and flinty our hearts are by nature, I should wonder how anyone could eat even his common food with any satisfaction, who has not some well-grounded hope of his being reconciled to God. Our Lord intimates thus much to us: for in his glorious prayer, after he has taught us to pray for our daily bread, immediately adds that petition, "Forgive us our trespasses"; as though our daily bread would do us no service, unless we were sensible of having the forgiveness of our sins.

To proceed; Saul has received meat, and is strengthened; and whither will he go now? To see the brethren. "Then was Saul certain days with the disciples that were at Damascus." If we know and love Christ, we shall also love and desire to be acquainted with the brethren of Christ: we may generally know a man by his company. And though all are not saints that associate with saints (for tares will be always springing up among the wheat till the time of harvest), yet, if we never keep company, but are shy and ashamed of the despised children of God, it is a certain sign we have not yet experimentally learned Jesus or received him into our hearts. My dear friends, be not deceived; if we are friends to the Bridegroom, we shall be friends to the children of the Bridegroom. Saul, as soon as he was filled with the Holy Ghost, "was certain days with the disciples that were at Damascus."

But who can tell what joy these disciples felt when Saul came among them? I suppose holy Ananias introduced him. I think I see the once persecuting zealot, when they came to salute him with a holy kiss, throwing himself upon each of their necks, weeping over them with floods of tears, and saying, "My brother, O my sister, can you forgive me? Can you give such a wretch as I the right hand of fellowship, who intended to drag you behind me bound unto Jerusalem?" Thus, I say, we may suppose Saul addressed himself to his fellow disciples; and I doubt not but they were as ready to forgive and forget as Ananias was, and saluted him with the endearing title of "Brother Saul." Lovely was this meeting; so lovely that it seemed Saul continued certain days with them, to communicate experiences, and to learn the way of God more perfectly; to pray for a blessing on his future ministry, and to praise Christ Jesus for what he had done for their souls. Saul, perhaps, had sat certain years at the feet of Gamaliel, but undoubtedly learned more these certain days, than he had learned before in all his life. It pleases me to think how this great scholar is transformed by the renewing of his mind. What a mighty change was here! That so great a man as Saul was, both as to his station in life and internal qualifications, and such a bitter enemy to the Christians; for him, I say, to go and be certain days with the people of this mad way, and to sit quietly, and be taught of illiterate men, as many of these disciples we may be sure were; what a substantial proof was this of the reality of his conversion!

What a hurry and confusion may we suppose the chief priests were now in! I warrant they were ready to cry out, What! Is he also deceived? As for the common people, who knew not the law, and are accursed, for them to be carried away, is no such wonder; but for a man bred up at the feet of Gamaliel, for such a scholar, such an enemy to the cause as Saul; for him to be led away with a company of silly, deceived men and women, surely it is impossible: we cannot believe it. But Saul soon convinces them of the reality of his becoming a fool for Christ's sake: for straightway, instead of going to deliver the letters from the high priests, as they expected, in order to bring the disciples that were at Damascus bound to Jerusalem, "he preached Christ in the synagogues, that he is the Son of God." This is another proof of his being converted. He not only conversed with Christians in private, but he preached Christ publicly in the synagogues; especially he insisted on the divinity of our Lord, proving, notwithstanding his state of humiliation, that he was really the Son of God.

But why did Saul preach Christ thus? Because he had felt the power of Christ upon his own soul. And here is the reason why Christ is so seldom preached, and his divinity so slightly insisted on in our synagogues: because the generality of those that pretend to preach him never felt a saving work of conversion upon their own souls. How can they preach, unless they are first taught of, and then sent by God? Saul did not preach Christ before he knew him; no more should anyone else. An unconverted minister, though he could speak with the tongues of men and angels, will be but as a sounding brass and tinkling cymbal to those whose senses are exercised to discern spiritual things. Ministers that are unconverted may talk and declaim of Christ, and prove from books that he is the Son of God; but they cannot preach with the demonstration of the Spirit and with power, unless they preach from experience, and have had a proof of his divinity, by a work of grace worked upon their own souls. God forgive those who lay hands on an unconverted man, knowing that he is such: I would not do it for a thousand worlds. Lord Jesus, keep your own faithful servants pure, and let them not be partakers of other men's sins!

Such an instance as was Saul's conversion, we may be assured, must make a great deal of noise; and, therefore, no wonder we are told, "But all that heard him were amazed, and said, 'Is not this he that destroyed them who called on this name in Jerusalem, and came hither for that intent, that he might bring them bound to the chief priests?'" (v. 21).

Thus it will be with all that appear publicly for Jesus Christ; and it is as impossible for a true Christian to be hid, as a city built upon a hill. Brethren, if you are faithful to [Christ], you must be reproached and have remarks made on you for Christ; especially if you have been remarkably wicked before your conversion. Your friends will say, is not this he, or she, who a little while ago would run to as great an excess of riot and vanity as the worst of us all? What has turned your brain? Or if you have been close, false, formal hypocrites, as Saul was, they will wonder that you should be so deceived, as to think you were not in a safe state before. No doubt, numbers were surprised to hear Saul, who was touching the law blameless, affirm that he was in a damnable condition (as in all probability he did) a few days before.

Brethren, you must expect to meet with many such difficulties as these. The scourge of the tongue is generally the first cross we are called to bear for the sake of Christ. Let not, therefore, this move you: it did not intimidate, no, it rather encouraged Saul: says the text, "But Saul increased the more in strength, and confounded the Jews who dwelt at Damascus, proving that this is very Christ." Opposition never yet did or ever will hurt a sincere convert: nothing like opposition to make the man of God perfect. None but a hireling, who cares not for the sheep, will be affrighted at the approach or barking of wolves. Christ's ministers are as bold as lions: it is not for such men as they to flee.

And therefore (that I may draw toward a conclusion) let the ministers and disciples of Christ learn from Saul, not to fear men or their revilings; but, like him, increase in strength, the more wicked men endeavor to weaken their hands. We cannot be Christians without being opposed: no; disciples in general must suffer; ministers in particular must suffer great things. But let not this move any of us from our steadfastness in the gospel. He that stood by and strengthened Saul will also stand by and strengthen us. He is a God mighty to save all that put their trust in him. If we look up with an eye of faith, we, as well as the first martyr Stephen, may see Jesus standing at the right hand of God, ready to assist and protect us. Though the Lord's seat is in heaven, yet he has respect to his saints in a special manner, when suffering here on earth: then the Spirit of Christ and of glory rests upon their souls. And, if I may speak my own experience, I never enjoy more rich communications from God than when despised and rejected of men for the sake of Jesus Christ. However little they may design it, my enemies are my greatest friends. What I most fear is a calm; but the enmity which is in the hearts of natural men against Christ, will not suffer them to be quiet long. No; as I hope the work of God will increase, so the rage of men and devils will increase also. Let us put on, therefore, the whole armor of God: let us not fear the face of men: "Let us fear him only, who can destroy both body and soul in hell." I say unto you, let us fear him alone. You see how soon God can stop the fury of his enemies.

You have just now heard of a proud, powerful zealot stopped in his full career, struck down to the earth with a light from heaven, converted by the almighty power of efficacious grace, and thereupon zealously promoting, even resolutely suffering for, the faith, which once with threatenings and slaughters he endeavored to destroy. Let this teach us to pity and pray for our Lord's most inveterate enemies. Who knows, but in answer thereunto, our Lord may give them repentance unto life? Most think that Christ had respect to Stephen's prayer, when he converted Saul. Perhaps for this reason God suffers his adversaries to go on, that his goodness and power may shine more bright in their conversion.

But let not the persecutors of Christ take encouragement from this to continue in their opposition. Remember, though Saul was converted, yet the high priest and Saul's companions were left dead in trespasses and sins. And if this should be your case, you will of all men be most miserable, for persecutors have the lowest place in hell. And if Saul was struck to the earth by a light from heaven, how will you be able to stand before Jesus Christ, when he comes in terrible majesty to take vengeance on all those who have persecuted his gospel? Then the question, "Why persecutest thou me?" will cut you through and through. The secret enmity of your hearts shall be then detected before men and angels, and you shall be doomed to dwell in the blackness of darkness forevermore. Kiss the Son, therefore, lest he be angry: for even you may yet find mercy, if you believe on the Son of God: though you persecute him, yet he will be your Jesus. I cannot despair of any of you, when I find a Saul among the disciples at Damascus. What though your sins are as scarlet, the blood of Christ shall wash them as white as snow. Having much to be forgiven, despair not; only believe, and, like Saul, of whom I have now been speaking, love much. He counted himself the chiefest sinner of all, and therefore labored more abundantly than all.

Who is there among you fearing the Lord? Whose hearts has the Lord now opened to hearken to the voice of his poor unworthy servant? Surely, the Lord will not let me preach in vain. Who is the happy soul that is this day to be washed in the blood of the Lamb? Will no poor sinner take encouragement from Saul to come to Jesus Christ? You are all thronging round, but which of you will touch the Lord Jesus? What a comfort will it be to Saul, and to your own souls, when you meet him in heaven, to tell him, that hearing of his was a means, under God, of your conversion! Doubtless it was written for the encouragement of all poor, returning sinners; he himself tells us so: for "in me God showed all long-suffering, that I might be an example to them that should hereafter believe." Was Saul here himself, he would tell you so, indeed he would; but being dead, by this account of his conversion he yet speaks. Oh, that God may speak by it to your hearts! Oh, that the arrows of God might this day stick fast in your souls, and you made to cry out, "Who art thou, Lord?" Are there any such among you? I think I feel something of what this Saul felt, when he said, "I travail in birth again for you, till Christ be formed again in your hearts." Oh, come, come away to Jesus, in whom Saul believed; and then I care not if the high priests issue out never so many writs or injuriously drag me to a prison. The thoughts of being instrumental in saving you will make me sing praises even at midnight. And I know you will be my joy and crown of rejoicing, when I am delivered from this earthly prison, and meet you in the kingdom of God hereafter.

Now to God the Father, God the Son, and God the Holy Ghost, be all honor, power, glory, might, majesty, and dominion, both now and forevermore. Amen.

Christ, the Believer's Wisdom, Righteousness, Sanctification, and Redemption

—ɯ—

But of him are ye in Christ Jesus, who of God is made unto us wisdom, and righteousness, and sanctification, and redemption. —1 CORINTHIANS 1:30

Of all the verses in the Book of God, this which I have now read to you, is, I believe, one of the most comprehensive: what glad tidings does it bring to believers! What precious privileges are they herein invested with! How are they here led to the fountain of them all, I mean, the love, the everlasting love of God the Father! "Of him are ye in Christ Jesus, who of God is made unto us wisdom, righteousness, sanctification, and redemption."

Without referring you to the context, I shall from the words,

First, point out to you the fountain, from which all those blessings flow, that the elect of God partake of in Jesus Christ, "who of God is made unto."

And, second, I shall consider what these blessings are, "wisdom, righteousness, sanctification, and redemption."

First, I would point out to you the fountain, from which all those blessings flow, that the elect of God partake of in Jesus, "who of God is made unto us"; the Father he it is who is spoken of here. Not as though Jesus Christ was not God also; but God the Father is the fountain of the Deity; and if we consider Jesus Christ acting as mediator, God the Father is greater than he; there was an eternal contract between the Father and the Son: "I have made a covenant with my chosen, and I have sworn unto David my servant"; now David was a type of Christ, with whom the Father made a covenant that if he would obey and suffer, and make himself a sacrifice for sin, he should "see his seed, he should prolong his days, and the pleasure of the Lord should prosper in his hands." This compact our Lord refers to, in that glorious prayer recorded in John 17; and therefore he prays for, or rather demands with a full assurance, all that were given to him by the Father: "Father, I will that they also whom thou hast given me, be with me where I am." For this same reason, the apostle breaks out into praises of God, even the Father of our Lord Jesus Christ;

for he loved the elect with an everlasting love, or, as our Lord expresses it, "before the foundation of the world"; and therefore to show them to whom they were beholden for their salvation, our Lord, in Matthew 25, represents himself saying, "Come, ye blessed children of my Father, receive the kingdom prepared for you from the foundation of the world." And thus, in reply to the mother of Zebedee's children, he says, "It is not mine to give, but it shall be given to them for whom it is prepared of the Father." The apostle therefore, when here speaking of the Christian's privileges, lest they should sacrifice to their own drag[nets], or think their salvation was owing to their own faithfulness, or improvement of their own free will, reminds them to look back on the everlasting love of God the Father, "who of God is made unto us. . . ."

Would to God this point of doctrine was considered more, and people were more studious of the covenant of redemption between the Father and the Son! We should not then have so much disputing against the doctrine of election, or hear it condemned (even by good men) as a doctrine of devils. For my own part, I cannot see how true humbleness of mind can be attained without a knowledge of it; and though I will not say that everyone who denies election is a bad man, yet I will say, with that sweet singer, Mr. Trail, it is a very bad sign: such a one, whoever he be, I think cannot truly know himself; for, if we deny election, we must, partly at least, glory in ourselves; but our redemption is so ordered that no flesh should glory in the divine presence; and hence it is that the pride of man opposes this doctrine, because, according to this doctrine, and no other, "he that glories, must glory only in the Lord." But what shall I say? Election is a mystery that shines with such resplendent brightness, that, to make use of the words of one who has drunk deeply of electing love, it dazzles the weak eyes even of some of God's dear children; however, though they know it not, all the blessings they receive, all the privileges they do or ill enjoy, through Jesus Christ, flow from the everlasting love of God the Father: "But of him are you in Christ Jesus, who of God is made unto us, wisdom, righteousness, sanctification, and redemption."

Second, I come to show what these blessings are, which are here, through Christ, made over to the elect.

1. And first, Christ is made to them *wisdom*; but wherein does true wisdom consist? Were I to ask some of you, perhaps you would say, in indulging the lust of the flesh, and saying to your souls, eat, drink, and be merry: but this is only the wisdom of brutes; they have as good a gust and relish for sensual pleasures, as the greatest epicure on earth. Others would tell me, true wisdom consisted in adding house to house, and field to field, and calling lands after

their own names: but this cannot be true wisdom; for riches often take to themselves wings, and fly away, like an eagle toward heaven. Even wisdom itself assures us, "that a man's life doth not consist in the abundance of the things which he possesses"; vanity, vanity, all these things are vanity; for, if riches leave not the owner, the owners must soon leave them; "for rich men must also die, and leave their riches for others"; their riches cannot procure them redemption from the grave, whither we are all hastening apace.

But perhaps you despise riches and pleasure, and therefore place wisdom in the knowledge of books: but it is possible for you to tell the numbers of the stars, and call them all by their names, and yet be mere fools; learned men are not always wise; what's more, our common learning, so much cried up, makes men only so many accomplished fools; to keep you therefore no longer in suspense, and withal to humble you, I will send you to a heathen to school, to learn what true wisdom is: "Know thyself" was a saying of one of the wise men of Greece; this is certainly true wisdom, and this is that wisdom spoken of in the text, and which Jesus Christ is made to all elect sinners: they are made to know themselves, so as not to think more highly of themselves than they ought to think. Before, they were darkness; now, they are light in the Lord; and in that light they see their own darkness; they now bewail themselves as fallen creatures by nature, dead in trespasses and sins, sons and heirs of hell, and children of wrath; they now see that all their righteousnesses are but as filthy rags; that there is no health in their souls; that they are poor and miserable, blind and naked; and that there is no name given under heaven, whereby they can be saved, but that of Jesus Christ. They see the necessity of closing with a Savior, and behold the wisdom of God in appointing him to be a Savior; they are also made willing to accept of salvation upon our Lord's own terms and receive him as their all in all; thus Christ is made to them wisdom.

2. Second, *righteousness.* "Who of God is made unto us wisdom, and righteousness": Christ's whole personal righteousness is made over to and accounted theirs. They are enabled to lay hold on Christ by faith, and God the Father blots out their transgressions, as with a thick cloud: their sins and their iniquities he remembers no more; they are made the righteousness of God in Christ Jesus, "who is the end of the law for righteousness to everyone that believeth." In one sense, God now sees no sin in them; the whole covenant of works is fulfilled in them; they are actually justified, acquitted, and looked upon as righteous in the sight of God; they are perfectly accepted in the beloved; they are complete in him; the flaming sword of God's wrath, which before moved every way, is now removed, and free access given to the Tree of

Life; they are enabled to reach out the arm of faith and pluck, and live forever-more. Hence it is that the apostle, under a sense of this blessed privilege, breaks out into this triumphant language: "It is Christ that justifies, who is he that condemns?" Does sin condemn? Christ's righteousness delivers believers from the guilt of it: Christ is their Savior, and is become a propitiation for their sins: who therefore shall lay anything to the charge of God's elect? Does the law condemn? By having Christ's righteousness imputed to them, they are dead to the law, as a covenant of works; Christ has fulfilled it for them, and in their stead. Does death threaten them? They need not fear: the sting of death is sin, the strength of sin is the law, but God has given them the victory by imputing to them the righteousness of the Lord Jesus.

And what a privilege is here! Well might the angels at the birth of Christ say to the humble shepherds, "Behold, I bring you glad tidings of great joy"; unto you that believe in Christ "a Savior is born." And well may angels rejoice at the conversion of poor sinners; for the Lord is their righteousness; they have peace with God through faith in Christ's blood, and shall never enter into condemnation. O believers! (for this discourse is intended in a special manner for you) lift up your heads; "rejoice in the Lord always; again I say, rejoice." Christ is made to you, of God, righteousness, what then should you fear? You are made the righteousness of God in him; you may be called, "The Lord our righteousness." Of what then should you be afraid? What shall separate you henceforward from the love of Christ? "Shall tribulation, or distress, or persecution, or famine, or nakedness, or peril, or sword? No, I am persuaded, neither death, nor life, nor angels, nor principalities, nor powers, nor things present, nor things to come, nor height, nor depth, nor any other creature, shall be able to separate you from the love of God, which is in Christ Jesus our Lord," who of God is made unto you righteousness.

This is a glorious privilege, but this is only the beginning of the happiness of believers: For,

3. Third, Christ is not only made to them righteousness, but *sanctification*; by sanctification, I do not mean a bare hypocritical attendance on outward ordinances, though rightly informed Christians will think it their duty and privilege constantly to attend on all outward ordinances. Nor do I mean by sanctification a bare outward reformation, and a few transient convictions, or a little legal sorrow; for all this an unsanctified man may have; but, by sanctification I mean a total renovation of the whole man: by the righteousness of Christ, believers come legally, by sanctification they are made spiritually alive; by the one they are entitled to, by the other they are made meet for glory. They are sanctified therefore throughout, in spirit, soul, and body.

Father Your Will Be In Me. Amen.

Their understandings, which were dark before, now become light in the Lord; and their wills, before contrary to, now become one with the will of God; their affections are now set on things above; their memory is now filled with divine things; their natural consciences are now enlightened; their members, which were before instruments of uncleanness, and of iniquity into iniquity, are now new creatures: "old things are passed away, all things are become new" in their hearts: sin has now no longer dominion over them; they are freed from the power, though not the indwelling of being, of it; they are holy both in heart and life, in all manner of conversation: they are made partakers of a divine nature, and from Jesus Christ, they receive grace; and every grace that is in Christ is copied and transcribed into their souls; they are transformed into his likeness; he is formed within them; they dwell in him, and he in them; they are led by the Spirit, and bring forth the fruits thereof; they know that Christ is their Emmanuel, God with and in them; they are living temples of the Holy Ghost. And therefore, being a holy habitation unto the Lord, the whole Trinity dwells and walks in them; even here, they sit together with Christ in heavenly places and are vitally united to him, their head, by a living faith; their Redeemer, their Maker, is their husband; they are flesh of his flesh, bone of his bone; they talk, they walk with him, as a man talks and walks with his friend; in short, they are one with Christ, even as Jesus Christ and the Father are one.

Thus is Christ made to believers sanctification. And, oh, what a privilege is this! to be changed from beasts into saints, and from a devilish, to be made partakers of a divine nature; to be translated from the kingdom of Satan, into the kingdom of God's dear Son! To put off the old man, which is corrupt, and to put on the new man, which is created after God, in righteousness and true holiness! Oh, what an unspeakable blessing is this! I almost stand amazed at the contemplation thereof. Well might the apostle exhort believers to rejoice in the Lord; indeed they have reason always to rejoice, yes, to rejoice on a dying bed; for the kingdom of God is in them; they are changed from glory to glory, even by the Spirit of the Lord: well may this be a mystery to the natural, for it is a mystery even to the spiritual man himself, a mystery which he cannot fathom. Does it not often dazzle your eyes, O you children of God, to look at your own brightness, when the candle of the Lord shines out, and your Redeemer lifts up the light of his blessed countenance upon your souls? Are not you astonished, when you feel the love of God shed abroad in your hearts by the Holy Ghost, and God holds out the golden scepter of his mercy, and bids you ask what you will, and it shall be given you? Does not that peace of God, which keeps and rules your hearts, surpass the utmost limits of your understandings? And is not the joy you feel unspeakable? Is it not full of glory? I am persuaded it is; and in your secret communion, when the Lord's love flows in upon your souls, you are as it were swallowed up in, or, to use the apostle's phrase, "filled with all the fullness of God." Are not you ready to cry out with Solomon, "And will the Lord, indeed, dwell thus with men?" How is it that we should be thus your sons and daughters, O Lord God almighty?

If you are children of God, and know what it is to have fellowship with the Father and the Son, if you walk by faith, and not by sight, I am assured this is frequently the language of your hearts.

But look forward, and see an unbounded prospect of eternal happiness lying before you, O believer! What you have already received are only the first-fruits, like the cluster of grapes brought out of the land of Canaan; only an earnest and pledge of yet infinitely better things to come: the harvest is to follow; your grace is hereafter to be swallowed up in glory. Your great Joshua, and merciful High Priest, shall administer an abundant entrance to you into the land of promise, that rest which awaits the children of God: for Christ is not only made to believers wisdom, righteousness, and sanctification, but also redemption.

But, before we enter upon the explanation and contemplation of this privilege, first, learn hence the great mistake of those writers and clergy, who, notwithstanding they talk of sanctification and inward holiness (as indeed sometimes they do, though in a very loose and superficial manner), yet they generally make it the cause, whereas they should consider it as the effect, of our justification. "Of him are ye in Christ Jesus, who of God is made unto us wisdom, righteousness, (and then) sanctification." For Christ's righteousness, or that which Christ has done in our stead without us, is the sole cause of our acceptance in the sight of God, and of all holiness worked in us: to this, and not to the light within, or anything worked within, should poor sinners seek for justification in the sight of God: for the sake of Christ's righteousness alone, and not anything worked in us, does God look favorably upon us; our sanctification at best, in this life, is not complete: though we be delivered from the power, we are not freed from the in-being of sin; but not only the dominion, but the in-being, of sin, is forbidden, by the perfect law of God: for it is not said, "Thou shalt not give way to lust," but, "Thou shalt not lust." So that while the principle of lust remains in the least degree in our hearts, though we are otherwise never so holy, yet we cannot, on account of that, hope for acceptance with God. We must first therefore look for a righteousness without us, even the righteousness of our Lord Jesus Christ: for this reason the apostle mentions it, and puts it before sanctification in the words of the text. And whosoever teaches any other doctrine does not preach the truth as it is in Jesus.

Second, from hence also, the Antinomians and formal hypocrites may be confuted, who talk of Christ outside, but know nothing, experimentally, of a work of sanctification worked within them. Whatever they may pretend to, since Christ is not in them, the Lord is not their righteousness, and they have no well-grounded hope of glory: for though sanctification is not the cause, yet it is the effect, of our acceptance with God: "who of God is made unto us righteousness and sanctification." He therefore that is really in Christ is a new creature; it is not going back to a covenant of works, to look into our hearts, and, seeing that they are changed and renewed, from thence form a comfortable and well-grounded assurance of the safety of our states: no, but this is what we are directed to in Scripture; by our bringing forth the fruits, we are to judge whether or no we ever did truly partake of the Spirit of God. "We know (says John) that we are passed from death unto life, because we love the brethren." And however we may talk of Christ's righteousness, and exclaim against legal preachers, yet, if we be not holy in heart and life, if we be not sanctified and renewed by the Spirit in our minds, we are self-deceivers; we are only formal hypocrites, for we must not put asunder what God has joined together; we must keep the medium between the two extremes; not insist so much, on the one hand, upon Christ without, as to exclude Christ within, as an evidence of our being his, and as a preparation for future happiness; nor, on the other hand, so depend on inherent righteousness or holiness worked in us, as to exclude the righteousness of Jesus Christ without us. But—

4. Fourth, let us now go on, and take a view of the other link, or rather the end, of the believer's golden chain of privileges, redemption. But we must look very high; for the top of it, like Jacob's ladder, reaches heaven, where all believers will ascend and be placed at the right hand of God: "who of God is made unto us wisdom, righteousness, sanctification, and redemption."

This is a golden chain indeed! And, what is best of all, not one link can ever be broken asunder from another. Was there no other text in the Book of God, this single one sufficiently proves the final perseverance of true believers; or never did God yet justify a man, whom he did not sanctify; nor sanctify one, whom he did not completely redeem and glorify. No! as for God, his way, his works, is perfect; he always carried on and finished the work he began; thus it was in the first, so it is in the new creation; when God says, "Let there be light," there is light, that shines more and more unto the perfect day, when believers enter into their eternal rest, as God entered into his. Those whom God has justified, he has in effect glorified: for as a man's worthiness was not the cause of God's giving him Christ's righteousness; so neither shall his unworthiness be a cause of his taking it away; God's gifts and callings are without repentance: and I cannot think they are clear in the notion of Christ's righteousness, who deny the final perseverance of the saints; I fear they understand justification in that low sense, which I understood it in a few years ago, as implying no more than remission of sins: but it not only signifies remission of sins past, but also a federal right to all good things to come. If God has given us his only Son, how shall he not with him freely give us all things? Therefore the apostle, after he says, "who of God is made unto us righteousness," does not say, "perhaps he may be made to us sanctification and redemption," but, "he is made"; for there is an eternal, indissoluble connection between these blessed privileges. As the obedience of Christ is imputed to believers, so his perseverance in that obedience is to be imputed to them also; and it argues great ignorance of the covenant of grace and redemption, to object against it.

By the word *redemption* we are to understand not only a complete deliverance from all evil, but also a full enjoyment of all good both in body and soul. I say, "both in body and soul," for the Lord is also for the body; the bodies of the saints in this life are temples of the Holy Ghost; God makes a covenant with the dust of believers; after death, though worms destroy them, yet, even in their flesh shall they see God. I fear, indeed, there are some Sadducees in our days, or at least heretics, who say either that there is no resurrection of the body, or that the resurrection is past already, namely, in our regeneration. Hence it is that our Lord's coming in the flesh, at the day of judgment, is denied; and consequently we must throw aside the Sacrament of the Lord's Supper. For why should we remember the Lord's death until he come to judgment, when he is already come to judge our hearts, and will not come a second time? But all this is only the reasoning of unlearned, unstable men, who certainly know not what they say, nor whereof they affirm. That we must follow our Lord in the regeneration, be partakers of a new birth, and that Christ must come into our hearts, we freely confess; and we hope, when speaking of these things, we speak no more than what we know and feel: but then it is plain that Jesus Christ will come, hereafter, to judgment, and that he ascended into heaven with the body which he had here on earth, for says he after his resurrection, "Handle me, and see; a spirit has not flesh and bones, as you see me have." And it is plain that Christ's resurrection was an earnest of ours, for, says the apostle, "Christ is risen from the dead, and become the firstfruits of them that sleep; and as in Adam all die (and are subject to mortality), so all that are in Christ (the second Adam, who represented believers as their federal head) shall certainly be made alive," or rise again with their bodies at the last day.

Here then, O believers, is one, though the lowest, degree of that redemption which you are to be partakers of hereafter; I mean, the redemption of your bodies: for this corruptible must put on incorruption; this mortal must put on immortality. Your bodies, as well as souls, were given to Jesus Christ by the Father; they have been companions in watching and fasting and praying: your bodies therefore, as well as souls, shall Jesus Christ raise up at the last day. Fear not, therefore, O believers, to look into the grave: for to you it is not other than a consecrated dormitory, where your bodies shall sleep quietly until the morning of the resurrection, when the voice of the archangel shall sound, and the trump of God give the general alarm, "Arise, you dead, and come to judgment"; earth, air, fire, water shall give up your scattered atoms, and both in body and soul shall you be ever with the Lord. I doubt not, but many of you are groaning under crazy bodies and complain often that the mortal body weighs down the immortal soul; at least this is my case; but let us have a little patience, and we shall be delivered from our earthly prisons; before long, these tabernacles of clay shall be dissolved, and we shall be clothed with our house which is from heaven; hereafter our bodies shall be spiritualized and shall be so far from hindering our souls through weakness, that they shall become strong; so strong, as to bear up under an exceeding and eternal weight of glory; others again may have deformed bodies, emaciated also with sickness, and worn out with labor at age; but wait a little, until your blessed change by death comes; then your bodies shall be renewed and made glorious, like unto Christ's glorious body: of which we may form some faint idea, from the account given us of our Lord's transfiguration on the mount, when it is said, "His raiment became bright and glistening, and his face brighter than the sun." Well then may a believer break out in the apostle's triumphant language: "O death, where is thy sting? O grave, where is thy victory?"

But what is the redemption of the body, in comparison of the redemption of the better part, our souls? I must therefore say to you believers, as the angel said to John, "Come up higher"; and let us take as clear a view as we can, at such a distance, of the redemption Christ has purchased for, and will shortly put you in actual possession of. Already you are justified, already you are sanctified, and thereby freed from the guilt and dominion of sin; but, as I have observed, the being and indwelling of sin yet remains in you. God sees it proper to leave some Amalekites in the land, to keep his Israel in action. The most perfect Christian, I am persuaded, must agree, according to one of* our articles, that "the corruption of nature remains even in the regenerate; that

*on the peace knowing America's Amalekites are a tool of God for those He loves & called according to his purpose

the flesh lusteth always against the spirit, and the spirit against the flesh." So that believers cannot do things for God with that perfection they desire; this grieves their righteous souls day by day and, with the holy apostle, makes them cry out, "Who shall deliver us from the body of this death?" I thank God, our Lord Jesus Christ will, but not completely before the day of our dissolution; then will the very being of sin be destroyed, and an eternal stop put to inbred, indwelling corruption. And is not this a great redemption? I am sure believers esteem it so: for there is nothing grieves the heart of a child of God so much as the remains of indwelling sin. Again, believers are often in heaviness through manifold temptations; God sees that it is needful and good for them so to be; and though they may be highly favored, and wrapped up in communion with God, even to the third heavens; yet a messenger of Satan is often sent to buffet them, lest they should be puffed up with the abundance of revelations. But be not weary, be not faint in your minds: the time of your complete redemption draws nigh. In heaven the wicked one shall cease from troubling you, and your weary souls shall enjoy an everlasting rest; his fiery darts cannot reach those blissful regions: Satan will never come anymore to appear with, disturb, or accuse the sons of God, when once the Lord Jesus Christ shuts the door. Your righteous souls are now grieved, day by day, at the ungodly conversation of the wicked; tares now grow up among the wheat; wolves come in sheep's clothing; but the redemption spoken of in the text will free your souls from all anxiety on these accounts; hereafter you shall enjoy a perfect communion of saints; nothing that is unholy or unsanctified shall enter into the holy of holies, which is prepared for you above: this, and all manner of evil whatsoever, you shall be delivered from, when your redemption is hereafter made complete in heaven; not only so, but you shall enter into the full enjoyment of all good. It is true, all saints will not have the same degree of happiness, but all will be as happy as their hearts can desire. Believers, you shall judge the evil, and familiarly converse with good, angels: you shall sit down with Abraham, Isaac, Jacob, and all the spirits of just men made perfect; and, to sum up all your happiness in one word, you shall see God the Father, Son, and Holy Ghost; and, by seeing God, be more and more like unto him, and pass from glory to glory, even to all eternity.

But I must stop—the glories of the upper world crowd in so fast upon my soul that I am lost in the contemplation of them. Brethren, the redemption spoken of is unutterable; we cannot here find it out; eye has not seen, nor ear heard, nor has it entered into the hearts of the most holy men living to conceive how great it is. Were I to entertain you whole ages with an account of it, when you come to heaven, you must say, with the Queen of Sheba, "Not half, no, not one thousandth part was told us." All we can do here is to go upon Mount Pisgah, and, by the eye of faith, take a distant view of the promised land: we may see it, as Abraham did Christ, afar off, and rejoice in it; but here we only know in part. Blessed be God, there is a time coming, when we shall know God, even as we are known, and God be all in all. Lord Jesus, accomplish the number of your elect! Lord Jesus, hasten your kingdom!

And now, where are the scoffers of these last days, who count the lives of Christians to be madness, and their end to be without honor? Unhappy men! You know not what you do. Were your eyes open, and had you senses to discern spiritual things, you would not speak all manner of evil against the children of God, but you would esteem them as the excellent ones of the earth, and envy their happiness: your souls would hunger and thirst after it: you also would become fools for Christ's sake. You boast of wisdom; so did the philosophers of Corinth: but your wisdom is the foolishness of folly in the sight of God. What will your wisdom avail you, if it does not make you wise unto salvation? Can you, with all your wisdom, propose a more consistent scheme to build your hopes of salvation on, than what has been now laid before you? Can you, with all the strength of natural reason, find out a better way of acceptance with God, than by the righteousness of the Lord Jesus Christ? Is it right to think your own works can in any measure deserve or procure it? If not, why will you not believe in him? Why will you not submit to his righteousness? Can you deny that you are fallen creatures? Do not you find that you are full of disorders and that these disorders make you unhappy? Do not you find that you cannot change your own hearts? Have you not resolved many and many a time, and have not your corruptions yet dominion over you? Are you not bondslaves to your lusts, and led captive by the devil at his will? Why then will you not come to Christ for sanctification? Do you not desire to die the death of the righteous, and that your future state may be like theirs? I am persuaded you cannot bear the thoughts of being annihilated, much less of being miserable forever. Whatever you may pretend, if you speak truth, you must confess that conscience breaks in upon you in more sober intervals whether you will or not, and even constrains you to believe that hell is no painted fire. And why then will you not come to Christ? He alone can procure you everlasting redemption. Haste, haste away to him, poor beguiled sinners. You lack wisdom; ask it of Christ. Who knows but he may give it you? He is able: for he is the wisdom of the Father; he is that wisdom which was from everlasting. You have no righteousness; away, therefore, to Christ: "He is the end of the law for righteousness to everyone that believeth." You are unholy: flee to the Lord Jesus: he is full of grace and truth; and of his fullness all may

2ND LAW OF THERMO-DYNAMICS

Was Whitfield, here, tapping out a warning to believers not to engage in "division" - must every generation learn not to?

receive that believe in him. You are afraid to die; let this drive you to Christ: he has the keys of death and hell; in him is plenteous redemption; he alone can open the door which leads to everlasting life.

Let not therefore the deceived reasoner boast any longer of his pretended reason. Whatever you may think, it is the most unreasonable thing in the world not to believe on Jesus Christ, whom God has sent. Why, why will you die? Why will you not come unto him, that you may have life? "Ho! everyone that thirsteth, come unto the waters of life, and drink freely: come, buy without money and without price." Were these blessed privileges in the text to be purchased with money, you might say, "We are poor, and cannot buy"; or, were they to be conferred only on sinners of such a rank or degree, then you might say, "How can such sinners as we expect to be so highly favored?" But they are to be freely given of God to the worst of sinners: "to us," says the apostle—to me a persecutor, to you Corinthians, who were "unclean, drunkards, covetous persons, idolaters." Therefore each poor sinner may say then, "Why not unto me?" Has Christ but one blessing? What if he has blessed millions already, by turning them away from their iniquities; yet he still continues the same: he lives forever to make intercession, and therefore will bless you, even you also. Though Esau-like you have been profane, and hitherto despised your heavenly Father's birthright; even now, if you believe, "Christ will be made to you of God, wisdom, righteousness, sanctification, and redemption."

But I must turn again to believers, for whose instruction, as I observed before, this discourse was particularly intended. You see, brethren, partakers of the heavenly calling, what great blessings are treasured up for you in Jesus Christ your head, and what you are entitled to by believing on his name. Take heed therefore that you walk worthy of the vocation wherewith you are called. Think often how highly you are favored, and remember, you have not chosen Christ, but Christ has chosen you. Put on (as the elect of God) humbleness of mind and glory, but let it be only in the Lord; for you have nothing but what you have received of God. By nature you were foolish, as legal, as unholy, and in as damnable a condition, as others. Be pitiful therefore, be courteous; and, as sanctification is a progressive work, beware of thinking you have already attained. Let him that is holy be holy still; knowing that he who is most pure in heart shall hereafter enjoy the clearest vision of God. Let indwelling sin be your daily burden; and not only bewail and lament, but see that you subdue it daily by the power of divine grace; and look up to Jesus continually to be the Finisher, as well as Author, of your faith. Build not on your own faithfulness, but on God's unchangeableness. Take heed of thinking you stand by the power of your own free will. The everlasting love of God the

Father must be your only hope and consolation;* let this support you under all trials. Remember that God's gifts and callings are without repentance; that Christ, having once loved you, will love you to the end. Let this constrain you to obedience and make you long and look for that blessed time, when he shall not only be your wisdom and righteousness and sanctification, but also complete and everlasting redemption.

Glory be to God in the highest!

* Many are those who are the biological seed of Abraham who will not be found at the consolidation.

Of Justification by Christ

—⟨W⟩—

But ye are washed, but ye are sanctified, but ye are justified in the name of our Lord Jesus Christ, and by the Spirit of our God. —1 CORINTHIANS 6:11

It has been objected by some who dissent from, what's more, I may add, by others also who actually are friends to, the present ecclesiastical establishment, that the ministers of the Church of England preach themselves, and not Christ Jesus the Lord; that they entertain their people with lectures of mere morality, without declaring to them the glad tidings of salvation by Jesus Christ. How well grounded such an objection may be is not my business to inquire. All I shall say at present to the point is, that whenever such a grand objection is urged against the whole body of the clergy in general, every honest minister of Jesus Christ should do his utmost to cut off all manner of occasion, from those who desire an occasion to take offense at us; that so by hearing us continually sounding forth the word of truth, and declaring with all boldness and assurance of faith, that "there is no other name given under heaven, whereby they can be saved, but that of Jesus Christ," they may be ashamed of this, their same confident boasting against us.

It was an eye to this objection, joined with the agreeableness and delightfulness of the subject (for who can but delight to talk of that which the blessed angels desire to look into?) that induces me to discourse a little on that great and fundamental article of our faith; namely, our being freely justified by the precious blood of Jesus Christ. "But ye are washed, but ye are sanctified, but ye are justified in the name of our Lord Jesus Christ, and by the Spirit of our God."

The words beginning with the particle *but* have plainly a reference to something before; it may not therefore be improper, before I descend to particulars, to consider the words as they stand in relation to the context. The apostle, in the verses immediately foregoing, had been reckoning up many notorious sins, drunkenness, adultery, fornication, and suchlike, the commission of which, without a true and hearty repentance, he tells the Corinthians, would entirely shut them out of the kingdom of God. But then, lest they should, on the one hand, grow spiritually proud by seeing themselves differ from their unconverted brethren, and therefore be tempted to set them at naught, and say with the self-conceited hypocrite in the prophet, "Come not nigh me, for I am holier than thou"; or, on the other hand, by looking back on the multitude of their past offenses, should be apt to think their sins were too many and grievous to be forgiven. He first, in order to keep them humble, reminds them of their sad state before conversion, telling them in plain terms, "such (or as it might be read, these things) were some of you"; not only one, but all that sad catalog of vices I have been drawing up, some of you were once guilty of; but then, at the same time, to preserve them from despair, behold he brings them glad tidings of great joy: "But ye are washed, but ye are sanctified, but ye are justified in the name of our Lord Jesus Christ, and by the Spirit of our God." *AMEN! I am one of these.*

The former part of this text, our being sanctified, I have in some measure treated of already; I would not enlarge on our being freely justified by the precious obedience and death of Jesus Christ: "But ye are justified in the name of our Lord Jesus Christ."

From which words I shall consider three things:

First, what is meant by the word *justified.*

Second, I shall endeavor to prove that all mankind in general, and every individual person in particular, stands in need of being justified.

Third, that there is no possibility of obtaining this justification, which we so much want, but by the all-perfect obedience and precious death of Jesus Christ.

First, I am to consider what is meant by the word *justified.*

"But ye are justified," says the apostle, *if you are in Jesus* which is, as though he had said, you have your sins forgiven, and are looked upon by God as though you never had offended him at all; for that is the meaning of the word *justified* in almost all the passages of holy Scripture where this word is mentioned. Thus, when this same apostle writes to the Romans, he tells them that "whom God called those he also justified." And that this word *justified* implies a blotting out of all *Call them today, Father, Call them all.* our transgressions is manifest from what follows, "them he also glorified," which could not be if a justified person was not looked upon by God as though he never had offended him at all. And again, speaking of Abraham's faith, he tells them that "Abraham believed on him that justifies the ungodly," who acquits and clears the ungodly man; for it is a law term, and alludes to a judge acquitting an accused criminal of the thing laid to his charge. Which expression the apostle himself explains by a quotation out of the Psalms: "Blessed is the man to whom the Lord imputeth no sin." From all which proofs, and many others that might be urged, it is evident that by being justified, we are to understand, being so acquitted in the sight of God as to be looked upon as though we never had offended him at all. And in this sense we are to understand that article, which we profess to believe in our creed, when each of us declare in his own person, I believe the forgiveness of sins.

This leads me to the second thing proposed, to prove that all mankind in general, and every individual person in particular, stands in need of being justified. *Who else is there?*

And indeed the apostle supposes this in the words of the text: "But ye are justified," thereby implying that the Corinthians (and consequently all mankind, there being no difference, as will be shown hereafter) stood in need of being justified.

But not to rest in bare suppositions, in my further enlargement on this head, I shall endeavor to prove that we all stand in need of being justified on account of the sin of our natures, and the sin of our lives.

1. First, I affirm that we all stand in need of being justified, on account of the sin of our natures: for we are all chargeable with original sin, or the sin of our first parents. Which, though a proposition that may be denied by a self-justifying infidel, who "will not come to Christ that he may have life," yet can never be denied by anyone who believes that St. Paul's epistles were written by divine inspiration; where we are told that "in Adam all died," that is, Adam's sin was imputed to all, and lest we should forget to make a particular application, it is added in another place that "there is none that doeth good (that is, by nature), no, not one: that we are all gone out of the way (of original righteousness) and are by nature the children of wrath." And even David, who was a man after God's own heart, and, if anyone could, might surely plead an exemption from this universal corruption, yet he confesses that "he was shapen in iniquity, and that in sin did his mother conceive him." And, to mention but one text more, as immediately applicable to the present purpose, St. Paul, in his Epistle to the Romans, says that "death came upon all men, for the disobedience of one, namely, of Adam, even upon those (that is, little children) who had not sinned after the similitude of Adam's transgression"; who had not been guilty of actual sin, and therefore could not be punished with temporal death (which came into the world, as this same apostle elsewhere informs us, only by sin) had not the disobedience of our first parents been imputed to them. So that what has been said in this point seems to be excellently summed up in that article of our church, where she declares that "Original sin standeth not in the following of Adam, but it is the fault and corruption of every man, that naturally is engendered of the offspring of Adam; whereby man is very far gone from original righteousness, and is of his

*It wasn't Eve's being deceived. Adam did not keep the serpent out and he was the one God gave the instructions to not Eve

own nature inclined to evil, so that the flesh lusteth always contrary to the spirit; and therefore in every person born into this world, it deserveth God's wrath and damnation."

I have been more particular in treating of this point, because it is the very foundation of the Christian religion: for I am verily persuaded, that it is nothing but a want of being well grounded in the doctrine of original sin, and of the helpless, no, even, I may say, damnable condition, each of us comes into the world in, that makes so many infidels oppose, and so many who call themselves Christians, so very lukewarm in their love and affections to Jesus Christ. It is this, and I could almost say, this only, that makes infidelity abound among us so much as it does. For alas! we are mistaken if we imagine that men now commence or continue infidels, and set up corrupted reason in opposition to divine revelation merely for want of evidence (for I believe it might easily be proved that a modern unbeliever is the most credulous creature living); no, it is only for want of a humble mind, of a sense of their original depravity, and a willingness to own themselves so depraved, that makes them so obstinately shut their eyes against the light of the glorious gospel of Christ. Whereas, on the contrary, were they but once pricked to the heart with a due and lively sense of their natural corruption and liableness to condemnation, we should have them no more scoffing at divine revelation, and looking on it as an idle tale; but they would cry out with the trembling jailer, "What shall I do to be saved?" It was an error in this fundamental point that made so many resist the evidence the Son of God himself gave of his divine mission, when he tabernacled among us. Every word he spoke, every action he did, every miracle he worked, proved that he came from God. And why then did so many harden their hearts, and would not believe his report? Why, he himself informs us, "They will not come unto me that they may have life." They will obstinately stand out against those means God had appointed for their salvation. And St. Paul tells us that "if the gospel be hid, it is hid to them that are lost; in whom the God of this world hath blinded the eyes of them which believe not, lest the light of the glorious gospel of Christ, who is the image of God, should shine upon them" (2 Cor. 4:3–4).

If it be asked, how it suits with the divine goodness to impute the guilt of one man's sin, to an innocent posterity, I should think it sufficient to make use of the apostle's words: "Nay, but O man, who art thou that repliest against God? Shall the thing formed say to him that formed it, why hast thou made me thus?" But to come to a more direct reply: persons would do well to consider that in the first covenant God made with man, Adam acted as a public person, as the common representative of all mankind, and consequently we must stand or fall with him. Had he continued in his obedience, and not eaten the forbidden fruit, the benefits of that obedience would doubtless have been imputed to us; but since he did not persist in it, but broke the covenant made with him, and us in him, who dares charge the righteous Judge of all the earth with injustice for imputing that to us also?

2. I proceed, second, to prove that we stand in need of being justified, on account of the sin of our lives.

That God, as he made man, has a right to demand his obedience, I suppose is a truth no one will deny: that he has also given us both a natural and a written law, whereby we are to be judged, cannot be questioned by anyone who believes St. Paul's Epistle to the Romans to be of divine authority; for in it we are told of a law written in the heart, and a law given by Moses; and that each of us has broken these laws is too evident from our sad and frequent experience. Accordingly the holy Scriptures inform us that "there is no man which liveth and sinneth not"; that "in many things we offend all"; that "if we say we have no sin, we deceive ourselves," and suchlike. And if we are thus offenders against God, it follows that we stand in need of forgiveness for thus offending him; unless we suppose God to enact laws, and at the same time not care whether they are obeyed or no, which is as absurd as to suppose that a prince should establish laws for the proper government of his country, and yet let every violator of them come off with impunity. But God has not dealt so foolishly with his creatures: no, as he gave us a law, he demands our obedience to that law and has obliged us universally and perseveringly to obey it, under no less a penalty than incurring his curse and eternal death for every breach of it: for thus speaks the Scripture, "Cursed is he that continueth not in all things that are written in the law to do them"; as the Scripture also speaks in another place, "The soul that sinneth, it shall die." Now it has already been proved that we have all of us sinned; and therefore, unless some means can be found to satisfy God's justice, we must perish eternally.

Let us then stand a while, and see in what a deplorable condition each of us comes into the world, and still continues, till we are translated into a state of grace. For surely nothing can well be supposed more deplorable than to be born under the curse of God; to be charged with original guilt; and not only so, but to be convicted as actual breakers of God's law, the least breach of which justly deserves eternal damnation. Surely this can be but a melancholy prospect to view ourselves in, and must put us upon contriving some means whereby we may satisfy and appease our offended Judge. But what must those means be? Shall we repent? Alas! there is not one word of repentance mentioned in the First Covenant: "The day that thou eatest thereof, thou shalt surely die." So that, if God be true, unless there be some way found out to satisfy divine justice, we must perish; and there is no room left for us to expect a change of mind in God, though we should seek it with tears. Well then, if repentance will not do, shall we plead the law of works? Alas! "By the law shall no man living be justified: for by the law comes the knowledge of sin." It is that which convicts and condemns, and therefore can by no means justify us; and "all our righteousnesses (says the prophet) are but as filthy rags." Wherewith then shall we come before the Lord and bow down before the most high God? Shall we come before him with calves of a year old, with thousands of rams, or ten thousands of rivers of oil? Alas! God has shown you, O man, that this will not avail, for he has declared, "I will take no bullock out of thy house, nor he goat out of thy fold: for all the beasts of the forests are mine, and so are the cattle upon a thousand hills." Will the Lord then be pleased to accept our firstborn for our transgression, the fruit of our bodies for the sin of our souls? Even this will not purchase our pardon: for he has declared that "the children shall not bear the iniquities of their parents." Besides, they are sinners, and therefore, being under the same condemnation, equally stand in need of forgiveness with ourselves. They are impure, and will the Lord accept the blind and lame for sacrifice? Shall some angel then, or archangel, undertake to fulfill the covenant which we have broken, and make atonement for us? Alas! they are only creatures, though creatures of the highest order; and therefore are obliged to obey God as well as we; and after they have done all, must say they have done no more than what was their duty to do. And supposing it was possible for them to die, yet how could the death of a finite creature satisfy an infinitely offended justice? Oh, wretched men that we are! Who shall deliver us? I thank God, our Lord Jesus Christ. Which naturally leads me to the—

Third thing proposed, which was to endeavor to prove that there is no possibility of obtaining this justification, which we so much want, but by the all-perfect obedience and precious death of Jesus Christ: "But ye are justified in the name of our Lord Jesus Christ."

But this having been in some measure proved by what has been said under the foregoing head, wherein I have shown that neither our repentance, righteousness, nor sacrifice, no not the obedience and death of angels, themselves, could possibly procure justification for us, nothing remains for me to do under this head, but to show that Jesus Christ has procured it for us.

And here I shall still have recourse "to the law and to the testimony." For after all the most subtle disputations on either side, nothing but the lively oracles of God can give us any satisfaction in this momentous point: it being such an inconceivable mystery, that the eternal, only begotten Son of God should die for sinful man, that we dare not have presumed so much as to have thought of it, had not God revealed it in his holy Word. It is true, reason may show us the wound, but revelation only can lead us to the means of our cure. And though the method God has been pleased to take to make us happy may be to the infidel a stumbling block, and to the wise opiniator and disputer of this world foolishness; yet wisdom, that is, the dispensation of our redemption, will be justified, approved of, and submitted to, by all her truly wise and holy children, by every sincere and upright Christian.

But to come more directly to the point before us. Two things, as was before observed, we wanted, in order to be at peace with God.

1. To be freed from the guilt of the sin of our nature.

2. From the sin of our lives.

And both these (thanks be to God for this unspeakable gift) are secured to believers by the obedience and death of Jesus Christ. For what says the Scripture?

1. As to the first, it informs us that "as by the disobedience of one man (or by one transgression, namely, that of Adam), many were made sinners; so by the obedience of one, Jesus Christ (therein including his passive as well as active obedience), many were made righteous." And again, "As by the disobedience of one man, judgment came upon all men unto condemnation"; or all men were condemned on having Adam's sin imputed to them; "so by the obedience of one, that is, Jesus Christ, the free gift of pardon and peace came upon all men (all sorts of men) unto justification of life." I say all sorts of men, for the apostle in this chapter is only drawing a parallel between the first and second Adam in this respect, that they acted both as representatives; and as the posterity of Adam had his sin imputed to them, so those for whom Christ died, and whose representative he is, shall have his merits imputed to them also. Those who run the parallel further, in order to prove universal redemption (whatever arguments they may draw for the proof of it from other passages of Scripture), if they would draw one from this for that purpose, I think they stretch their line of interpretation beyond the limits of Scripture.

2. Pardon for the sin of our lives was another thing, which we wanted to have secured to us, before we could be at peace with God.

And this, the holy Scriptures inform us, is abundantly done by the death of Jesus Christ. The evangelical prophet foretold that the promised Redeemer should be "wounded for our transgressions, and bruised for our iniquities; that the chastisement of our peace should be upon him; and that by his stripes

we should be healed" (Isa. 53:5). The angels at his birth said that he should **1.**
"save his people from their sins." And St. Paul declares that "this is a faithful
saying, and worthy of all acceptance, that Jesus Christ came into the world to
save sinners." And here in the words of the text, "Such (or, as I observed
before, these things) were some of you; but ye are washed. . . ." And again,
"Jesus Christ is the end of the law for righteousness to everyone that
believeth." And, to show us that none but Jesus Christ can do all this, the apostle St. Peter says, "Neither is their salvation in any other; for there is no other
name under heaven given among men, whereby we must be saved," but the
name of Jesus Christ.

How God will be pleased to deal with the Gentiles, who yet sit in darkness
and under the shadow of death, and upon whom the Sun of righteousness
never yet arose, is not for us to inquire. "What have we to do to judge those
that are without?" To God's mercy let us recommend them, and wait for a
solution of this and every other difficult point, till the great day of accounts,
when all God's dispensations, both of providence and grace, will be fully
cleared up by methods to us as yet unknown, because unrevealed. However,
this we know, that the Judge of all the earth will, most assuredly, do right.
But it is time for me to draw a conclusion.

I have now, brethren, by the blessings of God, discoursed on the words of
the text in the method I proposed. Many useful inferences might be drawn
from what has been delivered; but as I have detained you, I fear, too long
already, permit me only to make a reflection or two on what has been said,
and I am done.

If then we are freely justified by the death and obedience of Jesus Christ,
let us here pause a while; and as before we have reflected on the misery of a
fallen, let us now turn aside and see the happiness of the believing, soul. But
alas! how am I lost to think that God the Father, when we were in a state of
enmity and rebellion against him, should notwithstanding yearn in his bowels
toward us his fallen, his apostate, creatures; and because nothing but an infinite ransom could satisfy an infinitely offended justice, that [he] should send
his only and dear Son Jesus Christ (who is God, blessed forever, and who had
lain in his bosom from all eternity) to fulfill the covenant of works and die a
cursed, painful, ignominious death for us and for our salvation! Who can avoid
crying out at the consideration of his mystery of godliness. "Oh, the depth of
the riches of God's love" to us his wretched, miserable, and undone creatures!
"How unsearchable is his mercy, and his ways past finding out!" Now know
we of a truth, O God, that you have loved us, "since thou hast not withheld
thy Son, thine only Son Jesus Christ," from thus doing and dying for us.

1. If the angels in Heaven knew so did those cast out

But as we admire the Father sending, let us likewise humbly and thankfully adore the Son coming, when sent to die for man. But oh, what thoughts can conceive, what words express the infinite greatness of that unparalleled love, which engaged the Son of God to come down from the mansions of his Father's glory to obey and die for sinful man! The Jews, when he only shed a tear at poor Lazarus' funeral, said, "Behold how he loved him!" How much more justly then may we cry out, "Behold how he loved us!" When he not only fulfilled the whole moral law, but did not spare to shed his own most precious blood for us.

And can any poor truly convicted sinner, after this, despair of mercy? What, can they see their Savior hanging on a tree, with arms stretched out ready to embrace them, and yet, in their truly believing on him, doubt of finding acceptance with him? No, away with all such dishonorable, desponding thoughts. Look on his hands, bored with pins of iron; look on his side, pierced with a cruel spear, to let loose the sluices of his blood, and open a fountain for sin, and for all uncleanness; and then despair of mercy if you can! No, only believe in him, and then, though you have crucified him afresh, yet will he abundantly pardon you; "though your sins be as scarlet, yet shall they be as wool; though deeper than crimson, yet shall they be whiter than snow."

Which God of his infinite mercy grant through Jesus Christ our Lord; to whom with the Father and the Holy Ghost, three persons and one God, be ascribed, as is most due, all honor and praise, might, majesty, and dominion, now and forever. Amen. are Yours LORD

The Great Duty
of Charity Recommended

—◆—

Charity never faileth. —1 Corinthians 13:8

Nothing is more valuable and commendable, and yet not one duty is less practiced, than that of charity. We often pretend concern and pity for the misery and distress of our fellow creatures, but yet we seldom commiserate their condition so much as to relieve them according to our abilities; but unless we assist them with what they may stand in need of, for the body, as well as for the soul, all our wishes are no more than words of no value or regard, and are not to be esteemed or regarded; for when we hear of any deplorable circumstance, in which our fellow creatures are involved, be they friends or enemies, it is our duty, as Christians, to assist them to the utmost of our power.

Indeed, we are not, my brethren, to hurt ourselves or our families; this is not that charity which is so much recommended by St. Paul; no, but if we are any ways capable of relieving them without injuring either ourselves, or families, then it is our duty to do it; and this never fails, where it proceeds from a right end and with a right view.

St. Paul had been showing, in the preceding chapter, that spiritual gifts were diverse; that God had disposed of one blessing to one, and another to another; and though there was a diversity of blessings, God did not bestow them to one person, but gave to one a blessing which he denied to another, and gave a blessing or a gift to the other which might make him as eminent in one way as the other's gift made him so in another; but though there are these diverse spiritual gifts, they are all given for some wise end, even to profit withal, and to that end they are thus diversely bestowed. We are not, on the one hand, to hide those gifts which God has given us: neither are we, on the other, to be so lavish of them, as to spend them upon our lusts and pleasures, to satisfy our sensual appetites, but they are to be used for the glory of God, and the good of immortal souls. After he had particularly illustrated this, he comes to show that all gifts, however great they may be in themselves, are of no value unless we have charity, as you may see particularly, by considering from the beginning of this chapter.

But before I go any further, I shall inform you what the apostle means by charity; and that is, love, if there is true love, there will be charity; there will *the gift we all possess in Christ* be an endeavor to assist, help, and relieve according to that ability wherewith God has blessed us: and, since this is so much recommended by the apostle, let us see how valuable this charity is, and how commendable in all those who pursue it. I shall—

I. Consider this blessing as relation to the bodies of men.

II. I shall show how much more valuable it is, when relating to the souls of men.

III. Shall show you when your charity is of the right kind.

IV. Why this charity, or the grace of love, never fails.

V. Shall conclude all, with an exhortation to high and low, rich and poor, one with another, to be found in the constant practice of this valuable and commendable duty.

First, I shall consider this duty, as relating to the bodies of men. And—

1. Oh, that the rich would consider how praiseworthy this duty is, in helping their fellow creatures! We were created to be a help to each other; God has made no one so independent as not to need the assistance of another; the richest and most powerful man upon the face of this earth needs the help and assistance of those who are around him; and though he may be great today, a thousand accidents may make him as low tomorrow; he that is rolling in plenty today may be in as much scarcity tomorrow. If our rich men would be more charitable to their poor friends and neighbors, it would be a means of recommending them to the favor of others, if providence should frown upon them; but alas, our great men had much rather spend their money in a play-house, at a ball, an assembly, or a masquerade, than relieve a poor distressed servant of Jesus Christ. They had rather spend their estates on their hawks and hounds, on their whores and earthly, sensual, devilish pleasures, than comfort, nourish, or relieve one of their distressed fellow creatures. What difference is there between the king on the throne and the beggar on the dunghill, when God demands their breaths? There is no difference, my brethren, in the grave, nor will there be any at the day of judgment. You will not be excused because you have had a great estate, a fine house, and lived in all the pleasures that earth could afford you; no, these things will be one means of your condemnation; neither will you be judged according to the largeness of your estate, but according to the use you have made of it.

Now, you may think nothing but of your pleasures and delights, of living in ease and plenty, and never consider how many thousands of your fellow creatures would rejoice at what you are making waste of and setting no account by. Let me beseech you, my rich brethren, to consider the poor of the

*Whitefield was frickin "BLUNT" in what was the Victorian age

world, and how commendable and praiseworthy it is to relieve those who are distressed. Consider, how pleasing this is to God, how delightful it is to man, and how many prayers you will have put up for your welfare by those persons whom you relieve; and let this be a consideration to spare a little out of the abundance wherewith God has blessed you for the relief of his poor. He could have placed you in their low condition, and they in your high state; it is only his good pleasure that has thus made the difference, and shall not this make you remember your distressed fellow creatures?

Let me beseech you to consider, which will stand you best at the day of judgment, so much money expended at a horse race or a cockpit, at a play or a masquerade, or so much given for the relief of your fellow creatures, and for the distressed members of Jesus Christ.

I beseech you, that you would consider how valuable and commendable this duty is: do not be angry at my thus exhorting you to that duty, which is so much recommended by Jesus Christ himself, and by all his apostles: I speak particularly to you, my rich brethren, to entreat you to consider those that are poor in this world, and help them from time to time, as their necessity calls for it. Consider, that there is a curse denounced against the riches of those who do not thus do good with them; namely, "Go to now, you rich men, weep and howl for your miseries that shall come upon you; your riches are corrupted, your garments are moth-eaten, your gold and silver is cankered, and the rust of them shall be a witness against you, and shall eat your flesh, as it were fire; ye have heaped your treasure together for the last day." You see the dreadful woe pronounced against all those who hoard up the abundance of the things of this life, without relieving the distresses of those who are in want thereof: and the apostle James goes on also to speak against those who have acquired estates by fraud, as too many have in these days. "Behold, the hire [pay] of the laborers, which have reaped down your fields, which is by you kept back by fraud, crieth; and the cries of them who have reaped, are entered into the ears of the Lord God of Sabaoth. Ye have lived in pleasure on the earth, and been wanton; ye have nourished your hearts, as in the day of slaughter." Thus, if you go on to live after the lust of the flesh, to pamper your bellies, and make them a god, while the poor all around you are starving, God will make these things a witness against you, which shall be as a worm to your souls, and gnaw your consciences to all eternity; therefore let me once more recommend charity unto the bodies of men, and beseech you to remember what a blessed Lord Jesus Christ has promised unto those who thus love his members that "as they have done it to the least of his members, they have done it unto him."

* Father I forgive all who deliberately withhold my due. Forgive them LORD I ask.

I am not now speaking for myself; I am not recommending my little flock in Georgia to you; then you might say, as many wantonly do, that I wanted the money for myself; no, my brethren, I am now recommending the poor of this land to you, your poor neighbors, poor friends, yes, your poor enemies; they are whom I am now speaking for; and when I see so many starving in the streets and almost naked, my bowels are moved with pity and concern, to consider that many in whose power it is to lend their assisting hand should shut up their bowels of compassion, and will not relieve their fellow creatures, though in the most deplorable condition for the want thereof.

As I have thus recommended charity particularly to the rich among you, so now I would—

2. Second, recommend this to another set of people among us, who, instead of being the most forward in acts of charity, are commonly the most backward; I mean the clergy of this land.

Good God! How amazing is the consideration that those whom God has called out to labor in spiritual things should be so backward in this duty, as fatal experience teaches. Our clergy (that is, the generality thereof) are only seeking after preferment, running up and down, to obtain one benefice after another; and to heap up an estate, either to spend on the pleasures of life, or to gratify their sensual appetites, while the poor of their flock are forgotten; no, worse, they are scorned, hated, and disdained.

I am not now, my brethren, speaking of all the clergy; no, blessed be God, there are some among them who abhor such proceedings and are willing to relieve the necessary; but God knows, these are but very few, while many take no thought of the poor among them.

They can visit the rich and the great, but the poor they cannot bear in their sight; they are forgetful, willfully forgetful, of the poor members of Jesus Christ.

They have gone out of the old paths and turned into a new polite way, but which is not warranted in the Word of God: they are sunk into a fine way of acting; but as fine as it is, it was not the practice of the apostles or of the Christians in any age of the church; for they visited and relieved the poor among them; but how rare is this among us, how seldom do we find charity in a clergyman?

It is with grief I speak these things, but woeful experience is a witness to the truth thereof: and if all the clergy of this land were here, I would tell them boldly that they did not keep in the ways of charity, but were remiss in their duty; instead of "selling all and giving to the poor," they will not sell anything, nor give at all to the poor.

3. Third, I would exhort you who are poor to be charitable to one another. Though you may not have money, or the things of this life, to bestow upon one another; yet you may assist them, by comforting, and advising them not to be discouraged though they are low in the world; or in sickness you may help them according as you have time or ability. Do not be unkind to one another: do not grieve, or vex, or be angry with each other, for this is giving the world an advantage over you.

And if God stirs up any to relieve you, do not make an ill use of what his providence, by the hands of some Christian, has bestowed upon you. Be always humble and wait on God. Do not murmur or repine, if you see any relieved and you are not. Still wait on the Lord, and help one another, according to your abilities, from time to time.

Having showed you how valuable this is to the bodies of men, I now proceed—

Second, to show you how much more valuable this charity is when it extends to the souls of men.

And is not the soul more valuable than the body? It would be of no advantage, but an infinite disadvantage, to obtain all the world, if we were to lose our souls. The soul is of infinite value, and of infinite concern; and therefore we should extend our charity whenever we see it needful, and likewise should reprove, rebuke, and exhort with all godliness and love.

We should, my dear brethren, use all means and opportunities for the salvation of our own souls, and of the souls of others. We may have a great deal of charity and concern for the bodies of our fellow creatures, when we have no thought, or concern, for their immortal souls. But oh, how sad is it, to have thought for a mortal, but not for the immortal part; to have charity for the body of our fellow creatures, while we have no concern for their immortal souls; it may be, we help them to ruin them, but have no concern in the saving of them.

You may love to spend a merry evening, to go to a play or a horse race, with them; but on the other hand, you cannot bear the thoughts of going to a sermon or a religious society with them; no, you would sing the songs of the drunkard, but you will not sing hymns, with them; this is not polite enough; this is unbecoming a gentleman of taste, unfashionable, and only practiced among a parcel of enthusiasts and madmen.

Thus you will be so uncharitable as to join hand in hand with those who are hastening to their own damnation, while you will not be so charitable as to assist them in being brought from darkness to light, and from the power of

Satan unto God. But this, this, my dear brethren, is the greatest charity as can be, to save a soul from death: this is of far greater advantage, than relieving the body of a fellow creature; for the most miserable object as could be, death, would deliver it from all. But death, to those who are not born again, would be so far from being a release from all misery, that it would be an inlet to all torment, and that to all eternity. Therefore, we should assist, as much as possible, to keep a soul from falling into the hands of Satan, for he is the grand enemy of souls. How should this excite you to watch over your own and others' souls? For unless you are earnest with God, Satan will be too hard for you. Surely, it is the greatest charity to watch over one another's words and actions, that we may forewarn each other when danger is nigh, or when the enemy of souls approaches.

And if you have once known the value of your own souls, and know what it is to be snatched as brands out of the burning fire, you will be solicitous that others may be brought out of the same state. It is not the leading of a moral life, being honest, and paying every man his just due; this is not a proof of your being in a state of grace, or of being born again, and renewed in the spirit of your minds, no, you may die honest, just, charitable, and yet not be in a state of salvation.

It is not the preaching of that morality, which most of our pulpits now bring forth, that is sufficient to bring you from sin unto God. I saw you willing to learn, and yet were ignorant of the necessity of being born again, regenerated, of having all old things done away, and all things becoming new in your souls. I could not bear, my brethren, to see you in the highway to destruction, and none to bring you back. It was love to your souls, it was a desire to see Christ formed in you, which brought me into the fields, the highways, and hedges, to preach unto you Jesus, a crucified Jesus as dying for you. It was charity, indeed it was charity to your souls, which has exposed me to the present ill treatment of my letter-learned brethren.

Therefore, let me advise you to be charitable to the souls of one another; that is, by advising them with all love and tenderness, to follow after Christ, and the things which belong to their immortal peace, before they be forever hid from their eyes.

I now proceed, in the third place, to show when your charity is of the right kind.

And here, my brethren, I shall show, first, when it is not, and, second, when it is of the right kind.

★ Lord my heart is pricked, I have no concern often times for those I see on the road to destruction. I repent I choose to have Your heart for the lost.

1. First, your charity is not of the right kind when it proceeds from worldly views or ends.

If it is to be seen of men, to receive any advantage from them, to be esteemed, or to gain a reputation in the world; or if you have any pride in it, and expect to reap benefit from God merely for it; if all or each of these is the end of your charity, then it is all in vain; your charity does not proceed from a right end, but you are hereby deceiving your own souls. *Me too often* If you give an alms purely to be observed by man, or as expecting favor from God, merely on the account thereof, then you have not the glory of God, or the benefit of your fellow creatures at heart, but merely yourself: this, this is not charity. *ME again*

Nor, second, is that true charity when we give anything to our fellow creatures purely to indulge them in vice: this is so far from being charity, that it is a sin, both against God and against our fellow creatures. And yet, this is common, as it is sinful, to carry our friends, under a specious pretense of charity, to one or the other entertainment, with no other view but to make them guilty of excess. Hereby you are guilty of a double sin: we are not to sin ourselves, much less should we endeavor to make another sin likewise.

But, third, our charity comes from a right end, when it proceeds from love to God, and for the welfare both of the body and soul of our fellow creatures.

When this is the sole end of relieving our distressed fellow creatures, then our charity comes from a right end, and we may expect to reap advantage by it: this is the charity which is pleasing to God. God is well pleased, when all our actions proceed from love, love to himself, and love to immortal souls.

Consider, my dear brethren, that it was love for souls, that brought the blessed Jesus down from the bosom of his Father; that made him, who was equal in power and glory, to come and take upon him our nature; that caused the Lord of life to die the painful, ignominious, and accursed death of the cross. It was love to immortal souls that brought this blessed Jesus among us. And oh, that we might hence consider how great the value of souls was and is: it was that which made Jesus to bleed, pant, and die. And surely souls must be of infinite worth, which made the Lamb of God to die so shameful a death.

And shall not this make you have a true value for souls? It is of the greatest worth: and this, this is the greatest charity, when it comes from love to God, and from love to souls. This will be a charity, the satisfaction of which will last to all eternity. Oh, that this may make you have so much regard for the value of souls, as not to neglect all opportunities for the doing of them good: here is something worth having charity for, because they remain to all eternity. Therefore let me earnestly beseech you both to consider the worth of immortal souls and let your charity extend to them, that by your advice and admonition, you may be an instrument, in the hands of God, in bringing souls to the Lord Jesus.

I am in the next place to consider, fourth, why this charity or grace of love never fails.

And it never fails in respect of its proceeding from an unchangeable God. We are not to understand that our charity is always the same: no, there may, and frequently are, ebbs and flowings; but still it never totally fails; no, the grace of love remains forever. There is, and will be, a charity to all who have erred and run astray from God. We cannot be easy to see souls in the highway to destruction and not use our utmost endeavor to bring them back from sin, and show them the dreadful consequence of running into evil. Christians cannot bear to see those souls for whom Christ died perish for want of knowledge; and if they see any of the bodies of their fellow creatures in want, they will do the utmost in their power to relieve them.

Charity will never fail, among those who have a true love to the Lord Jesus and know the value of souls: they will be charitable to those who are in distress. And thus you see, that true charity, if it proceeds from a right end, never fails.

I now proceed, my brethren, in the last place, to exhort all of you, high and low, rich and poor, one with another, to practice this valuable and commendable duty of charity.

It is not rolling in your coaches, taking your pleasure, and considering the miseries of your fellow creatures that is commendable or praiseworthy; but the relieving your distressed poor fellow creatures is valuable and praiseworthy wherever it is found. But alas! how very few of our carefree and polite gentlemen consider their poor friends; rather they despise and do not regard them. They can indulge themselves in the follies of life and had much rather spend their estates in lusts and pleasures, while the poor all round them are not thought worthy to be set with the dogs of their flock. If you have an abundance of the things of this world, then you are esteemed as companions for the polite and carefree in life; but if you are poor, then you must not expect to find any favor, but be hated, or not thought fit for company or conversation: and if you have an abundance of the things of this life, and do not want any assistance, then you have many ready to help you. My dear brethren, I do not doubt but your own experience is a proof of my assertions; as also, that if any come into distress, then those who promised to give relief quite forget what they promise and will despise because providence has frowned. But this is not acting like those who are bound for the heavenly Jerusalem; thus our hearts and our actions give our lips the lie; for if we profess the name of Christ and do not depart from all iniquity, we are not those who are worthy of being esteemed Christians indeed.

For if we have not charity, we are not Christians: charity is the great duty of Christians; and where is our Christianity, if we want charity? Therefore let me beseech you to exercise charity to your distressed fellow creatures. Indeed, my dear brethren, this is truly commendable, truly valuable; and therefore, I beseech you, in the bowels of tender mercy to Christ, to consider his poor distressed members; exercise, exercise, I beseech you, this charity. If you have no compassion, you are not true disciples of the Lord Jesus Christ. I humbly beg you to consider those who want relief and are really destitute, and relieve them according to your abilities. Consider, that the more favorable providence has been to you, it should make you the more earnest and solicitous to relieve *anxiously* those whom you may find in distress: it is of the utmost consequence, what is *awaiting* well pleasing to your fellow creatures, and doing your duty to God.

When you are called from hence, then all riches and grandeur will be over; the grave will make no distinction; great estates will be of no significance in the other world; and if you have made a bad use of the talent which God has put into your hands, it will be only an aggravation of your condemnation at the great day of account, when God shall come to demand your souls, and to call you to an account, for the use to which you have put the abundance of the things of this life.

To conclude, let me once more beseech each of you to act according to the circumstances of life, which God, in his rich and free mercy, has given you.

If you were sensible of the great consequences which would attend your acting in this charitable manner, and considered it as a proof of your love to God—the loving his members—you could not be uncharitable in your tempers, nor fail to relieve any of your distressed fellow creatures.

Consider how easy it is for many of you, by putting your mites together, to help one who is in distress; and how can you tell, but that the little you give *collectively, not individually* may be the means of bringing one from distress into flourishing circumstances? And then, if there is a true spirit of a Christian in them, they can never be sufficiently thankful to God the Author, and to you as the instrument, in being so great a friend to them in their melancholy circumstances. Consider also, once more, how much better your account will be at the day of judgment, and what peace of conscience you will enjoy. How satisfactory must be the thought of having relieved the widow and the fatherless. This is recommended by the Lord Jesus Christ, and has been practiced in all ages of the church: and therefore, my brethren, be you now found in the practice of this duty. [LOVE] the distressed

I have been the larger upon this, because our enemies say we deny all moral actions; but, blessed be God, they speak against us without cause. We highly value them, but we say that faith in Christ, the love of God, and being born again are of infinite more worth; but you cannot be true Christians without having charity to your fellow creatures, be they friends or enemies, if in distress. And therefore exert yourselves in this duty, as is commanded by the blessed Jesus: and if you have true charity, you shall live and reign with him forever.

Now to God the Father, God the Son, and God the Holy Ghost, be all honor, power, glory, might, majesty, and dominion, both now and forevermore. Amen.

Satan's Devices

—m—

Lest Satan should get an advantage of us: for we are not ignorant of his devices. —2 CORINTHIANS 2:11

The occasion of these words was as follows: in the church of Corinth there was an unhappy person who had committed such incest, as was not so much as named among the Gentiles, in taking his father's wife; but either on account of his wealth, power, or some such reasons, like many notorious offenders nowadays, he had not been exposed to the censures of the church. St. Paul, therefore, in his first epistle, severely chides them for this neglect of discipline, and commands them, "in the name of our Lord Jesus Christ, when they were gathered together, to deliver such a one (whoever he was) to Satan, for the destruction of the flesh, that his spirit might be saved in the day of the Lord"; that is, they should solemnly excommunicate him, which was then commonly attended with some bodily disease. The Corinthians, being obedient to the apostle, as dear children, no sooner received this reproof, but they submitted to it, and cast the offending party out of the church. But while they were endeavoring to amend one fault, they unhappily ran into another; and as they formerly had been too mild and remiss, so now they behaved toward him with too much severity and resentment. The apostle therefore in this chapter, reproves this, and tells them that "sufficient to the offender's shame, was the punishment which had been inflicted of many": that he had now suffered enough; and that therefore lest he should be tempted to say with Cain, "My punishment is greater than I can bear," or to use the apostle's own words, "Lest he should be swallowed up with overmuch sorrow," they ought, now he had given proof of his repentance, to forgive him, to confirm their love toward him, and to restore him in the spirit of meekness; "lest Satan (to whose buffetings he was now given, by tempting him to despair) should get an advantage over us"; and so, by representing you as merciless and cruel, cause that holy name to be blasphemed, by which you are called, "for we are not ignorant of his devices": we know very well how many subtle ways he has to draw aside and beguile unguarded, unthinking men.

Thus then stand the words in relation to the context; but as Satan has many devices, and as his quiver is full of other poisonous darts besides those which he shoots at us to drive us to despair, I shall, in the following discourse,

First, briefly observe who we are to understand by Satan.

And, second, point out to you, what are the chief devices he generally makes use of to draw off converts from Christ and also prescribe some remedies against them.

First, who are we to understand by Satan?

The word *Satan,* in its original significance, meant an adversary; and in its general acceptance, is made use of, to point out to us the chief of the devils, who, for striving to be as God, was cast down from heaven, and is now permitted "with the rest of his spiritual wickednesses in high places, to walk up and down, seeking whom he may devour." We hear of him immediately after the creation, when in the shape of a serpent, he lay in wait to deceive our first parents. He is called Satan in the book of Job, where we are told that "when the sons of God came to present themselves before the Lord, Satan also came among them." As the Scripture also speaks in the book of Chronicles, "and Satan moved David to number the people." In the New Testament he goes under different denominations; sometimes he is called the evil one, because he is evil in himself, and tempts us to evil. Sometimes "the prince of the power of the air" and "the spirit that now ruleth in the children of disobedience," because he resides chiefly in the air, and through the whole world, and all that are not born of God, are said to lie in him.

He is an enemy to God and goodness; he is a hater of all truth. Why else did he slander God in paradise? Why did he tell Eve, "You shall not surely die"? And why did he promise to give all the kingdoms of the world, and the glories of them, to Jesus Christ, if he would fall down and worship him?

He is full of malice, envy, and revenge, for what other motives could induce him to molest innocent man in paradise? And why is he still so restless in his attempts to destroy us, who have done him no wrong?

He is a being of great power as appears in his being able to act on the imagination of our blessed Lord, so as to represent to him all the kingdoms of the world, and the glories of them, in a moment of time. As also in carrying his sacred body through the air up to a pinnacle of the temple, and his driving a herd of swine so furiously into the deep. What's more, so great is his might, that, I doubt not, was God to let him use his full strength, but he could turn the earth upside down or pull the sun from its orb. *Abt confusing, Satan then Jesus?*

But what he is most remarkable for is his subtlety; for not having power given him from above, to take us by force, he is obliged to wait for opportunities to betray us and to catch us by guile. He therefore made use of the serpent, which was subtle above all the beasts of the field, in order to tempt our first parents; and accordingly he is said, in the New Testament, "to lie in wait to deceive"; and, in the words of the text, the apostle says, "We are not igno-rant of his devices," thereby implying that we are more in danger of being seduced by his policy, than overborne by his power.

From this short description of Satan, we may easily judge whose children they are, who love to make a lie, who speak evil of, and slander their neighbor, and whose hearts are full of pride, subtlety, malice, envy, revenge, and all uncharitableness. Surely they have Satan for their father: for the tempers of Satan they know, and the works of Satan they do. But were they to see either themselves, or Satan as he is, they could not but be terrified at their own like-ness and abhor themselves in dust and ashes.   * 2nd Law of Thermodynamics!

But the justice of God in suffering us to be tempted, is vindicated from the following considerations: that we are here in a state of disorder; *that he has promised not to suffer us to be tempted above what we are able to bear; and not only so, but to him that overcoms he will give a crown of life.

The holy angels themselves, it should seem, were once put to a trial whether they would be faithful or not. The first Adam was tempted, even in paradise. And Jesus Christ, that second Adam, though he was a son, yet was carried, as our representative, by the Holy Spirit, into the wilderness, to be tempted of the devil. And there is not one single saint in paradise, among the goodly fellowship of the prophets, the glorious company of the apostles, the noble army of mar-tyrs, and the spirits of just men made perfect, who, when on earth, was not assaulted by the fiery darts of that wicked one, the devil.

What then has been the common lot of all God's children, and of the angels, even of the eternal Son of God himself, we must not think to be exempted from; no, it is sufficient if we are made perfect through temptations, as they were. And therefore since we cannot but be tempted, unless we could unmake human nature, instead of repining at our condition, we should rather be inquiring at what time of our lives Satan most violently assaults us. And what those devices are, which he commonly makes use of, in order to "get an advantage over us"?

As to the first question—what time of life?—I answer, we must expect to be tempted by him, in some degree or other, all our lives long. For this life being a continual warfare, we must never expect to have rest from our spiri-tual adversary the devil, or to say, our combat with him is finished, till, with our blessed Master, we bow down our heads and give up the ghost.

But since the time of our conversion, or first entering upon the spiritual life, is the most critical time at which he, for the most part, violently besets us, as well knowing, if he can prevent our setting out, he can lead us captive at his will; and since the wise son of Sirach particularly warns us, when we are going to serve the Lord, to prepare our souls for temptation, I shall, in answer to the other question, pass on to the—

Second general thing proposed; and point out those devices which Satan generally makes use of at our first conversion, in order to get an advantage over us.

But let me observe to you, that whatsoever shall be delivered in the following discourse is only designed for such as have actually entered upon the divine life; and not for carnal "almost Christians," who have the form of godliness, but never yet felt the power of it in their hearts.

This being premised, the first device I shall mention which Satan makes use of is to drive us to despair. *I Sam 30: 25 comes to mind*

When God the Father awakens a sinner by the terrors of the law, and by his Holy Spirit convinces him of sin, in order to lead him to Christ, and show him the necessity of a Redeemer, then Satan generally strikes in and aggravates those convictions to such a degree, as to make the sinner doubt of finding mercy through the Mediator.

Thus, in all his temptations of the holy Jesus, he chiefly aimed to make him question whether he was the Son of God, "If thou be the Son of God," ✱ do so and so. With many such desponding thoughts, no doubt, he filled the heart of the great St. Paul, when he continued three days, neither eating bread nor drinking water; and therefore he speaks by experience, when he says, in the words of the text, "We are not ignorant of his devices," that he would endeavor to drive the incestuous person to despair.

But let not any of you be influenced by him, to despair of finding mercy. For it is not the greatness or number of our crimes, but impenitence and unbelief, that will prove our ruin. No, were our sins more in number than the hairs of our head, or of a deeper dye than the brightest scarlet; yet the merits of the death of Jesus Christ are infinitely greater, and faith in his blood shall make them white as snow.

Answer always therefore his despairing suggestions, as your blessed Lord did, with an "It is written." Tell him, you know that your Redeemer lives, ever to make intercession for you; that the Lord has received from him double for all your crimes; and though you have sinned much, that is no reason why you should despair, but only why you should love much, having so much forgiven.

A second device that Satan generally makes use of, to get an advantage over young converts, is to tempt them to presume, or to think more highly of themselves than they ought to think.

When a person has for some little time tasted the good word of life and felt the powers of the world to come, he is commonly (as indeed well he may)

✱ He knew Jesus was he knew him from heaven,

most highly transported with that sudden change he finds in himself. But then Satan will not be wanting, at such a time, to puff him up with a high conceit of his own attainments as if he was some great person; and will tempt him to set at naught his brethren, as though he was holier than they.

Take heed therefore, and let us beware of this device of our spiritual adversary; for as before honor is humility, so a haughty spirit generally goes before a fall; and God is obliged, when under such circumstances, to send us some humbling visitation, or permit us to fall, as he did Peter into some grievous sin, that we may learn not to be too high minded.

To check therefore all suggestions to spiritual pride, let us consider that we did not apprehend Christ, but were apprehended of him. That we have nothing but what we have received. That the free grace of God has alone made the difference between us and others; and, was God to leave us to the deceitfulness of our own hearts but one moment, we should become weak and wicked, like other men. We should further consider, that being proud of grace is the most ready way to lose it. "For God resisteth the proud, and giveth more grace only to the humble." And were we endowed with the perfections of the seraphim, yet if we were proud of those perfections, they would but render us more accomplished devils. Above all, we should pray earnestly to almighty God, that we may learn of Jesus Christ, to be lowly in heart. That his grace, through the subtlety and deceivableness of Satan, may not be our poison. But that we may always think soberly of ourselves, as we ought to think.

A third device I shall mention, which Satan generally makes use of "to get an advantage over us," is to tempt us to uneasiness, and to have hard thoughts of God, when we are dead and barren in prayer.

Though this is a term not understood by the natural man, yet whosoever there are among you who have passed through the pangs of the new birth, they know full well what I mean, when I talk of deadness and dryness in prayer. And, I doubt not, but many of you, among whom I am not preaching the kingdom of God, are at this very time laboring under it.

For when persons are first awakened to the divine life, because grace is weak and nature strong, God is often pleased to vouchsafe them some extraordinary illuminations of his Holy Spirit; but when they are grown to be more perfect men in Christ, then he frequently seems to leave them to themselves; and not only so, but permits a horrible deadness and dread to overwhelm them; at which times Satan will not be wanting to vex and tempt them to impatience, to the great discomfort of their souls.

But be not afraid; for this is no more than your blessed Redeemer, that spotless Lamb of God, has undergone before you: witness his bitter agony in the garden, when his soul was exceedingly sorrowful, even unto death. When he sweat great drops of blood, falling on the ground; when the sense of the divinity was drawn from him; and Satan, in all probability, was permitted to set all his terrors in array before him.

Rejoice therefore, my brethren, when you fall into the like circumstances; as knowing that you are therein partakers of the sufferings of Jesus Christ. Consider that it is necessary such inward trials should come, to wean us from the immoderate love of sensible devotion, and teach us to follow Christ, not merely for his loaves, but out of a principle of love and obedience. In patience therefore possess your souls, and be not terrified by Satan's suggestions. Still persevere in seeking Jesus in the use of means, though it be sorrowing; and though through barrenness of soul, you may go mourning all the day long. Consider that the spouse is with you, though behind the curtain, as he was with Mary, at the sepulcher, though she knew it not. That he was withdrawn but for a little while, to make his next visit more welcome. That though he may now seem to frown and look back on you, as he did on the Syrophonecian woman, yet if you, like her, or blind Bartimeus, cry out so much the more earnestly, "Jesus, thou Son of David, have mercy on us," he will be made known unto you again, either in the temple, by breaking of bread, or some other way.

But among all the devices that Satan makes use of "to get an advantage over us," there is none in which he is more successful, or by which he grieves the children of God worse, than a fourth device I am going to mention: his troubling you with blasphemous, profane, unbelieving thoughts, and sometimes to such a degree, that they are as tormenting as the rack.

Some indeed are apt to impute all such evil thoughts to a disorder of body. But those who know anything of the spiritual life can inform you, with greater certainty, that for the generality, they proceed from that wicked one, the devil; who, no doubt, has power given him from above, as well now as formerly, to disorder the body, as he did Job's, that he may, with the more secrecy and success, work upon, ruffle, and torment the soul.

You that have felt his fiery darts can subscribe to the truth of this, and by fatal experience can tell how often he has bid you "curse God and die," and darted into your thoughts a thousand blasphemous suggestions, even in your most secret and solemn retirements; the bare [mere] looking back on which makes your very hearts to tremble.

I appeal to your own consciences: have not some of you, when you have been lifting up holy hands in prayer, been pestered with such a crowd of the most horrid insinuations, that you have been often tempted to rise off from your knees and been made to believe your prayers were an abomination to the Lord?

What's more, when, with the rest of your Christian brethren, you have crowded around the holy table and taken the sacred symbols of Christ's most blessed body and blood into your hands, instead of remembering the death of your Savior, have you not been employed in driving out evil thoughts, as Abraham was in driving away the birds that came to devour his sacrifice; and thereby have been terrified, lest you have eaten and drunk your own damnation?

But marvel not, as though some strange thing happened unto you; for this has been the common lot of all God's children. We read, even in Job's time, that "when the sons of God came to appear before their Maker (at public worship), Satan also came amongst them," to disturb their devotions.

And think not that God is angry with you for these distracting, though ever so blasphemous, thoughts: no, he knows it is not you, but Satan working in you; and therefore, notwithstanding he may be displeased with, and certainly will punish him, yet he will both pity and reward you. And though it be difficult to make persons in your circumstances to believe so; yet I doubt not but you are more acceptable to God when performing your holy duties in the midst of such involuntary distractions, than when you are wrapped up by devotion, as it were, into the third heavens; for you are then suffering, as well as doing the will of God, at the same time; and, like Nehemiah's servants at the building of the temple, are holding a trowel in one hand, and a sword in the other. Be not driven from the use of any ordinance whatever, on account of those abominable suggestions; for then you let Satan get his desired advantage over you; it being his chief design, by these thoughts, to make you fall out with the means of grace; and to tempt you to believe, you do not please God, for no other reason than because you do not please yourselves. Rather persevere in the use of the holy Communion (prayer) especially, and all other means whatever; and when these temptations have worked that resignation in you, for which they were permitted, God will visit you with fresh tokens of his love, as he met Abraham when he returned from the slaughter of the five kings; and will send an angel from heaven, as he did to his Son, on purpose to strengthen you.

Hitherto we have only observed such devices as Satan makes use of immediately by himself; but there is a fifth I shall mention, which is not the least, tempting us by our carnal friends and relatives.

This is one of the most common, as well as most artful, devices he makes use of, to draw young converts from God; for when he (Satan) cannot prevail over them by himself, he will try what he can do by the influence and mediation of others.

Thus he tempted Eve, that she might tempt Adam. Thus he stirred up Job's wife, to bid him "curse God and die." And thus he made use of Peter's tongue, to persuade our blessed Lord "to spare himself," and thereby decline those sufferings, by which alone we could be preserved from suffering the vengeance of eternal fire. And thus, in these last days, he often stirs up our most powerful friends and dearest intimates, to dissuade us from going in that narrow way, which alone leads unto life eternal.

But our blessed Lord has furnished us with a sufficient answer to all such suggestions. "Get you behind me, my adversaries," for otherwise they will be an offense unto you; and the only reason why they give such advice is because they "favor not the things that be of God, but the things that be of men."

Whoever, therefore, among you are resolved to serve the Lord, prepare your souls for many such temptations as these; for it is necessary that such offenses should come, to try your sincerity, to teach us to cease from man, and to see if we will forsake all to follow Christ. *those we think would stand w/us urge us to quit*

Indeed our modernizers of Christianity would persuade us that the gospel was calculated only for about two hundred years; and that now there is no need of hating father and mother, or of being persecuted for the sake of Christ and his gospel.

But such persons err, not knowing the Scriptures, and the power of godliness in their hearts; for whosoever receives the love of God in the truth of it, will find that Christ came to send not peace, but a sword upon earth, as much now as ever. That the father-in-law shall be against the daughter-in-law, in these latter as well as in the primitive times; and that if we will live godly in Christ Jesus, we must, as then, so now, from carnal friends and relations suffer persecution.

But the devil has a sixth device, which is as dangerous as any of the former, by not tempting us at all, or rather, by withdrawing himself for a while, in order to come upon us at an hour when we think not of it.

Thus it is said that he left Jesus Christ only for a season; and our blessed Lord has bid us to watch and pray always, that we enter not into temptation; thereby implying that Satan, whether we think of it or not, is always seeking how he may devour us.

If we would therefore behave like good soldiers of Jesus Christ, we must be always upon our guard, and never pretend to lay down our spiritual weapons of prayer and watching, till our warfare is accomplished by death; for if we do, our spiritual Amalek will quickly prevail against us. What if he has left us? It is only for a season; yet a little while, and, like a roaring lion, with double fury, he will break out upon us again. So great a coward as the devil is, he seldom leaves us at the first onset. As he followed our blessed Lord with one temptation after another, so will he treat his servants. And the reason why he does not renew his attacks is, sometimes, because God knows we are yet weak and unable to bear them; sometimes because our grand adversary thinks to beset us at a more convenient season.

Watch carefully over your heart, O Christian; and whenever you perceive yourself to be falling into a spiritual slumber, say to it, as Christ to his disciples, "Arise (my soul), why sleepest thou?" Awake, awake; put on strength, watch and pray, or otherwise the Philistines will be upon you and lead you whither you would not. Alas! Is this life a time to lie down and slumber in? Arise, and call upon your God, your spiritual enemy is not dead, but lurks in some secret place, seeking a convenient opportunity how he may betray you. If you cease to strive with him, you cease to be a friend of God; you cease to go in that narrow way which leads unto life.

Thus have I endeavored to point out to you some of those devices that Satan generally makes use of "to get an advantage over us"; many others there are, no doubt, which he often uses.

But these, on account of my youth and want of experience, I cannot yet apprise you of; they who have been listed for many years in their Master's service, and fought under his banner against our spiritual Amalek, are able to discover more of his artifices; and, being tempted in all things, like unto their brethren, can, in all things, advise and succor those that are tempted.

In the meanwhile, let me exhort my young fellow soldiers, who, like myself, are but just entering the field, and for whose sake this was written, not to be discouraged at the fiery trial wherewith they must be tried, if they would be found faithful servants of Jesus Christ. You see, my dearly beloved brethren, by what has been delivered, that our way through the wilderness of this world to the heavenly Canaan is beset with thorns, and that there are sons of Anak to be grappled with, before you can possess the promised land. But let not these, like so many false spies, discourage you from going up to fight the Lord's battles, but say with Caleb and Joshua, "Nay, but we will go up, for we are able to conquer them." Jesus Christ, that great captain of our salvation, has in our stead, and as our representative, baffled the grand enemy of mankind, and we have nothing to do but manfully to fight under his banner, and to go on from conquering to conquer. Our glory does not consist in being exempted from, but in enduring, temptations. "Blessed is the man (says the apostle) that endureth temptation"; and again, "Brethren, count it all joy, when you fall into diverse temptations." And in that perfect form our blessed Lord has prescribed to us, we are taught to pray, not so much to be delivered from all temptation, as "from the evil" of it. While we are on this side eternity, it must needs be that temptations come; and, no doubt, "Satan has desired to have all of us, to sift us as wheat." But wherefore should we fear? For he that is for us is by far more powerful, than all that are against us. Jesus Christ, our great High Priest, is exalted to the right hand of God, and there sits to make intercession for us, that our faith fail not.

Since then Christ is praying, whom should we fear? And since he has promised to make us more than conquerors, of whom should we be afraid? No, though a host of devils are set in array against us, let us not be afraid; though there should rise up the hottest persecution against us, yet let us put our trust in God. What though Satan, and the rest of his apostate spirits, are powerful, when compared with us; yet, if put in competition with the Almighty, they are as weak as the meanest worms. God has them all reserved in chains of darkness unto the judgment of the great day. So far as he permits them, they shall go, but no farther; and where he pleases, there shall their proud malicious designs be stayed. We read in the gospel that though a legion of them possessed one man, yet they could not destroy him; nor could they so much as enter into a swine, without first having leave given them from above. It is true, we often find they foil us, when we are assaulted by them; but let us be strong, and very courageous; for, though they bruise our heels, we shall, at length, bruise their heads. Yet a little while, and he that shall come, will come; and then we shall see all our spiritual enemies put under our feet. What if they do come out against us, like so many great Goliaths? Yet if we can go forth, as the stripling David, in the name and strength of the Lord of hosts, we may say, "O Satan, where is your power? O fallen spirits, where is your victory?"

Once more therefore, and to conclude: let us be strong and very courageous, and let us put on the whole armor of God, that we may be able to stand against the fiery darts of the wicked one. Let us renounce ourselves, and the world, and then we shall take away the armor in which he trusts, and he will find nothing in us for his temptations to work upon. We shall then prevent his malicious designs; and being willing to suffer ourselves, shall need less sufferings to be sent us from above. Let us have our loins girt about with truth and for a helmet, the hope of salvation; "praying always with all manner of supplication." Above all things, "Let us take the sword of the spirit, which is the Word of God," and "the shield of faith," looking always to Jesus, the Author and Finisher of our faith, who for the joy that was set before him, endured the cross, despising the shame, and is now sat down at the right hand of God.

To which happy place, may God of his infinite mercy translate us all, through our Lord Jesus Christ.

To whom, with the Father, and the Holy Ghost, three persons and one eternal God, be all honor and glory, now and forevermore. Amen.

On Regeneration

—m—

Therefore, if any man be in Christ, he is a new creature: old things are passed away; behold, all things are become new. —2 CORINTHIANS 5:17

The doctrine of our regeneration, or new birth in Christ Jesus, though one of the most fundamental doctrines of our holy religion, though so plainly and often pressed on us in sacred Writ that he who runs may read it; even though it is the very hinge on which the salvation of each of us turns, and a point too in which all sincere Christians, of every denomination, agree; yet it is so seldom considered, and so little experimentally understood by the generality of professors, that were we to judge of the truth of it, by the experience of most who call themselves Christians, we should be apt to imagine they had "not so much as heard" whether there be any such thing as regeneration or not. It is true, men for the most part are orthodox in the common articles of their creed; they believe "there is but one God, and one mediator between God and men, even the man Christ Jesus"; and that there is no other name given under heaven, whereby they can be saved, besides his. But then tell them they must be regenerated, they must be born again, they must be renewed in the very spirit, in the inmost faculties of their minds, before they can truly call Christ "Lord, Lord," or have an evidence that they have any share in the merits of his precious blood; and they are ready to cry out with Nicodemus, "How can these things be?" Or with the Athenians, on another occasion, "What wilt this bumbler say? He seemeth to be a setter-forth of strange doctrines," because we preach unto them Christ, and the new birth.

That I may therefore contribute my mite toward curing the fatal mistake of such persons, who would thus put asunder what God has inseparably joined together, and vainly think they are justified by Christ or have their sins forgiven and his perfect obedience imputed to them, when they are not sanctified, have not their natures changed, and made holy, I shall beg leave to enlarge on the words of the text in the following manner:

First, I shall endeavor to explain what is meant by being in Christ: "If any man be in Christ."

Second, what we are to understand by being a new creature: "If any man be in Christ, he is a new creature."

Third, I shall produce some arguments to make good the apostle's assertion.

And fourth, I shall draw some inferences from what may be delivered, and then conclude with a word or two of exhortation.

First, I am to endeavor to explain what is meant by this expression in the text: "If any man be in Christ."

Now a person may be said to be in Christ two ways.

First, only by an outward profession. And in this sense, everyone that is called a Christian, or baptized into Christ's church, may be said to be in Christ. But that this is not the sole meaning of the apostle's phrase before us is evident, because then everyone that names the name of Christ, or is baptized into his visible church, would be a new creature. Which is notoriously false, it being too plain, beyond all contradiction, that comparatively but few of those that are "born of water" are "born of the Spirit" likewise; to use another spiritual way of speaking, many are baptized with water, which were never baptized with the Holy Ghost.

To be in Christ therefore, in the full import of the word, must certainly mean something more than a bare outward profession, or being called after his name. For, as this same apostle tells us, "All are not Israelites that are of Israel," so when applied to Christianity, all are not real Christians that are nominally such. What's more, this is so far from being the case, that our blessed Lord himself informs us that many who have prophesied or preached in his name, and in his name cast out devils, and done many wonderful works, shall notwithstanding be dismissed at the last day, with "depart from me, I know you not, ye workers of iniquity."

It remains therefore that this expression, "if any man be in Christ," must be understood in a second and closer significance, to be in him so as to partake of the benefits of his sufferings; to be in him not only by an outward profession, but by an inward change and purity of heart, and cohabitation of his Holy Spirit; to be in him, so as to be mystically united to him by a true and lively faith, and thereby to receive spiritual virtue from him, as the members of the natural body do from the head, or the branches from the vine; to be in him in such a manner as the apostle, speaking of himself, acquaints us he knew a person was: "I knew a man in Christ," a true Christian; or, as he himself desires to be in Christ, when he wishes, in his Epistle to the Philippians, that he might be found in him.

This is undoubtedly the proper meaning of the apostle's expression in the words of the text; so that what he says in his Epistle to the Romans about

* oh that others would say this of me.

circumcision may very well be applied to the present subject; that he is not a real Christian who is only one outwardly; nor is that true baptism which is only outward in the flesh. But he is a true Christian who is one inwardly, whose baptism is that of the heart, in the spirit, and not merely in the water, whose praise is not of man but of God. Or, as he speaks in another place, "Neither circumcision nor uncircumcision availeth anything (of itself) but a new creature." Which amounts to what he here declares in the verse now under consideration, that if any man be truly and properly in Christ, he is a new creature.

Which brings me to show, second, what we are to understand by being a new creature.

And here it is evident at the first view, that this expression is not to be so explained as though there was a physical change required to be made in us; or as though we were to be reduced to our primitive nothings and then created and formed again. For, supposing we were, as Nicodemus ignorantly imagined, to enter a "second time into our mother's womb, and be born," alas! what would it contribute toward rendering us spiritually new creatures? Since "that which was born of the flesh would be flesh still," we should be the same carnal persons as ever, being derived from carnal parents, and consequently receiving the seeds of all manner of sin and corruption from them. No, it only means that we must be so altered as to the qualities and tempers of our minds, that we must entirely forget what manner of persons we once were. As it may be said of a piece of gold that was once in the ore, after it has been cleansed, purified, and polished, that it is a new piece of gold; as it may be said of a bright glass that has been covered over with filth, when it is wiped and so become transparent and clear, that it is a new glass. Or, as it might be said of Naaman, when he recovered of his leprosy and his flesh returned unto him like the flesh of a young child, that he was a new man; so our souls, though still the same as to offense, yet are so purged, purified, and cleansed from their natural dross, filth, and leprosy, by the blessed influences of the Holy Spirit, that they may be properly said to be made anew.

How this glorious change is worked in the soul cannot easily be explained, for no one knows the ways of the Spirit save the Spirit of God himself. Not that this ought to be any argument against this doctrine; for, as our blessed Lord observed to Nicodemus, when he was discoursing on this very subject, "The wind bloweth where it listeth, and thou hearest the sound thereof, but knowest not whence it cometh, and whither it goeth"; and if we are told of natural things, and we understand them not, how much less ought we to wonder, if we cannot immediately account for the invisible workings of the Holy Spirit? The truth of the matter is this: the doctrine of our regeneration, or new birth in Christ Jesus, is hard to be understood by the natural man. But that there is really such a thing, and that each of us must be spiritually born again, I shall endeavor to show under my—

Third general head, in which I was to produce some arguments to make good the apostle's assertion.

And here one would think it sufficient to affirm, first, that God himself, in his holy Word, has told us so. Many texts might be produced out of the Old Testament to prove this point, and indeed, one would wonder how Nicodemus, who was a teacher in Israel, and who was therefore to instruct the people in the spiritual meaning of the law, should be so ignorant of this grand article, as we find he really was, by his asking our blessed Lord, when he was pressing on him this topic, "How can these things be?" Surely he could not forget how often the psalmist had begged of God to make him "a new heart" and "to renew a right spirit within him"; as likewise how frequently the prophets had warned the people to make them "new hearts" and new minds, and so turn unto the Lord their God. But not to mention these and suchlike texts out of the Old Testament, this doctrine is so often and plainly repeated in the New, that, as I observed before, he who runs may read. For what says the great Prophet and Instructor of the world himself: "Except a man (everyone that is naturally the offspring of Adam) be born again of water and the Spirit, he cannot enter into the kingdom of God." And lest we should be apt to slight this assertion, and Nicodemus-like, reject the doctrine, because we cannot immediately explain "how this thing can be," our blessed Master therefore affirms it, as it were, by an oath, "Verily, verily I say unto you," or, as it may be read, "I the Amen; I who am truth itself say unto you, that it is the unalterable appointment of my heavenly Father, that 'unless a man be born again, he cannot enter into the kingdom of God.'"

Agreeable to this are those many passages we meet with in the Epistles, where we are commanded to be "renewed in the Spirit," or, which was before explained, in the inmost faculties of our minds; to "put off the old man, which is corrupt; and to put on the new man, which is created after God, in righteousness and true holiness"; that "old things must pass away, and that all things must become new"; that we are to be "saved by the washing of regeneration, and the renewing of the Holy Ghost." Or, I think, was there no other passage to be produced besides the words of the text, it would be full enough, since the apostle therein positively affirms that "if any man be in Christ, he is a new creature."

Multitudes of other texts might be produced to confirm this same truth; but those already quoted are so plain and convincing, that one would imagine no one should deny it; were we not told, there are some "who having eyes, see not, and ears, hear not," and that will not understand with their hearts, or hear with their ears, lest they should be converted, and Christ should heal them.

But I proceed to a second argument; and that shall be taken from the purity of God, and the present corrupt and polluted state of man.

God is described in holy Scripture (and I speak to those who profess to know the Scripture) as a Spirit; as a being of such infinite sanctity, as to be of "purer eyes than to behold iniquity"; as to be so transcendently holy, that it is said, "the very heavens are not clean in his sight; and the angels themselves he chargeth with folly." On the other hand, man is described (and every regenerate person will find it true by his own experience) as a creature altogether "conceived and born in sin"; as having "no good thing dwelling in him"; as being "carnal, sold under sin"; what's more, as having "a mind which is at enmity with God," and suchlike. And since there is such an infinite disparity, can anyone conceive how a filthy, corrupted, polluted wretch can dwell with an infinitely pure and holy God, before he is changed and rendered, in some measure, like him? Can he, who is of purer eyes than to behold iniquity, dwell with it? Can he, in whose sight the heavens are not clean, delight to dwell with uncleanness itself? No, we might as well suppose light to have communion with darkness, or Christ to have concord with Belial.

But I pass on to a third argument, which shall be founded on the consideration of the nature of that happiness God has prepared for those that unfeignedly love him.

To enter indeed on a minute and particular description of heaven would be vain and presumptuous, since we are told that "eye hath not seen, nor ear heard, neither hath it entered into the heart of man to conceive the things that are there prepared" for the sincere followers of the holy Jesus, even in this life, much less in that which is to come. However, this we may venture to affirm in general, that as God is a Spirit, so the happiness he has laid up for his people is spiritual likewise; and consequently, unless our carnal minds are changed, and spiritualized, we can never be made meet to partake of that inheritance with the saints in light.

It is doubtless for this reason that the apostle declares it to be the irrevocable decree of the Almighty, that "without holiness (without being made

* How then do we balance the Friend, John caught up to the third heaven. Is this not the heaven of paradise?

pure by regeneration, and having the image of God thereby reinstamped upon the soul) no man shall see the Lord." And it is very observable, that our divine Master, in the famous passage before referred to, concerning the absolute necessity of regeneration, does not say, "Unless a man be born again, he shall not," but "Unless a man be born again, he cannot enter into the kingdom of God." It is founded in the very nature of things, that unless we have dispositions worked in us suitable to the objects that are to entertain us, we can take no manner of complacency or satisfaction in them. For instance, what delight can the most harmonious music afford to a deaf, or what pleasure can the most excellent picture give to a blind, man? Can a tasteless palate relish the richest dainties, or a filthy swine be pleased with the finest garden of flowers? No, and what reason can be assigned for it? An answer is ready; because they have neither of them any tempers of mind correspondent or agreeable to what they are to be diverted with. And thus it is with the soul hereafter; for death makes no more alteration in the soul, than as it enlarges its faculties, and makes it capable of receiving deeper impressions either of pleasure or pain. If it delighted to converse with God here, it will be transported with the sight of his glorious Majesty hereafter. If it was pleased with the communion of saints on earth, it will be infinitely more so with the communion and society of holy angels, and the spirits of just men made perfect in heaven. But if the opposite of all this be true, we may assure ourselves the soul could not be happy, was God himself to admit it (which he never will do) into the regions of the blessed.

But it is time for me to hasten to the fourth argument: because Christ's redemption will not be complete in us, unless we are new creatures.

If we reflect indeed on the first and chief end of our blessed Lord's coming, we shall find it was to be a propitiation for our sins, to give his life a ransom for many. But then, if the benefits of our dear Redeemer's death were to extend no further than barely to procure forgiveness of our sins, we should have as little reason to rejoice in it as a poor condemned criminal that is ready to perish by some fatal disease would have in receiving a pardon from his judge. For Christians would do well to consider that there is not only a legal hindrance to our happiness, as we are breakers of God's law, but also a moral impurity in our natures, which renders us incapable of enjoying heaven (as has been already proved) till some mighty change has been worked in us. It is necessary therefore, in order to make Christ's redemption complete, that we should have a grant of God's Holy Spirit to change our natures, and so prepare us for the enjoyment of that happiness our Savior has purchased by his precious blood.

Accordingly the holy Scriptures inform us that whom Christ justifies, or whose sins he forgives, and to whom he imputes his perfect obedience, those he also sanctifies, purifies, and cleanses, and totally changes their corrupted natures. As the Scriptures also speak in another place, "Christ is to us justification, sanctification, and then redemption."

But, fourth, proceed we now to the next general thing proposed, to draw some inferences from what has been delivered; and, first, if he that is in Christ be a new creature, this may serve as a reproof for those who rest in a bare performance of outward duties, without perceiving any real inward change of heart.

We may observe a great many persons to be very punctual in the regular returns of public and private prayer, as likewise of receiving the holy Communion, and perhaps now and then too in keeping a fast. But here is the misfortune, they rest barely in the use of the means and think all is over when they have thus complied with those sacred institutions; whereas, were they rightly informed, they would consider that all the instituted means of grace, as prayer, fasting, hearing, and reading the Word of God, receiving the blessed Sacrament, and suchlike, are no further serviceable to us than as they are found to make us inwardly better, and to carry on the spiritual life in the soul.

It is true, they are means; but then they are only means; they are part, but not the whole, of religion; for if so, who more religious than the Pharisee? He fasted twice in the week and gave tithes of all that he possessed, and yet was not justified, as our Savior himself informs us, in the sight of God.

You perhaps, like the Pharisee, may fast often and make long prayers; you may, with Herod, hear good sermons gladly. But yet, if you continue vain and trifling, immoral or worldly minded, and differ from the rest of your neighbors barely in going to church, or in complying with some outward performances, are you better than they? No, in nowise; you are by far much worse; for if you use them, and at the same time abuse them, you thereby encourage others to think there is nothing in them and therefore must expect to receive the greater damnation.

But, second, if he that is in Christ be a new creature, then this may check the groundless presumption of another class of professors, who rest in the attainment of some moral virtues and falsely imagine they are good Christians, if they are just in their dealings, temperate in their diet, and do not hurt or violence to any man.

But if this was all that is requisite to make us Christians, why might not the heathens of old be good Christians, who were remarkable for these virtues? Or St. Paul before his conversion, who tells us that he lived in all good conscience? But we find he renounces all dependence on works of this nature, and only desires to be found in Christ, and to know the power of his resurrection, or have an experimental proof of receiving the Holy Ghost, purchased for him by the death, and ensured and applied to him by the resurrection, of Jesus Christ.

The sum of the matter is this: Christianity includes morality, as grace does reason; but if we are only mere moralists, if we are not inwardly worked upon, and changed by the powerful operations of the Holy Spirit, and our moral actions proceed from a principle of a new nature, however we may call ourselves Christians, we shall be found naked at the great day, and in the number of those who have neither Christ's righteousness imputed to them for their justification in the sight [of God], nor holiness enough in their souls as the consequence of that, in order to make them meet for the enjoyment of God.

Nor, third, will this doctrine less condemn those who rest in a partial amendment of themselves, without experiencing a thorough, real, inward change of heart.

A little acquaintance with the world will furnish us with instances of no small number of persons, who perhaps were before openly profane; but seeing the ill consequences of their vices, and the many worldly inconveniences it has reduced them to, suddenly, as it were, grow civilized; and thereupon flatter themselves that they are very religious, because they differ a little from their former selves, and are not so scandalously wicked as once they were: whereas, at the same time, they shall have some secret darling sin or other, some beloved Delilah or Herodias, which they will not part with; some hidden lust, which they will not mortify; some vicious habit, which they will not take pains to root out. But would you know, O vain man! whoever you are, what the Lord your God requires of you? You must be informed that nothing short of a thoroughly sound conversion will fit you for the kingdom of heaven. It is not enough to turn from profaneness to civility; but you must turn from civility to godliness. Not only some, but "all things must become new" in your soul. It will profit you but little to do many things, if yet some one thing you lack. In short, you must not only be an almost, but altogether a new, creature, or in vain you boast that you are a Christian.

Fourth, if he that is in Christ be a new creature, then this may be prescribed as an infallible rule for every person of whatever denomination, age, degree, or quality, to judge himself by; this being the only solid foundation whereon we can build a well-grounded assurance of pardon, peace, and happiness.

We may indeed depend on the broken reed of an external profession; we may think we are good enough, if we lead such sober, honest, moral lives, as many heathens did. We may imagine we are in a safe condition, if we attend on the public offices of religion and are constant in the duties of our closets. But unless all these tend to reform our lives and change our hearts and are only used as so many channels of divine grace—as I told you before, so I tell you again, Christianity will profit you nothing.

Let each of us therefore seriously put this question to our hearts: Have we received the Holy Ghost since we believed? Are we new creatures in Christ or no? At least, if we are not so yet, is it our daily endeavor to become such? Do we constantly and conscientiously use all the means of grace required thereto? Do we fast, watch, and pray? Do we, not lazily seek, but laboriously strive to enter in at the strait gate? In short, do we renounce our own righteousness, take up our crosses, and follow Christ? If so, we are in that narrow way which leads to life; the good seed is sown in our hearts, and will, if duly watered and nourished by a regular persevering use of all the means of grace, grow up to eternal life. But on the contrary, if we have only heard, and know not experimentally, whether there be any Holy Ghost; if we are strangers to fasting, watching, and prayer, and all the other spiritual exercises of devotion; if we are content to go in the broad way, merely because we see most other people do so, without once reflecting whether it be the right one or not; in short, if we are strangers, even enemies to the cross of Christ, by lives of worldly mindedness and sensual pleasure, and thereby make others think that Christianity is but an empty name, a bare formal profession; if this be the case, I say, Christ is as yet dead in vain to us; we are under the guilt of our sins and are unacquainted with a true and thorough conversion.

But, beloved, I am persuaded better things of you, and things that accompany salvation, though I thus speak; I would humbly hope that you are sincerely persuaded that he who has not the Spirit of Christ is none of his; and that, unless the Spirit, which raised Jesus from the dead, dwell in you here, neither will your mortal bodies be quickened by the same Spirit to dwell with him hereafter.

Let me therefore (as was proposed in the last place) earnestly exhort you, in the name of our Lord Jesus Christ, to act suitable to those convictions, and to live as Christians that are commanded in holy Writ to "put off their former conversation concerning the old man, and to put on the new man, which is created after God in righteousness and true holiness."

It must be owned indeed, that this is a great and difficult work; but, blessed be God, it is not impossible. Many thousands of happy souls have been assisted by a divine power to bring it about, and why should we despair of success? Is God's hand shortened, that it cannot save? Was he the God of our fathers? Is he not the God of their children also? Yes, doubtless, of their children also. It is a task likewise that will put us to some pain; it will oblige us to part with some lust, to break with some friend, to mortify some beloved passion, which may be exceedingly dear to us, and perhaps as hard to leave as to cut off a right hand or pluck out a right eye. But what of all this? Will not the being made a real living member of Christ, a child of God, and an inheritor of the kingdom of heaven, abundantly make amends for all this trouble? Undoubtedly it will.

The setting about and carrying on the great and necessary work, perhaps may, even assuredly will, expose us also to the ridicule of the unthinking part of mankind, who will wonder that we run not into the same excess of riot with themselves; and because we deny our sinful appetites and are not conformed to this world, being commanded in Scripture to do the one, and to have our conversation in heaven, in opposition to the other, they may count our lives folly and our end to be without honor. But will not the being numbered among the saints, and shining as the stars forever and ever, be a more than sufficient recompense for all the ridicule, calumny, or reproach we can possibly meet with here?

Indeed, were there no other reward attended a thorough conversion, but that peace of God, which is the unavoidable consequence of it, and which even in this life "passeth all understanding," we should have great reason to rejoice. But when we consider that this is the least of those mercies God has prepared for those that are in Christ and become new creatures; that this is but the beginning of an eternal succession of pleasures; that the day of our deaths, which the unconverted, unrenewed sinner must so much dread, will be, as it were, but the first day of our new births, and open to us an everlasting scene of happiness and comfort; in short, if we remember that they who are regenerate and born again have a real title to all the glorious promises of the gospel and are infallibly certain of being as happy, both here and hereafter, as an all-wise, all-gracious, all-powerful God can make them; I think everyone that has but the least concern for the salvation of his precious and immortal soul, having such promises, such a hope, such an eternity of happiness set before him, should never cease watching, praying, and striving, till he find a real, inward, saving change worked in his heart, and thereby knows of a truth, that he dwells in Christ, and Christ in him; that he is a new creature, therefore a child of God; that he is already an inheritor, and will before long be an actual possessor of the kingdom of heaven.

Which God of his infinite mercy grant through Jesus Christ our Lord; to whom with the Father and the Holy Ghost, three persons and one God, be ascribed, as is most due, all honor and praise, might, majesty, and dominion, now and forever. Amen.

Christians, Temples of the Living God

—m—

Ye are the temple of the living God. —2 CORINTHIANS 6:16

Isaiah, speaking of the glory of gospel days, said, "Men have not heard nor perceived by the ear, neither hath the eye seen, O God, besides thee, what he hath prepared for him that waiteth for him" (64:4). Could a world lying in the wicked one be really convinced of this, they would need no other motive to induce them to renounce themselves, take up their cross, and follow Jesus Christ. And had believers this truth always deeply impressed upon their souls, they could not but abstain from every evil, be continually aspiring after every good; and in a word, use all diligence to walk worthy of him who has called them to his kingdom and glory. If I mistake not, that is the end purposed by the apostle Paul, in the words of the text, "Ye are the temple of the living God"—words originally directed to the church of Corinth, but which equally belong to us, and to our children, and to as many as the Lord our God shall call. To give you the true meaning of, and then practically to improve them, shall be my endeavor in the following discourse.

It is thus that Christians are "the temple of the living God," of Father, Son, and Holy Ghost; they who once held a consultation to create are all equally concerned in making preparations for, and effectually bringing about, the redemption of man. The Father creates, the Son redeems, and the Holy Ghost sanctifies all the elect people of God. Being loved from eternity, they are effectually called in time, they are chosen out of the world, and not only by an external formal dedication at baptism, or at the Lord's Supper, but by a free, voluntary, unconstrained oblation, they devote myself, spirit, soul, and body, to the entire service of Him who has loved and given Himself for me.

This is true and undefiled religion before God our heavenly Father. This is the real Christian's reasonable service, or, as some think the word imports, this is the service required of us in the Word of God. It implies no less than a total renunciation of the world; in short, turns the Christian's whole life into one continued sacrifice of love to God; so that, "whether he eats or drinks, he does all to his glory." Not that I would hereby insinuate that to be Christians, or to keep to the words of our text, in order to be temples of the living God, we must become hermits, or shut ourselves up in nunneries or cloisters; this be far from me! No. The religion, which this Bible in my hand prescribes, is a social religion, a religion equally practicable by high and low, rich and poor, and which absolutely requires a due discharge of all relative duties, in whatsoever state of life God shall be pleased to place and continue us.

That some, in all ages of the church, have literally separated themselves from the world and, from a sincere desire to save their souls and attain higher degrees of Christian perfection, have wholly devoted themselves to solitude and retirement, is what I make no doubt of. But then such a zeal is in nowise according to knowledge; for private Christians, as well as ministers, are said to be "the salt of the earth" and the lights of the world, and are commanded to "let their light shine before men." But how can this be done, if we shut ourselves up, and thereby entirely exclude ourselves from all manner of conversation with the world? Or supposing we could take the wings of the morning and fly into the most distant and desolate parts of the earth, what would this avail us, unless we could agree with a wicked heart and wicked tempter not to pursue and molest us there?

So far should we be from thus getting ease and comfort, that I believe we should on the contrary soon find by our experience the truth of what a hermit himself once told me, that a tree which stands by itself is most exposed and liable to the strongest blasts. When our Savior was to be tempted by the devil, he was led by the Spirit into the wilderness. How contrary this to their practice, who go into a wilderness to avoid temptation! Surely such are unmindful of the petition put up for us by our blessed Lord, "Father, I pray not that thou wouldest take them out of the world, but that thou wouldest keep them from the evil." This then is to be a Christian indeed; to be in the world and yet not of it; to have our hands, according to our respective stations in life, employed on earth, and our hearts at the same time fixed on things above. Then, indeed, are we "temples of the living God," when with a humble boldness, we can say, with a great and good soldier of Jesus Christ: we are the same in the parlor, as we are in the closet; and can at night throw off our cares, as we throw off our clothes; and being at peace with the world, ourselves, and God, are indifferent whether we sleep or die.

Further, the Jewish temple was a house of prayer. "My house (says the great God) shall be called a house of prayer," and implies that the hearts of true believers are the seats of prayer. For this end was it built and adorned with such furniture. Solomon, in that admirable prayer which he put up to God at the dedication of the temple, said, "Hearken therefore unto the supplication of thy servant, and of thy people Israel, which they shall make toward this place." And hence I suppose it was that Daniel, that man greatly beloved, in the time of captivity, "prayed as aforetime three times a day with his face toward the temple." And what was said of the first [temple], our Lord applies to the second temple: "My house shall be called a house of prayer." On this account also, true believers may be styled, "the temple of the living God." For being wholly devoted and dedicated to God, even a God in Christ, their hearts become the seats of prayer, from where, as to many living altars, a perpetual sacrifice of prayer and praise (like unto, though infinitely superior to, the perpetual oblation under the Mosaic dispensation) is continually ascending, and offered up, to the Father of mercies, the God of all consolations. Such, and such only, who thus worship God in the temple of their hearts can truly be said to be made priests unto God, or be styled a royal priesthood; such, and such only, can truly be styled, "the temple of the living God," because such only pray to him, as one expresses it, in the temple of their hearts, and consequently worship him in spirit and in truth.

Let no one say that such a devotion is impracticable, or at least only practicable by a few, and those such who have nothing to do with the common affairs of life; for this is the common duty and privilege of all true Christians. "To pray without ceasing" and "to rejoice in the Lord always" are precepts equally obligatory on all that name the name of Christ. And though it must be owned, that it is hard for persons that are immersed in the world to serve the Lord without distraction; and though we must confess that the lamp of devotion, even in the best of saints, sometimes burns too dimly; yet those who are the temple of the living God find prayer to be their very element. And when those who make this objection once come to love prayer, as some unhappy men love swearing, they will find no more difficulty in praying to, and praising God always, than these unhappy creatures do in cursing and swearing always. What has been advanced is far from being a state peculiar to persons wholly retired from the world.

My brethren, the love of God is all in all. When once possessed of this, as we certainly must be, if we are "the temple of the living God," meditation, prayer, praise, and other spiritual exercises become habitual and delightful. When once touched with this divine magnet, forever after the soul feels a divine attraction and continually turns to its center, God, and if diverted therefrom by any sudden or violent temptation, yet when that obstruction is removed, like as a needle touched by a lodestone when your finger is taken away, turns to its rest, its center, its God, its All, again.

The Jewish temple was also a place where the great Jehovah was pleased in a more immediate manner to reside. Hence he is said to put and record his name there, and to sit or dwell between the cherubim; and when Solomon first dedicated it, we are told, "the house was filled with a cloud, so that the priests could not stand to minister by reason of the cloud, for the glory of the Lord had filled the house." And wherefore all this amazing manifestation of the divine glory? Even for this, O man, to show you how the high and lofty One that inhabits eternity would make believers' hearts his living temple, and dwell and make his abode in all those that tremble at his Word.

To this the apostle more particularly alludes in the words immediately following our text; for having called the Corinthians "the temple of the living God," he adds, "as God hath said, 'I will dwell in them, and I will walk in them, and I will be their God, and they shall be my people.'" Strange and strong expressions these! But strange and strong as they are, must be experienced by all who are indeed "the temple of the living God." For they are said, to be "chosen to be a holy habitation through the Spirit; to dwell in God and God in them; to have the witness in themselves, and to have God's Spirit witnessing with their spirits that they are the children of God." Which expressions import no more or less than that prayer of our Lord which he put up for his church and people a little before his bitter passion: "that they may be one, even as we are one, I in them, and thou in me, that they may be made perfect in one." This glorious passage our church adopts in her excellent Communion office, and is so far from thinking that this was only the privilege of apostles that she asserts, in the strongest terms, that it is the privilege of every worthy communicant. For then (says she) if we receive the Sacrament worthily, we are one with Christ, and Christ is one with us; we dwell in Christ, and Christ in us. And what is it, but that inspiration of the Holy Spirit, which we pray for in the beginning of that office, and that fellowship of the Holy Ghost, which the minister in the conclusion of every day's public prayer entreats the Lord to be with us all evermore?

Brethren, the time would fail me to mention all the Scriptures, and the various branches of our liturgy, articles, and homilies, that speak of this inestimable blessing, the indwelling of the blessed Spirit, whereby we do indeed become "the temples of the living God." If you have eyes that see, or ears that hear, you may view it almost in every page of the lively oracles, and every part of those offices, which some of you daily use, and hear read to you, in the public worship of almighty God. In asserting therefore this doctrine, we do not vent the whimsies of a disordered brain and heated imagination; neither do we broach any new doctrines, or set up the peculiar opinions of any particular sect or denomination of Christians whatsoever; but we speak the words of truth and soberness; we show you the right and good old way, even that in which the articles of all the reformed churches and all sincere Christians of all parties, however differing in other respects, do universally agree. We are now insisting upon a point, which may properly be termed the Christian shibboleth, something which is the grand criterion of our most holy religion; and on account of which, the holy Ignatius, one of the first fathers of the church, was used to style himself a "bearer of God," and the people to whom he wrote, "bearers of God": for this, as it is recorded of him, he was arraigned before Trajan, who imperiously said, "Where is this man that says he carries God about with him?" With a humble boldness, he answered, "I am he," and then quoted the passage in the text: "Ye are the temple of the living God; as God hath said, 'I will dwell in them, and walk in them, and I will be their God, and they shall be my people.'" Upon this, to cure him of his enthusiasm, he was condemned to be devoured by lions.

Blessed be God! We are not in danger of being called before such persecuting Trajans now: under our present mild and happy administration, the scourge of the tongue is all that they can legally lash us with. But if permitted to go further, we need not be ashamed of witnessing this good confession. Suffering grace will be given for suffering times; and if, like Ignatius, we are bearers of God, we also shall be enabled to say with him, when led to the devouring lions, "Now I begin to be a disciple of Christ."

But it is time for me, second, to make some practical improvement of what has been delivered. You have heard in what sense it is that real Christians are "the temple of the living God." Shall I ask, "Believe you these things?" I know and am persuaded that some of you do indeed believe them, not because I have told you, but because you yourselves have experienced the same.

I congratulate you from my inmost soul. Oh, that your hearts may be in tune this day to "magnify the Lord," and your spirits prepared to "rejoice in God your Savior." Like the virgin Mary, you are highly favored, and from henceforth all the generations of God's people shall call you blessed. You can call Christ Lord, by the Holy Ghost, and thereby have an internal, as well as external, evidence of the divinity, both of his person, and of his holy Word. You can now prove that despised Book, emphatically called the Scriptures, does contain the perfect and acceptable will of God. You have found the second Adam to be a quickening Spirit; he has raised you from death to life. And being thus taught, and born of God, however unlearned in other respects, you can say, "Is not this the Christ?" Oh, ineffable blessing! Inconceivable privilege! God's Spirit witnesses with your spirits, that you are the children of God. When you think of this, are you not ready to cry out with the beloved disciple, "What manner of love is this, that we should be called the children of

God!" I believe that holy man was in an ecstasy when he wrote these words; and though he has been in heaven so long, yet his ecstatic surprise is but now beginning, and will be but as beginning through the ages of eternity.

Thus shall it be with all you likewise, whom the high and lofty One, that inhabits eternity, has made his living temples. For he has sealed you to the day of redemption, and has given you the earnest of your future inheritance. His eyes and heart shall therefore be upon you continually: and in spite of all opposition from men or devils, the top stone of this spiritual building shall be brought forth, and you shall shout, "Grace, grace unto it": your bodies shall be fashioned like unto the Redeemer's glorious body, and your souls, in which (Oh, infinite condescension!) he now delights to dwell, shall be filled with all the fullness of God! You shall then go no more out; you shall then no more need the light of the sun or the light of the moon, for the Lord himself will be your temple, and the Lamb in the midst thereof shall be your glory. Dearly beloved in the Lord, what say you to these things? Do not your hearts burn within you while thinking of these deep, but glorious truths of God? While I am musing and speaking of them, I think a fire kindles even in this cold, icy heart of mine. Oh, what shall we render unto the Lord for all these mercies? Surely he has done great things for us: how great is his goodness and his bounty! Oh, the height, the depth, the length, and the breadth of the love of God! Surely it passes knowledge. Oh, for humility! And a soul-abasing, God-exalting sense of these things! When the blessed Virgin went into the hill country to pay a visit to her cousin Elizabeth, amazed at such a favor, she cried out, "Whence is it that the mother of my Lord vouchsafes to come to me?" And when the great Jehovah filled the temple with his glory, out of the abundance of his heart, King Solomon burst forth into this pathetic exclamation, "But will God in very deed dwell with men on the earth?" With how much greater astonishment ought we to say, "And will the Lord himself in very deed come to us?" Will the high and lofty One that inhabits eternity dwell in and make our earthly hearts his living temples? My brethren, from where is this? From any fitness in us foreseen? No, I know you disclaim such an unbecoming thought. Was it then from the improvement of our own free will? No, I am persuaded you will not thus debase the riches of God's free grace. Are you not all ready to say, "Not unto us, not unto us, but unto thy free, thy unmerited, thy sovereign, distinguishing love and mercy, O Lord, be all the glory"? It is this, and this alone, has made the difference between us and others. We have nothing but what is freely given us from above: if we love God, it is because God first loved us. Let us look then unto the rock from which we have been hewn, and the hole of the pit from which we have been dug. And if there be any consolation in

Christ, if any comfort of love, if any fellowship of the Spirit, if any bowels and mercies, let us study and strive to walk as becomes those who are made the temples of the living God, or, as the apostle elsewhere expresses himself, "a holy temple unto the Lord." What manner of persons ought such to be in all holy conversation and godliness? How holily and how purely should we live! As our apostle argues in another place, "For what fellowship hath righteousness and unrighteousness? What communion hath light with darkness? Or what concord hath Christ with Belial?" Shall those who are temples of the living God, suffer themselves to be dens of thieves and cages of unclean birds? Shall vain unchaste thoughts be suffered to dwell within them? Much less shall anything that is impure be conceived or acted by them? Shall we provoke the Lord to jealousy? God forbid! We all know with what distinguished ardor our blessed Redeemer purged an earthly temple; a zeal for his Father's house even ate him up: with what a holy vehemence did he overturn the tables of the moneychangers, and scourge the buyers and sellers out before him! Why? They made his Father's house a house of merchandise: they had turned the house of prayer into a den of thieves.

O my brethren, how often have you and I been guilty of this great evil? How often have the lust of the flesh, the lust of the eye, and the pride of life insensibly stolen away our hearts from God? Once they were indeed houses of prayer; faith, hope, love, peace, joy, and all the other fruits of the blessed Spirit lodged within them; but now, oh, now, it may be, thieves and robbers. *Hinc illae lachrymae* ["Hence these tears"]. Hence those hidings of God's face, that dryness, and deadness and barrenness of soul, those wearisome nights and days, which many of us have felt from time to time, and have been made to groan under. Hence those dolorous and heartbreaking complaints, "Oh, that I knew where I might find him! Oh, that it was with me as in days of old, when the candle of the Lord shone bright upon my soul!" Hence those domestic trials, those personal losses and disappointments: and to this perhaps some of us may add, hence all those public rebukes with which we have been visited: they are all only as so many scourges of small cords in the loving Redeemer's hands, to scourge the buyers and sellers out of the temple of our hearts. Oh, that we may know the rod and who has appointed it! He has chastised us with whips: may we be wise, and by a more close and circumspect walk prevent his chastising us in time to come with scorpions! But who is sufficient for this thing? None but you, "O Lord, to whom alone all hearts are open, all desires known, and from whom no secrets are hidden! Cleanse thou therefore the thoughts of our hearts by the inspiration of thy blessed Spirit, that henceforward we may more perfectly love thee and more worthily magnify thy holy name!"

But are not some of you ready to object, and to fear, that the Lord has forgotten to be gracious, that he has shut up his loving-kindness in displeasure, and that he will be no more entreated? Thus the psalmist once thought, when visited for his backslidings with God's heavy hand. But he acknowledged this to be his infirmity; and whether you think of it or no, I tell you, this is your infirmity. O you dejected, desponding, distrustful souls, hear the Word of the Lord, and call to mind his wonderful declarations of old to his people. "I, even I, am he that blotteth out thy transgressions. For a small moment have I forsaken thee, but with everlasting mercies will I gather thee. Can a woman forget her sucking child? Yes, she may, but the Lord will not forget you, O ye of little faith. For as a father pitieth his own children, so doth the Lord pity them that fear him. How shall I give thee up, O Ephraim? How shall I make thee as Admah? How shall I set thee as Zeboim?" And what is the result of all these interrogations? "My repentings are kindled together: I will not return to execute the fierceness of my anger against Ephraim: for I am God, and not man." And is not the language of all these endearing passages like that of Joseph to his self-convicted, troubled brethren: "Come near to me"? Oh, that it may be said of you, as it is said of them, "And they came near unto him." Then should you find by happy experience, that the Lord, the Lord God, merciful and gracious, is indeed slow to anger and of great kindness, and repents him of the evil. Who knows but he may come down this day, this hour, even this moment, and suddenly revisit the temple of your hearts? Who knows but he may revive his work in your precious souls, cause you to return to your first love, help you to do your first works, and even exceed your hopes, and cause the glory of this second visitation even to surpass that glory which filled your hearts, in that happy, never to be forgotten day, in which he first vouchsafed to make you his living temples? Even so, Father, let it seem good in your sight!

But the improvement of our subject must not end here. Hitherto I have been giving bread to the children; and it is my meat and drink so to do: but must nothing be said to those of you who are outside—I mean to such who cannot yet say that they are "the temple of the living God"? And oh, how great, put you all together, may the number of you be: by far, in all probability, the greatest part of this auditorium. Say not that I am uncharitable; the God of truth has said it: "Strait is the gate, and narrow is the way, which leadeth unto life, and few there be that find it." Suffer me to speak plainly to you, my brethren; you have heard what has been said upon the words of our text, and what must be worked in us, before we can truly say that we are "the temple of the living God." Is it so with you? Are you separated from the world and worldly tempers? Are your hearts become houses of prayer? Does the Spirit of

God dwell in your souls? And whether you eat or drink, or whatsoever you do, as to the habitual bent of your minds, do you do all to the glory of God? These are short, but plain, and let me tell you very important questions. What answer can you make to them? Say not, "Go your way, and at a more convenient season I will call for you." I will not, I must not suffer you to put me off so; I demand an answer in the name of the Lord of hosts. What say you? I think I hear you say, "We have been dedicated to God in baptism; we go to church or meeting; we say our prayers, repeat our creeds, or have subscribed the articles, and the confession of faith; we are quite orthodox, and great friends to the doctrines of grace; we do nobody any harm; we are honest moral people; we are church members; we keep up family prayer and constantly go to the table of the Lord." All these things are good in their places. But thus far, even much farther may you go, and yet be far from the kingdom of God. The unprofitable servant did no one any harm; and the foolish virgins had a lamp of an outward profession, and went up even to heaven's gate, calling Christ, "Lord, Lord." These things may make you whited sepulchers, but not "the temples of the living God." Alas! Alas! One thing you yet lack, the one chief thing, and without which all is nothing; I mean the indwelling of God's blessed Spirit, without which you can never become "the temples of the living God."

Awake therefore, you deceived formalists, awake; who, vainly puffed up with your model of performances, boastingly cry out, "The temple of the Lord, the temple of the Lord, the temple of the Lord we are." Awake, you outward-court worshipers: you are building on a sandy foundation: take heed lest you also go to hell by the very door of heaven. Behold, and remember, I have told you before.

And as for you who have done none of these things, who instead of making an outward profession of religion have as it were renounced your baptism, proclaim your sin like Sodom, and willfully and daringly live a life without God in the world; I ask you, how can you think to escape, if you persist in neglecting such a great salvation? Verily I should utterly despair of your ever attaining the blessed privilege of being temples of the living God, did I not hear of thousands, who through the grace of God have been translated from a like state of darkness into his marvelous light. Such, says the apostle Paul, writing to these very Corinthians who were now God's living temples (drunkards, whoremongers, adulterers, and suchlike), "such were some of you. But ye are washed, but ye are sanctified, but ye are justified in the name of the Lord Jesus, and by the Spirit of our God." Oh, that the same blessed Spirit may this day vouchsafe to come and pluck you also as brands out of the burning!

Behold, I warn you to flee from the wrath to come. Go home, and meditate on these things; and think whether it is not infinitely better, even here, to be temples of the living God, than to be bondslaves to every brutish lust, and to be led captive by the devil at his will. The Lord Jesus can, and if you fly to him for refuge, he will set your souls at liberty. He has led captivity captive; he has ascended up on high, on purpose to receive this gift of the blessed Spirit of God for men, "even for the rebellious," that he might dwell in your hearts by faith here, and thereby prepare you to dwell with him and all the heavenly host in his kingdom hereafter.

That this may be the happy lot of you all, may God of his infinite mercy grant, for the sake of his dear Son Christ Jesus our Lord; to whom with the Father, and the blessed Spirit, three persons, but one God, be ascribed all power, might, majesty, and dominion, now and forevermore. Amen! And amen!

Christ, the Only Preservative Against
a Reprobate Spirit

—⟳—

Know ye not your own selves, how that Jesus Christ is in you, except ye be reprobates? —2 CORINTHIANS 13:5

The doctrines of the gospel are doctrines of peace, and they bring comfort to all who believe in them; they are not like the law given by Moses, which consisted of troublesome and painful ceremonies; neither do they carry with them that terror which the law did, as, "Cursed is everyone who continueth not to do all things which are written in the book of the law." If you were to keep the whole law and break but in one point, you are guilty of the breach of all. The law denounces threatenings against all who do not conform to her strict commands; but the gospel is a declaration of grace, peace, and mercy; here you have an account of the blood of Christ, blood which speaks better things than that of Abel; for Abel's blood cried aloud from vengeance, vengeance. But Jesus Christ's cries mercy, mercy, mercy upon the guilty sinner. If he comes to Christ, confesses, and forsakes his sin, then Jesus will have mercy upon him: and if, my brethren, you are but sensible of your sins, convinced of your iniquities, and feel yourselves lost, undone sinners, and come and tell Christ of your lost condition, you will soon find how ready he is to help you; he will give you his Spirit; and if you have his Spirit you cannot be reprobates; you will find his Spirit to be quickening and refreshing; not like the spirit of the world, a spirit of reproach, envy, and all uncharitableness.

Most of your own experiences will confirm the truth hereof; for are not you reproached and slandered, and does not the world say all manner of evil against you merely because you follow Jesus Christ; because you will not go to the same excess of riot with them? While they are singing the songs of the drunkard, you are singing psalms and hymns; while they are at a playhouse, you are hearing a sermon; while they are drinking, reveling, and misspending their precious time, and hastening on their own destruction, you are reading, praying, meditating, and working out your salvation with fear and trembling. This is matter enough for a world to reproach you; you are not polite and fashionable enough for them. If you will live godly, you must suffer persecution; you must not expect to go through this world without being persecuted and reviled. If you were of the world, the world would love you; for it always loves its own; but if you are not of the world, it will hate you; it has done so in all ages, it never loved any but those who were pleased with its vanities and allurements. It has been the death of many a lover of Jesus, merely because they have loved him; and therefore, my brethren, do not be surprised if you meet with a fiery trial, for all those things will be a means of sending you to your Master the sooner.

The spirit of the world is hatred; that of Christ is love: the spirit of the world is vexation; that of Christ is pleasure: the spirit of the world is sorrow; that of Christ is joy: the spirit of the world is evil, and that of Christ is good: the spirit of the world will never satisfy us, but Christ's Spirit is all satisfaction: the spirit of the world is misery, that of Christ is ease. In one word, the spirit of the world has nothing lasting; but the Spirit of Christ is durable, and will last through an eternity of ages: the Spirit of Christ will remove every difficulty, satisfy every doubt, and be a means of bringing you to himself, to live with him forever and ever.

From the words of my text, I shall show you,

I. The necessity of receiving the Spirit of Christ.

II. Who Christ is, whose Spirit you are to receive.

And then shall conclude with an exhortation to all of you, high and low, rich and poor, to come unto the Lord Jesus Christ; and to beg that you may receive his Spirit, so that you may not be reprobates.

First, I am to show you the necessity there is of receiving the Spirit of Christ.

And here, my brethren, it will be necessary to consider you as in your first state; that is, when God first created Adam and placed him in the garden of Eden, and gave him a privilege of eating of all the trees in the garden, except the Tree of Knowledge of Good and Evil, which stood in the midst thereof. Our first parents had not been long in this state of innocence, before they fell from it, they broke the divine commands, and involved all their posterity in guilt; for as Adam was our representative, so we were to stand or fall in him; and as he was our federal head, his falling involved all our race under the power of death, for death came into the world by sin; and we all became liable to the eternal punishment due from God, for man's disobedience to the divine command.

Now as man had sinned, and a satisfaction was demanded, it was impossible for a finite creature to satisfy him, who was a God of so strict purity as not to behold iniquity; and man by the justice of God would have been sent down into the pit, which was prepared of old for the devil and his angels; but when justice was going to pass the irrevocable sentence, then the Lord Jesus Christ came and offered himself a ransom for poor sinners. Here was admirable condescension of the Lord Jesus Christ! That he who was in the bosom of his Father, should come down from all that glory, to die for such rebels as you and I are, who if it lay in our power, would pull the Almighty from his throne. Now can you think that if there was no need of Christ's death, can you think that if there could have been any other ransom found, whereby poor sinners might have been saved, God would not have spared his only begotten Son, and not have delivered him up for all that believe in him?

This, my brethren, I think proves to a demonstration, that it was necessary for Christ to die. But consider, it will be of no service to know that Christ died for sinners, if you do not accept of his Spirit, that you may be sanctified, and fitted for the reception of that Jesus, who died for all those who believe in him. The sin of your nature, your original sin, is sufficient to sink you into torments, of which there will be no end; therefore, unless you receive the Spirit of Christ, you are reprobates, and you cannot be saved. Nothing short of the blood of Jesus applied to your souls will make you happy to all eternity. Then, seeing this is so absolutely necessary, that you cannot be saved without having received the Spirit of Christ, but that you are reprobates, do not rest contented till you have good hopes, through grace, that the good work is begun in your souls; that you have received a pardon for your sins; that Christ came down from heaven, died, and made satisfaction for your sins. Don't flatter yourselves that a little morality will be sufficient to save you; that going to church, or prayers, and Sacrament, and doing all the duties of religion in an external manner, will ever carry you to heaven; no, you must have grace in your hearts; there must be a change of the whole man.

You must be born again and become new creatures, and have the Spirit of Christ within you; and until you have that Spirit of Christ, however you may think to the contrary, and please yourselves in your own imagination, I say, you are no better than reprobates. You may content yourselves with leading civil, outwardly decent lives, but what will that avail you, unless you have the Spirit of the Lord Jesus Christ in your hearts. His kingdom must be set up in your souls; there must be the life of God in the soul of man, else you belong not to the Lord Jesus Christ; and until you belong to him, you are reprobates.

This may seem as enthusiasm to some of you, but if it is so, it is what the apostle Paul taught; and therefore, my brethren, they are the words of truth. I beseech you, in the mercies of God in Christ Jesus, not to despise these words, as if they do not concern you but were only calculated for the first ages of Christianity and therefore of no significance. If you think thus, you are wronging your own souls; for whatever is written was written for you in these times, as well as for the Christians in the first ages of the church.

For the case stands thus between God and man: God at first made man upright, or, as the sacred penman expresses it, "In the image of God made he man"; his soul was the very copy, the transcript, of the divine nature. He who had, by his almighty power, spoken the world into being breathed into man the breath of spiritual life; and his soul became adorned with purity and perfection. This was the finishing stroke of the creation; the perfection both of the moral and material world; and it so resembled the divine original that God could not but rejoice and take pleasure in his own likeness; therefore we read that when God had finished the inanimate and brutish part of the creation, "he looked, and, behold, it was good." But when that lovely, Godlike creature man was made, "behold, it was very good."

Happy, unspeakably happy, to be thus partaker of a divine nature; and thus man might have continued still, had he continued holy; but God placed him in a state of probation, with a free grant to eat of every tree in the garden, except the Tree of Knowledge of Good and Evil. The day he did eat thereof he was not only to become subject to temporal, but spiritual death; and so lost that divine image, that spiritual life which God had breathed into him, and which was as much his happiness as his glory.

But man, unhappy man, being seduced by the devil, did eat of the forbidden fruit, and thereby became liable to that curse which the eternal God had pronounced on him for his disobedience. And we read that soon after Adam was fallen, he complained that he was naked; naked, not only as to his body, but naked and destitute of those divine graces which before beautified his soul.

An unhappy mutiny and disorder then fell upon this world; those briars and thorns which now spring up and overspread the earth were but poor emblems, lifeless representations of that confusion and rebellion which sprang up in, and overwhelmed, the soul of man immediately after the fall. He now sank into the temper of a beast and devil.

In this dreadful and disordered condition are all of us brought into the world. We are told, my brethren, that "Adam had a son in his own likeness," or with the same corrupt nature which he himself had sunk into after eating the forbidden fruit. And experience, as well as Scripture, proves, that we are altogether born in sin and therefore incapable, while in such a state, to have communion with God.

For as light cannot have communion with darkness, so God can have no communion with such polluted sons of Belial. Here, here, appears the great and glorious end, why Christ was manifest in the flesh, to put an end to these disorders and to restore us unto the favor of God. He came down from heaven and shed his precious blood upon the cross, to satisfy the divine justice of his Father, for our sins; and so he purchased this Holy Ghost, who must once more restamp the divine image on our hearts and make us capable of living with and enjoying of God. We must be renewed by the Spirit of God; he must dwell in us before we can be new creatures and be freed from a reprobate spirit: the Spirit of Christ must bring us home unto that fold where all his sheep are, and implant his grace in our hearts, and take from us that spirit of sin which reigns in us. And till this is rooted out of our hearts, however we may flatter ourselves with being good Christians, because we are good moralists and lead civil, moral, decent lives, yet if we live and die, my brethren, in this way, we are only flattering ourselves into hell.

I think I have proved, to a demonstration, the necessity there is of receiving the Spirit of Christ.

I now come to show you, second, who Christ is, whose Spirit you are to receive.

My brethren, Jesus Christ is coequal, coessential, coeternal, and consubstantial with the Father, very God of very God; and as there was not a moment of time in which God the Father was not, so there was not a moment of time in which God the Son was not. *Let that truly settle in.*

Arians and Socinians deny this Godhead of Christ and esteem him only as a creature. The Arians look on him as a titular deity, as a created and subordinate God; but if they would humbly search the Scriptures, they would find divine homage paid to Christ. He is called God in Scripture, particularly when the great evangelical prophet says, "He shall be called the mighty God, the everlasting Father, and the government shall be upon his shoulders": And Jesus Christ himself says that he is the "Alpha and Omega" and that "the world was made by him"; but though this be ever so plain, our carefree airy sparks of this age will not believe the Lord Jesus Chris to be equal with his Father, and that for no other reason, but because it is a fashionable and polite doctrine to deny his divinity and esteem him only as a created God.

Our Socinians do not go so far; they look upon Christ only to be a good man sent from God, to show the people the way they should go, on their forsaking of Judaism; that he was to be also an example to the world, and that his death was only to prove the truth of his doctrines. *(Jehovah Witnesses?)*

Many of those who call themselves members, yes, teachers of the Church of England, have got into this polite scheme. Good God! My very soul shudders at the thoughts of the consequence that will attend such a belief. O my

I wonder is this Arians the former ugliness of present day Arayans?

brethren, do not think so dishonorably of the Lord who bought you; of the Jesus who died for you: he must be all in all unto your souls, if ever you are saved by him. Christ must be your active, as well as passive, obedience; his righteousness must be imputed to you. The doctrine of Christ's righteousness being imputed is a comfortable, a desirable doctrine to all real Christians. And to you, sinners, who are inquiring what you must do to be saved, how uncomfortable would it be to tell you, by your own good works, when perhaps you have never done one good work in all your lives: this would be driving you to despair indeed; no, "believe in the Lord Jesus Christ and you shall be saved"; come to the Lord Jesus by faith, and he shall receive you. He is able and willing to save you.   *"in" or "on" is there a difference? Jesus is LORD*

This second person in the Trinity, who is God-man, the Mediator of the New Covenant; he, my brethren, has virtue enough, in his blood, to atone for the sins of millions of worlds. *Jesus* As man he died; he was crucified, nailed to, and pierced on the accursed tree; this was the love of the Lord Jesus Christ for you; and will you then have low and dishonorable thoughts of Jesus Christ, after his having done so much for you? O my dear brethren, don't be so polite as to deny the deity of Christ; though you may be counted fools in the eye of the world, yet in God's account, you shall be esteemed wise, wise for salvation.

You may now be looked upon as fools and madmen, as a parcel of rabble, and, in a short time, fit for Bedlam. They may say you are going to undermine the established church; but God knows the secrets of all hearts, knows our innocence. And I speak the truth in Christ, I lie not, I should rejoice to see all the world adhere to her articles; I should rejoice to see the teachers, the ministers of the Church of England preach up those very articles they have subscribed to; but those ministers who do preach them up, they esteem as madmen and look on them as the offscouring of the earth, unfit for company and conversation.

The evil things they say of me, blessed be God, are without foundation; I am a friend to the church homilies; I am a friend to her liturgy, and if they did not thrust me out of their churches, I would read it every day. *

My brethren, I am not for limiting the Spirit of God, but am for uniting all in the bonds of love; I love all that love the Lord Jesus Christ: this will make more Christians, than will the spirit of persecution.

The Pharisees may think it madness to mention persecution in a Christian country, but the spirit of persecution resides in many: their will is as great, but blessed be God, they want the power; if they had that, my brethren, fire and fagot is what we must expect, for the devil's temple is shaken. Many are coming unto Jesus; I hope many of you are already come, and many more

K Research note the Church of England's own version of Cancel culture

coming; this must make Satan rage, to see his kingdom weakened; he will stir up all his malice against the people of God. We must expect that a suffering time will certainly come; it is now hastening on, it is ripening apace; then it will be proved, to a demonstration, whether you are hypocrites or not; for suffering times are always trying times. O my brethren, do not be afraid of a little reproach, but look on it as a forerunner of what will be the attendant upon it.

Therefore let me, by way of application, exhort all of you, high and low, rich and poor, one with another, to come unto the Lord Jesus Christ, that he may give you strength to undergo whatsoever he, in his wisdom, calls you to. Come, come, my brethren, to Jesus Christ, and he will give you grace, which will make you willing and ready to suffer all things for Jesus Christ.

It is not being pointed at; it is not being despised and looked on as mad, and a deluded people. Alas! what does this signify to a soul who has Jesus Christ? Do not be afraid to confess the blessed Jesus; dare to be singularly good. Don't be afraid of singing of hymns, or of meeting together to build each other up in the ways of the Lord. Shine as lights in the world amid a crooked and perverse generation.

It is necessary that offenses should come, to try what is in our hearts and whether we will be faithful soldiers of Jesus Christ or not. Be not content with following Christ afar off, for then we shall, as Peter did, soon deny him; but let us be altogether Christians. Let our speech and all our actions declare to the whole world, whose disciples we are and that we have determined to know nothing but Jesus Christ and him crucified. Oh, then, then, will it be well with us; happy, unspeakably happy, shall we be, even here; and what is infinitely better, when others that despised us shall be calling for the mountains to fall on them, and the hills to cover them, we shall be exalted to sit down on the right hand of God and shine as the sun in the firmament, and live forever with our Redeemer. And will not this be a sufficient recompense for all the sufferings you have undergone here? Therefore do not strive to have the greatness, the riches, the honor, and pleasures of this world, but strive to have Jesus Christ.

Your friends and carnal acquaintance, and, above all, your grand adversary the devil, will be persuading you not to have Christ until you are grown old; he would have you lay up goods for many years; to see plays, play at cards; go to balls and masquerades; and to make you the more willing to draw you in, he calls sinful pleasures, innocent diversions.

A late learned rabbi of our church told the people, in a sermon, which I myself heard, that if people went to church of a Sunday and said the prayers while there, that it was no harm, neither would God count it a sin, to take their recreation after the service of the church was over. But I say, my brethren, and the command of God says so too, that the whole Sabbath must be kept holy; and that as God has allowed you six days for yourselves, to do the duties in those several stations wherein providence has placed you, he expects you should give him one day to himself; and will you waste that Sabbath which should be spent in gathering provisions for your souls? God forbid!

You had ten thousand times better be ignorant of all the polite diversions of the age, than to be ignorant of the Spirit of Christ's being within you, and that it must be, before you are new creatures and are in Christ; and if you have not an interest in Christ, you are lost, your damnation is hastening on. "He that believeth shall be saved, and he that believeth not shall be damned."

If you stand out against Christ, you are fighting against yourselves. Oh, come unto him, do not stay to bring good works with you, for they will be of no service; all your works will never carry you to heaven; they will never pardon one sin nor give you the least comfort in a dying hour; if you have nothing more than your own works to recommend you to God, they will not prevent your sinking in that eternal abyss, where there is no bottom.

But come unto Christ, and he will give you that righteousness which will stand you in good account at the great day of the Lord, when he shall come to take notice of them that love him and of those who have the wedding garment on.

Let all your actions spring from the love of Jesus; let him be the Alpha and Omega of all your actions; then, my brethren, our indifferent ones are acceptable sacrifices; but if this principle be wanting, our most pompous services avail nothing; we are only spiritual idolaters; we sacrifice to our own net, and make an idol of ourselves, by making ourselves, and not Christ, the spring of our actions; and therefore, my brethren, such actions are so far from being accepted by God, that according to the language of one of the articles of our church, "We doubt not but that they have the nature of sin, because they spring not from an experimental faith in, and knowledge of, Jesus Christ."

Were we not fallen creatures, we might then act upon other principles; but since we are fallen in Adam and are restored again only by the death of Jesus Christ, the face of things is entirely changed, and all we think, speak, or do, is only accepted in and through him.

Therefore, my brethren, I beseech you, in the bowels of love and compassion, that you would come unto Jesus: do not go away scoffing, offended, or blaspheming. Indeed, all I say is in love to your souls; and if I could be but an instrument of bringing you to Jesus Christ, if you were to be never so much exalted, I should not envy but rejoice in your happiness. If I was to make up the last of the train of the companions of the blessed Jesus, it would rejoice me to see you above me in glory. I do not speak out of a false humility, a pretended sanctity, no, God is my Judge; I speak the truth in Christ, I lie not, I would willingly go to prison, or to death for you, so I could but bring one soul from the devil's strongholds, into the salvation which is by Christ Jesus.

Come, then, unto Christ, everyone that hears me this night; I offer Jesus Christ, pardon, and salvation to all you who will accept thereof. Come, O you drunkards; lay aside your cups, drink no more to excess; come and drink of the water which Christ will give you, and then you will thirst no more. Come, O you thieves; let him that has stolen, steal no more, but fly unto Christ, and he will receive you. Come unto him, O you harlots; lay aside your lusts and turn unto the Lord, and he will have mercy upon you; he will cleanse you of all your sins and wash you in his blood. Come, all you liars; come, all you Pharisees; come, all you fornicators, adulterers, swearers, and blasphemers; come to Christ, and he will take away all your filth; he will cleanse you from your pollution, and your sins shall be done away. Come, come, my guilty brethren; I beseech you for Christ's sake, and for your immortal soul's sake, to come unto Christ. Do not let me knock at the door of your hearts in vain, but open and let the King of glory in, and he will dwell with you; he will come and sup with you this night; this hour, this moment he is ready to receive you, therefore come unto him.

Do not consult with flesh and blood, let not the world hinder you from coming to the Lord of life. What are a few transitory pleasures of this life worth? They are not worth your having, but Jesus Christ is a pearl of great price, he is worth the laying out all you have, to buy.

And if you are under afflictions, fly not to company to divert you, neither read what the world calls harmless books; they only tend to harden the heart and to keep you from closing with the Lord Jesus Christ.

When I was a child, even when I came to riper years, God knows, it is with grief I speak it, when ignorant of the excellency of the Word of God, I read as many of these harmless books as anyone; but now I have tasted the good Word of life and am come to a more perfect knowledge of Christ Jesus my Lord, I put away these childish, trifling things and am determined to read no other books but what lead me to a knowledge of myself and Jesus Christ.

I think I could speak till midnight unto you, my brethren; I am full of love toward you; let me beseech you to fly to Christ for succor: "Now is the accepted time, now is the day of salvation"; therefore delay not, but strive to enter in at the strait gate; do not go the broad way of the polite world, but choose to suffer affliction with the people of God, rather than to enjoy the pleasures of sin for a season. You will have a reward afterward that will make amends for all the taunts, jeers, and calamities you may undergo here.

And will not the presence of Christ be a sufficient reward for all you have suffered for his name's sake? Why will you not accept of the Lord of glory? Do not say you have not heard of Christ, for he is now offered to you, and you will not accept of him; do not blame my Master—he is willing to save you, if you will but lay hold on him by faith; and if you do not, your blood will be required of your own heads.

But I hope that you will not let the blood of Jesus be shed in vain and that you will not let my preaching be of no significance. Would you have me go and tell my Master, you will not come, and that I have spent my strength in vain? I cannot bear to carry so unpleasing a message unto him; I would not, indeed, I would not be a swift witness against any of you at the great day of accounts; but if you will refuse these gracious invitations and not accept of them, I must do it: and will it not move your tender hearts to see your friends taken up into heaven, and you yourselves thrust down into hell? But I hope better things of most of you, even that you will turn unto the Lord of love, the Jesus who died for you, that in the day when he shall come to take his people to the mansions of everlasting rest, you may hear his voice, "Come, ye blessed of my Father, enter into the kingdom prepared for you before the foundation of the world." And that we may all enter into that glory, do you, O Jesus, prepare us, by your grace; give us your Spirit; and may our hearts be united to you. May the word that has now been spoken take deep root in your people's hearts, that it may spring up and bring forth fruit, in some thirty-, in some forty-, and in some a hundredfold; do preserve them while in this life from all evil and keep them from falling, and at last present them faultless before your Father, when you come to judge the world, that where you are, they may be also. Grant this, O Lord Jesus Christ, with whatever else you see needful for us, both at this time and forevermore.

Now to God the Father, God the Son, and God the Holy Ghost, be ascribed all honor, power, glory, might, majesty, and dominion, both now and forevermore. Amen.

Intercession: Every Christian's Duty

—⚏—

Brethren, pray for us. —1 THESSALONIANS 5:25

If we inquire, why there is so little love to be found among Christians, why the very characteristic by which everyone should know that we are disciples of the holy Jesus is almost banished out of the Christian world, we shall find it, in a great measure, owing to a neglect or superficial performance of that excellent part of prayer: intercession or imploring the divine grace and mercy in behalf of others.

Some forget this duty of praying for others, because they seldom remember to pray for themselves: and even those who are constant in praying to their Father who is in heaven are often so selfish in their addresses to the throne of grace, that they do not enlarge their petitions for the welfare of their fellow Christians as they ought; and thereby fall short of attaining that Christian charity, that unfeigned love to their brethren, which their sacred profession obliges them to aspire after, and without which, though they should bestow all their goods to feed the poor and even give their bodies to be burned, yet it would profit them nothing.

Since these things are so, I shall from the words of the text (though originally intended to be more confined) endeavor, to show:

I. First, that it is every Christian's duty to pray for others as well as for himself.

II. Second, show, whom we ought to pray for, and in what manner we should do it.

III. And, third, I shall offer some motives to excite all Christians to abound in this great duty of intercession.

I. First, I shall endeavor to show that it is every Christian's duty to pray for others, as well as for himself.

Now prayer is a duty founded on natural religion; the very heathens never neglected it, though many Christian heathens among us do: and it is so essential to Christianity that you might as reasonably expect to find a living man without breath, as a true Christian without the spirit of prayer and supplication. Thus, no sooner was St. Paul converted, but "behold, he prayeth," says the Lord almighty. And thus will it be with every child of God, as soon as he becomes such: prayer being truly called, the natural cry of the newborn soul.

For in the heart of every true believer there is a heavenly tendency, a divine attraction, which as sensibly draws him to converse with God as the lodestone attracts the needle.

A deep sense of their own weakness and of Christ's fullness, a strong conviction of their natural corruption and of the necessity of renewing grace, will not let them rest from crying day and night to their almighty Redeemer, that the divine image, which they lost in Adam, may through his all-powerful mediation, and the sanctifying operation of his blessed Spirit, be begun, carried on, and fully perfected both in their souls and bodies.

Thus earnest, thus importunate, are all sincere Christians in praying for themselves; but then, not having so lively, lasting, and deep a sense of the wants of their Christian brethren, they are for the most part too remiss and defective in their prayers for them. Whereas, was the love of God shed abroad in our hearts, and did we love our neighbor in that manner in which the Son of God our Savior loved us, and according to his command and example, we could not but be as importunate for their spiritual and temporal welfare as for our own, and as earnestly desire and endeavor that others should share in the benefits of the death and passion of Jesus Christ as we ourselves.

Let not anyone think that this is an uncommon degree of charity; a high pitch of perfection, to which not everyone can attain: for if we are all commanded to "love our neighbor (that is, every man) even as ourselves," what's more, to "lay down our lives for the brethren," then it is the duty of all to pray for their neighbors as much as for themselves, and by all possible acts and expressions of love and affection toward them, at all times, to show their readiness even to lay down their lives for them, if ever it should please God to call them to it.

Our blessed Savior, as "he hath set us an example, that we should follow his steps" in everything else, so has he more especially in this: for in that divine, that perfect and inimitable, prayer (recorded in St. John 17) which he put up just before his passion, we find but few petitions for his own, though many for *speaking of Jesus* his disciples' welfare: and in that perfect form which he has been pleased to prescribe us, we are taught to say not "my" but "our Father," thereby to put us in mind, that, whenever we approach the throne of grace, we ought to pray not for ourselves alone, but for all our brethren in Christ.

Intercession then is certainly a duty incumbent upon all Christians.

II. Whom we are to intercede for, and how this duty is to be performed, comes next to be considered.

1. And, first, our intercession must be universal. "I will (says the apostle) that prayers, supplications, and intercessions be made for all men." For as God's mercy is over all his works, as Jesus Christ died to redeem a people out of all nations and languages; so we should pray that "all men may come to the knowledge of the truth, and be saved." Many precious promises are made in holy Writ, that the gospel shall be published through the whole world, that "the earth shall be covered with the knowledge of the Lord, as the waters cover the sea"; and therefore it is our duty not to confine our petitions to our own nation, but to pray that all those nations who now sit in darkness and in the shadow of death may have the glorious gospel shine out upon them, as well as upon us. But you need not that any man should teach you this, since you yourselves are taught of God, and of Jesus Christ himself, to pray that his kingdom may come; part of the meaning of which petition is that "God's ways may be known upon earth, and his saving health among all nations."

2. Next to the praying for all men, we should, according to St. Paul's rule, pray for kings; particularly for our present sovereign King George and all that are put in authority under him; that we may lead quiet lives, in all godliness and honesty. For if we consider how heavy the burden of government is, and how much the welfare of any people depends on the zeal and godly conversation of those that have the rule over them, if we set before us the many dangers and difficulties to which governors by their station are exposed, and the continual temptations they be under to luxury and self-indulgence, we shall not only pity, but pray for them: that he who preserved Esther, David, and Josiah, "unspotted from the world" amid the grandeur of a court, and gave success to their designs, would also preserve them holy and unblamable, and prosper all the works of their hands upon them.

3. But, third, you ought, in a more special manner, to pray for those, whom "the Holy Ghost hath made overseers over you." This is what St. Paul begs, again and again, of the churches to whom he writes. Says he in the text, "Brethren, pray for us," and again, in his Epistle to the Ephesians, "praying always, with all manner of supplication; and for me also, that I may open my mouth boldly, to declare the mystery of the gospel." And in another place, to express his earnestness in this request, and the great importance of their prayers for him, he bids the church "strive (or, as the original word signifies, be in an agony) together with him in their prayers." And surely, if the great St. Paul, that chosen vessel, that favorite of heaven, needed the most importunate prayers of his Christian converts, much more do the ordinary ministers of the gospel stand in need of the intercession of their respective flocks.

And I cannot but in a more special manner insist upon this branch of your duty, because it is a matter of such importance: for, no doubt, much good is frequently withheld from many, by reason of their neglecting to pray for their ministers, and which they would have received, had they prayed for them as they ought. Not to mention that people often complain of the want of diligent and faithful pastors. But how do they deserve good pastors, who will not earnestly pray to God for such? If we will not pray to the Lord of the harvest, can it be expected he will send forth laborers into his harvest?

Besides, what ingratitude is it, not to pray for your ministers! For shall they watch and labor in the Word and doctrine for you and your salvation, and shall not you pray for them in return? If any bestow favors on your bodies, you think it right, meet, and your bounden duty, to pray for them; and shall not they be remembered in your prayers, who daily feed and nourish your souls? Add to all this, that praying for your ministers will be a manifest proof of your believing that though Paul plant, and Apollos water, yet it is God alone who gives the increase. And you will also find it the best means you can use, to promote your own welfare; because God, in answer to your prayers, may impart a double portion of his Holy Spirit to them, whereby they will be qualified to deal out to you larger measures of knowledge in spiritual things, and be enabled more skillfully to divide the Word of truth.

Would men but constantly observe this direction: and when their ministers are praying in their name to God, humbly beseech him to perform all their petitions, or, when they are speaking in God's name to them, pray that the Holy Ghost may fall on all them that hear the Word, we should find a more visible good effect of their doctrine, and a greater mutual love between ministers and their people. For ministers' hands would then be held up by the people's intercessions, and the people will never dare to villify or traduce those who are the constant subjects of their prayers.

4. Next to our ministers, our friends claim a place in our intercessions; but then we should not content ourselves with praying in general terms for them, but suit our prayers to their particular circumstances. When Miriam was afflicted with a leprosy from God, Moses cried and said, "Lord, heal her." And when the nobleman came to apply to Jesus Christ, in behalf of his child, he said, "Lord, my little daughter lieth at the point of death, I pray thee to come and heal her." In like manner, when our friends are under any afflicting circumstances, we should endeavor to pray for them with a particular regard to those circumstances. For instance, is a friend sick? We should pray that if it be God's good pleasure, it may not be unto death; but if otherwise, that he would give him grace so to take his visitation, that, after this painful life ended, he

may dwell with him in life everlasting. Is a friend in doubt in an important matter? We should lay his case before God, as Moses did that of the daughters of Zelophehad, and pray that God's Holy Spirit may lead him into all truth and give all seasonable direction. Is he in want? We should pray that his faith may never fail, and that in God's due time he may be relieved. And in all other cases, we should not pray for our friends only in generals, but suit our petitions to their particular sufferings and afflictions; for otherwise, we may never ask perhaps for the things our friends most want.

It must be confessed that such a procedure will oblige some often to break from the forms they use; but if we accustom ourselves to it and have a deep sense of what we ask for, the most illiterate will not want [lack] proper words to express themselves.

We have many noble instances in holy Scripture of the success of this kind of particular intercession; but none more remarkable than that of Abraham's servant, in the book of Genesis, who, being sent to seek a wife for his son Isaac, prayed in a most particular manner in his behalf. And the sequel of the story informs us how remarkably his prayer as answered. And did Christians now pray for their friends in the same particular manner, and with the same faith as Abraham's servant did for his master, they would, no doubt, in many instances receive as visible answers, and have as much reason to bless God for them, as he had.

5. But as we ought thus to intercede for our friends, so in like manner must we also pray for our enemies. "Bless them that curse you (says Jesus Christ), and pray for them that despitefully use you, and persecute you." Which commands he enforced in the strongest manner by his own example: in the very agonies and pangs of death he prayed even for his murderers, "Father, forgive them, for they know not what they do!" This, it must needs be confessed, is a difficult duty, yet not impracticable, to those who have renounced the things of this present life (from an inordinate love of which all enmities arise) and who, knowing the terrible woes denounced against those who offend Christ's little ones, can, out of real pity and a sense of their danger, pray for those by whom such offenses come.

6. Last, and to conclude this head, we should intercede for all that are any ways afflicted in mind, body, or estate; for all who desire and stand in need of our prayers, and for all who do not pray for themselves.

And oh! that all who hear me would set apart some time every day for the due performance of this most necessary duty! In order to which—

III. I shall now proceed to show the advantages, and offer some considerations to excite you to the practice of daily intercession.

*And yet rob mccoy says they are not the enemy they are the opportunity—I say my enemies are my opportunities

Speaking of "intercession"

1. And first, it will fill your hearts with love one to another. He that every day heartily intercedes at the throne of grace for all mankind cannot but in a short time be filled with love and charity to all: and the frequent exercise of his love in this manner will insensibly enlarge his heart and make him partaker of that exceeding abundance of it which is in Christ Jesus our Lord! Envy, malice, revenge, and suchlike hellish tempers, can never long harbor in a gracious intercessor's breast; but he will be filled with joy, peace, meekness, long-suffering, and all other graces of the Holy Spirit. By frequently laying his neighbor's wants before God, he will be touched with a fellow feeling of them; he will rejoice with those that do rejoice, and weep with those that weep. Every blessing bestowed on others, instead of exciting envy in him, will be looked on as an answer to his particular intercession and fill his soul with joy unspeakable and full of glory.

Abound therefore in acts of general and particular intercessions; and when you hear of your neighbor's faults, instead of relating them to and exposing them before others, lay them in secret before God, and beg of him to correct and amend them. When you hear of a notorious sinner, instead of thinking you do well to be angry, beg of Jesus Christ to convert and make him a monument of his free grace; you cannot imagine what a blessed alteration this practice will make in your heart and how much you will increase day by day in the spirit of love and meekness toward all mankind!

But further, to excite you to the constant practice of this duty of intercession, consider the many instances in holy Scripture, of the power and efficacy of it. Great and excellent things are there recorded as the effects of this divine employ. It has stopped plagues; it has opened and shut heaven, and has frequently turned away God's fury from his people. How was Abimelech's house freed from the disease God sent among them, at the intercession of Abraham! When "Phineas stood up and prayed," how soon did the plague cease! When Daniel humbled and afflicted his soul and interceded for the Lord's inheritance, how quickly was an angel dispatched to tell him, "his prayer was heard"! And to mention but one instance more, how does God own himself as it were overcome with the importunity of Moses, when he was interceding for his idolatrous people, "Let me alone," says God!

This sufficiently shows, I could almost say, the omnipotency of intercession, and how we may, like Jacob, wrestle with God, and by a holy violence prevail both for ourselves and others. And no doubt it is owing to the secret and prevailing intercessions of the few righteous souls who still remain among us, that God has yet spared this miserably sinful nation: for were there not some such faithful ones, like Moses, left to stand in the gap, we should soon be destroyed, even as was Sodom, and reduced to ashes, like unto Gomorrah.

But, to stir you up yet further to this exercise of intercession, consider that, in all probability, it is the frequent employment even of the glorified saints: for though they are delivered from the burden of the flesh, and restored to the glorious liberty of the sons of God, yet as their happiness cannot be perfectly consummated till the resurrection of the last day, when all their brethren will be glorified with them, we cannot but think they are often importunate in beseeching our heavenly Father shortly to accomplish the number of his elect and to hasten his kingdom. And shall now we, who are on earth, be often exercised in this divine employ with the glorious company of the spirits of just men made perfect? Since our happiness is so much to consist in the communion of saints in the church triumphant above, shall we not frequently intercede for the church militant here below, and earnestly beg that we may all be one, even as the holy Jesus and his Father are one, that we may also be made perfect in one?

To provoke you to this great work and labor of love, remember, that it is the never-ceasing employment of the holy and highly exalted Jesus himself, who sits at the right hand of God, to hear all our prayers, and to make continual intercession for us! So that he who is constantly employed in interceding for others is doing that on earth which the eternal Son of God is always doing in heaven.

Imagine therefore, when you are lifting up holy hands in prayer for one another, that you see the heavens opened and the Son of God in all his glory, as the great High Priest of your salvation, pleading for you the all-sufficient merit of his sacrifice before the throne of his heavenly Father! Join then your intercessions with his, and beseech him, that they may, through him, come up as incense and be received as a sweet-smelling savor, acceptable in the sight of God! This imagination will strengthen your faith, excite a holy earnestness in your prayers, and make you wrestle with God, as Jacob did, when he saw him face to face and his life was preserved; as Abraham, when he pleaded for Sodom; and as Jesus Christ himself, when he prayed, being in an agony, so much the more earnestly the night before his bitter passion.

And now, brethren, what shall I say more, since you are taught of Jesus Christ himself to abound in love, and in this good work of praying one for another. Though ever so mean, though as poor as Lazarus, you will then become benefactors to all mankind; thousands, and twenty times ten thousands, will then be blessed for your sakes! And after you have employed a few years in this divine exercise here, you will be translated to that happy place, where you have so often wished others might be advanced, and be exalted to sit at the right hand of our all-powerful, all-prevailing Intercessor, in the king-dom of his heavenly Father hereafter.

However, I cannot but in a special manner press this upon you now, because all you, among whom I have now been preaching, in all probability will see me no more; for I am now going (I trust under the conduct of God's most Holy Spirit) from you, knowing not what shall befall me: I need there-fore your most importunate intercessions, that nothing may move me from my duty, and that I may not "count even my life dear unto myself, so that I may finish my course with joy, and the ministry I have received of the Lord Jesus, to testify the gospel of the grace of God!"

While I have been here, to the best of my knowledge, I have not failed to declare unto you the whole will of God; and though my preaching may have been a savor of death unto death to some; yet I trust it has been also a savor of life unto life to others; and therefore I earnestly hope that those will not fail to remember me in their prayers. As for my own part, the many unmerited kindnesses I have received from you will not suffer me to forget you: out of the deep, therefore, I trust shall my cry come unto God; and while the winds and storms are blowing over me, unto the Lord will I make my supplication for you. For it is but a little while, and "we must all appear before the judg-ment seat of Christ," where I must give a strict account of the doctrine I have preached, and you of your improvement under it. And oh, that I may never be called out as a swift witness against any of those for whose salvation I have sin-cerely, though too faintly, longed and labored!

It is true, I have been censured by some as acting out of sinister and self-ish views, but it is a small matter with me to be judged by man's judgment; I hope my eye is single; but I beseech you, brethren, by the mercies of God in Christ Jesus, pray that it may be more so! And that I may increase with the increase of grace in the knowledge and love of God through Jesus Christ our Lord.

And now, brethren, what shall I say more? I could wish to continue my dis-course much longer; for I can never fully express the desire of my soul toward you! Finally, therefore, brethren, "whatsoever things are holy, whatsoever things are pure, whatsoever things are honest, whatsoever things are of good report: if there be any consolation in Christ, if any fellowship of the spirit," if any hopes of our appearing to the comfort of each other at the awful tribunal of Jesus Christ, "think of the things that you have heard," and of those which your pastors have declared, and will yet declare unto you; and continue under their ministry to "work out your own salvation with fear and trembling," so that whether I should never see you anymore, or whether it shall please God to bring me back again at any time, I may always have the satisfaction of knowing that your conversation is such "as becometh the gospel of Christ."

I almost persuade myself that I could willingly suffer all things, so that it might any ways promote the salvation of your precious and immortal souls; and I beseech you, as my last request, "obey them that have the rule over you in the Lord", and be always ready to attend on their ministry, as it is your bounden duty. Think not that I desire to have myself exalted at the expense of another's character; but rather think this, not to have any man's person too much in admiration; but esteem all your ministers highly in love, as they justly deserve for their work's sake.

And now, "brethren, I commend you to God, and to the word of his grace, which is able to build you up, and give you an inheritance amongst all them that are sanctified." May God reward you for all your works of faith, and labors of love, and make you to abound more and more in every good word and work toward all men. May he truly convert all that have been convinced, and awaken all that are dead in trespasses and sins! May he confirm all that are wavering! And may you all go on from one degree of grace unto another, till you arrive unto the measure of the stature of the fullness of Christ; and thereby be made meet to stand before that God, "in whose presence is the fullness of joy, and at whose right hand there are pleasures forevermore!" Amen! Amen!

* have rule over you in the LORD. Worth having been repeated "In the LORD".

● ? the concept of Confirmation among Catholicism?

Persecution: Every Christian's Lot

—∿—

Yea, and all that will live godly in Christ Jesus shall suffer persecution.
—2 TIMOTHY 3:12

When our Lord was pleased to take upon himself the form of a servant, and to go about preaching the kingdom of God, he took all opportunities in public, and more especially in private, to caution his disciples against seeking great things for themselves, and also to forewarn them of the many distresses, afflictions, and persecutions, which they must expect to endure for his name's sake. The great apostle Paul therefore, the author of this epistle, in this as in all other things, following the steps of his blessed Master, takes particular care, among other apostolic admonitions, to warn young Timothy of the difficulties he must expect to meet with in the course of his ministry: "This know also, that in the last days perilous times shall come. For men shall be lovers of their own selves, covetous, proud, blasphemers, disobedient to parents, unthankful, unholy, without natural affection, truce breakers, false accusers, incontinent [lacking self-restraint], fierce, despisers of those that are good, traitors, heady, high-minded, lovers of pleasure more than lovers of God; having a form of godliness, but denying the power thereof: from such turn away. For of this sort are they who creep into houses, and lead captive silly women laden with sins, led away with diverse lusts, ever learning, and never able to come to the knowledge of the truth. Now, as Jannes and Jambres (two of the Egyptian magicians) withstood Moses (by working sham miracles), so do they also resist the truth; and (notwithstanding they keep up the form of religion) are men of corrupt minds, reprobate concerning the faith." But, in order to keep him from sinking under their opposition, he [Paul] tells him that though God, for wise ends, permitted these false teachers, as he did the magicians, to oppose for some time, yet they should now proceed no further: "For their folly (says he) shall be made manifest unto all men, as theirs (the magicians') also was," when they could not stand before Moses because of the boil, for the boil was upon the magicians as well as upon all the Egyptians. And then, to encourage Timothy yet the more, he propounds to him his own example: "But thou hast fully known my doctrine, manner of life, purpose, faith, long-suffering, charity, patience, persecutions, afflictions, which came unto me at Antioch, at Iconium, at Lystra; what persecutions I endured; but out of them all the Lord delivered me." And then, lest Timothy might think that this was only the particular case of Paul, says he, in the words of the text, "Yea, and all that will live godly in Christ Jesus shall suffer persecution."

The words, without considering them as they stand in relation to the context, contain an important truth, that persecution is the common lot of every godly man. This is a hard saying. How few can bear it? I trust God, in the following discourse, will enable me to make it good, by showing—

I. What it is to live godly in Christ Jesus.

II. The different kinds of persecution to which they who live godly are exposed.

III. Why it is that godly men must expect to suffer persecution.

Last, we shall apply the whole.

1. First, let us consider what it is to live godly in Christ Jesus. This supposes that we are made the righteousness of God in Christ, that we are born again, and are one with Christ by a living faith and a vital union, even as Jesus Christ and the Father are one. Unless we are thus converted and transformed by the renewing of our minds, we cannot properly be said to be in Christ, much less to live godly in him. To be in Christ merely by baptism and an outward profession is not to be in him in the strict sense of the word; no, "They that are in Christ are new creatures; old things are passed away, and all things are become new" in their hearts. Their life is hid with Christ in God; their souls daily feed on the invisible realities of another world. To "live godly in Christ" is to make the divine will, and not our own, the sole principle of all our thoughts, words, and actions; so that, "whether we eat or drink, or whatsoever we do, we do all to the glory of God." Those who live godly in Christ may not so much be said to live, as Christ to live in them: he is their Alpha and Omega, their first and last, their beginning and end. They are led by his Spirit as a child is led by the hand of its father; and are willing to follow the Lamb withersoever he leads them. They hear, know, and obey his voice. Their affections are set on things above; their hopes are full of immortality; their citizenship is in heaven. Being born again of God, they habitually live to, and daily walk with, God. They are pure in heart; and, from a principle of faith in Christ, are holy in all manner of conversation and godliness.

This is to "live godly in Christ Jesus"; and hence we may easily learn: why so few suffer persecution? Because so few live godly in Christ Jesus. You may live formally in Christ; you may attend on outward duties; you may live morally in Christ, you may (as they term it) do no one a harm and avoid persecution; but they "that will live godly in Christ Jesus shall suffer persecution."

2. Second, what is the meaning of the word *persecution,* and how many kinds there are of it, I come now to consider.

The word *persecution* is derived from a Greek word signifying to pursue, and generally implies pursuing a person for the sake of his goodness, or God's goodwill to him.

The first kind of it is that of the heart. We have an early example of this in the wicked one Cain, who, because the Lord had respect to Abel and his offering, and not to him and his offering, was very angry, his countenance fell, and at length he cruelly slew his envied brother. Thus the Pharisees hated and persecuted our Lord long before they laid hold on him: and our Lord mentions being inwardly hated of men, as one kind of persecution his disciples were to undergo. This heart enmity (if I may so term it) is the root of all other kinds of persecution, and is, in some degree or other, to be found in the soul of every unregenerated man; and numbers are guilty of this persecution, who never have it in their power to persecute any other way. What's more, numbers would actually put in practice all other degrees of persecution, had not the name of *persecution* become odious among mankind, and did they not hereby run the hazard of losing their reputation. Alas! how many at the great day, whom we know not now, will be convicted and condemned, that all their life harbored a secret evil will against Zion! They may now screen it before men; but God sees the enmity of their hearts and will judge them as persecutors at the great and terrible day of judgment.

A second degree of persecution is that of the tongue; "out of the abundance of the heart, the mouth speaketh." Many, I suppose, think it no harm to shoot out arrows, even bitter words, against the disciples of the Lord: they scatter their firebrands, arrows and death, saying, "Are we not in sport?" But, however they may esteem it, in God's account evil speaking is a high degree of persecution. Thus Ishmael's mocking Isaac is termed persecuting him. "Blessed are ye (says our Lord) when men shall revile you and persecute you, and shall say all manner of evil against you falsely for my name's sake," from which we may gather that reviling, and speaking all manner of evil for Christ's sake, is a high degree of persecution. For "a good name (says the wise man) is better than precious ointment," and, to many, is dearer than life itself. It is a great breach of the Sixth Commandment to slander anyone; but to speak evil of and slander the disciples of Christ merely because they are his disciples must be highly provoking in the sight of God; and such who are guilty of it (without repentance) will find that Jesus Christ will call them to an account and punish them for all their ungodly and hard speeches in a lake of fire and brimstone. This shall be their portion to drink.

The third and last kind of persecution is that which expresses itself in actions: as when wicked men separate the children of God from their company. "Blessed are ye (says our Lord) when they shall separate you from their company," or expose them to church censures, "They shall put you out of their synagogues"; threatening and prohibiting them from making an open profession of his religion or worship; or interdicting ministers for preaching his word, as the high priests threatened the apostles, and "forbad them anymore to speak in the name of Jesus"; and Paul breathed out threatenings and slaughters against the disciples of the Lord; or when they call them into courts, "You shall be called before governors," says our Lord; or when they fine, imprison, or punish them, by confiscation of goods, cruel scourging, and, last, death itself.

It would be impossible to enumerate in what various shapes persecution has appeared. It is a many-headed monster, cruel as the grave, insatiable as hell; and, what is worse, it generally appears under the cloak of religion. But, cruel, insatiable, and horrid as it is, they that live godly in Christ Jesus must expect to suffer and encounter with it in all its forms.

This is what we are to make good under our next general head.

3. Third, why is it that godly men must expect to suffer persecution?

And, first, this appears from the whole tenor of our Lord's doctrine. We will begin with his divine Sermon on the Mount. "Blessed are they who are persecuted for righteousness' sake; for theirs is the kingdom of heaven." So that, if our Lord spoke truth, we are not so blessed as to have an interest in the kingdom of heaven, unless we are or have been persecuted for righteousness' sake. What's more, our Lord (it is remarkable) employs three verses in this beatitude, and only one in each of the others; not only to show that it was a thing which men (as men) are unwilling to believe, but also the necessary consequence of it upon our being Christians. This is likewise evident from all those passages, wherein our Lord informs us that he came upon the earth, not to send peace, but a sword; and that the father-in-law should be against the mother-in-law, and a man's foes should be those of his own household. Passages, which though confined by false prophets to the first, I am persuaded will be verified by the experience of all true Christians in this, and every age of the church. It would be endless to recount all the places, wherein our Lord forewarns his disciples, that they should be called before rulers and thrust out of synagogues; what's more, that the time would come wherein men should think they did God service to kill them. For this reason he so frequently declared that "unless a man forsake all that he had, and even hated life itself, he could not be his disciple." And therefore it is worthy our observation, that in the remarkable passage, wherein our Lord makes such an extensive promise to those who left all for him, he cautiously inserts persecution. "And Jesus answered and said, 'Verily I say unto you, there is no man that hath left house, or brethren, or sisters, or father, or mother, or wife, or children, or lands, for my sake and the gospel's, but he shall receive an hundredfold now in this time; houses and brethren, and sisters and mothers, and children and lands, with persecutions (the word is in the plural number, including all kinds of persecution); and in the world to come eternal life." He that has ears to hear, let him hear what Christ says in all these passages, and then confess that all "who will live godly in Christ Jesus shall suffer persecution."

As this is proved from our Lord's doctrine, so it is no less evident from his life. Follow him from the manger to the cross and see whether any persecution was like that which the Son of God, the Lord of glory, underwent while here on earth. How was he hated by wicked men? How often would that hatred have excited them to lay hold of him had it not been for fear of the people? How was he reviled, counted and called a blasphemer, a winebibber, a Samaritan, even a devil, and, in one word, had all manner of evil spoken against him falsely? What contradiction of sinners did he endure against himself? How did men separate from his company and were ashamed to walk with him openly? Insomuch that he once said to his own disciples, "Will you also go away?" Again, how was he stoned, thrust out of the synagogues, arraigned as a deceiver of the people, a seditious and pestilent fellow, an enemy of Caesar, and as such scourged, blindfolded, spit upon, and at length condemned and nailed to an accursed tree? Thus was the Master persecuted, thus did the Lord suffer; and the servant is not above his Master, nor the disciple above his Lord: "If they have persecuted me, they will also persecute you," says the blessed Jesus. And again, "Every man that is perfect (a true Christian) must be as his Master"—or suffer as he did. For in all these things our Lord has set us an example, that we should follow his steps: and therefore, far be it that any who live godly in Christ Jesus should henceforward expect to escape suffering persecution.

But further: not only our Lord's example, but the example of all the saints that ever lived, evidently demonstrates the truth of the apostle's assertion in the text. How soon was Abel made a martyr for his religion? How was Isaac mocked by the son of the bondwoman? And what a large catalog of suffering Old Testament saints have we recorded in Hebrews 11! Read the Acts of the Apostles, and see how the first Christians were threatened, stoned, imprisoned, scourged, and persecuted even unto death. Examine church history in after ages, and you will find the murder of the innocents by Herod was but an earnest of the innocent blood which should be shed for the sake of Jesus. Examine the experience of saints now living on earth; and, if it were possible to consult the spirits of just men made perfect, I am persuaded each would concur with the apostle in asserting that "all who will live godly in Christ Jesus shall suffer persecution."

How can it be otherwise in the very nature of things? Ever since the fall, there has been an irreconcilable enmity between the seed of the woman and the seed of the serpent. Wicked men hate God and therefore cannot but hate those who are like him: they hate to be reformed and therefore must hate and persecute those who, by a contrary behavior, testify of them that their deeds are evil. Besides, pride of heart leads men to persecute the servants of Jesus Christ. If they commend them, they are afraid of being asked, "Why do not you follow them?" And therefore because they dare not imitate, though they may sometimes be even forced to approve their way, yet pride and envy make them turn persecutors. Hence it is that as it was formerly, so it is now, and so will it be to the end of time: "He that is born after the flesh (the natural man, does and) will persecute him that is born after the Spirit," the regenerate man. Because Christians are not of the world, but Christ has chosen them out of the world, therefore the world will hate them. If it be objected against this doctrine, that we now live in a Christian world and therefore must not expect such persecution as formerly, I answer: all are not Christians that are called so; and, till the heart is changed, the enmity against God (which is the root of all persecution) remains; and consequently Christians, falsely so called, will persecute as well as others. I observed therefore, in the beginning of this discourse, that Paul mentions those that had a form of religion as persons of whom Timothy had need be chiefly aware: for, as our Lord and his apostles were mostly persecuted by their countrymen the Jews, so we must expect the like usage from the formalists of our own nation, the Pharisees, who seem to be religious. The most horrid and barbarous persecutions have been carried on by those who have called themselves Christians; witness the days of Queen Mary; and the fines, banishments, and imprisonments of the children of God in the last century, and the bitter, irreconcilable hatred that appears in thousands who call themselves Christians, even in the present days wherein we live.

Persons who argue against persecution are not sufficiently sensible of the bitter enmity of the heart of every unregenerate man against God. For my own part, I am so far from wondering that Christians are persecuted, that I wonder our streets do not run with the blood of the saints: was men's power equal to their wills, such a horrid spectacle would soon appear.

But persecution is necessary in respect to the godly themselves. If we have not all manner of evil spoken of us, how can we know whether we seek only that honor which comes from above? If we have no persecutors, how can our passive graces be kept in exercise? How can many Christian precepts be put into practice? How can we love, pray for, and do good to, those who despitefully use us? How can we overcome evil with good? In short, how can we know we love God better than life itself? Paul was sensible of all this, and therefore so positively and peremptorily asserts that "all who live godly in Christ Jesus shall suffer persecution."

Not that I affirm, all are persecuted in a like degree. No: this would be contrary both to Scripture and experience. But though all Christians are not really called to suffer every kind of persecution, yet all Christians are liable thereto: and notwithstanding some may live in more peaceful times of the church than others, yet all Christians, in all ages, will find by their own experience, that, whether they act in a private or public capacity, they must, in some degree or other, suffer persecution.

Here then I would pause, and, last, by way of application, exhort all persons—first, to stand a while and examine themselves. For, by what has been said, you may gather one mark whereby you may judge whether you are Christians or not. Were you ever persecuted for righteousness' sake? If not, you never yet lived godly in Christ our Lord. Whatever you may say to the contrary, the inspired apostle, in the words of the text (the truth of which, I think, I have sufficiently proved), positively asserts that all who "will live godly in him shall suffer persecution." Not that all who are persecuted are real Christians; for many sometimes suffer, and are persecuted, on other accounts than for righteousness' sake. The great question therefore is: whether you were ever persecuted for living godly? You may boast of your great prudence and sagacity (and indeed these are excellent things) and glory because you have not run such lengths and made yourselves so singular, and liable to such contempt, as some others have. But, alas! this is not a mark of your being of a Christian, but of a Laodicean spirit, neither hot nor cold, and fit only to be spewed out of the mouth of God. That which you call prudence, is often only cowardice, dreadful hypocrisy, pride of heart, which makes you dread contempt, and afraid to give up your reputation for God. You are ashamed of Christ and his gospel; and in all probability, was he to appear a second time upon earth, in words, as well as works, you would deny him. Awake therefore, all you that live only formally in Christ Jesus, and no longer seek that honor which comes of man. I do not desire to court you, but I entreat you to live godly and fear not contempt for the sake of Jesus Christ. Beg of God to give you his Holy Spirit, that you may see through and discover the latent hypocrisy of your hearts, and no longer deceive your own souls. Remember you cannot reconcile two irreconcilable differences, God and mammon, the friendship of this world with the favor of God. Know you not who has told you that "the friendship of this world is enmity with God"? If therefore you are in friendship with the world, notwithstanding all your specious pretenses to piety, you are at enmity with God: you are only heart hypocrites; and "what is the hope of the hypocrite, when God shall take away his soul?" Let the words of the text sound an alarm in your ears. Oh, let them sink deep into your hearts; "Yea, and all that will live godly in Christ Jesus shall suffer persecution."

Second, from the words of the text, I would take occasion to speak to those who are about to list themselves under the banner of Christ's cross. What say you? Are you resolved to live godly in Christ Jesus, notwithstanding the consequence will be that you must suffer persecution? You are beginning to build; but have you taken our Lord's advice to "sit down first and count the cost"? Have you well weighed with yourselves that weighty declaration: "He that loveth father or mother more than me is not worthy of me"? And again, "Unless a man forsake all that he hath he cannot be my disciple"? Perhaps some of you have great possessions; will not you go away sorrowful, if Christ should require you to sell all that you have? Others of you again may be kinsmen, or some way related or under obligations, to the high priests, or other great personages, who may be persecuting the church of Christ. What do you say? Will you, with Moses, "rather choose to suffer affliction with the people of God, than enjoy the pleasures of sin for a season"? Perhaps you may say, "My friends will not oppose me." That is more than you know: in all probability your chief enemies will be those of your own household. If therefore they should oppose you, are you willing naked to follow a naked Christ? And to wander about in sheepskins and goatskins, in dens and caves of the earth, being afflicted, destitute, tormented, rather than not be Christ's disciples? You are now all following with zeal, as Ruth and Orpah did Naomi, and may weep under the Word; but are not your tears crocodiles' tears? And, when difficulties come, will you not go back from following your Lord, as Orpah departed from following Naomi? Have you really the root of grace in your hearts? Or are you only stony-ground hearers? You receive the Word with joy; but when persecution arises because of the Word, will you not be immediately offended? Be not angry with me for putting these questions to you. I am jealous over you, but it is with a godly jealousy: for, alas! how many have put their hands to the plow and afterward have shamefully looked back? I only deal with you, as our Lord did with the person that said, "Lord, I will follow thee withersoever thou wilt. The foxes have holes, and the birds of the air have nests, but the Son of man (says he) hath not where to lay his head." What say you? Are you willing to endure hardness, and thereby approve yourselves good soldiers of Jesus Christ? You now come on foot out of the towns and villages to hear the Word and receive me as a messenger of God: but will you not by and by cry out, "Away with him, away with him; it is not fit such a fellow should live upon the earth"? Perhaps some of you, like Hazael, may say, "Are we dogs, that we should do this?" But alas! I have met with many unhappy souls who have drawn back unto perdition and have afterward accounted me their enemy, for dealing faithfully with them; though once, if it were possible, they would have plucked out their own eyes, and have given them unto me. Sit down therefore, I beseech you, and seriously count the cost, and ask yourselves again and again, whether you count all things but dung and dross, and are willing to suffer the loss of all things, so that you may win Christ and be found in him; for you may assure yourselves, the apostle has not spoken in vain: "All that will live godly in Christ Jesus shall suffer persecution."

Third, the text speaks to you that are patiently suffering for the truth's sake: "Rejoice, and be exceeding glad; great shall be your reward in heaven." For to you it is given, not only to believe, but also to suffer, and perhaps remarkably too, for the sake of Jesus! This is a mark of your discipleship, an evidence that you do live godly in Christ Jesus. Fear not, therefore, neither be dismayed. Oh, be not weary and faint in your minds! Jesus, your Lord, your life, comes, and his reward is with him. Though all men forsake you, yet will not he: no; the Spirit of Christ and of glory shall rest upon you. In patience therefore possess your souls. Sanctify the Lord God in your hearts. Be in nothing terrified by your adversaries: on their part Christ is evil spoken of; on your part his is glorified. Be not ashamed of your glory, since others can glory in their shame. Think it not strange concerning the fiery trial, wherewith you are or may be tried. The devil rages, knowing that he has but a short time to reign. He or his emissaries have no more power than what is given them from above: God sets them their bounds, which they cannot pass; and the very hairs of your head are all numbered. Fear not; no one shall set upon you to hurt you, without your heavenly Father's knowledge. Do your earthly friends and parents forsake you? Are you cast out of the synagogues? The Lord shall reveal himself to you, as to the man that was born blind. Jesus Christ shall take you up. If they carry you to prison and load you with chains, so that the iron enter into your souls, even there shall Christ send an angel from heaven to strengthen you and enable you, with Paul and Silas, to "sing praises at midnight." Are you threatened to be thrown into a den of lions or cast into a burning fiery furnace, because you will not bow down and worship the beast? Fear not; the God whom you serve is able to deliver you: or, if he should suffer the flames to devour your bodies, they would only serve, as so many fiery chariots, to carry your souls to God. Thus it was with the martyrs of old; so that one, when he was burning, cried out, "Come, you papists, if you want a miracle, here, behold one! This bed of flames is to me a bed of down." Thus it was with almost all that suffered in former times: for Jesus, notwithstanding he withdrew his own divinity from himself, yet has always lifted up the light of his countenance upon the souls of suffering saints. "Fear not therefore those that can kill the body, and after that have no more that they can do; but fear him only, who is able to destroy both body and soul in hell." Dare, dare to live godly in Christ Jesus, though you suffer all manner of persecution.

But, fourth, are there any true ministers of Jesus Christ here? You will not be offended if I tell you that the words of the text are, in a special manner, applicable to you. Paul wrote them to Timothy; and we, of all men, that live godly in Christ Jesus, must expect to suffer the severest persecution. Satan will endeavor to bruise our heels, let who will escape: and it has been the general way of God's providence, in times of persecution, to permit the shepherds first to be smitten, before the sheep are scattered. Let us not therefore show that we are only hirelings, who care not for the sheep; but, like the great Shepherd and Bishop of souls, let us readily lay down our lives for the sheep. While others are boasting of their great preferments, let us rather glory in our great afflictions and persecutions for the sake of Christ. Paul rejoiced that he suffered afflictions and persecutions at Iconium and Lystra: out of all, the Lord delivered him; out of all, the Lord will deliver us and cause us hereafter to sit down with him on thrones, when he comes to judge the twelve tribes of Israel.

I could proceed; but I am conscious, in this part of my discourse, I ought more particularly to speak to myself, knowing that Satan has desired to have me, that he may sift me as wheat. Without a spirit of prophecy, we may easily discern the signs of the times. Persecutions even at the doors: the tabernacle of the Lord is already driven into the wilderness: the ark of the Lord is fallen into the unhallowed hands of uncircumcised Philistines. They have long since put us out of their synagogues, and high priests have been calling on civil magistrates to exert their authority against the disciples of the Lord. Men in power have been breathing out threatenings: we may easily guess what will follow, imprisonment and slaughter. The storm has been gathering some time; it must break shortly. Perhaps it may fall on me first.

Brethren therefore, whether in the ministry or not, I beseech you, "pray for me," that I may never suffer justly, as an evildoer, but only for righteousness' sake. Oh, pray that I may not deny my Lord in anywise, but that I may joy-fully follow him, both to prison and to death, if he is pleased to call me to seal his truths with my blood. Be not ashamed of Christ, or of his gospel, though I should become a prisoner of the Lord. Though I am bound, the Word of God will not be bound: no; an open, an effectual door is opened for preaching the everlasting gospel, and men or devils shall never be able to prevail against it. Only pray, that, whether it be in life or death, Christ may be glorified in me: then I shall rejoice, yes, and will rejoice.

And now, to whom shall I address myself next?

Fifth, to those, who persecute their neighbors for living godly in Christ Jesus. But what shall I say to you? Howl and weep for the miseries that shall come upon you; for a little while the Lord permits you to ride over the heads of his people; but, by and by, death will arrest you, judgment will find you, and Jesus Christ shall put a question to you, which will strike you dumb: "Why per-secuted you me?" You may plead your laws and your canons and pretend what you do is out of zeal for God; but God shall discover the cursed hypocrisy and serpentine enmity of your hearts, and give you over to the tormentors. It is well, if in this life God does not send some mark upon you. He pleaded the cause of Naboth, when innocently condemned for blaspheming God and the king; and our Lord sent forth his armies and destroyed the city of those who killed the prophets and stoned them that were sent unto them. If you have a mind therefore to fill up the measure of your iniquities, go on, persecute and despise the disciples of the Lord: but know, "that for all these things, God shall bring you to judgment." What's more, those you now persecute shall be in part your judges, and sit on the right hand of the Majesty on high, while you are dragged by infernal spirits into a lake that burns with fire and brimstone, and the smoke of your torment shall be ascending up forever and ever. Lay down therefore, you rebels, your arms against the most high God, and no longer per-secute those who live godly in Christ Jesus. The Lord will plead, the Lord will avenge, their cause. You may be permitted to bruise their heels, yet in the end they shall bruise your accursed heads. I speak not this, as though I were afraid of you; for I know in whom I have believed: only out of pure love I warn you, and because I know not but Jesus Christ may make some of you vessels of mercy and snatch you, even you persecutors, as firebrands out of the fire. Jesus Christ came into the world to save sinners, even persecutors, the worst of sin-ners: his righteousness is sufficient for them; his Spirit is able to purify and change their hearts. He once converted Saul; may the same God magnify his power, in converting all those who are causing the godly in Christ Jesus, as much as in them lies, to suffer persecution! The Lord be with you all. Amen.

A Georgia Sermon

—⚏—

Preached before the governor, and Council, and the House of Assembly, in Georgia, on January 28, 1770.

For who hath despised the day of small things? —ZECHARIAH 4:10

Men, brethren, and fathers, at sundry times and in diverse manners, God spake to the fathers by the prophets, before he spoke to us in these last days by his Son. And as God is a sovereign agent, and his sacred Spirit bloweth when and where it listeth, surely he may reveal and make known his will to his creatures, when, where, and how he pleases; "and who shall say unto him, 'What doest thou?'" Indeed, this seems to be one reason to display his sovereignty, why he chose, before the canon of Scripture was settled, to make known his mind in such various methods, and to such a variety of his servants and messengers.

Hence it is that we hear he talked with Abraham as "a man talketh with a friend." To Moses he spoke "face to face." To others by "dreams in the night" or by "visions" impressed strongly on their imaginations. This seems to be frequently the happy lot of the favorite evangelical prophet Zechariah. I call him evangelical prophet, because his predictions, however they pointed at some approaching or immediate event, ultimately terminated in him who is the Alpha and Omega, the beginning and the end of all the lively oracles of God. The chapter from which our text is selected, among many other passages, is a striking proof of this: an angel, that had been more than once sent to him on former occasions, appears again to him, by way of vision, and "waked him (to use his own words) as a man that is wakened out of his sleep." Prophets, and the greatest servants of God, need waking sometimes out of their drowsy frames.

I think I see this man of God starting out of his sleep and being all attention: the angel asked him, "What seest thou?" He answers, "I have looked, and behold, a candlestick all of gold," an emblem of the church of God, "with a bowl upon the top of it, and seven lamps thereon, and seven pipes to the seven lamps, which were upon the top thereof"; implying that the church, however reduced to the lowest ebb, should be preserved, be kept supplied and shining, through the invisible, but not less real because invisible, aids and operations of the blessed Spirit of God. The occasion of such an extraordinary vision, if we

OIL = SPIRIT

compare this passage with the second chapter of the prophecy of the prophet Haggai, seems to be this: it was now near eighteen years since the Jewish people had been delivered from their long and grievous Babylonian captivity; and being so long deprived of their temple and its worship, which fabric had been razed even to the ground, one would have imagined that immediately upon their return, they should have postponed all private works, and with their united strength have first set about rebuilding that once stately and magnificent structure. But they, like too many Christians of a like lukewarm stamp, though all acknowledged that this church work was a necessary work, yet put themselves and others off, with this godly pretense, "The time is not come, the time that the Lord's house should be built." The time is not come! What, not in eighteen years! For so long had they now been returned from their state of bondage: and pray, why was not the time come? The prophet Haggai tells them; their whole time was so taken up building for themselves ceiled [covered] houses, that they had no time left to build a habitation for their great and glorious benefactor, the mighty God of Jacob. *wow the church of the 20th century*

This ingratitude must not be passed by unpunished. Omniscience observes, Omnipotence resents it! And that they might read their sin in their punishment, as they thought it best to get rich and secure houses and lands and estates for themselves, before they set about unnecessary church work, the prophet tells them, "You have sown much, but bring in little: ye eat, but ye have not enough: ye drink, but ye are not filled with drink: ye clothe you, but there is none warm: and he that earneth wages, earneth wages to put it into a bag with holes." Still he goes on thundering and lightning, "'Ye looked for much, and lo it came to little: and when ye brought it home (pleasing yourselves with your fine crops), I did blow upon it. Why?' saith the Lord of hosts. 'Because of mine house that is waste, and ye run every man unto his own house.'" A thundering sermon this! Delivered not only to the common people, but also unto, and in the presence of "Zerubbabel, the son of Shealtiel, and Joshua, the son of Josedech, the high priest." The prophet's report is believed; and the arm of the Lord was revealed. "Zerubbabel, the son of Shealtiel, and Joshua, the son of Josedech (oh, happy times when church and state are thus combined) with all the remnant of the people, obeyed the voice of the Lord their God, and the words of Haggai the prophet." *YES!*

The spirit of Zerubbabel, and of Joshua, and the spirits of all the remnant of the people were stirred up, and they immediately came, disregarding, as it were, their own private buildings, "and did work in the house of the Lord of hosts their God." For a while they proceeded with vigor; the foundation of the house is laid, and the superstructure raised to some considerable height; but whether this fit of hot zeal soon cooled, as is too common, or the people were discouraged by the false representations of their enemies, which perhaps met with too favorable a reception as the court of Darius, it so happened that the hearts of the magistrates and ministers of the people waxed faint; and an awful chasm intervened, between the finishing and laying the foundation of this promising and glorious work.

Upon this, another prophet, even Zechariah (who with Haggai had been joint sufferer in the captivity) is sent to lift up the hands that hang down, to strengthen the feeble knees, and by the foregoing instructive vision, to reanimate Joshua and the people in general, and the heart of Zerubbabel, the son of Shealtiel, in particular, in spite of all discouragements, either from inveterate enemies or from timid unstable friends, or all other obstacles whatsoever. If Haggai thunders, Zechariah's message is as lightning. "This is the word of the Lord unto Zerubbabel, saying, 'Not by might, not by power (not by barely human power or policy) but by my spirit, saith the Lord of hosts; 'Who art thou, O great mountain? (thou Sanballat and thy associates, who have been so long crying out, 'What mean these feeble Jews?' However great, formidable, and seemingly insurmountable) before Zerubbabel thou shalt (not only be lowered and rendered more accessible, but) become a plain'"; your very opposition shall, in the end, promote the work, and help to expedite that very building, which you intended to put a stop to and destroy.

And lest Zerubbabel, through unbelief and outward opposition, or for want of more bodily strength, should think this would be a work of time, and that he should not live to see it completed in his days, "The word of the Lord came to Zechariah, saying, 'The hands of Zerubbabel have laid the foundation of this house; his hands also shall finish it, and he shall bring forth the headstone thereof with shoutings, crying, "Grace, grace unto it."'" Grace! Grace! unto it: a double acclamation, to show, that out of the abundance of their hearts, their mouths spoke; and this with shoutings and crying from all quarters. Even their enemies should see the hand and providence of God in the beginning, continuance, and ending of this seemingly improbable and impractical work; so that they should be constrained to cry, "Grace unto it," and wish both the work and the builders much prosperity. But as for its friends, they should be so transported with heartfelt joy in the reflection upon the signal providences which had attended them through the whole process, that they would shout and cry, "Grace, grace unto it"; or, "This is nothing but the Lord's doing; God prosper and bless this work more and more, and make it a place where his free grace and glory may be abundantly displayed." Then by a beautiful and pungent sarcasm, turning to the insulting enemies, he utters the spirited interrogation in my text, "Who hath despised the day of small things?" Who are you that vauntingly said, "What can these feeble Jews do, pretending to lay the foundation of a house which they never will have money, or strength, or power to finish?" Or, who are you, O timorous, shortsighted, doubting, though well-meaning people, who, through unbelief, were discouraged at the small beginnings and feebleness of the attempt to build a second temple? And, because you thought it could not come up to the magnificence of the first, therefore were discouraged from so much as beginning to build a second at all?

A close instructive question this; a question implying that whenever God intends to bring about any great thing, he generally begins with a day of small things.

As a proof of this, I will not lead you so far back, as to the beginning of time, when the everlasting "I AM" spoke all things into existence, by his almighty fiat; and out of a confused chaos, "without form and void," produced a world worthy of a God to create and of his favorite creature man, his vicegerent and representative here below, to inhabit and enjoy in it both himself and his God. And yet, though the heavens declare his glory, and the firmament shows his handiwork, though there is no speech nor language where their voice is not heard, and their line is gone out through all the earth; and by a dumb, yet persuasive language, proves the hand that made them to be divine; yet there have been, and are now, such fools in the world, as to "say in their hearts, 'There is no God,'" or so wise, as by their wisdom, not to know God or own his divine image to be stamped on that book wherein these grand things are recorded, and that in such legible characters that he who runs may read.

Neither will I divert your attention, honored fathers, to the histories of Greece and Rome or any of the great kingdoms and renowned monarchies, which constitute so great a part of ancient history, but whose beginnings were very small (witness Romulus' ditch), their progress as remarkably great, and their declension and downfall, when arrived at their appointed zenith, as sudden, unexpected, and marvelous. These make the chief subjects of the learning of our schools, though they make but a mean figure in sacred history, and would not perhaps have been mentioned at all, had they not been, in some measure, connected with the history of God's people, which is the grand subject of that much-despised book, emphatically called, the Scriptures. Whoever has a mind to inform himself of the one, may read Rollin's *Ancient History*, and whoever would see the connection with the other, may consult the learned Prideaux's admirable and judicious connection. Books which, I hope, will be strenuously recommended and carefully studied, when this present infant institution gathers more strength, and grows up into a seat of learning.

I can hardly forbear mentioning the final beginnings of Great Britain, now so distinguished for liberty, opulence, and renown; and the rise and rapid progress of the American colonies, which promises to be one of the most opulent and powerful empires in the world. But my present views, and the honors done this infant institution this day, and the words of my text, as well as the feelings of my own heart, and I trust, of the hearts of all that hear me, lead me to confine your meditations to the history of God's own peculiar people, which for the simplicity and sublimity of its language, the veracity of its author, and the importance and wonders of the facts therein recorded, if weighed in a proper balance, has not its equal under the sun. And yet, though God himself has become an author among us, we will not condescend to give his Book one thorough reading. Be astonished, O heavens, at this!

Who would have thought that from one, even from Abraham, and from so small a beginning as the emigration of a single private family, called out of a land wholly given to idolatry, to be sojourners and pilgrims in a strange land; who would have thought that from a man, who for a long season was written childless, a man whose first possession in this strange land was by purchasing a burying place for his wife, and in whose grave one might have imagined he would have buried all future expectations; who would have thought that from this very man and woman, according to the course of nature, both as good as dead, should descend a numerous offspring like unto the stars of heaven for multitude, and as the sand which is upon the seashore innumerable? What's more, who would have imagined that against all probability, and in all human appearance impossible, a kingdom should arise? Behold a poor captive slave, even Joseph, who was cruelly separated from his brethren, became second in Pharaoh's kingdom: he was sent before to work out a great deliverance, and to introduce a family which should take root, deep root downward and bear fruit upward, and fill the land. How could it enter into the heart of man to conceive that, when oppressed by a king who knew not Joseph, though they were the best, most loyal, industrious subjects this king had, when an edict was issued forth as impolitic as cruel (since the safety and glory of all kingdoms chiefly consist in the number of its inhabitants), that an outcast, helpless infant should be taken, and bred up in all the learning of the Egyptians, and in that very court from which, and by that very tyrant from whom, the edict came, and that the deliverer should be nurtured to be king in Jeshurun?

But time as well as strength would fail me, was I to give you a detail of all the important particulars respecting God's peculiar people; as their miraculous support in the wilderness, the events which took place while they were under a divine theocracy, and during their settlement in Canaan to the time of their return from Babylon, and from there to the destruction of their second temple, etc., by the Romans. Indeed, considering to whom I am speaking, persons conversant in the sacred and profane history, I have mentioned these things only to stir up your minds by way of remembrance.

But if we descend from the Jewish to the Christian era, we shall find that its commencement was, in the eyes of the world, a "day of small things" indeed. Our blessed Lord compares the beginning of its progress in the world, to a grain of mustard seed, which, though the smallest of all seeds when sown, soon becomes a great tree, and so spread that the "birds of the air," or a multitude of every nation, language, and tongue, came and lodged in its branches; and its inward progress in the believer's heart Christ likens to a little leaven which a woman hid in three measures of meal. How both the Jewish and Christian dispensations have been, and even to this day are, despised, by the wise disputers of this world, on this very account is manifest to all who read the lively oracles with a becoming attention. What ridicule, obloquy, and inveterate opposition Christianity meets with, in this our day, not only from the open deist, but from formal professors, is too evident to every truly pious soul.

And what opposition the kingdom of grace meets with in the heart is well known by all those who are experimentally acquainted with their hearts: they know, to their sorrow, what the great apostle of the Gentiles means by "the Spirit striving against the flesh, and the flesh against the Spirit."

But the sacred oracles and the histories of all ages acquaint us that God brings about the greatest thing, not only by small and unlikely means, but by ways and means directly opposite to the carnal reasonings of unthinking men: he chooses things that be not, to bring to naught those which are. How did Christianity spread and flourish by One who was despised and rejected of men, a man of sorrows, and acquainted with grief, and who expired on a cross? He was despised and rejected, not merely by the vulgar and illiterate, but the rabbis and masters of Israel, the scribes and Pharisees, who by the Jewish churchmen were held too in so high a reputation for their outward sanctity that it became a common proverb, "If only two went to heaven, the one would be a scribe, and the other a Pharisee." Yet there were they who endeavored to silence the voice of all his miracles and heavenly doctrine with, "Is not this the carpenter's son?" What's more, "He is mad, why hear you him? He hath a devil, and casteth out devils by Beelzebul the prince of the devils." And their despite not only followed him to, but after death, and when in the grave.

"We remember (said they) that this deceiver said, 'After three days I will rise again; command therefore that the sepulcher be made sure'"; but in spite of all your impotent precautions, in sealing the stone, and setting a watch, he burst the bars of death asunder and, according to his repeated predictions, proved himself to be the Son of God with power, by rising the third day from the dead. And afterward, in pretense of great multitudes, was he received up into glory; as a proof thereof, he sent down the Holy Ghost (on the mission of whom he pawned all his credit with his disciples) in such an instantaneous, amazing manner, as one would imagine should have forced and compelled all who saw it to own that this was indeed the finger of God.

And yet how was this grand transaction treated? With the utmost contempt, when instantaneously the apostles commenced as orators and linguists, and with a divine profusion spoke of the wonderful things of God: "These men (said some) are full of new wine." And yet by these men, mean fishermen, illiterate men, idiots, in the opinion of the scribes and Pharisees, and notwithstanding all the opposition of earth and hell, and that too only by the foolishness of preaching, did this grain of mustard seed grow up, till thousands, ten thousands of thousands, a multitude which no man can number, out of every nation, language, and people, came and lodged under the branches of it.

Neither shall it rest here; whatever dark parenthesis may intervene, we are assured that being still watered by the same divine hand, it shall take deeper and deeper root downward and bear more and more fruit upward, till the whole earth be filled with the knowledge of the Lord, as the waters cover the sea. Who shall live when God does this? Hasten, O Lord, that blessed time! Oh, let this thy kingdom come! Come, not only by the external preaching of the gospel in the world, but by its renovating, heart-renewing, soul-transforming power, to awakened sinners! For want of this, alas! alas! though we understood all mysteries, could speak with the tongues of men and angels, we should be only like sounding brass or so many tinkling cymbals.

And yet, what a "day of small things" is the first implantation of the seed of divine life in the soul of man? Well might our Lord, who alone is the author and finisher of our faith, compare it to a little leaven, which a woman took and hid in three measures of meal, till the whole was leavened. Low similes, mean comparisons these, in the eyes of those who, having eyes, see not; who, having ears, hear not; whose heart, being waxed gross, cannot, will not, understand! To such, it is despicable, mysterious, and unintelligible in its description; and, if possible, infinitely more so, when made effectual by the power of God, to the salvation of any individual soul. For the wisdom of God will always be foolishness to natural men. As it was formerly, so it is now; they who are born after the flesh will persecute those that are born after the Spirit: the disciple must be as his master: they that will live godly in him; they that live most godly in him, must, shall, suffer persecution. This is so interwoven in the very nature and existence of the gospel, that our Lord makes it one part of the Beatitudes, in that blessed sermon which he preached, when, to use the words of my old familiar friend the seraphic [James] Hervey, a mount was his pulpit, and the heavens his sounding board: a part, which, like others of the same nature, I believe, will be little relished by such who are always clamoring against those few highly favored souls who dare stand up and preach the doctrine of justification by faith alone in the imputed righteousness of Jesus Christ, and are reproached with not preaching, like their Master, morality, as they term it, in his glorious Sermon on the Mount; for did we more preach and more live it, we should soon find all manner of evil would be spoken against us for Christ's sake.

But shall this hinder the progress, the growth, and consummation? And shall the Christian therefore be dismayed and discouraged? God forbid! On the contrary, the weakest believer may, and ought, to rejoice and be exceedingly glad. And why? For a very good reason; because he that has begun the good work has engaged also to finish it; though Christ found him as black as hell, he shall present him, and every individual purchased with his blood, without spot or wrinkle, or any such thing, before the divine Presence. Oh, glorious prospect! How will the saints triumph, and the sons of God then shout for joy? If they shouted when God said, "Let there by light, and there was light," and if there is joy in heaven over one sinner only that repents, how will the heavenly arches echo and rebound with praise, when all the redeemed of the Lord shall appear together, and the Son of God shall say, "Of all these that thou hast given to me, have I lost nothing"? On the contrary, what weeping, wailing, and gnashing of teeth will there be, not only among the devil and his angels, but among the fearful and unbelieving, when they see that all the hellish temptations and devices, instead of destroying, were overruled to the furtherance of the gospel in general, and to the increase and growth of grace in every individual believer in particular. And how will despisers then behold and wonder and perish, when they shall be obliged to say, "We fools counted their lives madness, and their end to be without honor; but how are they numbered among the children of God, and how happy is their lot among the saints!"

But where am I going? Pardon me, my dear hearers, if you think this to be a digression from my main point. It is true, while I am musing, the fire begins to kindle: I am flying, but not so high, I trust, as to lose sight of my main subject. And yet, after meditating and talking of the rise and progress of the gospel of the kingdom, I shall find it somewhat difficult to descend so low, as to entertain you with the small beginnings of this infant colony, and of the orphan house, in which I am now preaching. But I should judge myself inexcusable on this occasion, if I did not detain you a little longer, in taking a transient view of the traces of divine providence, in the rise and progress of the colony in general, and the institution of this orphan house in particular. Children yet unborn, I trust, will have occasion to bless God for both.

The very design of this settlement, as charity inclines us to hope all things, was that it might be an asylum, and a place of business, for as many as were in distress; for foreigners, as well as natives; for Jews and Gentiles. On February 1, a day, the memory of which, I think, should still be perpetuated, the first embarkation was made with forty-five English families; men who had once lived well in their native country, and who, with many persecuted Saltzburghers, headed by a good old soldier of Jesus lately deceased, the Rev. Mr. Boltzius, came to find a refuge here. They came, they saw, they labored, and endeavored to settle; but by an essential, though well-meant defect, in the very beginning of the settlement, too well known by some now present, and too long, and too much felt to bear repeating, prohibiting the importation and use of Negroes, etc., their numbers gradually diminished, and matters were brought to so low an ebb that the whole colony became a proverb of reproach.

About this time, in the year 1737, being previously stirred up thereto by a strong impulse, which I could by no means resist, I came here, after the example of my worthy and reverend friends, Messieurs John and Charles Wesley, and Mr. Ingham, who, with the most disinterested views, had come hither to serve the colony, by endeavoring to convert the Indians. I came rejoicing to serve the colony also, and to become your willing servant for Christ's sake. My friend and father, good Bishop Bensen, encouraged me, though my brethren and kinsmen after the flesh, as well as religious friends, opposed it. I came, and I saw (you will not be offended with me to speak the truth) the nakedness of the land. Gladly did I distribute about the £400, which I had collected in England, among my poor parishioners. The necessity and propriety of erecting an orphan house was mentioned and recommended before my first embarkation. But thinking it a matter of too great importance to be set about unwarily, I deferred the further prosecution for this laudable design till my return to England in the year 1738, for to have priests' orders.

Miserable was the condition of many grown persons, as well as children, whom I left behind. Their cause I endeavored to plead, immediately upon my arrival; but being denied the churches, in which I had the year before collected many hundreds for the London charity schools, I endeavored to plead their cause in the fields. The people threw in their mites most willingly; once or twice, I think, £22 were collected in copper; the alms were accompanied with many prayers, which, as I told them, laid, I am persuaded, a blessed foundation to the future charitable superstructure. In a short time, though plucked as it were out of the fire, the collections and charitable contributions amounted to more than £1000.

With that I reimbarked, taking Philadelphia in my way, and upon my second arrival found the spot fixed upon; but alas! who can describe the low estate to which it was reduced! The whole country almost was left desolate, and the metropolis Savannah was but like a cottage in a vineyard, or as a lodge in a garden of cucumbers. Many orphans, whose parents had been taken from them by the distresses that naturally attend new settlements, were dispersed here and there in a very forlorn helpless condition; my bowels yearned toward them, and, animated by the example of the great Professor Franck, previous to bringing them here, I hired a house, furnished an infirmary, employed all that were capable of employment, and in a few weeks walked to the house of God with a large family of above sixty orphans, and others in as bad a condition.

On March 25, 1740, in full assurance of faith, I laid the foundation of this house; and in the year following, brought in my orphan family, who, with the workmen, now made up the number of 150: by the money which was expended on these, the remaining few were kept in the colony and were enabled to pay the debts they owed; so that in a representation made to the House of Commons by some, who for very good reasons wanted the constitution of the colony altered, they declared that the very existence of the colony was in a great measure, if not totally, owing to the building and supporting of the orphan house.

Finding the care of such a family incompatible with the care due to a parish, upon giving previous warning to the then trustees, I gave up the living of Savannah, which without fee or reward I had voluntarily taken upon me; I then ranged through the northern colonies and afterward once more returned home. What calumny, what loads of reproach, I for many years was called to undergo, in thus turning beggars for a family—few here present need to be informed—a family utterly unconnected by any ties of nature; a family, not only to be maintained with food, but clothed and educated also, and that too in the dearest part of his majesty's dominions, on a pine barren, and in a colony where the use of Negroes was totally denied; this appeared so very improbable that all beholders looked daily for its decline and annihilation.

But, blessed be God, the building advanced and flourished, and the wished-for period is now come, after having supported the family for thirty-two years, by a change of constitution and the smiles of government, with liberal donations from the northern, and especially the adjacent provinces, the same hands that laid the foundation are now called to finish it, by making an addition of a seat of learning, the whole products and profits of which are to go toward the increase of the fund, as at the beginning, for destitute orphans, or such youths as may be called of God to the sacred ministry of his gospel. I need not call on any here, to cry, "Grace, grace, unto it." For on the utmost scrutiny of the intention of those employed, and considering the various exercises they have been called to undergo, and the opposition the building has everywhere met with, we may justly say, "Not by might, nor by power, but by thy Spirit, O Lord," has this work been carried on thus far; it is his doing, let it be marvelous in our eyes. With humble gratitude therefore would we now set up our Ebenezer, and say, "Hitherto thou, Lord, hast helped us"; and wherefore should we doubt, but that he, who has thus far helped, will continue to help, when the weary heads of the first founders and present helpers, are laid in the silent grave.

I am very well aware, what an invidious task it must be to a person in my circumstances, thus to speak on an affair in which he has been so much concerned. Some may perhaps think I am become a fool in thus glorying. But as I am now, blessed be God, in the decline of life, and as, in all probability, I shall never be present to celebrate another anniversary, I thought it best to be a little more explicit, that if I have spoken anything but truth, I may be confronted; and if not, that future ages, and future successors, may see with what a purity of intention and what various interpositions of providence, the work was begun and has been carried on to its present height.

It was the reading of a like account, written by the late Professor Franck, that encouraged me. Who knows but hereafter the reading something of a similar nature may encourage others to begin and carry on a like work elsewhere? I have said its present height, for I would humbly hope that this is, comparatively speaking, only a "day of small things," only the dawn of brighter scenes. Private geniuses and individuals, as well as collective bodies, have, like the human body, the nonage, puerile, juvenile estate, before they arrive at their zenith and their lives as gradually they decline. But yet I would hope that both the province and Bethesda [orphan house] are but in their puerile or juvenile state. And long, long may they increase, and make large strides, till they arrive at a glorious zenith! I mean not merely in trade, merchandise, and opulence (though I would be far from secluding them from the province, and would be thankful for the advances it has already made), but a zenith of glorious gospel blessings, without which all outward emoluments are less than nothing, or as the small dust of the balance: "For what shall it profit a man, if he shall gain the whole world and lose his own soul?"

Who can imagine, that the prophet Zechariah would be sent to strengthen the hands of Zerubbabel, in building and laying the foundation of the temple, if that temple was not to be frequented with worshipers that worshiped the Father in spirit and truth. The most gaudy fabrics, stately temples, new moon Sabbaths, and solemn assemblies are only solemn mockeries God cannot away with. This God has shown by the destruction of both the first and second temples. What is become of the seven churches of Asia? How are all their golden candlesticks overthrown? "God is a Spirit, and they who worship him must worship him in spirit and truth." And no longer do I expect that this house will flourish, than when the power of religion is encouraged and promoted, and the persons educated here prosecute their studies, not only to be great scholars, but good saints.

Blessed be God! I can say with Professor Franck, that it is in a great measure owing to the disinterested spirit of my first fellow helpers, as well as those who are now employed, that the building has reached to its present height. This I am bound to speak, not only in honor to those who are now with God, but those at present before me.

Nor dare I conclude, without offering to your excellency, our peppercorn of acknowledgment for the countenance you have always shown Bethesda's institution, and the honor you did us last year, inlaying the first brick of yonder wings: in thus doing, you have honored Bethesda's God. May he long delight to honor you here on earth! And after a life spent to his glory, and your country's good, may he honor you to all eternity, in placing you at Christ's right hand in the kingdom above!

Next to your excellency, my dear Mr. President, I must beg your acceptance both of thanks and congratulation on the annual return of this festival. For you were not only my dear familiar friend and first fellow traveler in this infant province, but you were directed by providence to this spot, laid the second brick of this house, watched, prayed, and worked for the family's good: a witness of innumerable trials, partner of my joys and griefs; you will have now the pleasure of seeing the orphan house a fruitful bough, its branches running over the wall. For this, no doubt, God has smiled upon and blessed you, in a manner we could not expect, much less design; and may he continue to bless you with all spiritual blessings in heavenly places in Christ Jesus. Look to the rock from which you have been hewn, and may your children never be ashamed, that their father left his native country, and married a real Christian, born again under this roof. May Bethesda's God grant this may be the happy portion of your children, and children's children!

Gentlemen of his majesty's council, Mr. Speaker, and you members of the General Assembly, many thanks are owing to you, for your late address to his excellency in favor of Bethesda. Your joint recommendation of it, when I was last here, which, though in some measure through the bigotry of some, for the present is rendered abortive, by their wanting to have it confined to a party, yet I trust the event will prove that everything shall be overruled to the furtherance of the work. Here I repeat, what I have often declared, that as far as lies in my power before and after my decease, Bethesda shall be always on a broad bottom. All denominations have freely given; all denominations, all the continent, God being my helper, shall receive benefit from it. May Bethesda's God bless you all! In your private as well as public capacity; and as you are honored to be the representatives of a now flourishing increasing people: may you be directed in all your ways! May truth, justice, religion, and piety be established among you through all generations!

Last, my reverend brethren, and you inhabitants of the colony accept unfeigned thanks for the honor done me, in letting us see you at Bethesda this day. You, sir, for the sermon preached here last year. Tell it in Germany, tell my great, good friend, Professor Franck, that Bethesda's God, is a God whose mercy endures forever. Oh, let us have your earnest prayers! Encourage your people not to "despise the day of small things." "What hath God wrought?" From its infancy, this colony has been blessed with many faithful gospel ministers. Oh, that this may be a nursery to many more! This has been the case of the New England College for almost a century, and why not the Orphan House Academy at Georgia?

Men, brethren, fathers, as many of you, whether inhabitants or strangers, who have honored this day with your presence: give us the additional blessings of your prayers. And, oh, that Bethesda's God may make this day, though but a day of small things, productive of great things to the souls of all among whom I have been now preaching the kingdom of God. A great and good day will it be indeed, if Jesus Christ, our great Zerubbabel, should, by the power of the eternal Spirit, bless anything that has now been said, to cause every mountain of difficulty that lies in the way of your conversion, to become a plain. And what are you, O great mountain, whether the lust of the flesh, the lust of the eye, or the pride of life, sin, or self-righteousness? Before our Bethesda's God, you shall become a plain.

Brethren, my heart is enlarged toward you: it is written, blessed be God that it is written, "In the name of Jesus every knee shall bow, whether things in heaven, or things in earth, or things under the earth." Oh, that we may be made a willing people in the day of his power! Look, look unto him, all you that are placed in these ends of the earth. This house has often been a house of God, a gate of heaven, to some of your fathers. May it be a house of God, a gate of heaven, to the children also! "Come unto him, all ye that are weary and heavy laden, he will give you rest"; rest from the guilt, rest from the power, rest from the punishment of sin; rest from the fear of divine judgments here, rest with himself eternally hereafter. Fear not, though the beginnings are but small, Christ will not despise the day of small things. A bruised reed will he not break, and the smoking flax will he not quench, until he bring forth judgment unto victory. His hands that laid the foundation, also shall finish it: yet a little while and the top stone shall be brought forth with shouting, and men and angels join in crying, "Grace! Grace! unto it." That all present may be in this happy number, may God of his infinite mercy grant, through Jesus our Lord.

The Good Shepherd: A Farewell Sermon

—ɯ—

The last sermon which Whitefield preached in London, on Wednesday, August 30, 1769, before his final departure to America.

> "My sheep hear my voice, and I know them, and they follow me. And I give unto them eternal life, and they shall never perish, <u>neither shall any man pluck them out of my hand</u>." —JOHN 10:27–28 *How is this so, if "even the elect will be deceived"?*

It is a common and I believe, generally speaking, my dear hearers, a true saying, that <u>bad manners beget good laws</u>. Whether this will hold good in every particular, in respect to the affairs of this world, I am persuaded the observation is very pertinent in respect to the things of another: I mean bad manners, bad treatment, bad words, have been overruled by the <u>sovereign grace of God</u>, <u>to produce, and to be the cause of, the best sermons that were ever delivered from the mouth of the God-man, Christ Jesus.</u>

One would have imagined that as he came clothed with divine efficience, as he came with divine credentials, as he spoke as never man spoke, no one should have been able to have resisted the wisdom with which he spoke; one would imagine, they should have been so struck with the demonstration of the Spirit, that with one consent they should all own that he was "that prophet that was to be raised up like unto Moses." <u>But you seldom find our Lord preaching a sermon, but something or other that he said was caviled at; what's more, their enmity frequently broke through all good manners. They often therefore interrupted him while he was preaching</u>, which shows the enmity of their hearts long before God permitted it to be in their power to shed his innocent blood. If we look no further than this chapter, where he presents himself as a good Shepherd, one that laid down his life for his sheep, we see the best return he had was to be looked upon as possessed or distracted; for we are told that there was a division therefore again among the Jews for these sayings, and many of them said, "He hath a devil, and is mad; why hear ye him?" If the master of the house was served so, pray what are the servants to expect? Others, a little more sober minded, said, "These are not the words of him that hath a devil"; the devil never used to preach or act in this way; "<u>Can a devil open the eyes of the blind?</u>" So he had some friends among these rabble. This did not discourage our Lord; he goes on in his work; and <u>we shall never, never go on</u>

with the work of God, till, like our Master, we are willing to go through good and through evil report; and let the devil see we are not so complacent as to stop one moment for his barking at us as we go along.

We are told that our Lord was at Jerusalem at the feast of the dedication, and it was winter; the feast of dedication held, I think, seven or eight days, for the commemoration of the restoration of the temple and altar, after its profanation by Antiochus. Now this was certainly a mere human institution and had no divine image, had no divine superscription upon it; and yet I do not find that our blessed Lord and Master preached against it; I do not find that he spent his time about this; his heart was too big with superior things; and I believe when we, like him, are filled with the Holy Ghost, we shall not entertain our audiences with disputes about rites and ceremonies, but shall treat upon the essentials of the gospel, and then rites and ceremonies will appear with more indifference. Our Lord does not say that he would not go up to the feast, for, on the contrary, he did go there, not so much as to keep the feast, as to have an opportunity to spread the gospel net; and that should be our method, not to follow disputing; and it is the glory of the Methodists, that we have been now forty years, and, I thank God, there has not been one single pamphlet written by any of our preachers about the nonessentials of religion.

Our Lord always made the best of every opportunity; and we are told, "he walked in the temple in Solomon's porch." One would have thought the scribes and Pharisees would have put him in one of their stalls and have complimented him with desiring him to preach: no, they let him walk in Solomon's porch. Some think he walked by himself, nobody choosing to keep company with him. I think I see him walking and looking at the temple, and foreseeing within himself how soon it would be destroyed; he walked pensively, to see the dreadful calamities that would come upon the land, for not knowing the day of its visitation; and it was to let the world see he was not afraid to appear in public: he walked, as much as to say, Have any of you anything to say to me? and he put himself in their way, that if they had any things to ask him, he was ready to resolve them; and to show them, that though they had treated him so ill, yet he was ready to preach salvation to them.

In verse 24 we are told, "Then came the Jews round about him, and said unto him, 'How long dost thou make us doubt?'" They came round about him when they saw him walking in Solomon's porch; "Now," say they, "we will have him, now we will attack him." And now was fulfilled that passage in the Psalms: "They compassed me about like bees" to sting me, or rather like wasps. Now, say they, we will get him in the middle of us, and see what sort of a man he is; we will see whether we cannot conquer him; they came to him, and they say, "How long dost thou make us to doubt?" Now this seems a plausible question, "How long dost thou make us to doubt?" Pray, how long, sir, do you intend to keep us in suspense? Some think the words will bear this interpretation: pray, sir, how long do you intend thus to steal away our hearts? They would represent him to be a designing man, like Absalom, to get the people on his side, and then set up himself for the Messiah; thus carnal minds always interpret good men's actions. But the meaning seems to be this; they were doubting concerning Christ; doubting Christians may think it is God's fault that they doubt, but, God knows, it is all their own. "How long dost thou make us to doubt?" I wish you would speak a little plainer, sir, and not let us have any more of your parables. Pray, let us know who you are, let us have it from your own mouth; "if thou be the Christ, tell us plainly"; and I do not doubt, but they put on a very sanctified face, and looked very demure; "If thou be the Christ, tell us plainly," intending to catch him: if he does not say he is the Christ, we will say he is ashamed of his own cause; if he tells us plainly that he is the Christ, then we will impeach him to the governor; we will go and tell the governor that this man says he is the Messiah; now we know of no Messiah, but what is to jostle Caesar out of his throne.

The devil always wants to make it believed that God's people, who are the most loyal people in the world, are rebels to the government under which they live; "If thou be the Christ, tell us plainly." Our Lord does not let them wait long for an answer; honesty can soon speak: "I told you, and ye believed not; the works that I do in my Father's name, they bear witness of me." Had our Lord said, "I am the Messiah," they would have taken him up; he knew that, and therefore he joined "the wisdom of the serpent" with "the innocence of the dove"; says he, "I appeal to my works and doctrine, and if you will not infer from them that I am the Messiah, I have no further argument." "But," he adds, "ye believe not, because ye are not of my sheep." He complains twice; for their unbelief was the greatest grief of heart to Christ: then he goes on in the words of our text, "My sheep hear my voice, and I know them, and they follow me. And I give unto them eternal life, and they shall never perish, neither shall any pluck them out of my hand." "My sheep hear my voice"; you think to puzzle me, you think to chagrin me with this kind of conduct, but you are mistaken; you do not believe on me, because you are not of my sheep. The great Mr. Stoddard of New England (and no place under heaven produces greater divines than New England) preached once from these words, "But ye believe not, because ye are not of my sheep"; a very strange text to preach upon, to convince a congregation! Yet God so blessed it, that two or three hundred souls were awakened by that sermon: God grant such success to attend the labors of all his faithful ministers.

"My sheep hear my voice, and they follow me." It is very remarkable, there are but two sorts of people mentioned in Scripture: it does not say that the Baptists and Independents, nor the Methodists and Presbyterians; no, Jesus Christ divides the whole world into but two classes, sheep and goats: the Lord give us to see this morning to which of these classes we belong.

But it is observable, believers are always compared to something that is good and profitable, and unbelievers are always described by something that is bad, and good for little or nothing.

If you ask me why Christ's people are called sheep, as God shall enable me, I will give you a short, and I hope it will be to you an answer of peace. Sheep, you know, generally love to be together; we say a flock of sheep; we do not say a herd of sheep; sheep are little creatures, and Christ's people may be called sheep, because they are little in the eyes of the world, and they are yet less in their own eyes. Oh, some people think, if the great men were on our side, if we had king, lords, and commons on our side, I mean if they were all true believers. Oh, if we had all the kings upon the earth on our side! Suppose you had: alas! alas! do you think the church would go on the better? Why, if it were fashionable to be a Methodist at court, if it were fashionable to be a Methodist abroad, they would go with a Bible or a hymn book, instead of a novel; but religion never thrives under too much sunshine. "Not many mighty, not many noble, are called, but God hath chosen the foolish things of the world to confound the wise, and God hath chosen the weak things of the world to confound the things which are mighty." Dr. [Isaac] Watts says, "Here and there I see a king, and here and there a great man, in heaven, but their number is but small."

Sheep are looked upon to be the most harmless, quiet creatures that God has made. Oh, may God, of his infinite mercy, give us to know that we are his sheep, by our having this blessed temper infused into our hearts by the Holy Ghost. "Learn of me," says our blessed Lord. What to do? To work miracles? No. "Learn of me, for I am meek and lowly in heart." A very good man, now living, said once, if there be any particular temper I desire more than another, it is the grace of meekness, quietly to bear bad treatment, to forget and to forgive: and at the same time that I am sensible, I am injured, not to be overcome of evil, but to have grace given me to overcome evil with good. To the honor of Moses, it is declared, that he was the meekest man upon earth. Meekness is necessary for people in power; a man that is passionate is dangerous. Every governor should have a warm temper, but a man of an unrelenting, unforgiving temper is no more fit for government than Phaethon to drive the chariot of the sun; he only sets the world on fire.

You all know that sheep, of all creatures in the world, are the most apt to stray and be lost; Christ's people may justly, in that respect, be compared to sheep; therefore in the introduction to our morning service, we say, "We have erred and strayed from thy ways like lost sheep." Turn out a horse or a dog, and they will find their way home, but a sheep wanders about; he bleats here and there, as much as to say, "Dear stranger, show me my way home again"; thus Christ's sheep are too apt to wander from the fold; having their eye off the great Shepherd, they go into this field and that field, over this hedge and that, and often return home with the loss of their wool.

But at the same time sheep are the most useful creatures in the world; they manure the land, and thereby prepare it for the seed; they clothe our bodies with wool, and there is not the least part of a sheep but is useful to man. O my brethren, God grant that you and I may, in this respect, answer the character of sheep. The world says that because we preach faith, we deny good works; this is the usual objection against the doctrine of imputed righteousness, but it is a slander, an impudent slander. It was a maxim in the first Reformers' time, that though the Arminians preached up good works, you must go to the Calvinists for them. Christ's sheep study to be useful, and to clothe all they can; we should labor with our hands, that we may have to give to all those that need.

Believers consider Christ's property in them; he says, "my sheep." Oh, blessed be God for that little, dear, great word *my*. We are his eternal election: "the sheep which thou hast given me," says Christ. They were given by God the Father to Christ Jesus, in the covenant made between the Father and the Son from all eternity. They that are not led to see this, I wish them better heads; though, I believe, numbers that are against it have got better hearts: the Lord help us to bear with one another where there is an honest heart.

He calls them "my sheep"; they are his by purchase. O sinner, sinner, you are come this morning to hear a poor creature take his "last farewell"; but I want you to forget the creature that is preaching; I want to lead you further than the tabernacle. Where do you want to lead us? Why, to Mount Calvary, there to see at what an expense of blood Christ purchased those whom he calls his own; he redeemed them with his own blood, so that they are not only his by eternal election, but also by actual redemption in time; and they were given to him by the Father, upon condition that he should redeem them by his heart's blood. It was a hard bargain, but Christ was willing to strike the bargain, that you and I might not be damned forever.

They are his, because they are enabled in a day of God's power voluntarily to give themselves up unto him; Christ says of these sheep, especially, that "they hear his voice, and that they follow him." Will you be so good as to mind that? Here is an allusion to a shepherd; now in some places in Scripture, the shepherd is represented as going after his sheep (2 Sam. 7:8; Ps. 78:71). That is our way in England; but in the Eastern nations, the shepherds generally went before; they held up their crook, and they had a particular call that the sheep understood. Now, says Christ, "My sheep hear my voice." "This is my beloved Son," says God, "hear ye him." And again, "The dead shall hear the voice of the Son of God, and live." Now the question is, what do we understand by hearing Christ's voice?

First, we have Moses' voice; we hear the voice of the law; there is no going to Mount Zion but by the way of Mount Sinai; that is the right straight road. I know some say, they do not know when they were converted; those are, I believe, very few: generally, no, I may say almost always, God deals otherwise. Some are, indeed, called sooner by the Lord than others, but before they are made to see the glory of God, they must hear the voice of the law; so you must hear the voice of the law, before ever you will be savingly called unto God. You never throw off your cloak in a storm, but you hug it the closer; so the law makes a man hug close his corruptions (Rom. 7:7–9), but when the gospel of the Son of God shines into their souls, then they throw off the corruptions which they have hugged so closely; they hear his voice saying, "Son, daughter, be of good cheer; your sins, which are many, are all forgiven you." "They hear his voice"; that bespeaks the habitual temper of their minds: the wicked hear the voice of the devil, the lusts of the flesh, the lusts of the eye, and the pride of life; and Christ's sheep themselves attended to it before conversion; but when called afterward by God, they hear the voice of a Redeemer's blood speaking peace unto them; they hear the voice of his Word and of his Spirit.

The consequence of hearing his voice, and the proof that we do hear his voice, will be to follow him. Jesus said unto his disciples, "If any man will come after me, let him deny himself, and take up his cross and follow me." And it is said of the saints in glory, that "they followed the Lamb whithersoever he went." Wherever the shepherd turns his crook, and the sheep hear his voice, they follow him; they often tread upon one another and hurt one another; they are in such haste in their way to heaven. Following Christ means following him through life, following him in every word and gesture, following him out of one clime into another. "Bid me come to thee upon the water," said Peter: and if we are commanded to go over the water for Christ, God, of his infinite mercy, follow us! We must first be sure that the great Shepherd points his crook for us: but this is the character of a true servant of Christ, that he endeavors to follow Christ in thought, word, and work.

Now, my brethren, before we go further, as this is the last opportunity I shall have of speaking to you for some months, if we live; some of you, I suppose, do not choose, in general, to rise so soon as you have this morning; now I hope the world did not get into your hearts before you left your beds; now you are here, do let me entreat you to inquire whether you belong to Christ's sheep, or no. Man, woman, sinner, put your hand to your heart and answer me. Did you ever hear Christ's voice so as to follow him, to give up yourself without reserve to him? I verily do believe from my inmost soul (and that is my comfort, now I am about to take my leave of you), that I am preaching to a vast body, a multitude of dear, precious souls, who, if it were proper for you to speak, would say, "Thanks be unto God, that we can follow Jesus in the character of sheep, though we are ashamed to think how often we wander from him, and what little fruit we bring unto him"; if that is the language of your hearts, I wish you joy; welcome, welcome, dear soul, to Christ. Oh, blessed be God for his rich grace, his distinguishing, sovereign, electing love, by which he has distinguished you and me. And if he has been pleased to let you hear his voice, though the ministration of a poor miserable sinner, a poor, but happy pilgrim, may the Lord Jesus Christ have all the glory.

If you belong to Jesus Christ, he is speaking of you; for, says he, "I know my sheep. I know them"; what does that mean? Why, he knows their number; he knows their names; he knows everyone for whom he died; and if there were to be one missing for whom Christ died, God the Father would send him down again from heaven to fetch him. "Of all," says he, "that thou hast given me, have I lost none." Christ knows his sheep; he not only knows their number, but the words speak the peculiar knowledge and notice he takes of them; he takes as much care of each of them, as if there were but that one single sheep in the world. To the hypocrite he says, "Verily I know you not"; but he knows his saints; he is acquainted with all their sorrows, their trials, and temptations. He bottles up all their tears; he knows their domestic trials; he knows their inward corruptions; he knows all their wanderings; and he takes care to fetch them back again. I remember, I heard good Dr. Marryat, who was a good market language preacher, once say at Pinner's Hall (I hope that pulpit will be always filled with such preachers), "God has got a great dog to fetch his sheep back," says he. Do not you know, that when the sheep wander, the shepherd sends his dog after them, to fetch them back again? So when Christ's sheep wander, he lets the devil go after them, and suffers him to bark at them, who, instead of driving them farther off, is made a means to bring them back again to Christ's fold.

There is a precious word I would have you take notice of: "I know them," that may comfort you under all your trials. We sometimes think that Christ does not hear our prayers, that he does not know us; we are ready to suspect that he has forgotten to be gracious; but what a mercy it is that he does know us. We accuse one another, we turn devils to one another, are accusers of the brethren; and what will support two of God's people when judged by one another but this: "Lord, you know my integrity, you know how matters are with me"?

But, my brethren, here is something better, here is good news for you; what is that? Say you: why, "I give unto them eternal life, and they shall never perish, neither shall any pluck them out of my hand." Oh, that the words may come to your hearts with as much warmth and power as they did to mine thirty-five years ago. I never prayed against any corruption I had in my life, so much as I did against going into holy orders so soon as my friends were for having me go: and Bishop Benson was pleased to honor me with peculiar friendship, so as to offer me preferment, or do anything for me. My friends wanted me to mount the church speedily; they wanted me to knock my head against the pulpit too young; but how some young men stand up here and there and preach, I do not know how it may be to them; but God knows how deep a concern entering into the ministry and preaching was to me; I have prayed a thousand times, till the sweat has dropped from my face like rain, that God, of his infinite mercy, would not let me enter the church before he called me to, and thrust me forth in, his work. I remember once in Glouces- ter (I know the room, I look up at the window when I am there and walk along the street; I know the window, the bedside, and the floor, upon which I have lain prostrate), I said, "Lord, I cannot go, I shall be puffed up with pride and fall into the condemnation of the devil; Lord, do not let me go yet." I pleaded to be at Oxford two or three years more; I intended to make 150 ser- mons, and thought I would set up with a good stock in trade, but I remember praying, wrestling, and striving with God; I said, "I am undone; I am unfit to preach in your great name; send me not, pray, Lord, send me not yet." I wrote to all my friends in town and country, to pray against the bishop's solicitations, but they insisted I should go into orders before I was twenty-two. After all the solicitations, these words came into my mind, "My sheep hear my voice, and none shall pluck them out of my hand." Oh, may the words be blessed to you,* my dear friends, that I am parting with, as they were to me when they came warm upon my heart; then, and not till then, I said, "Lord, I will go; send me

* that still- small voice which has spoken to billions through the ages when you will." I remember when I was in a place called Dover Island, near Georgia, we put in with bad winds; I had 150 in family to maintain, and not a single farthing to do it with, in the dearest part of the king's dominions; I remember, I told a minister of Christ, now in heaven, "I had these words once, sir, 'Nothing shall pluck you out of my hand.'" "Oh," says he, "take comfort from them; you may be sure God will be as good as his word, if he never tells you so again." And our Lord knew his poor sheep would be always doubting they should ever reach heaven, therefore says he, "I give to them eternal life, and they shall never perish."

Here are in our text three blessed declarations, or promises:

First: "I know them."

Second: "They shall never perish"; though they often think they shall perish by the hand of their lusts and corruptions; they think they shall perish by the deceitfulness of their hearts; but Christ says, "They shall never perish." I have brought them out of the world to myself, and do you think I will let them go to hell after that? "I give to them eternal life"; pray, mind that; not "I will" but "I do." Some talk of being justified at the day of judgment; that is nonsense; if we are not justified here, we shall not be justified there. He gives them eternal life, that is, the earnest, the pledge, and assurance of it. The indwelling of the Spirit of God here is the earnest of glory hereafter.

Third: "Neither shall any pluck them out of my hand." He holds them in his hand, that is, he holds them by his power; none shall pluck them there. There is always something plucking at Christ's sheep; the devil, the lust of the flesh, the lust of the eye, and the pride of life, all try to pluck them out of Christ's hand. O my brethren, they need not pluck us, yet we help all three to pluck ourselves out of the hand of Jesus; but "None shall pluck them out of my hand," says Christ. "I give to them eternal life. I am going to heaven to prepare a place for them, and there they shall be." O my brethren, if it were not for keeping you too long, and too much exhausting my own spirits, I could call upon you to leap [for joy] for you; there is not a more blessed text to support the final perseverance of the saints; and I am astonished any poor souls, and good people I hope too, can fight against the doctrine of the perseverance of the saints. What if a person say they should persevere in wickedness? Ah! that is an abuse of the doctrine; what, because some people spoil good food, are we never to eat it? But, my brethren, upon this text I can leave my cares, and all my friends, and all Christ's sheep, to the protection of Christ Jesus' never-failing love.

I thought this morning, when I came here, riding from the other end of the town, it was to me like coming to be executed publicly; and when the carriage turned just at the end of the walk, and I saw you running here, Oh, think I, it is like a person now coming just to the place where he is to be executed. When I went up to put on my gown, I thought it was just like dressing myself to be made a public spectacle to shed my blood for Christ. I take all heaven and earth to witness, and God and the holy angels to witness, that though I had preferment enough offered me, that though the bishop took me in his arms, and offered me two parishes before I was two-and-twenty, and always took me to his table; though I had preferment enough offered me when I was ordained, you, O God, know that when the bishop put his hand upon my head, I looked for no other preferment than publicly to suffer for the Lamb of God: in this Spirit I came out, in this Spirit I came up to this metropolis. I was thinking, when I read of Jacob's going over the brook with a staff, that I could not say I had so much as a staff, but I came up without a friend; I went to Oxford without a friend; I had not a servant, I had not a single person to introduce me, but God, by his Holy Spirit, was pleased to raise me up to preach for his great name's sake: through his divine Spirit I continue to this day and feel my affections are as strong as ever toward the work and the people of the living God. The congregations at both ends of the town are dear to me: God has honored me to build this and the other place; and, blessed be his name, when he called me to Georgia at first, and I left all London affairs to God's care, when I had most of the churches in London open to me, and had twelve or fourteen constables to keep the doors, that people might not crowd too much; I had offers of hundreds then to settle in London, yet I gave it all up to turn pilgrim for God, to go into a foreign clime; and I hope with that same single intention I am going now.

Now I must come to the hardest part I have to act; I was afraid when I came out from home, that I could not bear the shock, but I hope the Lord Jesus Christ will help me to bear it, and help you to give me up to the blessed God, let him do with me what he will. This is the thirteenth time of my crossing the mighty waters; it is a little difficult at this time of life; and though my spirits are improved in some degree, yet weakness is the best of my strength: but I am clear as light in my call and God fills me with a peace that is unutterable, which a stranger intermeddles not with: into his hands I commend my spirit; and I beg that this may be the language of your hearts: Lord, keep him, let nothing pluck him out of your hands. I expect many a trial while I am on board; Satan always meets me there, but that God who has kept me, I believe, will keep me. I thank God, I have the honor of leaving everything quite well and easy at both ends of the town; and, my dear hearers, my prayers to God shall be that nothing may pluck you out of Christ's hands. Witness against me, if I ever set up a party for myself. Did ever any minister, or could any minister in the world, say that I ever spoke against anyone going to any dear minister? I thank God that he has enabled me to be always strengthening the hands of all, though some have afterward been ashamed to own me. I declare to you, that I believe God will be with me and will strengthen me; and I believe it is in answer to your prayers that God is pleased to revive my spirits: may the Lord help you to pray on. If I am drowned in the waves, I will say, while I am drowning, "Lord, take care of my London; take care of my English friends; let nothing pluck them out of your hands."

And as Christ has given us eternal life, O my brethren, some of you, I doubt not, will be gone to him before my return; but, my dear brethren, my dear hearers, never mind that; we shall part, but it will be to meet again forever. I dare not meet you now; I cannot bear your coming to me, to part from me; it cuts me to the heart and quite overcomes me, but by and by all parting will be over, and all tears shall be wiped away from our eyes. God grant that none that weep now at my parting may weep at our meeting at the day of judgment; and if you never were among Christ's sheep before, may Christ Jesus bring you now. Oh, come, come, see what it is to have eternal life; do not refuse it; haste, sinner, haste away: may the great, the good Shepherd, draw your souls. Oh! if you never heard his voice before, God grant you may hear it now; that I may have this comfort when I am gone, that I had the last time of my leaving you, that some souls are awakened at the parting sermon. Oh, that it may be a farewell sermon to you; that it may be a means of your taking a farewell of the world, the lust of the flesh, the lust of the eye, and the pride of life. Oh, come! Come! Come! to the Lord Jesus Christ; to him I leave you.

And you, dear sheep, that are already in his hands, oh, may God keep you from wandering; God keep you near Christ's feet; I do not care what shepherds keep you, so as you are kept near the great Shepherd and Bishop of souls. The Lord God keep you, lift up the light of his countenance upon you, and give you peace. Amen.

*I just don't sense this is puffed up words. I can't help but feel he senses Satan has tried much to silence to destroy him— what's left but to cast him into the sea.